*The Channel Four Racing Companion 1992*

*The*
# CHANNEL FOUR

ALSO FROM CHANNEL FOUR RACING BY SEAN MAGEE

*The Channel Four Book of Racing* (1989, revised edition 1990)

*The Channel Four Book of the Racing Year* (1990)

# RACING COMPANION 1992

## EDITED BY SEAN MAGEE

SIDGWICK & JACKSON LIMITED · LONDON
*in association with* CHANNEL FOUR TELEVISION COMPANY LIMITED

First published in Great Britain in 1992 by Sidgwick & Jackson Limited,
Cavaye Place, London SW10 9PG

ISBN 0 283 06120 0

Photoset by Parker Typesetting Service, Leicester
Printed by Mackays of Chatham PLC, Chatham, Kent

*The front cover photograph shows Generous winning the Ever Ready Derby in June 1991.*

*Picture Acknowledgements*

All the black and white pictures are reproduced by permission of Gerry Cranham, with the
following exceptions: Brough Scott and John Lawrence in the Horse and Hound Cup 1967
reproduced by permission of Jim Meads; the final jumping meeting at Hurst Park and Eph
Smith winning at Alexandra Park in 1959 reproduced by permission of the Hulton Picture
Company; Red Cast at Wye and Democrat with Lord Kitchener are from private
collections.
    The colour pictures are reproduced by permission of Ronald Frain, Colin Turner, Les
Hurley, Philippa Gilchrist, Lesley Sampson, Kenneth Bright and Eric Leslie Gibbs.

# CONTENTS

# INTRODUCTION

The aim of *The Channel Four Racing Companion 1992* is to provide enthusiasts with a guide to the racing year ahead along with articles, information and recollections of the major events of 1991 – a memorable racing year by anyone's standards.

The information supplied is as up-to-date as we can make it at the end of 1991, but details are subject to change: sponsors come and go and the names of races can be altered; minor changes in the fixture list may occur; and you never know – some sleek Classic hope mentioned among Jim McGrath's prospects for 1992 may be sent to race in America before he can show his worth on the home front. So please consider some of the information to be provisional.

We hope that *The Channel Four Racing Companion* will enhance your enjoyment of racing in 1992 – whether on the racecourse or watching on television.

Several people have helped in the preparation of this *Companion*. Special thanks are due to Andrew Franklin, Teresa Wadeson and Sue Nicolle at Channel Four Racing, and to the presenters for their contributions to the book. Gerry Cranham was yet again a ready and willing supplier of photographs. Phillip Jones gave all sorts of assistance, notably in the preparation of the quiz. Chris Jones compiled the lists of past winners of big races, and Edward James provided the glossaries and all the hard graft on the racecourses section: he wrote most of the course descriptions, though not the paean of praise to the meat pie at Ludlow, a pleasure he has yet to experience.

My greatest debt is to Ingrid Connell at Sidgwick and Jackson, who displayed patience and understanding which would have had Griselda spitting with envy.

S.M.

# HORSES FOR 1992

Jim McGrath *looks ahead to the 1992 Flat season with recommendations of a few to follow, and the other Channel Four Racing presenters each nominate one to keep an eye on.*

At the advent of the new season, optimism amongst the flat-race fraternity is usually at its peak. Even the smallest of strings have at least one four-legged youngster reputedly 'flying' or 'catching pigeons'. The bigger stables probably have several. Also, there's almost invariably a whole host of horses who, to trot out (geddit?) another racing cliché, 'have come on a ton since last year' and of which one, maybe more, are saddled with yet another in 'might even be a Classic horse'! If I had a tenner for the number of times that such sentiments have been pronounced in my hearing I'd be wealthy enough not to need to write this. But alas, that's not the case; so it's my turn, here and now, to inflict a posse of probable Classic winners, nap-hand gatherers, record-breakers: in short, sure-fire certainties for the months ahead. Before I begin, another old racing saw – 'the definition of a pessimist is an optimist on his way home from the races'. Don't say you haven't been warned!

Let's begin with a couple of Classic possibles, Bonny Scot and Rainbow Corner. Top of my list is Luca Cumani's **Bonny Scot**, a compact, attractive son of Commanche Run, winner of the St Leger in 1984 and, the following year, of the Benson and Hedges Gold Cup and the Phoenix Champion Stakes. Bonny Scot's dam, Scot's Lass, from the family of Reform, was the winner of a maiden race over thirteen furlongs at Bath in the autumn of 1985. It's not a pedigree that suggests precocity and, indeed, Bonny Scot's two-year-old campaign was restricted to three late-season races, of which he won two. Easily the more significant of those victories was gained in the Sporting Life Zetland Stakes at Newmarket in November which he took easily, beating a useful colt, Captain Horatius, one and a half lengths, the pair drawing upwards of eight lengths clear of a useful field. Thoughts that Bonny Scot will actually win the Derby are optimistic. However, in view of his achievements so far, and the near certainty that he'll progress significantly over a mile and a half plus, it's not unreasonable to envisage his developing into a major contender for the St Leger at Doncaster.

Unlike Bonny Scot, **Rainbow Corner** (the Noble Lord's one to follow) took on the best of his age last season. On the third of three appearances as a juvenile he lined up in the Ciga Grand Criterium on 5 October. Like four other members of the field he found Arazi far too good an opponent. Nonetheless, in reaching second place, three lengths behind the winner, Rainbow Corner impressed me as a colt with a bright future. For much of the Criterium he was struggling, probably still green, yet battled on splendidly under powerful riding from Pat Eddery and, in the end, caught Seattle Rhyme for second. Rainbow Corner is a big, good-looking colt by Rainbow Quest (a major influence for stamina, incidentally) who looks sure to train on. With Arazi likely to be prepared for the Kentucky Derby, Rainbow Corner should be up to winning one of the leading trials in France at least. On form to date there's no doubt he's a good-class colt. Who knows, he may even atone for the dismal showing in last season's Derby by his stable-companion Toulon.

It's quite likely that **Desert Sun**, trained by Henry Cecil, featured on many lists of Horses to Follow for 1991. A magnificent dark bay, with a captivating, raking action, at one time last spring he was favourite for the Two Thousand Guineas. After a good second to Marju in the Craven Stakes, Desert Sun was extremely disappointing in his next two races. Fortunately, his final appearance, at Doncaster in September, proved unquestionably that he's still a high-class colt. He slaughtered subsequent Sun Chariot Stakes winner Ristna, producing a sharp turn of foot, after being held up. Judged on that display, never mind his Craven Stakes second, Desert Sun should be well able to win pattern races outside Group One status at around a mile, possibly even slightly further.

Pattern races are most unlikely to feature on **Duke of Eurolink**'s agenda. At this stage he's a twice-raced maiden whose performances in sizeable fields of maidens at Newmarket last October earned him a Timeform rating in the sixties. On both occasions Duke of Eurolink looked backward, somewhat babyish, but, nonetheless he shaped, as the saying goes, pleasingly. He needs one more run to secure a handicap mark and, unless my reckoning is well wide of the mark, should be worth looking out for in races over middle distances.

I won't take all the credit (nor the blame!) for **Never A Care**'s inclusion. On several occasions prior to this filly's debut at Chepstow last October John Francome told me to look out for her. Never A Care's trainer Barry Hills rents a yard from John, so naturally the Greatest

Jockey, possessed of a keen eye and a sharp brain, remembers anything of significance he's told or he sees. Despite that, neither he nor I spotted Never A Care's appearance in, ironically, the 'Pat Eddery 200-In-A-Season Stakes' at Chepstow on 22 October. Eddery, retained by Never A Care's owner, Khalid Abdullah, deserted her for the favourite Karen Louise. Never A Care, ridden by Robert Street and starting at 33-1, hacked up by six lengths. Apparently Barry Hills felt his filly had begun to lose her form; in short he felt she'd 'gone' for the season but, wanting to give her racecourse experience, let her take her chance. If this is what an 'out-of-form' Never A Care can do, what will she achieve when in full bloom? That's impossible to forecast; but it's pretty likely Pat Eddery will be back in the saddle and that she won't be 33-1 either!

Admittedly the last three in this offering are all somewhat (or should I say even more) chancy selections. In the cases of **Desert Splendour**, trained by Clive Brittain, and **Gulmarg**, now trained by Mark Tompkins, I'm playing a hunch. Two seasons ago both had excellent campaigns, Desert Splendour landing valuable nurseries and Gulmarg, a year older, winning at Thirsk and Wolverhampton, having earlier finished second in the Britannia Handicap at Royal Ascot. Last season neither did themselves anything like justice. To be fair, each had a lengthy spell absent from the track and, because of their successes in 1990, struggled in the handicap too. However, they begin 1992 lowered considerably. Gulmarg, bought by Mark Tompkins at the Newmarket Autumn Sales, should be effective at around a mile; Desert Splendour possibly over a couple of furlongs further.

I suppose my final selection proves that, in spite of seventeen years' working at Timeform, I'm just as much of a dreamer as the vast majority of racehorse owners. **Reasons For Love**, a two-year-old filly by Common Grounds and trained by Jonjo O'Neill, is the choice. Why? Well, for goodness sake, I own her and want you to share in her glories too. Mind you, if she follows in the hoofprints of the two two-year-olds I had in training in 1991, her best chance of winning a race is probably inside a greyhound!

*The rest of the Channel Four Racing team nominate:*

**Arazi** (*three-year-old colt trained by Francois Boutin*)

You won't get rich backing Arazi in 1992, but he has to be the horse whose appearances are most keenly awaited. Great horses are few and far between, and after his run at the Breeders' Cup there's no doubt that this is a great one. Catch him while you can – and let's just hope we get to see him run in England.

DEREK THOMPSON

## Casteddu (*three-year-old colt trained by Pip Payne*)

Casteddu enjoyed a good first season in 1991. In the frame in his first two races in maiden and graduation company, he finished third in the Coventry Stakes behind Dilum and Dr Devious – form which speaks for itself. After three months' rest, Casteddu duly won maiden and graduation races before being laid out to win the Racecall Gold Trophy at Redcar in October. He'll race in the highest class in 1992 in races up to a mile, possibly beyond that later in the season. His early target will be the Two Thousand Guineas, probably preceded by the European Free Handicap, given a reasonable chance at the weights.

JOHN TYRREL

## Marling (*three-year-old filly trained by Geoff Wragg*)

Whether Marling stays a mile and becomes a Classic filly or whether sprinting turns out to be her game (like her dam Marwell), she's one to keep on the right side. She was very impressive when beating Culture Vulture in the Queen Mary Stakes at Royal Ascot, then came back after a break to win the Cheveley Park Stakes in great style. She looks as though she'll improve through the winter, and her reappearance will be keenly awaited.

JOHN FRANCOME

## Mutharram (*three-year-old colt trained by John Gosden*)

The Gosden stable are the most progressive of all the big teams. Mutharram has won just two minor races at Leicester, but he could be a big fish before too long.

BROUGH SCOTT

## Ponsardin (*three-year-old colt trained by Sir Mark Prescott*)

Ponsardin, whose dam won five races including a Group Three for the shrewdest placer of horses in the game, is 'small, stocky, tough and game' according to Sir Mark. So watch out if Ponsardin is the day's steamer!

JOHN MCCRIRICK

**Rainbow Corner** (*three-year-old colt trained by André Fabre*)

Rainbow Corner is trained in France but belongs to Khalid Abdullah and is therefore likely to do some of his racing in England. If good enough, he will also have the advantage of being ridden by Pat Eddery. When Rainbow Corner ran second to Arazi in the Ciga Grand Criterium he only just beat Seattle Rhyme but finished better than anything else – except, of course, the winner. Although his dam, the fast King's Lake filly Kingscote, did not train on, Rainbow Corner (by Rainbow Quest) is bred to stay a mile and a half. He is a grand looking colt and a very good walker who, with luck, may avoid meeting Arazi too many times in 1992.

JOHN OAKSEY

**Scandalmonger** (*three-year-old colt trained by Barry Hills*)

This Robert Sangster colt ran twice as a two-year-old: seventh in a 20-runner Newmarket maiden then last of six behind Mutharram at Leicester. He'll need to improve on that to make an impression in 1992 but looks the type to do so, and should make up into a nice three-year-old.

GRAHAM GOODE

# RACING IN 1991

*A brief recollection by Sean Magee of some of the major events of the year.*

Three horses dominated the Flat season in 1991 – Arazi, Generous and Suave Dancer. But the beginning and end of the racing year are deep in the heart of mid-winter jumping action, and the same old familiar face dominated each end of 1991.

Desert Orchid bade farewell to his doting public at Kempton Park on Boxing Day (though his retirement was not confirmed until the following day). He never looked like landing a fifth King George VI Chase and took a crashing fall when out of contention at the third last, but the rapture which greeted his springing to his feet and cantering riderless but unscathed past the massed stands would not have been much greater had he won.

The year began five days after Dessie's fourth King George, and the early months saw no slackening of his hold on the public imagination: a survey in March revealed that the horse was recognized by a greater percentage of the population than the Chancellor of the Exchequer. After an unsurprising defeat in a two-mile chase at Ascot, Desert Orchid returned to glory when rallying courageously up the Sandown Park hill to give Nick The Brief 15 pounds and a three-quarter-length beating in the Agfa Diamond Chase in February.

By Gold Cup day, the Cheltenham Festival had already produced plenty of excitement and high-class racing. Destriero won the meeting's curtain-raiser, the Trafalgar House Supreme Novices' Hurdle, to land a mammoth gamble (probably around a million pounds) for his owner, Irish carpet magnate Noel Furlong, who had to settle the small matter of £500,000 outstanding VAT before he could enter the country. Then Remittance Man won his sixth race off the reel (and secured the NH Channel Four Trophy) with a scintillating performance in the Arkle Chase, and another new star was born when Morley Street won the Champion Hurdle in fine style: starting 4-1 favourite, he went clear before the last and held on up the hill to win from Nomadic Way, runner-up for the second successive year.

Also runner-up two years running in a big Cheltenham race was Waterloo Boy, second to Katabatic in the Queen Mother Champion Chase after going down to Barnbrook Again in 1990. But the performance which really took the eye on the middle day of the Festival was that of Martin Pipe's Rolling Ball in the Sun Alliance Chase, who shrugged off a bad mistake at halfway to make all the running and score in the style of a future star. High hopes were also entertained of Oh So Risky after a brilliant win in the Daily Express Triumph Hurdle.

The feeling persisted before the Gold Cup that Desert Orchid was simply not the same horse at Cheltenham as he was elsewhere, and he started second favourite at 4-1 behind 5-2 chance Celtic Shot, with only Cool Ground (7-1) also under 10-1 in a field of fourteen. But the finish was fought out between Garrison Savannah, trained by Jenny Pitman and ridden by her son Mark, and the six-year-old French challenger The Fellow. Garrison Savannah had a good lead at the last, but The Fellow, running up the stands side, battled every inch of the run-in and failed only by a short head. Desert Orchid plugged on gamely to be third, fifteen lengths in arrears: 'I was proud of the way he ran,' said David Elsworth, and nobody expected to see Desert Orchid at Cheltenham again.

But the prospect of seeing Garrison Savannah go for the Grand National beckoned, and with just 11st 1lb to carry on 6 April he seemed to have a major chance of becoming only the second horse ever to win the Gold Cup and the National in the same year. Having started 7-1 joint second favourite (Bonanza Boy was marginally preferred in the market), he jumped well throughout, and at the last of the thirty fences another tidy leap put him well clear of his nearest pursuer, Seagram. Setting off up the long run-in, Garrison Savannah looked a nailed-on certainty to join Golden Miller in the record books, but at the elbow he suddenly 'died' on Mark Pitman, and Nigel Hawke roused Seagram to a final effort. He went sailing by the Gold Cup winner, and such was the collapse of Garrison Savannah's run that Seagram was five lengths clear at the line. The third horse, Auntie Dot, was the first mare to be placed in the National since Eyecatcher in 1977.

And a real eyecatcher at the Liverpool meeting was the performance of Blazing Walker in the Glenlivet Melling Chase – his sixth victory in a row and one which proclaimed another star of the future.

Seagram reappeared in the Whitbread Gold Cup at Sandown, but Liverpool had taken its toll and he could finish only fourth behind Cahervillahow and Docklands Express – or, as the amended result would have it, behind Docklands Express and Cahervillahow. For this was one of the most controversial races of the year. At the last fence Cahervillahow (on the stands side) and Docklands Express were practically inseparable, with Seagram just behind, and in a desperate struggle up the hill to the line Cahervillahow just held his rival at bay by three quarters of a length. But Cahervillahow had drifted over towards the far rail on the run-in, taking the smaller Docklands Express with him, and though the stewards disallowed an objection by Anthony Tory, rider of the runner-up, they judged that the winner had accidentally interfered with the second, and as this interference had affected the result, the placings had to be reversed.

Poor Cahervillahow deserved a change of luck. He had been withdrawn in error from the Cheltenham Gold Cup and then run second to Seagram in the National Hunt Handicap Chase at the Festival, and had been beaten a short head by Omerta in the Irish Grand National at Fairyhouse.

Omerta himself, though well beaten in the Whitbread, had made his mark on the season when winning the Fulke Walwyn Kim Muir Challenge Cup at Cheltenham ridden by the then almost unknown amateur Adrian Maguire – a Martin Pipe horse which paid over 25-1 on the Tote! After Fairyhouse he started at 2-1 in the Scottish National at Ayr, finishing five lengths second to 40-1 outsider Killone Abbey.

As for the human champions, it was the same old story. Martin Pipe was top trainer with a new record total of 230 winners, nearly twice as many as his nearest rival Gordon Richards. And Peter Scudamore was champion jockey with 141 winners despite several weeks on the sidelines through injury – notably after breaking his leg through a fall from Black Humour at Market Rasen in November 1990.

By the time jumping ended on 1 June, the Flat (on turf) had been going for over two months. It had started with the most valuable British win yet for a lady jockey when Alex Greaves brought 22-1 shot Amenable through to win the Lincoln despite what many thought was a highly unfavourable draw.

At Newmarket's Craven Meeting the performance which impressed most people was that of Marju in the Craven Stakes. Unfancied in the race after supposedly being on less than top form at home, he surged through to beat hot favourite Desert Sun and become favourite for the Two Thousand Guineas – for which another possible was the volcanic grey Mystiko, winner of the Free Handicap.

The picture for the One Thousand Guineas became clearer after Shadayid had run away from her rivals in the Fred Darling Stakes at Newbury, and the 1991 Classics began true to form. Shadayid started at 6-4 on and never looked like being beaten, powering up the Newmarket hill under Willie Carson to beat Lester Piggott and Kooyonga – grandfathers first and second!

Piggott's return to action added a great deal of interest and excitement to the Flat scene, and though he was not to win an English Classic in 1991, he rode in four and was placed in two. By the time of the Guineas Piggott had already been associated with a special landmark – he was on board Golan Heights at Newmarket in April when that horse became Julie Cecil's first winner as a trainer.

The Two Thousand Guineas provided the first of a series of stirring finishes in the big Flat races of 1991. With 6-4 favourite Marju sustaining a leg injury and playing no significant part, it was left to Mystiko (Michael Roberts) and Lycius (Steve Cauthen) to fight out a memorable climax: hugging the rails, Mystiko started to go clear inside the final furlong, then Steve Cauthen detached Lycius from the pack and went in hot pursuit. For a moment Lycius looked certain to win, but could not quite get past the grey and was beaten by a head. Generous caught some shrewdies' attention in fourth. (It was the first time since 1950 that both Guineas had gone to greys.)

Meanwhile, in France the Francois Boutin colt Hector Protector was carrying all before him, though some felt that his scrambling victory in the Poule d'Essai des Poulains (the French Two Thousand Guineas) did not advertise him as a world-beater. It was, however, his eighth win from as many starts, and the announcement that he would come to England for the Derby was keenly welcomed.

The seasonal debuts (or not) of many Derby hopes worked their usual mischief, and the ante-post market featured a succession of favourites which for one reason or another (usually inability to justify home reputation through racecourse performance) fell by the wayside. Remember Suomi, the horse whose flop on his seasonal debut at Sandown had Luca Cumani complaining about how work-watchers artificially inflate regard for a horse? Then there were Polish King, Wakashan, Hip To Time and Opera House – all strongly fancied for Epsom but failing to get within sniffing distance of the place.

Of the traditional Derby prep races apart from the Guineas, Sandown's Thresher Classic Trial went to Hailsham – who later won the Italian Derby. The Lingfield Derby Trial boosted the claim of Corrupt and erased that of Young Buster. The Dante Stakes produced a 20-1 shock in the shape of Environment Friend. Then there was Cruachan, whose facile win in the Glasgow Stakes at the York May Meeting raised Guy Harwood's hopes of a first Derby – only for them to be dashed when the horse was injured a few days before his date at Epsom. But for many (including, it has to be said, J. McCririck), the most significant Derby trial was the Chester Vase, in which Toulon, owned by Khalid Abdullah and trained in France by André Fabre, overcame all sorts of trouble in running at the final bend to beat Luchiroverte and Peking Opera and catapult himself to Derby favouritism.

On the Sunday before the Derby the Prix du Jockey-Club at Chantilly had seen a horse of quite exceptional speed scythe his way through his rivals to win by four lengths. This was Suave Dancer, who earlier in the season had been hailed as the best three-year-old seen in France for many a long year.

If the Ever Ready Derby were to produce a worthy rival for this French colt it would have to be something very special, and so it proved. In a field of thirteen, Toulon and Corrupt started joint favourites on 4-1, with Mystiko 5-1, Hector Protector 6-1 and Generous 9-1. The age-old question of 'What does Lester ride?', unspoken for the last five years, was revived with great enthusiasm – more enthusiasm, probably, than greeted the answer: Hokusai.

Mystiko led from the stalls and was still in front coming round Tattenham Corner, but even at that stage there was really only one horse in it. Generous and Alan Munro were poised just off the pace, and once they had struck the front with two furlongs to go, that was that. The chestnut came away from his rivals and powered towards the line in the manner of an exceptional horse. Marju ran on to take second place, five lengths behind the winner, and seven lengths further back Star Of Gdansk just kept Hector Protector out of third.

Three days later the Gold Seal Oaks – the thousandth Classic in Great Britain – produced a near-sensation when 50-1 shot Jet Ski Lady led all the way to surge home ten lengths clear of Shamshir and the non-staying Shadayid (evens favourite). Though at the time it left most punters scratching their heads – or cursing their judgement if they'd backed the winner at the Tote odds of 15½-1 – the way in which Jet Ski Lady demolished her Oaks field was one of the highlights of the 1991 Flat season.

Plenty more were to follow, of course. Royal Ascot had a pulsating finish between Marju and Second Set in the St James's Palace Stakes and an even greater race when Kooyonga reversed Newmarket placings with Shadayid in the Coronation Stakes. The Gold Cup was one of those races which made you wish you studied the form book more closely: Indian Queen, who beat Arzanni in yet another marvellous finish, started at 25-1 despite being the only Group One winner in the race. There was a controversial finish to the Hardwicke Stakes when Rock Hopper got the race on the disqualification of Topanoora, brilliant sprint performances from Polish Patriot in the Cork and Orrery and from Elbio in the King's Stand, and memorable two-year-olds in Dilum and Marling. There was also the curious sight of 1990 Cheltenham Gold Cup winner Norton's Coin running at Royal Ascot partnered by Lester Piggott: they finished eighth in the Queen Alexandra Stakes.

Generous reappeared in the Budweiser Irish Derby for a showdown with Suave Dancer, on whom Walter Swinburn took the ride in place of the injured Cash Asmussen. But Alan Munro won the tactical battle of wits, shooting Generous into the lead early on and then thrusting clear once Suave Dancer had tried to get on terms in the straight. There was no longer any doubt that Generous was an outstanding colt, and his first encounter with older horses in the King George was eagerly awaited.

Meanwhile we had an Eclipse Stakes to relish, with Environment Friend, an almost unconsidered 28-1 outsider after flopping in the Derby, prevailing after a marvellous battle with Stagecraft through the final furlong.

The July Meeting at Newmarket brought its usual share of delights. Rock Hopper just pipped Mukddaam in the Princess of Wales's Stakes and Only Yours returned to form in the Child Stakes. But the star turn came from the volatile Polish Patriot, who beat a strong field for the July Cup (including Lycius, Elbio, Polar Falcon and Chicarica) with authority. Sadly he sustained an injury during the race which spelt the end of his racing career.

Then attention switched back to Ireland when Possessive Dancer – bred by Walter Swinburn – got the better of Jet Ski Lady in a great battle for the Irish Oaks: if nothing else, the race showed Jet Ski Lady's Epsom win to be no fluke.

Generous duly took on his elders in the King George VI and Queen Elizabeth Diamond Stakes at Ascot at the end of July and comprehensively demolished them, showing a staggering turn of foot to leave some of the best middle-distance horses in Europe toiling in his wake. Sanglamore was second, seven lengths behind the Derby winner, Rock Hopper third and Terimon fourth. It was the performance of the season to that point – and for many remained the racing moment of 1991.

By the end of July, Dilum was widely regarded as the best two-year-old seen out in England, and an authoritative victory in the Richmond Stakes at Goodwood strengthened the view. Other highlights of the Goodwood July Meeting were Second Set winning the Sussex Stakes from Shadayid and Priolo, and Ruby Tiger slamming her Nassau Stakes rivals by seven lengths: but she had suffered a cracked bone in her knee and was out for the season.

The big talking point at the York August Meeting was the going: had the course been watered too much, with the result that the ground was false? Although the going was officially good, times were generally slow. Trainers complained, and controversy raged. But some jockeys showed great enterprise during the meeting, none more so than Michael Roberts, who rode a magnificent tactical race to send good old Terimon into the lead early in the International Stakes and defy his better fancied rivals to catch him. Only 1990 Derby winner Quest For Fame could get anywhere near him, and Terimon won his first Group One race. Jet Ski Lady and Magnificent Star fought out a superb tussle for the Yorkshire Oaks, with Magnificent Star getting the verdict by a short head, and the meeting's third Group One race, the Nunthorpe Stakes, went to Sheikh Albadou and Pat Eddery, who beat the two-year-old Paris House, partnered by the riding find of the season, Darryll Holland. The Ebor went to another young star in the making when Francis Norton made most of the running on Deposki, but the Dilum bubble burst when Paul Cole's colt could finish only fourth of five in the Gimcrack.

Sheikh Albadou was out again in the Ladbroke Sprint Cup at Haydock but could not match the speed of French challenger Polar Falcon. Shadayid was third and Mystiko fourth, the second meeting of the two Guineas winners (after the Sussex Stakes).

A brief scare about the state of the ground on the opening day of the Doncaster September Meeting brought woeful memories of the 1989 subsidence, but all was well and racing continued uninterrupted. Notable memories included an authoritative victory by Rodrigo De Triano in the Champagne Stakes and an extraordinary climax to the Doncaster Cup, when a whirlwind effort by the Champion Hurdler Morley Street so nearly grabbed the prize from Great Marquess, who clung on by a short head.

The St Leger, sponsored for the first time by Coalite, attracted a less than glittering field but produced a great finish, with Toulon and Pat Eddery always holding Saddlers' Hall and John Reid once the two horses had drawn clear in the closing stages. Lester Piggott was third on Micheletti.

Ascot's Brent Walker Festival was somewhat overshadowed in prospect by the difficulties besetting the sponsoring company, and on the day by appalling weather. Selkirk battled through driving rain to win the Queen Elizabeth II Stakes from Kooyonga and Shadayid, and the other Group One contest, the Fillies' Mile, went to Culture Vulture, but only after the demotion of first-past-the-post Midnight Air, who had knocked Paul Cole's filly sideways as Pat Eddery drew out to challenge early in the straight. Eddery was suspended for eight days.

The Newmarket October Meeting saw two notable two-year-old performances. The unbeaten Marling ran on stoutly to beat Absurde in the Cheveley Park Stakes, and Rodrigo De Triano landed the Middle Park handily from Lion Cavern. But almost as much attention was paid to the Tattersalls Tiffany Highflyer Stakes, the prize money for which carried huge bonuses for runners bought at the Highflyer Sales. A high-class field was attracted by the swag, with Young Senor landing first prize of £30,218 plus a £500,000 bonus when beating Dr Devious. Robert Sangster's Soiree was only sixth, but picked up a bonus of £100,000 as the first eligible filly home! Hot favourite for the Cambridgeshire, one of the big betting races of the year, was Palatial Style, but it was Mary Reveley's Mellottie, second in 1990, who landed the spoils, by a short head from High Premium. With the second and third trained by Lynda Ramsden (who announced earlier in the year that she would be giving up training, then in December announced that she would not), the first three in the Cambridgeshire were all trained by women.

But throughout the early autumn anticipation was building up towards the Prix de l'Arc de Triomphe, and at Longchamp on the first Sunday of October came the moment of truth. Generous was there to set the seal on his greatness, but Suave Dancer, fresh from an easy victory in the Irish Champion Stakes, was reported to have improved since the Irish Derby. Add the likes of In The Groove (winner of the Coronation Cup), Pistolet Bleu, the 1990 St Leger winner Snurge, Toulon, the Prix Vermeille winner Magic Night, Quest for Fame and Jet Ski Lady, and the Arc field was truly representative of the best horses in Europe.

Confidence in the British camp was high after Culture Vulture had won her second Group One race in nine days in the Prix Marcel Boussac and John Gosden's Keen Hunter had taken the Abbaye from Sheikh Albadou. But just as Generous, steered round the outside by Alan Munro, seemed about to launch his attack at the entrance to the straight, his effort fizzled out, and all the glories of his midsummer campaign were momentarily forgotten as Cash Asmussen brought Suave Dancer from the back of the field to slice his way to the front in a few strides with a stupendous burst of speed.

The debate over what had happened to Generous raged for weeks. Even at the beginning of December, just when we thought it was safe to concentrate on the jumpers, a petulant speech at a racing writers' lunch by Anthony Penfold, racing manager to Generous's owner Fahd Salman, complained about the colt not winning a Cartier award, and denigrated the Arc as being 'a race run in the shadows'. But the shadows on Arc day 1991 were cast by the brilliance of Suave Dancer.

It had been announced after the King George that Generous would be retired at the end of the season (unlike Suave Dancer, who remains in training) because 'he has nothing left to prove', and although there was hope that he would run in the Champion Stakes and redeem his reputation, that was not to be. It transpired that Generous was indeed a sick horse on Arc day, and it is his remarkable turn of foot in the Derby, Irish Derby and King George which will live on in the memory. (He was unanimously elected Horse of the Year by the Racegoers' Club in a poll for which neither Arazi nor Suave Dancer was eligible.) And when the International Classifications were published in January 1992, Generous was officially rated at 137, one pound superior to Suave Dancer: only Dancing Brave, Shergar and El Gran Señor had been rated higher since the Classifications began in 1977.)

In Generous's absence the Champion Stakes at the Newmarket Houghton Meeting went to French challenger Tel Quel, Sheikh Mohammed's first Group One winner of the season in England. Tel Quel came late under rising French jockey Thierry Jarnet to deprive Cruachan and hold off the fast-finishing In The Groove. Other highlights of the meeting were the victory of Dr Devious over Great Palm in the Dewhurst, the rehabilitation of Mystiko in the Challenge Stakes, and Go South at 40–1 winning the Cesarewitch under Nicky Carlisle.

England's last Group One race of the year, the Racing Post Trophy, fell to the relentless stride of Seattle Rhyme, who looked a useful prospect for the 1992 Derby.

But come the beginning of November, the attention of the racing world shifted to Churchill Downs, Kentucky, venue of the 1991 Breeders' Cup, and specifically to Arazi, the exceptional French two-year-old who had beaten Seattle Rhyme in the Grand Criterium at Longchamp the day before the Arc and had only once been beaten in seven races.

In the Breeders' Cup Juvenile Arazi would be racing for the first time on dirt, had the outside draw in a hectic race which would involve racing around two 180-degree bends, and in the opinion of some (including, it was said, his trainer Francois Boutin) had done quite enough for the season already. The way in which the colt overcame these disadvantages has already entered racing legend. Pushed along to get a decent position by the first bend, Arazi seemed to have difficulty keeping up with the pace by the time the runners had reached the back straight. He was second last and, as Graham Goode called it, 'not really racing with any enthusiasm'. Then he hit his stride and produced the most extraordinary run seen for many a long year. Moving to the inside, to the outside, back halfway towards the inner and then back to the outside, he picked off horse after horse, so that by the turn into the straight he had effortlessly pulled his way to the head of affairs. Then, despite being on the wrong leg and thus getting carried wide round the final bend, he simply came away from his rivals in the straight and won, with rider Pat Valenzuela pulling him up, by 4¾ lengths.

Beside that the rest of the marvellous Breeders' Cup programme pales somewhat, but the event had begun with a superb victory from Sheikh Albadou (ridden by Pat Eddery) in the Sprint, only the second ever British victory in a Breeders' Cup race on the Flat, and the first ever on dirt. Europe also won the Turf with Miss Alleged (in which Quest For Fame was a game third), but our challengers disappointed in the Mile behind Opening Verse (who had been second to Nashwan in the Eclipse when trained by Henry Cecil). The world's richest race, the Breeders' Cup Classic, was won by Black Tie Affair from Twilight Agenda.

The Flat season in Great Britain closed nine days after the Breeders' Cup, a million miles from Churchill Downs on a gloomy Monday at Folkstone. It had been a memorable season, for humans as well as horses.

Pat Eddery was champion jockey yet again, with 165 winners, and passed the 3000-winner mark. Darryll Holland was champion apprentice. Willie Carson again won the most prize money for his patrons. John Lowe rode his thousandth winner. Jimmy Bleasdale announced his retirement on account of the side effects of head injuries. Bill Shoemaker, the winning-most jockey in history, was left partially paralysed after a car crash in California in March.

Paul Cole was leading trainer, thanks substantially to the exploits of Generous and Dilum, but other trainers to hit the headlines were Jack Berry, who had his best season and smashed existing records for the fastest 50 winners and then the fastest 100, and Richard Hannon, who scored his first century of winners on 20 September and passed the £1 million mark in winnings the following day. Frankie Durr announced his retirement.

Away from the racetrack, the Home Affairs Committee of the House of Commons conducted an in-depth examination of the racing business and made certain recommendations for reform to the Home Secretary, who paid little heed. The Racecourse Association commissioned a survey of why people go – and do not go – racing: predictably, the sport was still perceived as class-ridden, but less predictable was the revelation that two out of three racegoers felt they got value for money, and one out of three expressed themselves happy with course catering. The Aliysa case rumbled on, with the Aga Khan (who had removed all his horses in training from Britain) failing to have her disqualification from the 1989 Oaks overturned in the High Court. And Dancing Brave was exported to continue his stud career in Japan.

Meanwhile the National Hunt season had resumed. But the opening fixture at Bangor-on-Dee on 2 August made the headlines for the worst reason: jockey Sharron Murgatroyd suffered a fall which left her paralysed. Worse was to come. On Boxing Day conditional jockey Philip Barnard died from serious injuries incurred through a fall from Sayyure at Wincanton. He was twenty-four.

By the turn of the year the early stages of the jumping season had seen the emergence of a possible new star in the gigantic shape of Kings Fountain, winner of the H & T Walker Handicap Chase at Ascot and the A. F. Budge Gold Cup at Cheltenham. The Hennessy went to Martin and Pipe and Peter Scudamore with Chatam, and the same pair brought the rejuvenated Carvill's Hill back to winning form at Chepstow, first in the Rehearsal Chase and then with a stunning twenty-length victory over Party Politics in the Coral Welsh National. Five days later The Fellow turned in a smooth performance to beat Docklands Express and Remittance Man in the King George, and the pace of the jumping season moved up a gear.

The racing year in 1991 may have been an especially memorable one, but its last three months suggested that 1992 could be even better, and it certainly began on the right note. On New Year's Day the brilliant 1990 One Thousand Guineas and Oaks winner Salsabil gave birth to a filly foal by Nashwan. Had the foal been born a day earlier she would officially have become a yearling on 1 January and thus hardly a racing proposition, but her exquisite sense of timing – not to mention her breeding – makes her one to look out for in 1994!

# MAGIC MOMENTS OF 1991

*Each of the Channel Four Racing presenters chooses his top racing memory from last year.*

## DEREK THOMPSON

*Mystiko's victory in the Two Thousand Guineas.*

On *The Morning Line* on Two Thousand Guineas day Jim McGrath pronounced that Mystiko had no chance (sorry to remind you, Jimbo!), but I thought he'd win – and said so. Jockey Michael Roberts had told me he considered Mystiko far and away the best horse he'd ever ridden, and that was good enough for me. It was also a great result for Clive Brittain. There's no harder worker in racing, nor a nicer guy: I just wish all people in racing were like Clive!

## BROUGH SCOTT

*Star Player winning the Chester Cup*

The best moment about interviews is when the event and the people take them over. It was like that when Star Player landed a West Country coup at Chester. Not just jockey Frankie Dettori, but trainer John Baker and seemingly half of Somerset crammed into the tiny winner's circle. The place was sunny, crowded, and awash with happiness.

## JOHN TYRREL

*Cabochon's Ascot Stakes*

It is a rare – if not unique – occurrence for the holder of the post of Her Majesty's Representative at Ascot to have a winner at the Royal Meeting, and yet another thread was added and spun into the rich tapestry of the best four days' racing anywhere in the world when the home-bred

Cabochon won the Ascot Stakes in 1991 in the colours of Colonel Sir Piers Bengough. For me it was a memorable race – the memory assisted by a fiver each way at 15-2.

# GRAHAM GOODE

## *Jack Berry's ton-up*

The three-runner Gaetan Billard Champagne Sprint Handicap at Hamilton Park on 17 July 1991 was not the most complicated commentating task I had last year, but the result – a two-length victory for Our Fan, ridden by John Carroll – made the race something special. Our Fan was Jack Berry's one hundredth winner of the season, beating Henry Cecil's record for the fastest century by six days. The reception given this feat by the crowd was marvellous, and soon it was drinks all round on Jack – it seemed that everyone round the weighing room had a glass of champagne in their hand.

# JIM MCGRATH

## *Generous in the King George VI and Queen Elizabeth Diamond Stakes*

When you go racing day in, day out you don't often get very moved by what you see. But Generous at Ascot really rang bells for me. The result was not at all unexpected, but the manner in which he won the King George – that utter annhilation of his rivals – was simply superb. It was a staggering performance.

# JOHN OAKSEY

## *Further Flight in the Goodwood Cup*

The Goodwood Cup has always been one of my favourite flat races, and even reduced to two miles it is still a glorious sight – the most 'scenic' race in the whole form book. Further Flight must have given Michael Hills a deeply enviable thrill in the 1991 running – coming through from last to first in about a furlong and making his nine opponents look like frogs struggling in treacle. Apart, perhaps, from Arazi's opponents at Churchill Downs, no group of horses was overtaken in more spectacular style all season. I would love to own Further Flight, who was unluckily disqualified in France then ended the year gloriously by winning two Group races. Given the chance, he might make Morley Street think twice over hurdles.


## JOHN FRANCOME

*Lester Piggott at Doncaster*

For me the greatest sight of 1991 was Lester Piggott winning the Reference Point Sceptre Stakes on St Leger day on You Know The Rules. He'd dropped the filly out early on, and even well inside the final furlong she seemed to have no chance. Willie Carson and Silver Braid had the race sewn up, then Lester brought You Know The Rules flying through and put her nose in front right on the line to win by a short head. It was the season's most spectacular example of the Piggott perfect timing in action, and it's amazing to see him still doing it.


## JOHN MCCRIRICK

*Arazi in the Breeders' Cup Juvenile*

Breathtaking – literally. That was Arazi at Churchill Downs. Jet-lagged, on dirt for the first time, from a hideous outside stall 14, this equine freak, already crowned Europe's champion, scythed snipe-like through America's best, leaving astonished racegoers drained and gasping for oxygen. The old Kentucky home of the Thoroughbred had never witnessed his like before.

# STATISTICS OF 1991

*Chris Jones, who provides Channel Four Racing with much of its statistical information, introduces the facts and figures that made 1991 such a significant year.*

In 1991 the frenetic action on the racecourse was matched in the record books. Barriers continued to fall wherever Martin Pipe and Peter Scudamore went. In the spring of the 1990/91 National Hunt season, Pipe achieved the fastest-ever double century, breaking his own record by five days. He finished the season with 230 wins and total prize money of £1,203,014, becoming the first jumps trainer to net a seven-figure sum.

Peter Scudamore managed to win his sixth National Hunt Jockeys' Championship in a row, despite missing ten weeks of the season with a broken leg.

Gordon Richards had his best-ever season in numerical terms: he reached his second century in April and finished the season with 118 wins. Only three other jumping trainers have had a hundred wins in a year – Michael Dickinson, Arthur Stephenson and that man Pipe.

On the flat, racehorse of the year Generous ended his career a millionaire – his total of £1,119,944 puts him third on the all-time British list. (Only Pebbles and Ibn Bey surpassed his total.) Paul Cole's champion set the record winning distance in the King George VI and Queen Elizabeth Diamond Stakes when he beat Sanglamore by seven lengths in July.

Cole became Champion Trainer (in prize-money terms) for the first time, but also achieved a personal record. On the last day of the turf season, Confronter gave him his thousandth winner.

Alan Munro, aside from his exploits with Generous, achieved a couple of other notable feats. In October, he reached his first century, and finished the turf season with 109 wins. In June, though, he notched a rarer record, when joining the select band of jockeys to win six races in a day.

Munro's six came at Lingfield and Goodwood, but it's worth remembering that in 1990 Pat Eddery did the same at Wolverhampton and Windsor, and Willie Carson rode six winners on the same card, at Newcastle.

Five wins on one card was definitely the order of the day in the first half of the 1991/92 National Hunt Season. Peter Scudamore started the trend at Devon and Exeter in late August, and was followed in October at Kelso by Peter Niven. By the end of 1991 Niven had repeated the feat twice – at Doncaster and Sedgefield.

The summer of 1991 was one of career milestones and numerical records. Pat Eddery, champion jockey for the fourth successive year (165 wins by the end of the turf season), reached his three-thousandth winner at Bath on 22 July. He now stands fifth in the list of British career totals, behind Sir Gordon Richards, Lester Piggott, Willie Carson and Doug Smith.

Richard Hannon notched up his first century in September, and finished the turf campaign with 126 winners to his name. He was one of only three centurions in 1991 (the others were Jack Berry and Henry Cecil), and ended up second in the list of money-earners. Hannon is only the eleventh British trainer since 1900 to record a hundred winners, and all but two of them are still training.

Whilst not quite managing one hundred two-year-old winners, Jack Berry surpassed the previous record (his own) with a score of 90. His total score for the season was 143, and he broke Henry Cecil's records for the fastest 50 and fastest 100.

In May, Walter Swinburn emulated Willie Carson when riding and breeding a Classic winner. Carson achieved the feat with Minster Son in the 1988 St Leger. Swinburn bred Possessive Dancer, on whom he won the Italian Oaks: Steve Cauthen rode the filly to victory in the Irish Oaks. Gary Carter entered the history books in June when he became only the second jockey to win at three British courses in a day. His feat – at Southwell, York and Doncaster – equals that of Paul Cook, who won at Sandown, Bath and Nottingham in July 1981.

It was also a year of remarkable starting prices: Jet Ski Lady's Oaks victory set a record for the race of 50–1. And when Indian Queen won the Gold Cup, her 25–1 return equalled the record for that race. Indian Queen was only the third female Gold Cup-winner this century, after Quashed (1936) and Gladness (1958).

The season came to a climax in Kentucky, where European horses had their most successful Breeders' Cup yet. Morley Street started things going when he won the Steeplechase in Maryland. Churchill Downs, however, saw the real action, with victories for Sheikh Albadou from England and Arazi and Miss Alleged from France.

Records are not what they were. These days, new ones seem to be made almost weekly. Ancient achievements are surpassed, and higher goals are set. The sport moves on, to ever greater things. Who knows what's to come in 1992? We live in interesting times.

# *1991 Flat Statistics*

In Great Britain to 31 December, including all-weather racing

## OWNERS

In order of win and place prize money.
(The horse contributing the greatest amount of prize money is given in brackets.)

|  |  | RACES WON | £ |
|---|---|---|---|
| 1 | Sheik Mohammed (Tel Quel) | 139 | 1,836,590 |
| 2 | Hamdan Al-Maktoum (Shadayid) | 92 | 1,338,766 |
| 3 | Fahd Salman (Generous) | 48 | 1,159,353 |
| 4 | K. Abdullah (Toulon) | 71 | 801,650 |
| 5 | Maktoum Al Maktoum (Rock Hopper) | 33 | 643,532 |
| 6 | R.E. Sangster (Rodrigo De Triano) | 54 | 570,606 |
| 7 | The Dowager Lady Beaverbrook (Terimon) | 13 | 498,282 |
| 8 | David Thompson (Polar Falcon) | 17 | 374,085 |
| 9 | A.F. Budge (Equine) Ltd (River Falls) | 25 | 373,534 |
| 10 | George Strawbridge (Selkirk) | 10 | 356,212 |
| 11 | Ecurie Fustok (Made Of Gold) | 16 | 353,308 |
| 12 | Lord Weinstock (Saddlers' Hall) | 16 | 276,762 |
| 13 | Luciano Gaucci (Dr Devious) | 6 | 240,851 |
| 14 | W.J. Gredley (Environment Friend) | 5 | 236,679 |
| 15 | Richard L. Duchossois (Second Set) | 10 | 222,801 |

# TRAINERS

## In order of win and place prize money

| | | WINS | RUNS | % | £ | £1 LEVEL STAKE |
|---|---|---|---|---|---|---|
| 1 | P. F. I. Cole | 73 | 392 | 19 | 1,520,617 | −31.18 |
| 2 | R. Hannon | 126 | 958 | 13 | 1,342,392 | −149.52 |
| 3 | M. R. Stoute | 83 | 413 | 20 | 1,283,193 | −57.70 |
| 4 | C. E. Brittain | 53 | 545 | 10 | 1,164,499 | −117.41 |
| 5 | J. L. Dunlop | 58 | 366 | 16 | 1,040,654 | −64.14 |
| 6 | L. M. Cumani | 72 | 334 | 22 | 1,009,207 | −63.43 |
| 7 | H. R. A. Cecil | 119 | 381 | 31 | 983,715 | +17.10 |
| 8 | B. W. Hills | 99 | 491 | 20 | 919,606 | +7.81 |
| 9 | J. Berry | 143 | 837 | 17 | 873,219 | −184.88 |
| 10 | D. R. C. Elsworth | 40 | 354 | 11 | 796,850 | −93.91 |
| 11 | J. H. M. Gosden | 86 | 384 | 22 | 662,863 | −5.87 |
| 12 | I. A. Balding | 53 | 362 | 15 | 638,839 | −46.92 |
| 13 | A. Fabre | 5 | 12 | 42 | 634,709 | +15.94 |
| 14 | G. Harwood | 55 | 326 | 17 | 621,994 | −47.76 |
| 15 | G. Wragg | 51 | 220 | 23 | 553,492 | +28.18 |

# JOCKEYS

| | | WINS | RIDES | % | 2ND | 3RD | £1 LEVEL STAKE |
|---|---|---|---|---|---|---|---|
| 1 | Pat Eddery | 165 | 807 | 20 | 130 | 76 | −137.58 |
| 2 | W. Carson | 155 | 890 | 17 | 130 | 93 | −181.35 |
| 3 | M. Roberts | 118 | 864 | 14 | 109 | 96 | −13.71 |
| 4 | A. Munro | 110 | 789 | 14 | 92 | 79 | −74.06 |
| 5 | S. Cauthen | 107 | 472 | 23 | 79 | 57 | −15.41 |
| 6 | R. Cochrane | 102 | 718 | 14 | 103 | 84 | −28.08 |
| 7 | T. Quinn | 99 | 731 | 14 | 93 | 90 | −77.28 |
| 8 | L. Dettori | 94 | 708 | 13 | 94 | 85 | −204.89 |
| 9 | G. Duffield | 88 | 648 | 14 | 47 | 63 | −113.08 |
| 10 | J. Carroll | 87 | 585 | 15 | 76 | 66 | −189.61 |
| 11 | D. Holland | 83 | 556 | 15 | 68 | 61 | −2.15 |
| 12 | J. Reid | 80 | 676 | 12 | 94 | 74 | −94.55 |
| 13 | G. Carter | 75 | 611 | 12 | 59 | 59 | −181.68 |
| 14 | B. Raymond | 74 | 678 | 11 | 66 | 78 | −194.69 |
| 15 | W. Ryan | 72 | 494 | 15 | 69 | 46 | −210.61 |

# APPRENTICES

| | | WINS | RIDES | % | 2ND | 3RD |
|---|---|---|---|---|---|---|
| 1 | D. Holland | 83 | 556 | 15 | 68 | 61 |
| 2 | J. K. Fanning | 43 | 526 | 8 | 46 | 43 |
| 3 | F. Norton | 40 | 384 | 10 | 36 | 23 |
| 4 | R. Perham | 36 | 528 | 14 | 25 | 24 |
| 5 | Alex Greaves | 34 | 284 | 12 | 35 | 42 |

## HORSES

In order of win and place prize money

|   |   | WINS | RUNS | £ |
|---|---|---|---|---|
| 1 | Generous | 2 | 3 | 639,145 |
| 2 | Shadayid | 2 | 7 | 296,868 |
| 3 | Marju | 2 | 6 | 278,098 |
| 4 | Tel Quel | 1 | 1 | 262,350 |
| 5 | Selkirk | 2 | 6 | 252,480 |
| 6 | Kooyonga | 1 | 3 | 242,722 |
| 7 | Rock Hopper | 4 | 7 | 239,644 |
| 8 | Terimon | 2 | 7 | 228,774 |
| 9 | Environment Friend | 2 | 7 | 222,465 |
| 10 | Toulon | 2 | 3 | 205,049 |

# *1990/91 National Hunt Statistics*

In Great Britain

## OWNERS

In order of win and place prize money.
(The horse contributing the greatest amount of prize money is given in brackets.)

|   |   | RACES WON | £ |
|---|---|---|---|
| 1 | P. Piller (Blazing Walker) | 33 | 275,871 |
| 2 | Sir Eric Parker (Seagram) | 6 | 164,540 |
| 3 | B. A. Kilpatrick (Sabin du Loir) | 15 | 153,738 |
| 4 | Pell-Mell Partners (Katabatic) | 13 | 150,110 |
| 5 | Michael Jackson Bloodstock (Morley Street) | 5 | 146,774 |
| 6 | Autofour Engineering (Garrison Savannah) | 1 | 135,718 |
| 7 | A. F. Budge (Equine) Ltd (Uncle Ernie) | 23 | 124,929 |
| 8 | Pipe Scudamore Racing plc (Hopscotch) | 36 | 121,896 |
| 9 | John R. Upson (Thar-An-Barr) | 21 | 116,702 |
| 10 | R. H. Baines (Docklands Express) | 4 | 103,321 |
| 11 | R. Burridge (Desert Orchid) | 2 | 93.095 |
| 12 | M. R. Deeley (Waterloo Boy) | 4 | 91,759 |
| 13 | Mrs Shirley Robins (Wonder Man) | 14 | 88,845 |
| 14 | J. P. McManus (Blitzkrieg) | 5 | 84,591 |
| 15 | Paul Mellon (Crystal Spirit) | 4 | 81,937 |

# TRAINERS

In order of win and place prize money, and including all-weather hurdles

|   |                    | WINS | RUNS | %  | £         | £1 LEVEL STAKE |
|---|--------------------|------|------|----|-----------|----------------|
| 1 | M. C. Pipe         | 230  | 782  | 29 | 1,203,014 | −4.02          |
| 2 | G. W. Richards     | 118  | 493  | 24 | 524,591   | −14.31         |
| 3 | W. A. Stephenson   | 83   | 505  | 16 | 458,927   | −199.56        |
| 4 | Mrs J. Pitman      | 43   | 294  | 15 | 437,959   | −58.34         |
| 5 | G. B. Balding      | 48   | 340  | 14 | 379,035   | −167.12        |
| 6 | O. Sherwood        | 56   | 261  | 21 | 373,375   | −25.39         |
| 7 | N. J. Henderson    | 49   | 264  | 19 | 372,098   | −53.44         |
| 8 | J. T. Gifford      | 62   | 451  | 14 | 371.710   | −107.54        |
| 9 | D. Nicholson       | 55   | 277  | 20 | 343,079   | −55.88         |
| 10| D. H. Barons       | 34   | 215  | 16 | 277,431   | +22.17         |
| 11| D. R. C. Elsworth  | 23   | 131  | 18 | 267,531   | −19.50         |
| 12| J. A. C. Edwards   | 54   | 311  | 17 | 252,810   | −59.75         |
| 13| K. C. Bailey       | 33   | 189  | 17 | 248,567   | +11.79         |
| 14| J. G. FitzGerald   | 45   | 216  | 21 | 226,816   | −28.64         |
| 15| R. Akehurst        | 35   | 217  | 16 | 215,624   | +46.51         |

# JOCKEYS

|   |                  | WINS | RIDES | %  | 2ND | 3RD | £1 LEVEL STAKE |
|---|------------------|------|-------|----|-----|-----|----------------|
| 1 | P. Scudamore     | 141  | 420   | 34 | 53  | 37  | +9.74          |
| 2 | R. Dunwoody      | 127  | 646   | 20 | 122 | 78  | −156.92        |
| 3 | N. Doughty       | 96   | 349   | 28 | 62  | 38  | +51.35         |
| 4 | P. Niven         | 86   | 423   | 20 | 65  | 61  | −4.85          |
| 5 | G. McCourt       | 83   | 435   | 19 | 84  | 54  | +8.27          |
| 6 | M. Dwyer         | 81   | 380   | 21 | 64  | 51  | −63.60         |
| 7 | J. Osborne       | 62   | 353   | 18 | 58  | 37  | −23.00         |
| 8 | M. Perrett       | 58   | 272   | 21 | 27  | 31  | −81.56         |
| 9 | C. Grant         | 57   | 348   | 16 | 41  | 41  | −92.37         |
| 10| S. Smith Eccles  | 56   | 236   | 24 | 38  | 27  | −8.06          |
| 11| H. Davies        | 51   | 379   | 13 | 36  | 37  | −125.50        |
| 12| L. Wyer          | 44   | 248   | 18 | 36  | 38  | −45.76         |
| 13| L. Harvey        | 42   | 276   | 15 | 34  | 37  | −44.84         |
| 14| J. Frost         | 39   | 276   | 14 | 42  | 25  | −70.16         |
| 15| B. Powell        | 38   | 452   | 8  | 54  | 45  | −236.18        |

# AMATEUR RIDERS

|   |                 | WINS | RIDES | %  | 2ND | 3RD |
|---|-----------------|------|-------|----|-----|-----|
| 1 | Mr K. Johnson   | 24   | 151   | 16 | 21  | 16  |
| 2 | Mr A. Farrant   | 13   | 70    | 19 | 11  | 9   |
| 3 | Mr S. Swiers    | 12   | 110   | 11 | 13  | 14  |
| 4 | Miss S. Billot  | 9    | 36    | 25 | 6   | 4   |
| 5 | Mr J. Bradburne | 8    | 72    | 11 | 10  | 9   |

# HORSES

## In order of win and place prize money

|    |                    | WINS | RUNS | £       |
|----|--------------------|------|------|---------|
| 1  | Morley Street      | 5    | 7    | 145,402 |
| 2  | Seagram            | 3    | 9    | 137,858 |
| 3  | Garrison Savannah  | 1    | 3    | 135,718 |
| 4  | Katabatic          | 3    | 7    | 106,964 |
| 5  | Docklands Express  | 4    | 8    | 103,321 |
| 6  | Blazing Walker     | 6    | 7    | 98,090  |
| 7  | Desert Orchid      | 2    | 6    | 93,095  |
| 8  | Sabin du Loir      | 3    | 8    | 85,409  |
| 9  | Crystal Spirit     | 4    | 6    | 81,937  |
| 10 | Remittance Man     | 6    | 6    | 80,214  |

# THE CHANNEL FOUR RACING CHAMPION TIPSTER COMPETITION

The Champion Tipster competition was inaugurated by Channel Four Racing in August 1990. Each month participating viewers make selections for each of the live races shown by Channel Four, and the prize goes to the person who shows the greatest profit to a notional £1 stake on each selection.

**The Champion Tipsters in 1991 were:**

JANUARY   **Brian Hazelwood,** Banbury, Oxfordshire                £36.73

FEBRUARY   **Michael Jones,** Farsley, Leeds                       £55.00

MARCH   **John Vaughan,** Newcastle-under-Lyme, Staffs             £56.00

APRIL   **Mrs Sylvia Dugard,** Freeland, Oxfordshire              £64.00

MAY   **John Gould,** Northampton                                  £52.00

JUNE   **Peter Hopgood,** Barford St Martins, Salisbury           £81.50

JULY   **Ken Cowell,** London NW8                                  £42.00

AUGUST   **Ronald Sexton,** Thame, Oxfordshire                    £32.38

SEPTEMBER   **Ronald Field,** Coleshill, Birmingham               £69.67

OCTOBER   **Robert Preddy,** Swindon, Wiltshire                   £88.38

NOVEMBER   **Gerald Johnstone,** Blyth, Northumberland            £34.63

DECEMBER   **David Hughes,** Liverpool                            £38.90

# THE CHANNEL
# FOUR TROPHY

The Channel Four Trophy, established in 1985, is awarded twice a year. For the Flat, it goes to the owner of the British-trained horse who wins the greatest number of races during the Flat (turf) season; for National Hunt, to the owner of the British-trained horse who wins the greatest number of races between the end of the Flat (turf) season and Whitbread Gold Cup day. (Victories on all-weather surfaces do not apply, though wins overseas do.) In the event of a tie, placings are taken into account.

## *Table of Winners*

### FLAT

| YEAR | HORSE (AGE) | WINS (STARTS) | OWNER | TRAINER |
|------|-------------|---------------|-------|---------|
| 1985 | Chaplin's Club (5) | 9 (20) | P. D. Savill | D. W. Chapman |
| 1986 | Moon Madness (3) | 6 (8) | Duchess of Norfolk | J. L. Dunlop |
| 1987 | Perion (5) | 7 (13) | E. and B. Productions | G. Lewis |
| 1988 | Time To Go Home (2) | 9 (22) | P. D. Savill | R. Hollinshead |
| 1989 | Judgement Call (2) | 6 (13) | P. D. Savill | M. H. Easterby |
| 1990 | Timeless Times (2) | 16 (21) | Times of Wigan | W. O'Gorman |
| 1991 | Sense of Priority (2) | 6 (12) | P. D. Savill | M. H. Easterby |

## NATIONAL HUNT

| YEAR | HORSE (AGE) | WINS (STARTS) | OWNER | TRAINER |
|------|-------------|---------------|-------|---------|
| 1985/86 | Pearlyman (7) | 5 (7) | Mrs P. Shaw | J. A. C. Edwards |
| 1986/87 | Mandavi (6) | 6 (12) | Mrs K. Anderson | N. J. Henderson |
| 1987/88 | Rinus (7) | 8 (14) | A. M. Proos | G. Richards |
| 1988/89 | Roll-a-Joint (11) | 7 (10) | R. Thomas Williams | C. L. Popham |
| 1989/90 | The Leggett (7) | 6 (8) | A. E. Ford | M. C. Pipe |
| 1990/91 | Remittance Man (7) | 6 (6) | J. E. H. Collins | N. J. Henderson |

# The 1991 Winners

REMITTANCE MAN (Prince Regent – Mittens)
owned by J. E. H. Collins; trained by N. J. Henderson

Remittance Man must rank as one of the most worthy, and classy, winners of the National Hunt Channel Four Trophy, winning all his six races in the 1990/91 season. His crowning glory last year was a six-length victory in the Waterford Castle Arkle Challenge Trophy Chase at the Cheltenham Festival, a fitting end to a brilliant season.

In November 1990 Remittance Man impressed observers at Leicester on his chasing debut before stepping up in distance to two and a half miles in the Hopeful Chase at Newbury. He then won the Rovacabin Noel Novices' Chase at Ascot by eight lengths from Morley Street.

Desert Orchid dominated proceedings on Boxing Day at Kempton, but Remittance Man tasted victory too in the Wayward Lad Novices' Chase, which he took by twelve lengths. This impressive performance was a significant success in its own right and, along with a thirty-length win in the Galloway Braes Novices' Chase at Kempton two months later, provided a springboard to the National Hunt Festival.

Cheltenham put Remittance Man up against novices who had run only over two miles, such as Uncle Ernie and Last o' The Bunch, not surprisingly viewed as his main rivals. Gradually improving his position throughout the race and always going smoothly, he took the lead on the downhill run. Swinging for home, Uncle Ernie drew level and a close finish looked likely, but jumping told. Remittance Man put in a superb leap at the last and quickened away on landing to win easily.

## REMITTANCE MAN IN 1990/91

6 runs          6 wins

| | | |
|---|---|---|
| 19 November | Leicester | Douglas Concrete Novices' Chase   2 miles |
| 24 November | Newbury | Hopeful Chase   2½ miles |
| 15 December | Ascot | Rovacabin Noel Novices' Chase   2½ miles |
| 26 December | Kempton | Warners Wayward Lad Novices' Chase 2½ miles |
| 23 February | Kempton | Galloway Braes Novices' Chase   2½ miles |
| 12 March | Cheltenham | Waterford Castle Arkle Challenge Trophy Chase   2 miles |

## SENSE OF PRIORITY (Primo Dominie – Sense of Pride)
owned by P. D. Savill; trained by M. H. Easterby

Peter Easterby's Sense of Priority had close competition in last season's Channel Four Trophy, but his securing the title continues two trends obvious in the competition.

Then a two-year-old gelding and graduate of the Tattersalls October Yearling Sale, Sense of Priority provided the Trophy with its fourth successive two-year-old winner.

The sequence was begun in 1988 by Time To Go Home, and continued by Judgement Call the following year and the history-making Timeless Times in 1990.

There is, however, another thread running through the seven-year history of the competition: Peter Savill. The businessman based in the Cayman Islands won the Trophy in its inaugural year, thanks to Chaplin's Club, and since then has owned both Time To Go Home (1988) and Judgement Call (1989), as well as Sense of Priority.

The Flat Channel Four Trophy last season was a close-fought affair and resulted in a six-way tie at the top of the table. Under the rules of the competition, places are then used in deciding the outcome. Not until his last run, at Catterick on 18 October, did Sense of Priority secure the title, when a second place nosed him ahead of Titch Wizard, Laurel Queen, Paris House, Doublova and Red Rosein, all of whom also had six wins.

## SENSE OF PRIORITY IN 1991

| 12 runs | | 6 wins | 3 seconds | 2 thirds |

Wins:

| 30 May | Carlisle | Langdale Maiden Auction Stakes 5 furlongs |
| 6 June | Beverley | Etton Claiming Stakes 5 furlongs |
| 12 June | Beverley | Flexible Part-Time Study Selling Stakes 5 furlongs |
| 3 July | Catterick | Northern Echo Stakes 7 furlongs |
| 10 September | Carlisle | Greylag Claiming Stakes 7 furlongs |
| 21 September | Catterick | Beldale Nursery Handicap 7 furlongs |

# THE CARTIER AWARDS

The Cartier Awards were set up in 1991 as a European equivalent to the prestigious Eclipse Awards in the USA.

The Awards are based on three criteria: a points system derived from the Pattern races, a ballot of the top European racing journalists, and votes from the readers of the magazine *Pacemaker Update International*.

The results of the Cartier Awards for the 1991 Flat season were:

**EUROPEAN HORSE OF THE YEAR**
**Arazi** (30 points)
Suave Dancer (11)
Generous (7)

**TWO-YEAR-OLD COLT**
**Arazi** (30)
Rodrigo De Triano (10.5)
Seattle Rhyme (6.5)
Paris House (0.5)
Magic Ring (0.5)

**TWO-YEAR-OLD FILLY**
**Culture Vulture** (30)
Marling (15)
Musicale (2)
Twafeaj (1)

**THREE-YEAR-OLD COLT**
**Suave Dancer** (25)
Generous (20)
Sheikh Albadou (2)

**THREE-YEAR-OLD FILLY**
**Kooyonga** (20)
Shadayid (16)

*Three-year-old filly (cont.)*
Magic Night (11)
Danseuse du Soir (1)

**OLDER HORSE**
**Terimon** (15)
Rock Hopper (15)
Epervier Bleu (5)
In The Groove (1.5)
Kartajana (1)
Polar Falcon (0.5)

[Following the tie for first place, Terimon was chosen over Rock Hopper by the Cartier Awards jury.]

**SPRINTER**
**Sheikh Albadou** (30)
Polish Patriot (8)
Keen Hunter (6)
Polar Falcon (2)
Elbio (2)

**STAYER**
**Turgeon** (30)
Further Flight (10)

*Stayer (cont.)*
Victoire Bleue (5.5)
Indian Queen (2.5)

NORTH AMERICAN HORSE
OF THE YEAR
**Black Tie Affair** (12)
Lite Light (10)
In Excess (9)
Dance Smartly (5)
Arazi (3)
Versailles Treaty (1)

CARTIER AWARD OF
MERIT
**Henri Chalhoub –**
'for having the courage and
sportsmanship to keep his good
horse Suave Dancer in training
for another season'

# ADIEU TO DESSIE

John Oaksey *bids a fond farewell to the most popular horse of recent times.*

Richard Burridge, one of Desert Orchid's owners, is a highly successful and imaginative scriptwriter. But on 21 January 1983, standing beside his father and David Elsworth by the last flight of a two-mile novice hurdle at Kempton Park, he would have needed much more than a vivid imagination to foresee how their lives were going to be transformed by the grey four-year-old gelding who lay motionless at their feet.

At that moment, in fact, it seemed far from certain that Desert Orchid would 'transform' anything much at all. This had been the first race of his life, and until falling heavily just behind the leaders, he had put up an extremely promising performance. But he lay still much too long for anyone's peace of mind, including the Kempton vet's. 'You always hope they are just winded', says Elsworth, 'and more often than not they are. But for at least ten minutes – they felt like hours – it did not look at all good to us that day . . .'.

It was the last race of a cheerless January afternoon, and for most of the Kempton crowd getting out of the car park and home to a nice warm fire probably seemed at least as important as whether some unheard-of 50–1 outsider had done himself any lasting damage. A few concerned bystanders did raise a cheer when, eventually, the fallen grey got up, but it is only now, nine years and seventy-one races later, that the rest of us know just how grateful the sporting world should be that he *was* 'only winded'. In the nine seasons which followed that violent, potentially disastrous start, Desert Orchid has given the human race at least as much pleasure and excitement as any horse in Thoroughbred history.

Of course, you can dispute that claim and argue about it to your heart's content. 'The greatest equine entertainer of them all' is an imaginary title anyway – and could never be more than a matter of opinion. Arkle was a better steeplechaser than Desert Orchid, and, starring in five Grand Nationals, Red Rum played to a bigger audience. Before television, Brown Jack and Golden Miller would have been contenders.

Who knows – and, to tell the truth, who cares? All we know for certain is that the horse who survived that crashing Kempton fall turned out to have much more than his fair share of the qualities which enable any athlete to catch and hold the affection and admiration of a public outside the confines of his own specialized world.

Of course, excellence is one of them, and Desert Orchid's finest hours in terms of weight-conceding merit – the Racing Post Chase and Irish Grand National, for instance – are the rocks on which his reputation is founded. So, needless to say, are his four King George VI Chases, his Gold Cup and his Whitbread.

But there are others too – qualities and characteristics which I believe combine with his record to justify the word 'unique'. Soundness and durability are not the least of them, although these days they are regrettably among the rarest. Desert Orchid did not, admittedly, run well in Dawn Run's 1984 Champion Hurdle, but he started second favourite for it and almost ever since, for no fewer than *nine* seasons, has been at or near the top of whatever tree he was being asked to climb.

'Whatever tree . . . Whatever distance.' It never made much difference to the style and panache with which each succeeding different task was accomplished or gallantly attempted. A brilliantly quick jumper of hurdles, Desert Orchid was, to begin with, almost too bold a novice chaser. He managed to lose Colin Brown altogether once at Ascot, and quite often made his backers, if not his rider, close their eyes.

But although that boldness never vanished, it has been increasingly tempered with twinkle-toed cunning and, as the need for stamina increased with distance, economy of effort.

Just because Desert Orchid first made his name as a flamboyant front runner, it was easy to dismiss him as an exhibitionist tearaway – unlikely to stay beyond two miles and practically certain to hoist the white flag if taken on and headed. David Elsworth disagreed. When Desert Orchid was only five and had never jumped a fence, even at home, the trainer was quoted as follows in a Timeform interview: 'I have always regarded him as a potential chaser; a three-mile chaser at that.'

All his life, in fact, with the exception of his clairvoyant handler, Desert Orchid has been proving so-called experts wrong. He did it in his first spreadeagling King George. He did it again in the Whitbread, and when they said he was 'gone' in autumn 1990 he did it in style on Boxing Day. He did it by winning 'left-handed' at Liverpool, and given the chance I agree with David that he probably would have done it in the Grand National.

As for 'hoisting white flags', one of many things Desert Orchid has in common with Arkle is a point-blank refusal to accept that any task is beyond him. As evidence of his dour, dogged courage, I am not sure whether giving Panto Prince 22lbs, Pegwell Bay 18lbs or Gold Bearer 36lbs (in the Peregrine Handicap Chase at Ascot) would come top of my list. Probably the last because, owing to an uncharacteristic mistake at the fourth last, he had to fight back to give Gold Bearer more than two and a half stone from what looked an utterly hopeless position.

Those were triumphs over the handicapper. On Gold Cup day 1989 it was the bog-like ground, the left-hand bends, and an inspired Yahoo. No one lucky enough to see how Desert Orchid overcame those obstacles up the Cheltenham hill will easily believe that there has ever been a braver horse.

But courage and a superb constitution are not by any means the only gifts the Fates have given Desert Orchid. As I once wrote about Mill Reef, 'A racehorse's fate depends, often too closely for his own good, on the character, preferences and background of the human beings into whose hands he happens to fall'. Desert Orchid's breeder and owners do not happen to be quite a rich as Paul Mellon, but in almost every other respect their beloved grey, like Mill Reef, 'was born with a silver manger in his box'.

Much of the stubborn courage Desert Orchid has so often shown in defeat and victory alike is probably inherited from his grandmother Grey Orchid. According to family legend, she had icicles hanging from her shaggy coat when James Burridge found her in a field near Newark, and she certainly came over backwards, throwing him into a providential dungheap, the first time he tried to get on her.

Both Grey Orchid and her daughter Flower Child were so headstrong that hunting them was a hazardous, not particularly enjoyable pastime, so after winning two small chases with Charlie James, Flower Child was covered, at the ripe old age of eleven, by Grey Mirage.

It was a year later that the ungainly result of that mating so impressed James Burridge's son Richard that he bought a majority share. 'Desert Orchid suddenly took off across the field,' Richard remembers, 'and I've never seen anything move like it.' Highly articulate and used to importunate journalists, Richard Burridge has been a first-rate 'front' for his famous grey. But the best and biggest stroke of luck ever to befall our hero was the Burridges' choice of trainer.

David Elsworth's instinctive understanding of the horse has already been referred to. No one could possibly have masterminded Desert Orchid's career more successfully, and with a less sympathetic trainer his bright flame might so easily have burnt itself out long ago.

No trainer is better than his staff, and David's head lad Rodney Boult, who rides the grey in all his work at home, has his own very special place in this story. Without Rodney's strong arms and silken hands, Desert Orchid would have bored holes in numerous horizons. The close invaluable morning bond between them makes it all the sadder that, by one of Fate's most sadistic coincidences, Rodney has never seen his great friend win. All seven times he has actually gone to the races, Desert Orchid has been beaten. Now, reluctantly, even Rodney regards himself as a Jonah.

One lad, Gary Morgan, and two lasses, Jackie Parrish and Janice Coyle, have had the privilege of looking after Desert Orchid. They spent more time and hard work on him than anyone and, though occasionally cantankerous and alarmingly apt to escape from his box, he has repaid them pretty handsomely.

Six men have ridden Desert Orchid in races – Richard Linley in one hurdle race when Colin Brown was busy elsewhere, Graham Bradley in one chase, and Brian Rouse in his only Flat race, the Sagaro Stakes at Ascot. But Colin Brown, Simon Sherwood and Richard Dunwoody are, of course, the three who have shared his finest hours.

For the last two, stylists both, it has looked, except perhaps for the burden of public expectation, a deeply enviable job. Sherwood and Dunwoody both suit Desert Orchid perfectly – but it must be remembered that the finished article they had at their disposal was fashioned and educated in the first place by Colin Brown. The early risks and knocks were his – and Desert Orchid is a credit to his teacher.

He is, in fact, as much a credit to all the lucky humans who have worked with him as he been a delight to those who only watch. The whole racing scene will be duller and less colourful without him.

# A WEEK IN THE LIFE OF BIG MAC

John McCririck *offers a rare glimpse behind the pages of his crammed diary.*

## Wednesday, 16 October 1991

Whether publicity actually sells books is debatable, but for my first (and last) literary endeavour, *John McCririck's World of Betting: Double Carpet and All That*, anyone who would listen to the arm-waving fatso's ravings, from the Wogan and Jonathan Ross chat shows to local TV and radio and hacks from Fleet Street to Falmouth – all are enlisted.

In a sustained media blitz, with campaign swings taking in up to a dozen interviews a day, the tome detailing a lifetime of 'suffering', sex (the grateful Booby, among numerous others, features prominently here) and gambling's myriad global facets – some humorous, others informative – make up a good read.

That's the selling line, anyway, and some smashing reviews (thanks, all!) back it up.

And so does the spectacular *World of Betting* video, though – as hordes of Big Mac groupies have found to their intense dismay, footage of my hunky physique nude is slightly blurred!

Monday was the round of radio stations and newspapers in Birmingham and Wolverhampton. Tuesday Coventry – with the worst traffic system in the country – then Nottingham. Today it's Cheltenham, the greatest racing amphitheatre on the outskirts of one of England's more genteel towns. And again I attempt to liven up the natives during a morning signing session at Waterstone's sedate bookshop by screaming and shouting 'all my sex life is here', which evokes instant ripostes such as 'full of blank pages, is it?' or, more generously, 'manage two paragraphs, then?' Very droll! The morose Booby remains pining at home ('The Trap') in London, and the publishers have thoughtfully supplied their minder in the shape of a dishy, nubile 'Hippopotamus' – Alex Hippisley-Something Or Other – whose fortunate lot is to steer me from place to place through the promotional circus.

In the afternoon it's off to the more familiar surroundings of Prestbury Park, where a signing marathon at the Turf Newspapers kiosk on the course leaves them sold out of books (how many?, you ask).

But just as the Hippopotamus and I are planning our idyllic sojourn in Hawaii, who should turn up but the Booby, having dutifully driven from London to pick up her gorgeous hunk and take him home.

No more books to sign, but plenty of work still to get through, for tomorrow is the opening day of one of Channel Four's big fixtures, and there's homework to be done: stats, stats, and more stats.

And the Booby has been alone for two nights . . .

## Thursday, 17 October

Opening day of the Houghton Meeting at Newmarket. As usual there's an early morning conference at which presenters and production staff sift through the running order of the programme – prepared in advance by producer Andrew Franklin – and discuss details such as who we'll interview for 'windows' – inserts prior to most races.

Today a crew from BBC Television's *Pebble Mill* is filming a piece on racecourse betting, with dishy, fun-loving presenter Judy Spiers following me around to sample various joys and frustrations of the on-course jungle.

Top priority is still Channel Four Racing, and after another rapid book signing and haranguing of bemused punters, time to skip nimbly back to the hacks' box for more work on two racecards which form the sheet anchor of the afternoon's information. On one card are entered appropriate details of information and statistics to be spouted *before* the race, on the other those details for afterwards, updated according to who has won and lost. Also to be entered are notes of betting moves, SPs, big bets, etc.

Then it's time to be wired and miked up, and the next two hours are spent ducking and weaving gracefully around the betting ring blabbing all the latest news on air – with that Pebble Mill crew never far away. Strange, but I can't help feeling that tantalisingly attractive Judy Spiers fancies me something rotten.

At the end of the transmission shattered nerves are soothed as usual by a modest Lusitania (Havana, of course) cigar, then it's off for dinner at Little Wilbraham's brilliant Hole In The Wall, where the legendary Nancy, scorning menus, calls out the 'runners and riders' at our table. As you would expect, I eat sparingly, as tomorrow is another busy day . .

## Friday, 18 October

Dewhurst Stakes day. A similar Channel Four Racing routine to yesterday, but there's a special appointment in the evening. Clare Balding, daughter of Royal trainer Ian, is an undergraduate at nearby Cambridge University, and as part of their Turf Club's racing weekend has arranged a horsey quiz at St John's College. Teams from different universities are joined by Turf 'celebrities' such as 'Greatest Jockey' Francome, the all-seeing, all-knowing form guru 'Jimbo' Jim McGrath, my ex-fag at Harrow (or was I his?) Julian Wilson, and the irrepressible 'Foxy' Richard Fox, who joins me on the Bristol team. Stern question-master keeping a semblance of decorum is Channel Four's race commentator Graham 'Owl' Goode ('GG'). With little help from me our lot, thanks notably to a trivia whizzkid from Ireland, wins on the bridle – just the aperitif for a tasty repast.

## Saturday, 19 October

Eyelids flutter open well before dawn, to the sight of the exhausted Booby pouring my tea before lugging all the morning papers into our hotel room. These are scanned for the *Morning Line* slot while she lays out a choice of my outfits for the day.

As one of *Arena* magazine's Fifty Best-Dressed Men in Britain in 1991 – an accolade for which I was always long odds on – I have to pay very careful attention to my garb. Hugh McIlvanney in the *Observer* a few years ago wrote that Channel Four's man in the betting ring 'dresses in a way that suggests he has covered himself with glue and dived through a wardrobe – and a desperate eccentric's wardrobe at that.' What he meant to say was that I dress in the best traditions of an English gentleman, and for Cesarewitch day my tasteful outfit is completed by a discreet red hat, the headgear which English gentlemen sport when taking tiffin in our colonies out East.

All prepared, I'm driven by the Booby to the Rowley Mile, arriving at about 7.30 a.m. There's plenty to do, not only in advance of the live *Morning Line* but even during it: the Cesarewitch is one of the big betting races of the year, and a very open Champion Stakes adds to early-morning activity at the bookmakers. So, having done the paper review during the first half of the programme, it's time to phone around for early market moves, possibly even sussing out the day's 'steamer'.

Off air, it's back to the group of Channel Four production vans behind the Silver Ring, where the first target has to be the chuck wagon. My usual nibble on race-day mornings is a bacon and sausage roll on arrival at the course, then the same again to top up after the *Morning Line*. But today is an extra-busy day – better make it two sausages, but definitely no fat on the bacon!

It's a raw, cold day but the racing is superb and our near-three-hour programme rushes by. Then the Booby drives to our local Indian for a quick batch of poppadums, tandoori chicken and malai korma – and on to more personal business upstairs in 'The Trap'.

## Sunday, 20 October

Home on the Sabbath – though when those politicians finally allow us freedom to go racing on Sundays I'll happily seek out an alternative day of rest. Until then, Sunday is spent at our tiny mews house so flatteringly filmed for Yorkshire TV's *Through the Keyhole*, where the loving Booby hovers devotedly and the yellow Labradors Grub and Smelly, pestered by our playful tabby Found (pronounced 'Fee-ownd'), complete the picture of domestic bliss. No wonder I've unanimously been voted Husband of the Year for the 21st consecutive time!

But there's still work to be done, and the first task is to start preparing my two-page 'At Large' spread for next Saturday's *Racing Post*. This consists of extracts from newspapers, illuminated by my sagacious and deeply informed comments, usually collated by Thursday morning. This time, however, the bulk of it has to be done early as on Tuesday I'm trolling off on my annual round-the-globe trip.

## Monday, 21 October

Tomorrow Las Vegas, but today Glasgow, for a sporting 'Any Questions?' show on Scottish Television. I inadvertently happen to mention the *World of Betting* book and video.

## Tuesday, 22 October

The day of departure. Every year, as soon as the busy schedule of Channel Four Racing leading up to the Cesarewitch is behind me, I make a little excursion – mainly holiday, some work – which lasts five weeks.

After messing around in las Vegas for a few days it's back across to Louisville at the beginning of November for Breeders' Cup VIII at Churchill Downs. The Booby won't be coming on the first leg of the trip, but flies out to supervise packing and travel arrangements in Kentucky.

Then as soon as the Breeders' Cup is over I'll sling her back on the plane and make my solitary way to San Francisco and Hawaii for recuperation from the rigours of the year before going on to the Japan Cup in Tokyo.

With ten flights ahead, I'm not about to trust luggage to the uncertain fate which could await it beyond check-in desks, so travel – as always – is with hand baggage only. All worldly needs for the next five weeks are neatly packed (by the Booby) into a few carry-on bags.

It's therapeutic for her, you understand, to be charged with packing, as the job keeps her mind off how much she'll miss her boy while he's away from her arms.

She drives me to Heathrow, smiling bravely. But once the check-in formalities have been completed and the light of her life is ready to go through to the departure lounge, a tell-tale tear fills her eye, and I console her tenderly. Then I yank myself away from the clutch of her loving embrace and stride off, turning to give her one last wave.

Bye, bye, Booby! I might even take pity on you and return.

# 'YOU ARE A JOCKEY?'

*Between them the Channel Four Racing presenters can boast a wide experience of race-riding.* Sean Magee *looks at their careers in the saddle.*

When John McCririck landed at Narita Airport, Tokyo, *en route* for the 1987 Japan Cup, he was quizzed by a customs officer about the purpose of his visit. Big Mac blustered his way through a convoluted explanation of how he was there to cover the race for Channel Four: 'Long live the Emperor! Japanese horses are the best. I'm here for the Japan Cup.'

'Ah so!', exclaimed the customs officer: 'You are a jockey?'

John McCririck may cut an unlikely figure for a jockey, but among his Channel Four colleagues there is a wealth of experience and achievement in the saddle. John Francome of course has pride of place – seven times Champion Jockey under National Hunt rules. But many viewers of Channel Four Racing may not be aware of just how good an amateur rider was 'The Noble Lord', John Oaksey. Brough Scott rode exactly 100 winners as an amateur and then a professional jockey before his career was cut short by injury, and Derek Thompson rode as an amateur – on the Flat and over jumps – for several years.

McCririck dubs John Francome as 'Greatest Jockey', and it takes just a quick glance at the facts and figures to see why. Only the second jockey in history (after Stan Mellor) to top a thousand winners, John's career total of 1138 winning rides in Britain remained a record for a National Hunt jockey until Peter Scudamore overtook that figure in November 1989, and his strike rate of winners to rides is better than those of Sir Gordon Richards and Lester Piggott.

John Francome never won the Grand National, that ultimate goal of a jump jockey's career. He rode Fred Winter's Rough and Tumble into third place behind Rubstic in 1979 and went one better on the same horse a year later, finishing second to Ben Nevis in 1980 as one of only four finishers. But he won most of National Hunt racing's other glittering prizes: the Cheltenham Gold Cup on Midnight Court in 1978, the Champion Hurdle on Sea Pigeon in 1981 (bringing that old hero with a wonderfully timed late surge to head Pollardstown close home in what for many was Francome's finest hour), the King George VI Chase on Wayward Lad (1982) and on Burrough Hill Lad (1984), the Hennessy on Brown Chamberlin (1983) and Burrough Hill Lad (1984), the Schweppes Gold Trophy on Donegal Prince (1982) and the Welsh National on Narvik (1980) and Burrough Hill Lad (1983).

John's riding career spanned nearly fifteen years between his first race ride at Worcester on 2 December 1970 and his last at Cheltenham on 9 April 1985. The Worcester debut proved a winning one, Multigrey landing the Long Distance Opportunity Handicap Hurdle by two and a half lengths from the favourite Banquo, ridden by Taffy Salaman. John recalled that dream start in his autobiography *Born Lucky*:

> Just after I had weighed in I met David Mould and asked him how he thought I had done. 'You looked bloody awful,' he said in his Cockney accent. . . . Apart from being one of the best jockeys that I ever saw ride, he was also the most stylish and so I spared him the embarrassment of telling him that it was him I watched most often and on whom I was trying to model myself!

Style was to become John Francome's hallmark as a jockey, but not before he'd had a sharp introduction to the downside of jump racing. His second ride – and his first for Fred Winter, whose Lambourn stable he joined in 1969 after winning international honours as a junior show jumper – was on a horse named King Street in a novice chase at Cheltenham ten days after that Worcester victory. 'Always in rear, fell 11th' says the form book gloomily, and that tumble left John with a broken wrist.

Yet in all he rode 575 winners for Fred Winter, more than half his career total. In his early years at Uplands he was associated with those grand old campaigners Osbaldeston and Sonny Somers, but it was his riding of Bula and especially Lanzarote which put Francome firmly on the map. In 1975, on the retirement of Richard Pitman, John became Fred Winter's retained jockey, and he ended the 1974/75 season second in the jockeys' table behind Tommy Stack.

The following season he was Champion Jockey for the first time with 96 winners, and further championships followed in 1978/79 and 1980/81. In the 1981/82 term a long lead was whittled away by a young upstart named Peter Scudamore who, having trailed John in the first half of the season, struck a seam of winners in the New Year and took the lead in March after John had been sidelined by a fall.

John came back, but with five weeks of the season to go Scu was still twenty winners ahead. Then a bad fall at Southwell put the leader out of action for the rest of the term, and the initiative in a topsy-turvy championship swung back Francome's way. But time was rapidly running out, and it was with just four days of the season left that John pulled level at Uttoxeter – then announced that he was hanging up his boots for the season, thus leaving the championship tied between himself and Scudamore. From one who in his career attracted more than his fair share of criticism and muttering, it was a supremely sporting gesture towards his stricken rival – though there were predictable grumbles in the sporting press from mean-spirited punters who had backed John to win the title race!

He topped the table outright three more times in the following three seasons.

It was a fall at Chepstow on 9 April 1985 which convinced him that enough was enough: 'I parted company with The Reject at the open ditch in the straight and as he did so he galloped all over me. I am not superstitious as a rule but I took this as a hint that it was time to pack up and so that's what I did.'

It had been a great career. While considering Sea Pigeon the best horse he ever partnered, he does not share the popular view that the 1981 Champion Hurdle was the best race he ever rode. Rather he recalls fondly a ride around Fontwell on Sea Image. 'He was my favourite horse – very tough, very game – but that day he jumped badly, got stuck in the mud, and we had no right to win. We won a race we should not have done – and I'm proud of that ride.'

Pundits and punters are agreed that Francome was the supreme stylist among jump jockeys, his show-jumping experience doubtless contributing to his unparalleled ability to put a horse at a fence or hurdle in such a way as to give it the maximum chance of jumping cleanly. But whether he was the best ever is the stuff of lasting debate, not least because of the extraordinary subsequent achievements of Peter Scudamore.

On John Francome's retirement John Oaksey wrote in *Horse and Hound* of 'the amazing grace he introduced to the art of presenting a galloping horse at a steeplechase fence' and offered an appreciation of Francome's character: 'In the conventional, hidebound, often pompous world of racing, his highly developed sense of the ridiculous combined dangerously with a tendency to disregard both rules and officials for whom he felt no particular respect.' John Oaksey's tribute concluded:

We should be deeply grateful for the luck of watching him so much –
and grateful too that, unlike Lester Piggott's, his method can be
copied.

No one is ever as likely to do it as well, but men will try and as long
as they are trying the art of cross-country race-riding will not die.

The Noble Lord is far too modest to suggest that any aspiring jockey
use as a model his own riding style – which, he proudly recalls, was
described by Fulke Walwyn as 'a fine example of the Old English Lav-
atory seat' – but his record as an amateur jockey is one of the most
impressive of the post-war period. That he cannot say precisely how many
winners he rode is in keeping with the Corinthian spirit (something over
200, he thinks), but the record books bear witness to the quality as much
as the quantity.

His first winner came on Next Of Kin at the Pegasus Club point-to-
point at Kimble in 1951, and by the end of the Fifties he was one of the
best amateur riders under National Hunt Rules. His name will always be
associated with Taxidermist, on whom he won the Whitbread Gold Cup
and the Hennessy Gold Cup in 1958. Unearth murky footage of that
Hennessy – run at Cheltenham before moving to Newbury in 1960 – and
at the last fence you simply cannot believe that Taxidermist is the winner:
he jumps the last in sixth place, then sprouts wings to scorch up the hill
and pip the Gold Cup winner Kerstin on the line to win by a short head. It
was some finishing effort, and Taxidermist's pilot admits: 'When I am
depressed, I show myself the film of it.'

John Oaksey – who rode as John Lawrence until succeeding to his
father's title in 1970 – won other big races: the 1958 Imperial Cup on
Flaming East, the Foxhunters at Liverpool on Subaltern in 1966 and on
Bullock's Horn in 1973, and the Cheltenham Foxhunters on Bullock's
Horn the same year. But if there is one race for which his career in the
saddle is recalled, it has to be the 1963 Grand National.

Riding the seven-year-old Carrickbeg, John crossed the last of the
thirty fences in the lead, and up the run-in seemed assured of success –
only to have the race snatched away from him in the dying strides by the
late rally of 66–1 outsider Ayala, who passed him practically in the
shadow of the post to win by three-quarters of a length.

'Sick as a parrot' was not a phrase current in those days, but such a
sentiment would have been understandable after being so cruelly
deprived of the sweetest prize of all. Instead, John wrote for *Horse and
Hound* an account of his ride on Carrickbeg which is a classic of racing
literature, an unforgettable evocation of how the race unfolded towards its

dramatic climax. The description of the closing stages after the last fence is compellingly painful, as Carrickbeg gallops for glory:

> His stride had still not faltered and, straightening round the elbow half-way home with the roar of the crowd rising to a crescendo in our ears, the only feeling I remember was one of wild, incredulous hope that the dream first dreamt on a nursery rocking horse long ago was really coming true.
>
> Until this moment, sustained by my horse's strength and by the heat of battle, I had felt no real physical strain, but now, all at once, the cold, clammy hand of exhaustion closed its grip on my thighs and arms.
>
> Even to swing the whip had become an effort and the only thing that kept me going was the unbroken rhythm of Carrickbeg's heroic head, nodding in time with his stride. And, suddenly, even that was gone.
>
> With a hundred yards to go and still no sound of pursuit, the prize seemed within our grasp. Eighty, seventy, sixty perhaps – and then it happened. In the space of a single stride I felt the last ounce of Carrickbeg's energy drain away and my own with it. One moment we were a living, working combination, the next a struggling, beaten pair. There was still hope – but not for long. . . .
>
> To my dying day I shall never forget the sight of Ayala's head beside my knee. Two heartbeats later he was half a length in front . . .

Carrickbeg broke down at Sandown Park the following January and never got the chance to make amends in the National.

The other famous race with which John Oaksey's name will always be associated came in April 1974, in the Whitbread Gold Cup at Sandown Park. Riding Proud Tarquin, on whom just a week earlier he had come a four-length second to Red Rum in the Scottish National at Ayr, John had a slight advantage at the final fence over Ron Barry and that great performer The Dikler. But immediately after landing over the last Proud Tarquin, on The Dikler's inside, veered towards the stands, and his rival moved left to avoid a bump.

The two horses did not touch, and in a flash Proud Tarquin's erratic course had been righted. He ran straight as a gun-barrel up the hill to hold The Dikler by a head, but the stewards decided that Proud Tarquin's momentary loss of steering had cost The Dikler the race. Proud Tarquin was demoted to second, and nearly twenty years later the decision still rankles: John never tires of pointing out that two of the Sandown stewards who made that controversial judgement had no experience of steeplechasing and were young enough to be his sons.

Their decision 'either proves their balanced wisdom – or, as I believe, suggests that they ought to be tapping their way down Piccadilly with white sticks.'

But there are plenty of other abiding memories of John Lawrence/ John Oaksey in the saddle. He rode the winner of the Moët and Chandon Silver Magnum at Epsom – the 'Amateurs' Derby' – four times and was champion amateur under NH Rules twice, in 1957/58 and in 1970/71. On the latter occasion he pipped Graham MacMillan for the title at Market Rasen on the final evening of the season after Terry Biddlecombe had donated a ride which turned out to be John's championship clincher.

Then there was the occasion at Cheltenham when John pulled up Pioneer Spirit after the second last fence, despite having a gigantic lead over his only remaining rival in an amateurs' chase, in the mistaken belief that he had taken the wrong course. That was simply not his day: he was fined £25 for his embarrassing deed, and that evening forgot to turn the bath taps off while taking a phone call: the bath overflowed and brought half the ceiling of the room beneath crashing down.

Injury forced John Oaksey's retirement from the saddle in November 1975, some twenty years after he had first ridden under Rules. In addition to Taxidermist, Carrickbeg and Proud Tarquin, he retains a special affection for Happy Medium (on whom he won several races and who was a particularly exhilarating ride around John's beloved Sandown Park), that fine hunter chaser Rosie's Cousin, Tuscan Prince (now a twenty-eight-year-old pensioner at Oaksey), and Bullock's Horn, on whom he won those Foxhunters Chases at Cheltenham and Liverpool. Half a dozen horses were still in contention at the last at Liverpool, but Bullock's Horn stayed on up the yawning run-in that had found out Carrickbeg and got up to beat Dubaythorn by a head. 'I wasn't ashamed of that,' admits John when recalling the Foxhunters; but for the race which gave him most satisfaction he nominates a chase at Fontwell won by Solimyth: 'I got almost everything there was to get out of Solimyth', and in the Fontwell Chase in October 1965 John Lawrence forced the nine-year-old up on the run-in to beat John Cook on Wayward Queen and Stan Mellor on Auto Fly by half a length and the same.

For an amateur to have beaten professionals of the calibre of Mellor and Cook in a tight finish is a cause for understandable satisfaction, but there is also a lasting pleasure for John Oaksey in the result of the 1967 Horse and Hound Cup at Stratford, which he won on Cham. The stylish and somewhat younger amateur with whom he was locked in battle at the final fence was one Brough Scott.

Brough Scott rode exactly 100 winners under Rules during an eight-

year career, half as amateur and half as professional. For Brough, as for
so many jump jockeys, the point-to-point field provided the nursery for
the riding under Rules, and he had his first ride in the Members race at
the Bullingdon point-to-point in February 1962, in his first year at
Oxford. His mount Red Squirrel duly obliged, to be followed by a winner
at the Oxford University fixture at Wroughton.

While an undergraduate at Oxford he rode out regularly with nearby
trainer Derek Ancil, driving the twenty-odd miles to Middleton Stoney
each morning in a battered green mini-van. (In his Oxford days John
Oaksey had made the slightly longer trip to the Bicester stable of Cecil
Bonner in a Wolseley Hornet.) But the mini-van was put to other uses,
notably a curious duty connected with Brough's position as Master of the
Oxford Drag Hunt. 'I couldn't understand why I was so unsuccessful with
girls, until I realized that this was not entirely unconnected with my
having to make regular trips in the van to the station to collect the wolf's
pee sent down from London Zoo for the Drag Hunt. Occasionally there'd
be a message attached: "This week it's panther". Whatever animal it had
come from, the aroma tended to linger in the van.'

Brough's first ride under Rules was on Tamhill in the Cadman
Novices' Hurdle at the now defunct course at Woore on 21 March 1963
(John Oaksey's 34th birthday). His first winner under Rules came when
Arcticeelagh, owned by his father and trained by Frenchie Nicholson at
Cheltenham, landed the Richard Marler Memorial Cup for amateur
riders over ten furlongs at Lingfield Park on 24 August 1963, beating the
odds-on favourite Redoubt by a neck at odds of 33–1.

His first National Hunt win came on the same horse and by the same
margin, after a similarly stirring finish to the Monmouth Handicap Hurdle at Chepstow on 26 October 1963. (To put this in historical context:
Arkle and Mill House had their first meeting five weeks later.) Brough
had ridden, by his own admission, a brilliant finish to get up close home,
but there was a mild sting in the tail. In the euphoria of victory he had not
registered that the stewards were interviewing the rider of the second,
whose form-book description 'nt qckn nr fin' was subsequently explained
all too well: the jockey whom Brough had pipped in that rousing climax
had been stood down for not trying!

After Oxford, Brough spent a year as assistant trainer to Tim Forster,
and became a professional jockey in 1967, riding principally for the
Chepstow yard of Colin Davies. In his first season as a pro he won the
1968 Imperial Cup at Sandown Park on Persian Empire. A useful performer on the Flat (he had been runner-up in the Free Handicap in 1966),
Persian Empire was still a novice when he won the Imperial Cup, then

one of the most competitive and prestigious races in the calendar. And his pilot was not in the best of shape: 'I'd got mangled in a fall at Doncaster – kicked in the throat, broken arm – and had to ride at Sandown with my arm strapped up in a plaster splint. But I got away with it.'

Four days later Brough came third in the Champion Hurdle on Black Justice, nine lengths behind Persian War – who was to take the hurdling crown three years in succession. Owned like Persian Empire by the volatile Henry Alper, Persian War had been moved to Colin Davies after a disagreement between the owner and the previous handler Brian Swift, but the great hurdler came with his own jockey – Jimmy Uttley – and Brough did not get to ride him in a race.

He did ride Persian War in some of his work, though, and considers him the best horse he ever sat on. For the best he rode in action he nominates Black Justice: 'If he'd jumped better and acted on the ground he'd certainly have won that Champion Hurdle.' One of the best chasers he rode was The Otter, on whom he won the Mandarin Chase at Newbury in 1969.

But he'd always vowed that he would not go on riding if head or back injuries recurred, and after 'a big black brute called Bonnie Highlander' had given him a crashing fall at Warwick on 13 March 1971 the choice was obvious: quit while still in one piece.

For a promising career to have reached its unarguable conclusion at Brough's age of twenty-eight was galling, but to be riding in one of the golden periods of British jump racing alongside the likes of Bob Davies, Terry Biddlecombe and Stan Mellor (not to mention John Oaksey) was a wonderful experience.

Yet ask Brough for a particularly cherished memory from his riding days and you'll be offered not some powerhouse finish to beat Stan Mellor or Jeff King in a big race, but a thirteen-year-old gelding called Mr Wonderful and the Severnside Handicap Chase (Division Two) at Worcester on Monday 27 January 1969. 'I'd lost the job at Colin Davies's. I'd been hurt in a fall and had been off for two or three months, and that January was struggling to try and get going again. On the Saturday I'd had a good ride in the Great Yorkshire Chase at Doncaster on Indamelia – fourth behind Playlord and Ron Barry. On the Sunday I rode Black Justice into third in a big French hurdle race at Pau. On the Monday it was Mr Wonderful at Worcester. He was a big black horse – not a frightening ride, but occasionally he would miss one out. He made all the running, but at the last open ditch my saddle broke at the tree. I kicked my feet out of the irons and jumped the last few without stirrups. I really kicked him into the last, and he came up. He was all out on the run-in but held on to win by a head. That was one of those days – they can't take that away from me!'

Brough's own verdict on his riding career: 'I wasn't the best jockey in the world, but I wasn't the worst.'

The form book does not record whether Derek Thompson greeted Classified with a hearty 'Hey, big fella!' before getting the leg-up for the Madhatters Private Sweepstakes on the flat at Plumpton on 4 March 1980, but if Thommo did so the shock certainly transformed the horse's form. Classified had had a few undistinguished outings on the Flat but had not previously run under National Hunt Rules – though he was to become one of the most popular and consistent horses in training, running third in the 1986 Grand National. For the Plumpton race he started at 14–1 (from 20s), with Long Wharf – ridden by the Prince of Wales in the days before his brief experience as a jump jockey – the 13–8 favourite.

Derek brought Classified into the lead with over a furlong to run, to score by two lengths from HRH on Long Wharf, and the grossness of his *lèse-majesté* in beating the heir to the throne was augmented by his flies popping open on the way to the start. One newspaper the next day ran the headline: 'The Outsider Who Flashed Past The Prince'.

That victory was Derek Thompson's sole success from around fifty rides on the Flat and over jumps as an amateur jockey. After learning his riding in the Pony Club and at local gymkhanas, he moved on to 14.2 hands show-jumping, and had his first race ride at the South Durham point-to-point at Sedgefield at the age of sixteen in 1966. He later became assistant trainer to Denys Smith at Bishop Auckland and to Pierre Sanoner at Chantilly. That Plumpton excitement apart, Derek's major riding memory is of competing against one of the very best jump jockeys of the lot: 'I remember Terry Biddlecombe's arse getting further and further away from me . . .'.

And what of the rest of the Channel Four team?

After leaving school in 1971, Jim McGrath had a spell with trainer Bill Marshall, 'the best education for life I've ever had'. But the moment of truth came when he was exercising a Sea Bird colt named Mighty Seaman. Walking round the roads Mighty Seaman was placid enough, but when it was suggested to Jim that he might like to try a canter the horse took off and carted the would-be apprentice all the way back to the yard, where Jim was unceremoniously deposited on the ground outside Mighty Seaman's box. 'I decided then that my feet would stay on the ground. Racing is a serious business, and trainers have enough to put up with without enthusiastic amateurs making a nuisance of themselves riding their horses.'

Jim has two horses in training with Jonjo O'Neill but is strictly a visitor with carrots and Polos. Isn't he tempted to line up with Francome, Oaksey and Scott in those charity races? 'One day, perhaps, when I've made my millions – but we'll probably have donated Oaksey to the National Horseracing Museum before I make my comeback!'

Graham Goode had riding school experience as a youngster and has ridden polo ponies – though (Jilly Cooper please note) not on the polo field. His last competitive ride was when he represented the University of Leicester against the University of Nottingham in an against-the-clock show jumping contest, but he no longer rides regularly – 'dangerous things, horses'.

It's a while since John Tyrrel could do eight stone, but this graduate of Captain Younghusband's Riding Academy at Aldenham (near Radlett in Hertfordshire) can at least claim a varied experience in the saddle: he caught the eye of many expert judges when partnering donkeys on the sands at Scarborough, but for John the realization that he would not be much of a threat to Gordon Richards came on a riding school hack some time around 1945: 'Such were my skills in the saddle that as soon as I had mounted it, the animal promptly leant against the stable wall and dozed off.'

And, since we must ask, what about John McCririck? Although he will not definitely rule out ever having sat on a horse, he proclaims that 'the peak of my riding career was getting up on that mechanical horse on *Wogan* – a sight which must have startled the few viewers we had'.

So the chances of seeing Big Mac given the leg-up by John Dunlop on to some sleek Maktoum specimen for the annual charity race at Ascot's September Meeting remain remote. But over the last few years the Shadwell Estates Private Sweepstakes has provided some memorable moments, none more so than the 1991 running when John Francome was winning so easily on Shaleel that he had time to goose rival jockey Robin Gray as he went past!

For once the stewards did not call John in.

# WHERE DO THEY GO TO?

*The fate of racehorses after their time on the track is over fascinates many racing fans.* Michael Tanner *describes some of the less familiar second careers which horses have taken up.*

'My plan is to work 'em as long as they'll go and then sell 'em for what they'll fetch, at the knacker's or elsewhere.' The callous attitude of Anna Sewell's obnoxious cab-driver Nicholas Skinner – which drew from Black Beauty the heartrending cry, 'Oh, if men were more merciful they would shoot us before we come to such misery' – does not, thank heaven, constitute the unequivocal human response to all racehorses once they are past their prime.

However, relatively few colts and fillies possess the necessary credentials to prosper at stud; not every old gelding will be greeted by a loving owner at the gate of a capacious paddock with the promise of some decent hunting. Indeed, after inhabiting the equivalent of a five-star hotel, the prospect of switching to an open-air life could be exactly *not* what a retired racehorse requires. There are many circumstances – and there's no point shirking the fact – in which it might be more charitable to put horses down. All too easily the cast-off racer could embark on a downward spiral of sales rings which invariably ends in the kind of wretchedness Black Beauty so desperately feared.

But there *is* life after racing for the racehorse, and pretty diverse have been the occupations. The fate of literature's equine darling is an apt reminder, for example, that the 1908 Grand National winner Rubio once earned his corn by pulling an omnibus. While it's true that this bizarre alternative employment occurred in the course of Rubio's racing life (the National hero of 1924 escaped from an even more plebeian labour, for Master Robert had been required to pull a plough), genuine instances of unusual second careers, ranging from police mount to ceremonial charger, are equally plentiful. In Canada recently the Ontario division of the Canadian Thoroughbred Horse Society held a sale entitled 'Thoroughbreds for Sport and Leisure', specifically to redirect former racehorses into suitable walks of life.

The next best thing to being in training is to be with others who are. Hence the ideal existence for the retired racehorse is as a trainer's hack. As David Nicholson, who for years used his former stalwart What A Buck in this capacity, argues: 'The horse is living in an environment to which he is accustomed and is kept fit and busy.' Being close to the action, however, occasionally proves too much for some. Fulke Walwyn's great horse Mandarin never accepted his non-combative role on the Lambourn gallops and was soon pensioned off, a fate also in store for a second Walwyn favourite, Special Cargo. The Queen Mother's Whitbread winner was to be Julie Cecil's hack: he lasted a week. After a rush of blood drove him into joining some two-year-olds in their gallop the old rascal suffered immediate expulsion from Warren Place. By contrast, another Sandown specialist became the most instantly recognizable hack in Newmarket. Back in the 1970s Tingle Creek used to attack the Railway Fences like a wayward firecracker, and the flashy chestnut with the big white face can still prove a handful – as frequent partner Don Cantillon has testified. 'Oh, my God, does he not come out of his box of a morning fit to give the jockey a heart attack. If you've had a night on the booze he's a sod to face . . . but words can't describe him.'

Up in Yorkshire one more veteran regularly savours familiar surroundings. Every summer Lord Derby's Teleprompter travels north from his owner's Newmarket stud to go gently through the motions with the rest of Bill Watt's string at Hurgill Lodge, outside Richmond. 'He's treated as if he's in training. He does nothing other than canter, just routine exercise. I feel his legs and give him a carrot each evening and he's never looked better.' One of Teleprompter's winter companions at the Woodland Stud used to be Lord Derby's Wiveton until he, along with half brother Voracity, was presented to the nearby British Racing School in the hope he would become a fully-fledged schoolmaster.

The School has around forty ex-racehorses. 'It's an ideal Old People's Home: it's for the old but it's not a Rest Home,' explains the Director, Major Barney Griffiths. 'It keeps them going. As long as they are sound in mind they are suitable. They may run away with the kids but as long as they pull up sensibly at the end of the gallop that's all right.' The roster includes some well-known performers. Path Of Peace won the 1982 County Hurdle in addition to the November Handicap and Great Yorkshire Handicap on the Flat. Shiny Copper also scored at the 1982 Cheltenham Festival (Triumph Hurdle), while top-class hurdling form is represented by Migrator, who numbered Sea Pigeon and Broadsword among his victims in thirteen victories over timber. He and Path Of Peace (both foaled in 1976) are two years older than Shiny Copper but they can look forward to a few more years of active service. 'We've still got Efficacy, who will be twenty-seven in 1992 – Johnny Gilbert used to ride him when the School first began at Stoneleigh in 1972. They won't go on to anything else when they finish here. They'll either return to their owner or be put down.'

How else might the racehorse's competitive juices be recycled? The obvious outlet for the energies of one sound in mind and body would seem another equestrian discipline – dressage, eventing or showjumping. The quality is always desirable: on the other hand, racing will have developed the wrong muscles and possibly a dubious temperament to boot. In short, any switch ought to be made early and successful transitions are few and far between. In 1991, however, the eight-year-old Roi de Soleil won the Osberton Three-Day Event by a wide margin, largely due to an exhibition of flat-race speed over the cross-country phase, where he was the only competitor to go clear inside the time. This son of Ile de Bourbon had achieved nothing in fourteen racecourse appearances: he was a tricky ride and clearly disliked the game. Nowadays, according to his new owner Andrew Nicholson, 'he is doing something that he enjoys and is easily within his capabilities and he is only too willing to concentrate his mind. He's got the scope and ability to go to the top.' A second convert in this area is the former Cumani-trained Crown Flirt, who split a pastern and ran just the once. Renamed Benney's Boy, he recovered sufficiently to complete the cross-country at Badminton in 1989 as a ten-year-old and win pure dressage classes at Stoneleigh in 1990.

Benney's Boy was also no mean showjumper, but the most notable recruit to this branch of equestrianism in recent years was unquestionably Jenny Pitman's National winner Corbiere, who spent six months with Mike Florence after his retirement in 1987. 'He was an athlete who would have been a star in any equestrian sphere. He was a natural – he won his National on jumping – and was good enough to be a Grade A showjumper. All I had to do was to get him to change his length of stride and be more controlled and balanced, jump off his hocks now and again. We won three or four good classes together.'

Mrs Pitman's reluctance to see pensioners 'sulking in a field' led to Pat Cash and Gainsay finding employment with the Mounted Division of the Metropolitan Police. They followed in the hoofprints of Casamayor, whom Peter Bailey trained to be fourth in the 1979 Cheltenham Gold Cup. The Argentinian-bred gelding defied his Timeform squiggle for unreliability by carrying the Commissioner himself at the Trooping of the Colour and seeing action during the 1986 Wapping riots. In 1991 the Met also enrolled the seven-year-old South Parade, a winner on the Flat and over hurdles with Willie Jarvis and Toby Balding respectively, before a strained tendon brought about his premature retirement.

Grand Canyon was an infinitely better performer on the racecourse than Casamayor but he could never match the latter's equanimity on Horse Guards' Parade. In four injury-plagued seasons during the 1970s this dark brown – almost black – New Zealander showed both durability and versatility to win nineteen races on the Flat, over hurdles and over jumps in England, Italy, France and the USA, most notably taking two Colonial Cups. After yet another setback in the spring of 1980 his colouring came to the rescue and owner Pat Samuel's wish that he be found a berth in the Household Cavalry was fulfilled.

Thanks to the good offices of the Queen Mother and Colonel Andrew Parker-Bowles of the Blues and Royals (whose chargers are black), Grand Canyon was accepted into No.2 Troop RH G/D. On arrival at Knightsbridge Barracks he was allocated the box opposite the great seventeen-hands Drum Horse Claudius and entrusted to Lieuteuant Sam Bullard.

We were together for two and a half years and did duty at state occasions and the Changing of the Guard, but he was very bouncy and couldn't be risked at something like Trooping the Colour. He showed scant respect for military protocol. He could not understand why two horses had to stand next to each other facing in opposite directions at the Changing of the Guard ceremony. He first tried to eat the other officer's boot and then his charger's tail. He wanted to turn round and line up for a race! The sword also worried him: slapping against his flank, it probably reminded him of a whip. So we tied the scabbard to the spur with a bit of invisible nylon. He also hated turning in the regulation clockwise direction so we had a pact to turn the other way and nobody ever commented on it, surprisingly. They gave him up in the end. He always wanted to jog everywhere and once when he heard the band strike up the National Anthem outside Buckingham Palace he nearly carted me down the Mall. Eventually he came to us in Norfolk and my father Gerry hunted him until one day the horse just lay down in his field and died.

Grand Canyon's brush with pageantry was surpassed by the experiences of Democrat, the best two-year-old of 1899. In the hands of Tod

Sloan this American-bred chestnut gelding won seven of his last eight races, including the Coventry, Champagne, Middle Park and Dewhurst. Three of these victories were over future Triple Crown winner Diamond Jubilee. Installed as winter favourite for the Derby, he subsequently lost his form completely and Diamond Jubilee's trainer Richard Marsh was able to acquire him for only 290 guineas at the Newmarket October Sales of 1901 'in the belief that he simply could not have gone hopelessly to the dogs.' Even a trainer of Marsh's talents failed to revitalize Democrat: 'yet he was a delightful creature. A quieter and better mannered animal you could not have wished for.'

Democrat's story took its final twist the following summer. Marsh was introduced to Lord Kitchener, shortly off to India as Commander-in-Chief. Kitchener asked the trainer if he could purchase on his behalf a Thoroughbred likely to make a decent ceremonial charger. Marsh replied that he knew one who would be just the ticket and offered Democrat as a gift. 'Democrat arrived all right and is a charming horse,' wrote Kitchener to Marsh. 'I think he will suit me admirably.' About a year afterwards Marsh received a further letter from his lordship along with a photograph of the new liaison prior to the Delhi Durbar of January 1903, 'as a slight token of the great pleasure you have given me in providing me with such a splendid horse.' Democrat carried the C-in-C at all manner of parades throughout his six-year stay in India (besides winning prizes at local shows) and was immortalized in the magnificent equestrian bronze of Kitchener which stood in Calcutta.

Democrat's high profile came about more by accident than design. These days any celebrity has public relations potential, and that includes equine celebrities. Red Rum was the trailblazer in this regard, opening, it seemed, either a betting shop or a charity function every other week. 'Over the years Red has done and seen it all,' says Don McCain, 'from wives arranging for him to appear at their husbands' birthday parties to probably the strangest of the lot – the day he was made a clan chieftain at the Highland Games.' At a fee of up to £1000 (plus expenses) it is no wonder Red Rum has his own company and an agent. Dangerous or tasteless promotions are out, however. A lucrative offer to pose with a Page Three girl on his back was politely rejected as was another offer of £500,000 from a Japanese visitor who wanted him for the star attraction at a safari park: 'I'll always remember one old lady taking a swing at Mr Aoki with her handbag and yelling, "Remember Pearl Harbor".'

One of Rummy's most recent undertakings was to promote the cause of Farriers in company with Desert Orchid, his natural successor in the equine celebrity stakes. The White Wonder of Whitsbury has, moreover, already dabbled in politics. In June 1991 he escorted a 250,000-signature petition to 10 Downing Street in support of retaining the legislation which prevents the export of live horses for slaughter. 'Desert Orchid has become the symbol for all that is best in British horses – bravery, beauty, celebrity and success,' said Colonel George Stephen, chief executive of the International League for the Protection of Horses: 'While he will never face the threat of being sold off for meat, there are an awful lot of horses, not quite as good as him, who have done their stuff by mankind and who have gone for slaughter.'

Desert Orchid's horizons appear boundless. Goodness only knows what worthy causes he will endorse in the future: for sure he will never be idle.

# THESE WE HAVE LOVED

*Thirteen British racecourses have closed down since 1960. Here Channel Four Racing's resident Turf historian* John Tyrrel *and former jockey* Caroline Baldock *consider the fate of some much-missed tracks.*

The *Sporting Life* on Tuesday 15 September 1970 carried this impassioned letter on one of the burning issues of the day, the imminent closure of Alexandra Park racecourse:

> The decision to shut down Alexandra Park will come as a shock to the many people for whom the evening fixtures so near to London were their only opportunity of attending a meeting.
>
> Of course, Ally Pally was the subject of ribald comments from all quarters due to its primitive amenities.
>
> These were undeniably Dickensian, but the lethargic management had become a byword and the authorities concerned appeared to make no innovation or improvement in an attempt to modernise either the course itself or the general facilities.
>
> The 'night lark' was unpopular with the professional element, who are no doubt pleased at the course's demise, and its defence was therefore in the hands of those whose voice still enjoys such little support among so many of the sport's hierarchy – the ordinary racegoer.
>
> Surprisingly Lord Wigg, their much-vaunted champion – a position he has fully earned throughout his distinguished public career – has refused to step in.
>
> Apparently a mere £5000 a year would have sufficed. This sum is easily found for one 'prestige' race attracting a handful of runners but is evidently unavailable to continue to give pleasure to thousands.

Considering the Levy Board money comes, in the main, from those very people who will now be hardest hit by the closure, it would be informative were the reasons to be fully explained.

Could it be that the Levy Board's tie-up with Epsom and Sandown makes them less inclined to help a nearby course whose evening fixtures did little to swell their coffers? . . .

The success of Windsor's evening meetings has proved the market is there.

Can no voice now be raised in protest against this arbitrary decision which deprives so many when so little is required?

This heartfelt plea was signed, from London W1, by someone called John McCririck . . .

But Ally Pally was just one of a baker's dozen of courses which have ceased operations since 1960:

Buckfastleigh (last meeting, 27 August 1960)
Hurst Park (10 October 1962)
Woore (1 June 1963)
Manchester (9 November 1963)
Lincoln (21 May 1964)
Lewes (14 September 1964)
Bogside (10 April 1965)
Rothbury (also 10 April 1965)
Birmingham (21 June 1965)
Alexandra Park (8 September 1970)
Wye (2 May 1974)
Lanark (18 October 1977)
Stockton (16 June 1981)

What caused their disappearance?

The Jockey Club was not considered to have emerged with much credit from the hearings by the Parliamentary Select Committee enquiring into racing in 1991. On reflection, this was probably inevitable in an era where much thinking is based on the false values of the Sixties tinged by the ignorance of the Eighties. The bookmaking industry didn't impress either, but they have not been controlling a high-gambling sport for nearly 250 years, although they have have lived off it happily enough.

It is hard to imagine racing surviving in its present form in the butter-fingered hands of the governing bodies of several games and sports we could mention, but the Club's quiet style and aristocratic confidence has made it an obvious Aunt Sally, at the same time cloaking many examples of forward thinking.

When racecourses were going to the wall in the early Sixties, the Jockey Club was almost by custom charged with indifference. This was not the case, as they had addressed the problem of inefficient racetracks nearly twenty years earlier.

A reorganisation committee set up in 1941 reported two years later that some courses were no longer required and should be abolished forthwith. These tracks were those with poor standards for horse and public alike, which could not reasonably expect to cater for the demands of a sophisticated racegoer in post-war Britain.

The committee visualised a trust which would enable the Club to purchase a number of courses which would then be run by the Club for the good of racing at large (rather than lining the pockets of shareholders and directors), much in the manner that United Racecourses, a Levy Board subsidiary, operates today.

If this far-sighted plan had prevailed, it would have prevented courses from falling into the hands of speculators with no interest in racing but a keen desire to 'develop' the land for building or commerce. However, it was wartime and the scheme required Treasury approval. Understandably more concerned with Hitler than with Hurst Park, the plan was thwarted in 1944 by a Coalition Government taking the usual view adopted by administrations of any political colour, that racing is a rich man's sport well able to take care of itself – a philosophy which still applies in modern times.

The chance was lost, the post-war boom produced a euphoria not emulated until the mid-Eighties, but the chickens came home to roost with a vengeance in 1962 when it was estimated that it would cost £15,000,000 to bring every course in the country up to acceptable standards. With the bookmakers' contribution to the Levy running at £892,617, which was £35,376 less than the Tote input of £927,993 with a fractional share of the market, the sum was clearly unattainable.

Buckfastleigh, a minor National Hunt track, was in 1960 the first to go, but it was the urban courses which were the most vulnerable. As the scope of travel widened and more people went by car rather than train, so the suburban green spaces beckoned to the builder. Hurst Park capitulated in 1962, followed by Manchester in 1963 and Birmingham two years later.

Lincoln and Lewes folded in 1964, not the victims of urban sprawl but of under-funding which could so easily have been avoided had the 1943 scheme found favour. By now the Levy Board held the purse-strings, with the thankless task of cutting a coat according to a cloth not only lacking in quality but width as well. The derisory and shameful contribution to racing by the bookmakers had been greatly enhanced by Lord Wigg when he became chairman of the Levy Board in 1967, but it was a case of bolting a stable door with the horse halfway down the High Street.

In October 1962, the curtain fell on Hurst Park. Punters backing the coincidence bets of Lastime and Final Bloom were disappointed, but Fidelio won the Gainsborough Stakes, Bill Williamson rode a double and the letters 'RIP' were hoisted in the number board, with a horseshoe wreath adorning the winning post. The turf was removed to lay the foundation of Ascot's new 'Blackpool with the tide out' National Hunt course, and the grandstand relocated to Mansfield Town Football Club.

Hurst Park had been opened in 1890, to replace Croydon, and was modelled on Sandown Park, the first of the 'drawing room' courses where women could attend the races in safety. The site was at Hampton, or 'Appy 'Ampton in the jargon of the cockney racegoers who patronised the original course on the gentle banks of the Middlesex side of the river Thames, once the home of David Garrick and the country retreat of Nell Gwyn. Even such an unlikely racing buff as Charles Dickens found time to go to the sports in 1831.

The first five meetings at Hurst Park in 1890 were all National Hunt fixtures, and flat racing started in 1891. The Inauguration Handicap was won by Colonel North's Rough And Ready, and in July Tom Cannon's True Blue III won the Victoria High Weight Handicap, worth 200 sovereigns and the precursor of the Victoria Cup, Hurst Park's most famous race – now run at Ascot together with another Hurst survivor, the White Rose Stakes.

Naturally enough the names of the races enjoyed a strong Tudor flavour, with the Henry VIII Stakes and five events named after his matrimonial escapades; the Boleyn, the Aragon, the Seymour, the Cleeves and the Howard were all remembered. Doubtless the final consort was considered to be one over Parr. Garrick, who built the Temple to Shakespeare on the river bank, was honoured with a seller.

In 1933 Gordon Richards was at Hurst Park when he equalled Fred Archer's record of 246 winners in a season. Emerging from the rigours of the Second World War, racing at Hurst was swiftly restored and 50,000 people attended the Easter fixture in 1946. But perhaps it is as a National Hunt track that the course will chiefly be remembered. The Triumph Hurdle, now a Cheltenham feature, was a main event together with the long forgotten National Trial Handicap Chase.

The roll of honour for the Triumph has a distinctly Gallic feel with winners including Beaver II, Cantab, Kwannin, Clair Soleil, Abrupto and Grey Tank, all bred across the Channel.

H. M. Queen Elizabeth the Queen Mother was a frequent visitor. Monaveen, the first horse owned by the then Queen in partnership with her daughter Princess Elizabeth, won the Queen Elizabeth Handicap Chase in 1949, only to fall at the water with fatal results a year later. Compensation came with Laffy, Devon Loch, Gay Record and The Rip.

But by the 1961/2 National Hunt season the shadows were deepening. Wates Ltd purchased the property and soon the bulldozers were razing the memories of Garrick and Sweet Nell of Old Drury, providing homes for 2700. Only Sandown and Kempton now survived from the mid-nineteenth-century tracks such as Egham, Reigate, Guildford, and Croydon. The new 'Winning Post' Inn may well be haunted by the ghosts of Lochroe, Golden Miller, Tulyar, Halloween, Pandofell, and Whinstone Hill, to say nothing of the redoubtable Captain Ryan Price, a latrine orderly when the course was under military occupation.

The demise of Alexandra Park, otherwise 'Ally Pally', was a very different matter. The words of the old music hall song which one of the co-authors used to sing a few decades ago on the stage – 'They made me a present of Mornington Crescent, They threw it a brick at a time, The night I appeared as Macbeth' – could well have been the theme for the starter, Geoffrey Freer.

Except for five-furlong races, all the starts at this deleterious dump were in the front of the stands. If the favourite was left, and not always as the fault of the unfortunate official, there would be a torrent of abuse and unfriendly objects from London 'sportsmen' which nevertheless left Mr Freer unperturbed. He had formerly started races at Ostend, and always asserted that he had constructed a nice villa from the missiles hurled at him in the course of his duties.

Alexandra Park was described with typical eccentricity as the 'Longchamp of London' by Labour Cabinet minister Richard Crossman, who had grandiose plans to make it a top-class racecourse (an ambition akin to running the Grand National at Bangor-on-Dee), but the decision by the Jockey Club in September 1970 to withdraw the track's licence to operate surprised few. Jockeys hated it as the camber of the 'frying pan' circular course at the end of the 'handle' was lethal after a shower of rain, the Levy Board were paying £5000 a year to keep it open with little income as most of the meetings were evening fixtures after the betting shops had closed, and not even George Wigg was prepared to come to the rescue.

Some tried – including Jarvis Astaire, who put up £100,000 for a modernisation package – and one of racing's most sophisticated and amiable figures, Doug Marks, regretted the passing of the North London track as 'it was so easy to win there and handy for the West End for dinner with Paul Cole in some swank restaurant on the way home'. Even so, it was at Ally Pally that the man who won two wartime Classics on Godiva was given the worst fall of his career when an apprentice miscounted the number of circuits to be negotiated on the 'frying pan' and cut across as Marks was turning up 'the handle'.

Always a place to attract horses for courses, Alexandra Park specialists included Cider Apple, Auction Pool, Friars Daughter and subsequent Two Thousand Guineas winner Right Tack. As early as 1919, the *Muswell Hill Record* had concluded that matters had 'sunk to a low ebb' as the racing was watched by German prisoners of war from the terrace of their prison in the Palace, later the first home of BBC Television.

Pioneering the cause of evening racing in the metropolis merely made things worse as the ruffianism and chicanery increased. More than one Bishop of London tried to have the track closed and, not the finest advertisement for the sport, the end had to come.

If Ally Pally was no great loss, the same cannot be said of Lanark, a course steeped in the history of Scottish racing. Many English raiders used to cross the Border, causing a bellman to go round the town crying 'Close your shutters, and bolt your doors, the English thieves are coming'. With this exhortation in mind, some races were confined to animals bred in Scotland. The Silver Bell, Lanark's premier race, was instituted by King William the Lion in 1165, but there are few records prior to 1628, and the first fixture to feature in the *Calendar* was in 1785.

In the mid nineteenth century a syndicate of innkeepers and traders was running the races, with financial help from local lairds when the books didn't balance. By the early twentieth century, this primitive form of sponsorship had given way to a more professional and substantial administration under the control of Sir Loftus Bates, the greatest racing supremo of his day, and quite possibly the best ever. The racing was run as only Bates could, but by the end of the Second World War facilities were desperately outdated.

Action was taken, and a year after King George VI had won the Silver Bell with Kingstone in 1946, improvements including hot baths in the jockeys' room were completed, the Racecourse Company wound up and the future of the track placed in the hands of trustees. For a time Lanark bathed in the afterglow of the war as servicemen spent their gratuities and crowds of 40,000 were recorded. On one such occasion, two of the three officiating stewards were stuck in the traffic until after the third race, but nobody noticed.

However, by the late Sixties the spectators had dwindled to around 2000 for a Saturday meeting, and in midweek it was two men and a dog. When the dog stayed at home, the Levy Board decided that loans totalling £40,000 had been chucking good money after bad, and the track spluttered on without support until the death knell tolled in October 1977.

A year before, Caroline had ridden at Lanark, an experience she reports in her own words:

It was always a mystery to me as to why Lanark should close. It is one of the southern-most of the Scottish courses, the turf was excellent and the hospitality up to the highest of Scottish standards. The course offered a straight five furlong with a ten furlongs round, which has a three-and-a-half-furlong straight run-in. The stands were adequate and the stables were at least secure. My only ride up there as a professional jockey proved that the jockeys of olden days had a great deal more to contend with than their counterparts today. The headlines the next day in the *Sporting Life* read, 'BIG FIELDS WITHOUT STALLS MAKE RACING A FARCE', rather suggesting that racing was indeed something of a farce before the invention of starting stalls.

The Turf authorities had in their wisdom decided to send the only free set of stalls and handlers from Pontefract direct to Redcar and so avoid a double journey back to Lanark. It proved to be bad decision, as not only did the lack of stalls cause havoc at Lanark but Redcar's racing was called off.

The first race had a false start and the horses milled around hopelessly at the post. But the real jewel in this disorganised crown was the 4.15, the Symington Handicap, one mile with a value of £600. I set off on Loughborough George, a one-time sprinter owned by that well-known racing character, Richmond Sturdy. I say one-time, because Loughborough George was still a colt and at seven years old was distinctly bored with racing round tracks in answer to the frantic efforts of his jockeys and had his heart firmly fixed on a large field and retirement. We cantered down to the start and there milled around until the field assembled, being told by the starter Captain Hibbert-Foy to take up the positions afforded to us by the draw. Mine was six, and so I was supposed to sit six spaces out from the outside rail.

Lanark favours high draws. Mark Birch was riding a horse called Embargo which unfortunately got too enthusiastic and took off with him, refusing to pull up at the start. No one took much notice until someone shouted, ' Clear, the course, stand back!', and Mark Birch shot past us being carted on his second circuit, to the sarcastic and witty encouragement of his fellow jockeys.

The precise words used are unprintable.

Time and again the starter called us in and the jockeys crowded over on the inside, breaking before the flag was lowered, and time and again we were called back. I remember watching George – his ears pricked, feet set squarely on the turf – refusing to be upset by all this flap, watching the ensuing chaos with what must have been mild amusement. The seventh call-in worked and an exhausted starter declared the race commenced. George was off and I steered over to the rails somewhat behind the rest of the field.

Little does the punter realise what goes on in that *mêlée* on the course. The thunder of hooves and shouts of the jockeys are deafening and, I suppose, resemble the old-fashioned cavalry charge. I can quite understand the usefulness of being hard of hearing. We had not gone very far before someone shouted, 'faller!', and George neatly skirted round the figure of S. Salmon whose saddle had slipped on Ruffino, rendering his continuance in the race a trifle pointless. That obstacle dealt with, George and I were neatly cut up by a fellow jockey who seemed to take exception at the idea of having to ride with women – but I got my own back as George came to the bend, which he zipped round. Pulling away ahead of the offender, I had time for a passing remark. We headed for the straight, by now tailed off but not last (we finished fifteenth of twenty-two, George put his head down and I, in a thoughtless gesture, went to raise my stick to give him a little encouragement, but fate played my hand. A rib cracked two days earlier (by George when he lashed out during a mild bout of colic) sent a sharp reminder through my body, so I rode him out hands and heels. Back in the paddock a well-known trainer came up to me and trainer Louie Dingwall as I unsaddled, and hinted that I had actually managed to get round. 'Yes', I replied, 'unlike some of them.' I can safely say that none of the false starts were caused by George, bless his heart, and you can imagine the headlines if they had been!

The race was won by Lindsay Charnock on Abercata, trained by Eric Collingwood. Tragically, one year later the same meeting was the last ever to be held at Lanark. Dutch Martyr, trained by G. Robinson and ridden by John Lowe, ran in the last Symington Handicap as he had also run in the previous year, 1976, when ridden by George Duffield. Mark Birch and Lindsay Charnock rode at that last meeting too, and must have recalled the dreadful fiasco at the start the previous year.

Postscript: Upon our return home the pain from the broken rib forced me to seek expert advice at Bournemouth Hospital. I explained to the doctor where I had been kicked and that I had just returned from riding in a race at Lanark, having driven the horsebox there and back. He kindly suggested that it was my brain which needed examining, not my chest.

And so to Wye, the final link in our tale. The last meeting was held in May 1974 on a track always regarded as a gaff and the subject of some fierce comment by F. H. Bayles, the famous geologist of the Turf, in 1903:

It is a fixture which hardly comes within the element of steeplechasing proper. It would be better placed among the Hunt meeting class. It has its own clientèle who welcome the chance of winning a small race with a very moderate animal, and the class of owner who advocates the reduction of steeplechase jockeys' fees.

In this latter comment, Bayles was grappling with one of the hot potatoes of racing politics at the time, and coming down 'with all the firmness of a Cromwell' on the side of the jockeys. He went on to say that the going was always good on the soup plate track, only 1 mile and 88 yards round, but adding in his waspish way that 'the drawback to the place is that the course trifles with horses as is the case at Plumpton'.

One horse never trifled with at Wye was Red Cast, holder of the course record and winner of more than half a dozen hunter chases and twenty point-to-points. A beautifully balanced animal, he loved the tight turns at the Kent course and ran his last race at the age of sixteen. Now an elegant thirty, he enjoys his retirement with his owner and former jockey Bob Hacking, a steward at Lingfield and Folkestone and a former steward at Wye.

Wye owed its popularity to several things. It was close to a railway, allowing easy access for townspeople, small enough to have a very friendly atmosphere, and excellent value for money as punters could drive their cars into the middle of the course, picnic and watch the horses going past at least twice. There is a lot to be said for giving the public value for money, and although Wye may not have been the best equipped course in the country, it certainly provided excellent entertainment. Mrs Long, whose family owned the course, explained that the Jockey Club had refused to license the track unless certain improvements were made, such as a new weighing room and resetting the camber on the corner, which like Alexandra Park sloped the wrong way, often causing horses to slip if conditions were unfavourable. New safety posts and rails would have to replace the concrete ones which were adequate but a trifle unforgiving if diced with at speed, and the course owners would be expected to fund the improvements.

In the light of these demands the course closed, and all that remains now are two rows of old pitch-blackened stables with solid doors which are firmly barred, containing only memories, cobwebs and farmyard furniture.

The stands have been pulled down and now only the base of the stands, weighing room and conveniences remain together with a pile of rotting concrete girders by the row of trees, waiting for nature to conceal their true form. Part of the old course is still cropped short by sheep, but most of it has gone under the plough.

Could it happen again? Unlikely in spite of the current doom and gloom. Admittedly, Epsom, Sandown and Kempton are reportedly up for grabs, but for racing only; most of the minor National hunt tracks survive well enough on the big Bank Holiday paydays, and enterprising management can make all the difference, as Stan Clarke has shown at Uttoxeter. Pending a proper financial deal with the leeches of bookmaking, racing can and must stand on its own feet.

# A RACING QUIZ

Here are 100 questions to test the memory cells of racing fans, from the novice to the expert.

The first forty are about the racing year 1991, and the rest concern a wide range of horses, races, people and terms. Throughout the quiz easier questions are mixed in with harder, so keep going!

The answers can be found on page 246.

## THE RACING YEAR 1991

1   Who in 1991 became only the second Flat jockey ever to ride winners at three different courses on the same day?

2   Which horse started favourite for the 1991 King George VI Chase?

3   Which horse won the Coral Welsh National in 1991?

4   Who rode Julie Cecil's first winner as a trainer in April 1991?

5   Who rode the winner of the Gold Seal Oaks in 1991?

6   What unusual incident occurred during the running of the 1991 St Leger?

7   On which course did Willie Carson ride a five-timer (from seven rides) in 1991, following a six-timer (also from seven rides there the previous year?

8   Which horse in 1991 became the first American-trained winner of an Irish Classic?

9   Which was the only horse to beat Arazi in 1991?

10   Which horse in 1991 became the first European-trained winner of a Breeders' Cup race on dirt?

11   Which stallion, a King George and Arc winner, was sold to continue his stud career in Japan in October 1991?

12   On which course was the Irish Champion Stakes run in 1991?

13   Who was the only jockey apart from Cash Asmussen to ride Suave Dancer in 1991?

14   On which course were the City & Suburban and Great Metropolitan Handicaps run in 1991?

15   What is the nationality of Peter Piller, leading owner of the 1990/91 National Hunt season?

16    Which jockey incurred a ten-day suspension on the very last day of the 1991 Flat turf season?

17    Apart from Generous, which English-trained horse won three Group One races in Europe in 1991?

18    Name the David Elsworth-trained filly who won the Tote-Portland Handicap and the Ladbroke Ayr Gold Cup in 1991.

19    Which former international footballer trained the winner of the Tattersalls Breeders Stakes, worth over IR£200,000 to the winner, at The Curragh in August 1991?

20    Which English-trained horse won two Group One races within eight days in 1991?

21    Name the Englishman who trained the winner of the 1991 Prix de l'Arc de Triomphe.

22    Lester Piggott rode a Derby winner in 1991. In which country?

23    Which horse in 1991 became the first female winner of the Ascot Gold Cup for thirty-three years?

24    Which two horses started joint favourites for the 1991 Derby?

25    What record is held by Seattle Dancer, sire of Seattle Rhyme, winner of the 1991 Racing Post Trophy?

26    Which horse defeated Desert Orchid in the race that bore Dessie's name at Wincanton in October 1991?

27    Which new bet was introduced by the Tote in 1991?

28    Which recent winner of the Derby was put down in December 1991 after an accident at the Dalham Hall Stud in Newmarket?

29    Name the runner-up to Generous in the Derby . . .

30    And in the King George VI and Queen Elizabeth Diamond Stakes.

31    Who rode the winner of the 1991 Lincoln Handicap?

32    What significant milestone did Pat Eddery reach in July 1991?

33    Which three English Group One races were won by French-trained horses in 1991?

34    Which two English Group One races were won by Irish-trained horses in 1991?

35    Which trainer saddled eight runners in one race in 1991?

36    On which course did the 1991 Flat turf season end?

37    On which course did the 1991/92 National Hunt season open?

38    Which jump jockey rode his 800th winner in November 1991?

39    Name the horses who fought out the controversial finish to the 1991 Whitbread Gold Cup.

40    The winning jockey in the Tote Ebor Handicap was an apprentice claiming the five-pound allowance. Name him.

# GENERAL

41  To the end of 1991, how many English Classics had Sheikh Mohammed won with colts?

42  Which was the only English Classic to be run outside England?

43  For which odds is 'ear 'ole' the slang?

44  And 'double carpet'?

45  Which course is to become Britain's third All-Weather track in 1993?

46  Which horse ran each year at the National Hunt Festival at Cheltenham in the nine years from 1983 to 1991 inclusive?

47  Which horse was Willie Carson's first Derby winner?

48  When was the Breeders' Cup first staged?

49  Name the only British-trained horse to have won two Breeders' Cup races.

50  Name the only two other horses to have won two Breeders' Cup races.

51  Six jockeys rode Desert Orchid during his racing career. Name them.

52  What was the last year in which the Flat jockeys' championship went to a rider born in England?

53  Which horse finished first in the 1989 Oaks but was subsequently disqualified for failing a drugs test?

54  Name the two horses which jointly hold the twentieth-century record for the most wins in a Flat season.

55  Which famous public school did the BBC's Julian Wilson and Channel Four's John McCririck attend?

56  Of which major international race was Mairzy Doates, ridden by Cash Asmussen, the first winner?

57  Complete the following sponsorship sequence – Timeform, Observer, William Hill . . .

58  Likewise, what comes next in this sequence – Massey-Ferguson, Kennedy Construction, Still Fork Trucks, Glen International . . .?

59  In which year did betting shops become legal in Britain?

60  Which former Champion Hurdler and Cheltenham Gold Cup winner was fatally injured in a fall in the French Champion Hurdle in 1986?

61  What was the first commercially sponsored race?

62  Where was the Hennessy Gold Cup first run?

63  Up to 1991, who was the last winner of the Daily Express Triumph Hurdle to go on to win the Champion Hurdle?

64    Which three champion racehorses are commemorated by statues at Cheltenham racecourse?

65    On which two racecourses are there statues of Red Rum?

66    On which racecourse is a statue of Desert Orchid to be found?

67    Whose colours are: emerald green, royal blue sleeves, white cap, emerald green spots?

68    Likewise: green, pink sash and cap, white sleeves?

69    And again: dark blue, grey sleeves and cap?

70    On which racecourse would you find The Bushes?

71    Likewise – the Pond Fence?

72    And again – the Chair?

73    Name the two racecourses in Wales.

74    On which racecourse are the following races run: Brigadier Gerard Stakes and Tingle Creek Chase?

75    And: Magnet Cup and Dante Stakes?

76    And: King's Own Scottish Borderers' Cup and Morebattle Hurdle?

77    Which horse won America's prestigious Horse of the Year award five times in a row between 1960 and 1964?

78    Name the only horse ever to beat Brigadier Gerard.

79    Which English-trained gelding won the Arlington Million in 1984?

80    What was the last British racecourse to close?

81    Who trains at Warren Place?

82    And at Moss Side Racing Stables?

83    And at Cotswold House, Condicote?

84    Name the first English-trained horse to win the Prix du Jockey-Club.

85    Which major international race is run on the first Tuesday in November?

86    Name the five racecourses in Scotland.

87    How old was Lester Piggott when he rode his first winner?

88    And how old was Lester Piggott when he rode his first Derby winner?

89    The famous 1984 Whitbread Gold Cup was won by the Queen Mother's Special Cargo, trained by Fulke Walwyn. Two short heads away came his stable companion Diamond Edge. Which horse finished between these two?

90    When Equinoctial won a hurdle race at Kelso in November 1990 he returned the longest winning starting price ever in Britain. What was it?

91    The last French-trained winner of the Prix de l'Abbaye was also the last two-year-old to win the race. Name her.

92   What are the three races that make up the American Triple Crown?
93   And who was the last horse to land the American Triple Crown?
94   Name the two racetracks in Hong Kong.
95   What was the name of the horse at the centre of the famous betting coup at Cartmel in August 1974?
96   What are the equivalent odds of a Tote return of £6.50?
97   How many bets are there in a Super Yankee?
98   Name the last French-trained winner of the Derby.
99   Who before Quest For Fame was the last Derby winner to be kept in training as a four-year-old?
100  Who was the horse who provided Steve Cauthen with his first English Classic winner?

**RACECOURSES OF THE
BRITISH ISLES**

Flat
*National Hunt*
**Flat and National Hunt**

Courses which stage fixtures covere[
Channel Four Racing in 1992 are s[
in boxes.

Perth

Hamilton Park    ● Edinburgh
                 *Kelso*
Ayr

                 Newcastle
Carlisle         *Hexham*
                 *Sedgefield*        Redcar
*Cartmel*        Catterick Bridge    *Thirsk*
Down Royal                  *Ripon*
Downpatrick      *Wetherby*          York
Sligo                               *Beverley*
Dundalk                     *Pontefract*
Roscommon   Navan   Bellewstown
Ballinrobe          Laytown    *Liverpool*
Galway      Fairyhouse          Haydock Park   Doncaster
Kilbeggan   Naas            *Bangor-on-Dee*   Chester   Southwell
The Curragh   Leopardstown                              (A/W)
              Punchestown       *Uttoxeter*   Nottingham   Market Rasen
Limerick   Thurles                                        Fakenham
Listowel   Tipperary         Wolverhampton    Leicester   Yarmouth
Tralee     Clonmel   Gowran Park   *Ludlow*              *Huntingdon*
Mallow              Wexford    *Worcester*   *Stratford*   Newmarket
Killarney           Waterford and Tramore   *Hereford*   Towcester
                                   *Cheltenham*
                    Chepstow          Windsor   Kempton Park
                              Ascot
                    *Bath*   Newbury          Sandown Park
                                        Epsom   Lingfield Park (A/W
                         *Salisbury*   Goodwood         Folkesto
                    *Taunton*   *Wincanton*        *Plumpton*
                    *Devon and Exeter*                *Brighton*
                                        *Fontwell Park*
                    *Newton Abbot*

# RACECOURSES IN GREAT BRITAIN

The following pages offer the essential information about the 59 racecourses in Britain and their 1992 fixture lists.

We have *not* included details of entrance charges, as at some courses these vary considerably depending on the meeting, and are in any case subject to alteration. Do not hesitate to phone the racecourse at the number given to enquire about charges – or indeed about anything else – before planning your day at the races.

As John McCririck would encourage you – Come Racing!

## *Ascot*

### FLAT AND NATIONAL HUNT

ADDRESS Ascot Racecourse, Ascot, Berkshire SL5 7JN
TELEPHONE 0344 22211
LOCATION Ascot is 6 miles south-west of Windsor, 3 miles east of
  Bracknell, with easy access from both the M3 (junction 3) and M4
  (junctions 6 or 7)
NEAREST STATION Ascot (from Waterloo): ten minutes' walk to course
FAMILY FACILITIES supervised crèche and playground (accompanied
  children of 16 or under are admitted free)
ENCLOSURES Members, Grandstand, Silver Ring, Course
CLERK OF THE COURSE Capt. the Hon. Nicholas Beaumont

ASCOT has been Britain's premier racecourse since its founding by Queen Anne in 1711,and although the Royal Meeting (16–19 June in 1992) remains a high point of the Turf as well as the social year, the overall standard of racing at the course is extremely high. The Royal Meeting apart, Ascot stages three Group One races: the King George VI and Queen Elizabeth Diamond Stakes at the end of July (the country's top middle-distance race for three-year-olds and upwards), the Queen Elizabeth II Stakes and the Fillies' Mile at the end of September on the day known since 1987 as the Festival of British Racing.

Ascot is a right-handed course, of a galloping nature, and provides a very fair test for horses at all distances and under both codes. Beyond the winning post the ground sweeps down towards the apex of the triangular course at Swinley Bottom, then gradually rises to the turn into the straight and rises further until levelling out just before the line.

For racegoers, as for horses, Ascot takes some beating. The facilities are excellent, it is (usually!) easy to get about, and all the enclosures afford good views of the racing. For jumping, the parade ring moves from the summer location on the west side of the grandstand to right in front of the stand, where there is access for Silver Ring patrons.

## FIXTURES 1992

JANUARY
10  (Fri) NH (PML Day)
11  (Sat) NH (Victor Chandler Chase)
FEBRUARY
5  (Wed) NH (Charterhouse Day)
MARCH
28  (Sat) NH (Letheby & Christopher Long Distance Hurdle)
APRIL
8  (Wed) NH (Bollinger Novices' Chase)
28  (Tue evening) NH (Spring Evening Meeting)
29  (Wed) Flat (Insulpak Victoria Cup)
JUNE
16  (Tue) Royal Meeting (St James's Palace Stakes)
17  (Wed) Royal Meeting (Coronation Stakes)
18  (Thu) Royal Meeting (Gold Cup)
19  (Fri) Royal Meeting (King's Stand Stakes)

20  (Sat) Flat (Grand Metropolitan Handicap)
JULY
24  (Fri) Flat (Virginia Water Stakes)
25  (Sat) Flat (King George VI and Queen Elizabeth Diamond Stakes)
SEPTEMBER
24  (Thu) Flat (Hoover Cumberland Lodge Stakes)
25  (Fri) Flat (Charity Day – Ascot Action For Ability)
26  (Sat) Flat (Festival of British Racing)
OCTOBER
9  (Fri) Flat (October Stakes)
10  (Sat) Flat (Bovis Handicap)
21  (Wed) NH (United Construction Chase)
NOVEMBER
20  (Fri) NH (Racecall Hurdle)
21  (Sat) NH (H&T Walker Gold Cup)
DECEMBER
19  (Sat) NH (SGB Chase)

# *Ayr*

## FLAT AND NATIONAL HUNT

ADDRESS Ayr Racecourse, Whitletts Road, Ayr KA8 0JE
TELEPHONE 0292 264179
LOCATION the racecourse is on the eastern side of Ayr just off the A77;
   Ayr is about 35 miles south-west of Glasgow
NEAREST STATION Ayr (from Glasgow)
FAMILY FACILITIES supervised playground
ENCLOSURES Club, Paddock, Silver Ring
CLERK OF THE COURSE S. Morshead
GENERAL MANAGER M. Kershaw

A YR is a superb racecourse for horses and spectators alike. The left-handed track is oval in shape and just over 12 furlongs round. With its long straights, easy bends and gentle undulations, it is a very fair course suited to long-striding horses with plenty of stamina. The turf is excellent and the going rarely firm.

All the stands command a good view of the racing, and the atmosphere is vibrant and enthusiastic, especially at the principal fixture, September's Western Meeting.

Jumping at Ayr is of a high standard: the course is on the inside of the flat course and the fences are very fair (it was the first racecourse to dispense with the water jump). The feature race of the season is the Scottish National, run at Ayr since the closure of Bogside in 1965 and won by such esteemed horses as Red Rum and Merryman II.

## FIXTURES 1992

JANUARY
   2 (Thu) NH
   25 (Sat) NH
FEBRUARY
   8 (Sat) NH
MARCH
   7 (Sat) NH
APRIL
   10 (Fri) NH (Scottish Champion
      Hurdle)
   11 (Sat) NH (William Hill Scottish
      National)
JUNE
   19 (Fri) Flat
   20 (Sat) Flat

JULY
   18 (Sat) Flat (Scottish Classic)
   20 (Mon) Flat
   21 (Tue) Flat
   24 (Fri evening) Flat
   25 (Sat) Flat
SEPTEMBER
   16 (Wed) Flat
   17 (Thu) Flat
   18 (Fri) Flat (Ladbroke Ayr Gold Cup)
   19 (Sat) Flat
OCTOBER
   10 (Sat) NH
NOVEMBER
   13 (Fri) NH
   14 (Sat) NH

# *Bangor-on-Dee*

## NATIONAL HUNT

ADDRESS Bangor-on-Dee Racecourse, Bangor-on-Dee, nr Wrexham, Clywd LL13 0DA

TELEPHONE 0978 780323 Race days only; 0948 860438 Secretary; 0981 250436 Clerk of Course

LOCATION the racecourse is 22 miles north of Shrewsbury, and 5 miles south-east of Wrexham on the B5069. Good link from north via Chester Bypass.

NEAREST STATION Wrexham

FAMILY FACILITIES car parks have good view of course: ideal for picnics in late spring and early autumn

ENCLOSURES Paddock (Tattersalls), course

CLERK OF THE COURSE B. R. Davies

THE essential things to know about Bangor-on-Dee are (a) that it is near Wrexham, and not at the Bangor near Anglesey, and (b) that it has no grandstand. It is also the course where the National Hunt season now begins, on the Friday of the Goodwood July Meeting. No grandstand apart, racegoers enjoy perfectly good facilities, and can watch the racing from the side of the hill which looks down the home straight (making race-reading in the closing stages difficult) or, away from the main enclosure, can stretch out and picnic on the mound alongside the straight. There is thus a very casual atmosphere, not unlike that of a point-to-point.

The course is left-handed, triangular and mostly flat, the bends quite sharp and the fences easy.

## FIXTURES 1992

FEBRUARY
7  (Fri) NH (Gredington Handicap Chase)
MARCH
4  (Wed) NH
21  (Sat) NH
APRIL
11  (Sat) NH (McAlpine Day)
MAY
1  (Fri evening) NH

9  (Sat) NH (N.W. Area point-to-point Final)
JULY
31  (Fri) NH
AUGUST
15  (Sat) NH
SEPTEMBER
12  (Sat) NH
OCTOBER
10  (Sat) NH (Willis Faber

Handicap Chase)
30  (Fri) NH (Corbett Bookmakers Handicap Chase)
NOVEMBER
27  (Fri) NH
DECEMBER
16  (Wed) NH

# *Bath*

## FLAT

ADDRESS Bath Racecourse, Lansdown, Bath, Avon
TELEPHONE 0225 424609 or 0451 20517
LOCATION the racecourse is about 2 miles north-west of the city at
  Lansdown, which is 2 miles off the A46; the A46 links direct with
  junction 18 of the M4
NEAREST STATION Bath (from London Paddington)
FAMILY FACILITIES picnic area, centre of course
ENCLOSURES Club, Tattersalls, Silver Ring
CLERK OF THE COURSE Capt. C. B. Toller

SINCE 1811 Bath Races have been held on the downland at Lansdown, 780 feet above sea level. While the setting is extremely appealing, views are less than ideal: the stands are fairly low and the horses are obscured by the running rail and the gradual rise of the straight. Because of Lansdown's height above sea level and the openness of its setting it is advisable to take warm clothing.

At just over 1½ miles round the left-handed track is galloping and demanding, though the bend into the home straight is very sharp; the straights are long and the final four furlongs rise gradually. In sprints low numbers are often preferred, for there is a kink in the track a furlong out which favours horses drawn on the inside.

## FIXTURES 1992

APRIL
  28  (Tue) Flat
MAY
  9  (Sat) Flat
  18  (Mon) Flat
JUNE
  13  (Sat) Flat
  26  (Fri evening) Flat

JULY
  4  (Sat) Flat
  8  (Wed) Flat
  20  (Mon) Flat
AUGUST
  11  (Tue) Flat
SEPTEMBER
  14  (Mon) Flat
  28  (Mon) Flat

# Beverley
## FLAT

ADDRESS Beverley Race Company Ltd, 19 North Bar Within, Beverley, North Humberside HU17 8DB

TELEPHONE 0482 867488 or 882645 (racedays only)

LOCATION Beverley is about 10 miles north of Hull; the racecourse is on the western side of the town off the A1035, which can be reached via the B1230, from junction 38 of the M62

NEAREST STATION Beverley

ENCLOSURES Club, Tattersalls, Silver Ring, Third Ring (including picnic park)

CLERK OF THE COURSE J. G. Cleverly

T HE town of Beverley has long been associated with horses. A track was laid out here even before the end of the seventeenth century, such was the popularity of matching horses, and in its prime at the beginning of the nineteenth century it was the hunting, coursing, racing and breeding centre of the East Riding. Although the facilities are rather outdated, the racecourse is colourful, if cramped.

The right-handed course undulates slightly, is 13 furlongs round and provides a fair test for the horses. The straight 5-furlong track is very testing, however, particularly in soft going, since it rises steadily from start to finish.

## FIXTURES 1992

MARCH
27  (Fri) Flat
28  (Sat) Flat
APRIL
23  (Thu) Flat
MAY
8  (Fri) Flat
9  (Sat) Flat
19  (Tue) Flat
JUNE
3  (Wed evening) Flat
4  (Thu) Flat
10  (Wed) Flat

JULY
3  (Fri evening) Flat
4  (Sat) Flat
13  (Mon evening) Flat
14  (Tue) Flat
28  (Tue) Flat
AUGUST
12  (Wed) Flat
13  (Thu) Flat
SEPTEMBER
16  (Wed) Flat
17  (Thu) Flat

# Brighton
## FLAT

ADDRESS Brighton Racecourse, Brighton, Sussex BN2 2XZ
TELEPHONE 0273 603580 (racedays); 0444 441111 (Clerk of the
  Course)
LOCATION the racecourse is on the eastern side of the town, just off the
  A27 (Brighton-Lewes road)
NEAREST STATION Brighton
FAMILY FACILITIES temporary play area in July and August
ENCLOSURES Club, Tattersalls
CLERK OF THE COURSE C. E. Griggs

B RIGHTON's track is similar to that at Epsom; it is 1½ miles in
length and suited to compact, well-made horses who are able to cope
with the two sharpish bends and exaggerated undulations. It is a fast
course: the straight falls steeply downhill before rising at the distance and
finally levelling out in the last furlong.

Brighton races have a distinctive holiday atmosphere; once renowned
for race gangs, Brighton is now a popular and pleasant course. The stands
offer a fine view of the course (although sea mists occasionally roll in and
obscure everything) and the facilities are good.

## FIXTURES 1992

| MARCH | | JULY | |
|---|---|---|---|
| 26 | (Thu) Flat | 2 | (Thu evening) Flat |
| APRIL | | 23 | (Thu) Flat |
| 2 | (Thu) Flat | AUGUST | |
| 13 | (Mon) Flat | 4 | (Tue) Flat |
| MAY | | 5 | (Wed) Flat |
| 7 | (Thu) Flat | 6 | (Thu) Flat |
| 27 | (Wed) Flat | 25 | (Tue) Flat |
| 28 | (Thu) Flat | 26 | (Wed) Flat |
| JUNE | | SEPTEMBER | |
| 15 | (Mon) Flat | 23 | (Wed) Flat |
| 23 | (Tue) Flat | 29 | (Tue) Flat |

# *Carlisle*
## FLAT AND NATIONAL HUNT

ADDRESS Grandstand Office Carlisle Racecourse, Durdar Road,
Carlisle, Cumbria CA2 4TS
TELEPHONE 0228 22973
LOCATION the racecourse is 2 miles south of the town on Durdar Road,
and is only 2 miles from junction 42 of the M6
NEAREST STATION Carlisle
ENCLOSURES Club, Paddock
CLERK OF THE COURSE Major T. R. Riley

THE 12½ furlong round, pear-shaped track at Carlisle is particularly testing and undulates severely throughout. On entering the straight, 3½ furlongs from home, the horses meet a very stiff climb that runs nearly all the way to the finish. This climb is more pronounced on the steeplechase course and makes sure that a horse gets every bit of the trip: many a horse has won here with a late flourish, and Carlisle is suited to a long-striding horse with plenty of stamina. The going is subject to extreme variations and can change dramatically since it stands on 9 inches of soil over clay.

## FIXTURES 1992

JANUARY
13   (Mon) NH
FEBRUARY
4   (Tue) NH
MARCH
6   (Fri) NH
APRIL
18   (Sat) NH
20   (Mon Bank Holiday) NH
24   (Fri) Flat
MAY
7   (Thu) Flat
8   (Fri) Flat
28   (Thu) Flat
JUNE
6   (Sat evening) Flat

24   (Wed) Flat (Carlisle Bell)
25   (Thu) Flat (Cumberland Plate)
JULY
24   (Fri) Flat
SEPTEMBER
8   (Tue) Flat
26   (Sat) NH
28   (Mon) NH
OCTOBER
9   (Fri) NH
NOVEMBER
9   (Mon) NH
26   (Thu) NH
DECEMBER
30   (Wed) NH

# *Cartmel*

## NATIONAL HUNT

ADDRESS Cartmel Racecourse, Cartmel, nr Grange-over-Sands,
   Cumbria
TELEPHONE 05395 36340 (racedays) or 09312 392
LOCATION the racecourse is 1 mile west of the town, which is itself about
   20 miles south-west of Kendal; it is a little over 10 miles from the M6
   (junction 36) via the A590
NEAREST STATIONS Cark-in-Cartmel or Grange-over-Sands
ENCLOSURES Paddock, Course
CLERK OF THE COURSE Major T. R. Riley

L IVERPOOL apart, Cartmel is the least-used racecourse in the
   country, with just five days scheduled for 1992 – two meetings on
and around the Whit and August Bank Holidays. Cartmel is immensely
popular, partly because of the rarity value of racing there, but the course
also has a unique charm which attracts fervent support. An intimate track
set in wooded Cumbrian parkland, it has a left-handed circuit of a little
over a mile which favours the handy sort of horse. But the fences are stiff,
and the run-in – half a mile – is the longest in the country.

## FIXTURES 1992

| MAY | | AUGUST | |
|---|---|---|---|
| 23 | (Sat) | 29 | (Sat) |
| 25 | (Mon Bank Holiday) | 31 | (Mon Bank Holiday) |
| 27 | (Wed) | | |

# *Catterick Bridge*

## FLAT AND NATIONAL HUNT

ADDRESS The Racecourse, Catterick Bridge, Richmond, North
   Yorkshire
TELEPHONE 0748 811478
LOCATION the racecourse is about 10 miles south of Darlington and 1
   mile north-west of Catterick; the course is adjacent to the A1 but
   access is from the A6136
NEAREST STATION Darlington
ENCLOSURES Club, Tattersalls, Course

CLERKS OF THE COURSE J. F. Sanderson (Flat)
C. Enderby (N.H.)

A T just under 11 furlongs round, Catterick Bridge is an exceptionally fast and sharp track. It is suited to nippy, well-made horses who are able to cope with the undulations and ready pace. Although the fences are small, experience in both rider and horse is invaluable here, and many a poor jumper has come to grief. Front-runners often do well at Catterick. The subsoil of gravel ensures fine drainage and the going is usually good.

## FIXTURES 1992

JANUARY
 1 (Wed Bank Holiday) NH
17 (Fri) NH
18 (Sat) NH
FEBRUARY
 8 (Sat) NH
20 (Thu) NH
MARCH
 4 (Wed) NH
25 (Wed) Flat
APRIL
22 (Wed) Flat
MAY
21 (Thu) Flat
JUNE
 5 (Fri) Flat
 6 (Sat) Flat
JULY
 1 (Wed evening) Flat

 2 (Thurs) Flat
15 (Wed) Flat
16 (Thu) Flat
29 (Wed) Flat
AUGUST
11 (Tue evening) Flat
SEPTEMBER
19 (Sat) Flat
OCTOBER
16 (Fri) Flat
17 (Sat) Flat
24 (Sat) NH
NOVEMBER
21 (Sat) NH
23 (Mon) NH
DECEMBER
 2 (Wed) NH
18 (Fri) NH
31 (Thu) NH

# *Cheltenham*

## NATIONAL HUNT

ADDRESS Cheltenham Racecourse, Prestbury Park, Cheltenham, Gloucestershire GL50 4SH
TELEPHONE 0242 513014
LOCATION the racecourse is 1½ miles north of the town on the A435, with easy access from the M5 (junctions 10 or 11)
NEAREST STATION Cheltenham (from London Paddington)
FAMILY FACILITIES children under 16 free of charge (except at NH Festival)
ENCLOSURES Club, Tattersalls, Fosters Enclosure

CLERK OF THE COURSE P. W. F. Arkwright
GENERAL MANAGER E. W. Gillespie

CHELTENHAM now has three courses: the Old Course, the New Course (very similar in terrain to the Old Course but using separate ground for most of the circuit) and the Park Course, opened in October 1991 to provide a less demanding test early in the season. Both the Old and New courses are tailor-made for exciting racing: the runners make a long uphill climb to the furthest point from the stands, then turn left-handed to charge downhill before reaching the straight and the grind up the final hill to the post. The ability to see out the trip is paramount, though chasers also need to jump well: the fences are particularly well made and unforgiving of sloppy jumping. Indeed, anything less would be inappropriate, for Cheltenham is the premier jumping track in Britain.

The Cheltenham year culminates in the glorious National Hunt Festival in March, but the standard of racing at the course is very high throughout the season. Facilities for racegoers are first-rate, and the surroundings – notably the wonderful backdrop of Cleeve Hill – make this a course with a feel all its own: at Cheltenham you know you're at the Mecca of the sport.

## FIXTURES 1992

JANUARY
 1 (Wed Bank Holiday) NH (ASW Chase)
 25 (Sat) NH (Charterhouse Mercantile Chase)
MARCH
 10 (Tue) NH Festival (Smurfit Champion Hurdle)
 11 (Wed) NH Festival (Sun Alliance Chase, Queen Mother Champion Chase)
 12 (Thu) NH Festival (Tote Cheltenham Gold Cup, Daily Express Triumph Hurdle)
APRIL
 15 (Wed) NH (South Wales Showers Chase)

 16 (Thu) NH (Howard E. Perry Hunters Chase)
 29 (Wed evening) NH (Rover Cars Hunters Evening)
SEPTEMBER
 30 (Wed) NH
OCTOBER
 1 (Thu) NH
 14 (Wed) NH
NOVEMBER
 13 (Fri) NH (Countryside Day)
 14 (Sat) NH (Mackeson Gold Cup)
DECEMBER
 11 (Fri) NH
 12 (Sat) NH (A. F. Budge Gold Cup)
 31 (Thu) NH

# *Chepstow*

## FLAT AND NATIONAL HUNT

ADDRESS Chepstow Racecourse, Chepstow, Gwent NP6 5YH
TELEPHONE 0291 622260
LOCATION Chepstow is 1 mile north-west of Chepstow town on the
A466, and is easily accessible from the M4 (junction 22) – just west of
the Severn Bridge
NEAREST STATION Chepstow (from Newport): 1 mile from course
ENCLOSURES Members, Tattersalls, Silver Ring
CLERK OF THE COURSE R. Farrant

SET in attractive parkland, Chepstow is well known for the consider-
able undulations throughout the course. On the straight mile, for
example, the horses run up and down three stiff rises and falls before
reaching the winning post. On the Flat a good gallop is usually assured,
making for a strong test of stamina. However, a good gallop is not always
guaranteed in jump races where the foibles of the course often upset the
pace.

Although horses do disappear from sight early in the home straight this
does not detract from the excitement of racing at Chepstow, and races
such as the Welsh National are among the highlights of the year.

## FIXTURES 1992

JANUARY
  7  (Tue) NH
 21  (Tue) NH
FEBRUARY
  1  (Sat) NH (John Hughes Grand
     National Trial)
 15  (Sat) NH
MARCH
  7  (Sat) NH (Polycell Hurdle)
 14  (Sat) NH
APRIL
 20  (Mon Bank Holiday) NH (Welsh
     Champion Hurdle)
 21  (Tue) NH
MAY
  5  (Tue) NH
 25  (Mon Bank Holiday) Flat
JUNE
 11  (Thu evening) Flat

 27  (Sat) Flat
 30  (Tue) Flat
JULY
  9  (Thu evening) Flat
 16  (Thu evening) Flat
AUGUST
 31  (Mon Bank Holiday) Flat
SEPTEMBER
 12  (Sat) Flat
OCTOBER
  3  (Sat) NH (Timeform Hurdle)
 13  (Tue) Flat
 20  (Tue) Flat
NOVEMBER
  7  (Sat) NH (Tote Silver Trophy)
DECEMBER
  5  (Sat) NH
 28  (Mon Bank Holiday) NH (Coral
     Welsh National)

# Chester
### FLAT

ADDRESS The Racecourse, Chester CH1 2LY
TELEPHONE 0244 323170
LOCATION the racecourse is in the south-west of the city on the A548
   Queensferry road; it is served by the M56 (junction 15)
NEAREST STATION Chester General (from London Euston): 1 mile
   from course
ENCLOSURES County Stand, Tattersalls, Dee Stand, open course
CLERK OF THE COURSE Capt. C. B. Toller

CHESTER is an extraordinary racecourse. Situated between the
banks of the River Dee and the old Roman walls of the city, it is the
tightest Flat track in the country, with a circuit of scarcely more than one
mile and a run from the final bend of just over a furlong. Consequently it
favours the handy, nimble sort of horse who can break quickly and has no
difficulty holding a position. The draw is a crucial factor here, especially
in shorter races, where runners with an inside berth (low numbers) have a
distinct advantage.

A course steeped in history, Chester can claim to stage the oldest race
meeting still run at its original location, but it is keeping up with the times
in its facilities (notably the new County Stand) and has an atmosphere all
its own. The big May Meeting (featuring the Chester Vase and the
Chester Cup) is the track's high point of the year, but its evening
meetings are also extremely popular: a crowd of 17,000 turned up for one
evening meeting in 1991 despite very small fields. So get there early!

## FIXTURES 1992

MAY
   5  (Tue) Flat (Dalham Chester Vase)
   6  (Wed) Flat (Ladbroke Chester Cup,
       Shadwell Stud Cheshire Oaks)
   7  (Thu) Flat (Ormonde EBF Stakes,
       Dee Stakes)
JUNE
  24  (Tue evening) Flat

JULY
  10  (Fri evening) Flat
  11  (Sat) Flat
AUGUST
  21  (Fri) Flat
  22  (Sat) Flat
OCTOBER
  20  (Tue) Flat
  21  (Wed) Flat

*Racecourses continued on page 89*

# THE BONUSPRINT/ CHANNEL FOUR RACING RACEHORSE PHOTOGRAPHY AWARDS

Since 1988 BonusPrint, Europe's largest colour photo-processing company, has combined with Channel Four Racing to promote the annual racehorse photography awards scheme, open to all professional racing photographers.

For each of the six months from April to September a monthly prize of £250 is awarded to the photographer responsible for what the judging panel considers the best photo, and each month's winner and runner-up qualify for the best racing photograph of the year, for which the prize is £1,000 and a crystal trophy. There are also awards for the runner-up and the third-placed, and for the best portfolio of photos.

**The 1991 awards went to:**

*Winner*     Ronald Frain (for the photograph opposite)
*Runner-up*  Mel Fordham
*Third*      Colin Turner
*Portfolio*  Philippa Gilchrist

The colour photographs on the following pages are all entries to the BonusPrint/Channel Four Racing competition in 1991.

'Heading for the lollipop' by Ronald Frain: Brighton racecourse, May 1991. (Photograph of the Year, 1991)

'Win(some) treble' by Ronald Frain: Royal Ascot, June 1991.

'The best view in racing' by Colin Turner: Kingsley Stud Farm,
Westward Ho!, Devon.

'It's true – from this height you can see Hereford Cathedral!'
by Les Hurley: Mr K. Green and Slaney Prince at Hereford,
August 1991.

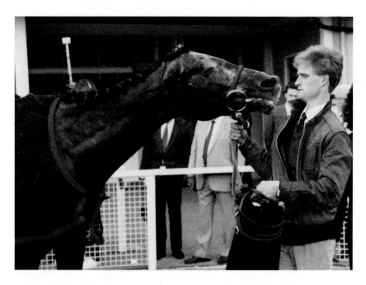

The 1991 Portfolio Award went to Philippa Gilchrist for a collection which included these three photographs. *Above:* 'Give me a kiss, sweetheart!': Bighayir in the unsaddling enclosure at Epsom, June 1991. *Below:* 'Pat Eddery and Darryll Holland battle it out': Darryll Holland on Stately March (right) beats Pat Eddery on Dokkha Oyston at Goodwood, May 1991. *Opposite:* 'Ooops, Frankie – haven't you forgotten something?': Lanfranco Dettori at Epsom.

'I always said water jumps would be popular in front of the stands' by
Lesley Sampson: Memsahib about to shed Willie Carson after winning at
Lingfield Park in May 1991.

'Good afternoon, Harvey' by Kenneth Bright: Willie Carson after winning
on Subsonic at Newcastle, the fourth of his five winners at the course on 1
October 1991.

'A cheeky end to the season' by Eric Gibbs: Jacqui Oliver and Noel Luck at
Stratford, June 1991.

'Evening racing' by Ronald Frain: Windsor, July 1991.

# Devon and Exeter
## NATIONAL HUNT

ADDRESS The Racecourse, Kennford, nr. Exeter
TELEPHONE 0392 832599
LOCATION Devon and Exeter is 5 miles south-west of Exeter, on the
   A38 (the main Exeter-Plymouth road)
NEAREST STATION Exeter St David's
ENCLOSURES Members, Tattersalls, Course
CLERK OF THE COURSE R. H. Merton

SET amidst the gorse and heather at Haldon, Devon and Exeter is one
of the country's most attractive courses and, like many of the smaller
British courses, has a strong local character.

The course is right-handed, two miles round and fairly stiff, providing
a good test of stamina; after the downhill stretch in the back straight
(where the horses disappear from view for a while) the track rises steadily,
levels out around the bend and then rises again all the way up the straight
to the finish.

The feature race of the season, the Plymouth Gin Haldon Gold Cup,
has attracted some big names recently: Sabin du Loir (twice a winner of
this race), Desert Orchid (who drew a bigger crowd than did the Queen
when attending the racecourse), Waterloo Boy and Beech Road.

## FIXTURES 1992

JANUARY
   1  (Wed Bank Holiday) NH
MARCH
   19  (Thu) NH
APRIL
   3  (Fri) NH
MAY
   4  (Mon Bank Holiday) NH
AUGUST
   5  (Wed) NH
   26  (Wed) NH

SEPTEMBER
   9  (Wed) NH
   16  (Wed) NH
   29  (Tue) NH
OCTOBER
   13  (Tue) NH
   23  (Fri) NH
NOVEMBER
   3  (Tue) NH
   24  (Tue) NH
DECEMBER
   4  (Fri) NH

# Doncaster
## FLAT AND NATIONAL HUNT

ADDRESS Doncaster Racecourse, Leger Way, Doncaster DN2 6BB
TELEPHONE 0302 320066
LOCATION the racecourse is on the eastern side of the town just off the
   A638, with easy access from the M18 (junctions 3 and 4)
NEAREST STATION Doncaster Central
FAMILY FACILITIES playground, crèche
ENCLOSURES Club, Grandstand, Second Enclosure
CLERK OF THE COURSE J. F. Sanderson

HOME of the oldest Classic, Doncaster is proud of its history and its reputation as one of the fairest racecourses in the country. A pear-shaped left-handed circuit of nearly 2 miles round, its wide track and easy turn into the 4½-furlong straight make it a course where trouble in running should be easily avoided, and the only significant undulation is the slight rise and fall towards the end of the back straight. The steeplechase fences have been criticised for being too easy, and horses can sometimes get away with liberties here which would bring them down at Cheltenham or Ascot. Under both codes, Doncaster suits the longstriding, galloping horse.

For racegoers the facilities are good, primarily in the modern grandstand, and a particularly welcome feature is the siting of the parade ring in front of the stands. But don't try the 'Do you know who I am?' routine to get into Members' without the required tie: until his neck was properly equipped, Gazza himself was denied entrance to that hallowed sanctum in July 1991.

## FIXTURES 1992

JANUARY
   25  (Sat) NH (William Hill Golden
       Spurs)
FEBRUARY
   22  (Sat) NH
   24  (Mon) NH
MARCH
    7  (Sat) NH
   19  (Thu) Flat
   20  (Fri) Flat
   21  (Sat) Flat (William Hill Lincoln
       Handicap)

MAY
    4  (Mon Bank Holiday) Flat (AT
       PONTEFRACT)
   23  (Sat) Flat
   25  (Mon Bank Holiday) Flat
JUNE
   12  (Fri evening) Flat
   26  (Fri) Flat
   27  (Sat evening) Flat
JULY
   22  (Wed) Flat
   23  (Thu evening) Flat

SEPTEMBER
9 (Wed) Flat (A. F. Budge Park Hill Stakes)
10 (Thu) Flat (Doncaster Cup, Kiveton Park Stakes)
11 (Fri) Flat (Laurent-Perrier Champagne Stakes)
12 (Sat) Flat (Coalite St Leger Stakes)

OCTOBER
23 (Fri) Flat
24 (Sat) Flat (Racing Post Trophy)

NOVEMBER
6 (Fri) Flat
7 (Sat) Flat (William Hill November Handicap)

DECEMBER
11 (Fri) NH
12 (Sat) NH

# Edinburgh
## FLAT AND NATIONAL HUNT

ADDRESS Musselburgh Racecourse, Linkfield Road, Musselburgh, East Lothian
TELEPHONE 031 665 2859 or non-racedays 0292 264179
LOCATION Musselburgh is 5 miles east of Edinburgh
NEAREST STATION Musselburgh (from Edinburgh Waverley)
ENCLOSURES Members, Paddock
CLERK OF THE COURSE S. Morshead
GENERAL MANAGER M. Kershaw

A right-handed course about 10 furlongs round, Edinburgh has sharp bends and tends to suit the handy sort of horse. There has been jumping here only since 1987, and the standard of racing under both codes is moderate. But the course has a certain antique charm, viewing is good, and the location hard by the seashore at Musselburgh can protect the course from fierce weather nearby. So even if central Edinburgh is under a foot of snow, don't assume that they can't race at Musselburgh.

## FIXTURES 1992

JANUARY
3 (Fri) NH
9 (Sat) NH
30 (Thu) NH
FEBRUARY
14 (Fri) NH
22 (Sat) NH
APRIL
13 (Mon) Flat
MAY
18 (Mon) Flat

30 (Sat) Flat
JUNE
15 (Mon) Flat
22 (Mon) Flat
JULY
6 (Mon) Flat
13 (Mon) Flat
31 (Fri evening) Flat
AUGUST
28 (Fri evening) Flat

SEPTEMBER
21 (Mon) Flat
OCTOBER
19 (Mon) Flat
NOVEMBER
5 (Thu) Flat
DECEMBER
7 (Mon) NH
12 (Sat) NH
21 (Mon) NH

# *Epsom*
## FLAT

ADDRESS United Racecourses Ltd, Racecourse Paddock, Epsom, Surrey KT18 5NJ
TELEPHONE 03727 26311
LOCATION the racecourse is 2 miles south of the town on the B290, and is only 5 miles from the M25 (junctions 8 or 9)
NEAREST STATION Tattenham Corner (from London Bridge, Charing Cross, Victoria or Waterloo, change at Purley)
ENCLOSURES Club, Grandstand, Paddock, Lonsdale Stand
CLERK OF THE COURSE R. M. O. Webster

THERE are two significant innovations at Epsom in 1992. The new Members' Stand will be opened, and for the first time the course will stage evening meetings – on 1 and 29 July. It will be interesting to see how racegoers respond to the evening fixtures, for it is often felt that the vast stands of Epsom – the grandstand was extensively refurbished in 1991 – lack atmosphere except on Derby Day (and some years even then).

The Derby course illustrates the unique nature of this track: uphill on leaving the stalls and into a slight right-hand bend, then across to the other rail to start the long but irregular downhill sweep towards Tattenham Corner. The straight – just under 4 furlongs long – has a very marked camber from the stands side towards the Downs, and after running downhill for most of its length goes slightly uphill just before the winning post. No wonder so many tired horses become unbalanced in the closing stages, and no wonder the Derby is described as a unique test of the Thoroughbred. The straight 5 furlong course is exceptionally fast.

## FIXTURES 1992

JUNE
3  (Wed) Flat (Ever Ready Derby)
4  (Thu) Flat (Hanson Coronation Cup)
5  (Fri) Flat
6  (Sat) Flat (Gold Seal Oaks)

JULY
1  (Wed evening) Flat
29  (Wed evening) Flat
AUGUST
31  (Mon Bank Holiday) Flat
SEPTEMBER
1  (Tue) Flat

# *Fakenham*
## NATIONAL HUNT

ADDRESS The Racecourse, Fakenham, Norfolk NR21 7NY
TELEPHONE 0328 862388
LOCATION Fakenham is 25 miles north-west of Norwich; the racecourse
   is 1 mile south of the town on the B1146
NEAREST STATION King's Lynn or Norwich
FAMILY FACILITIES parking within racecourse enclosures enables
   families to use their cars throughout the day
ENCLOSURES Members, Grandstand and Paddock, Course
   (Grandstand/Paddock and Course are combined on non-Bank
   Holidays)
CLERK OF THE COURSE P. B. Firth

SET alongside the river Wensum, Fakenham is one of only two
Norfolk racecourses. The amenities and facilities at this small and
attractive course were quickly upgraded following Victor Lucas's appointment as Clerk of the Course here in 1965, and it is now a good minor
racecourse. The horses are never far from the stands on the exceptionally
tight track. It is just over 1 mile round, square in shape and sharp in
character, suited to compact and handy types. Front-runners often do
well here.

## FIXTURES 1992

| | |
|---|---|
| FEBRUARY | MAY |
| 14  (Fri) NH | 25  (Mon Bank Holiday) NH |
| MARCH | OCTOBER |
| 13  (Fri) NH | 19  (Mon) NH |
| APRIL | DECEMBER |
| 20  (Mon Bank Holiday) NH | 18  (Fri) NH |

# *Folkestone*
## FLAT AND NATIONAL HUNT

ADDRESS Folkestone Racecourse, Westenhanger, Hythe, Kent
TELEPHONE 0303 66407 (racedays); 0444 441111 (Clerk of the Course)
LOCATION the racecourse is 6 miles west of the town at Westenhanger,
   with easy access from the M20 (junction 11)
NEAREST STATION Westenhanger

ENCLOSURES Club, Tattersalls and Paddock, Course
CLERK OF THE COURSE C. E. Griggs

SINCE the closure of Wye, Folkestone is the only racecourse in Kent. The course itself is just over 10 furlongs round, has sharp bends and undulates throughout. It is not a demanding track and is not suited to long-striding horses.

With its impressive new stand in the Tattersalls and Paddock enclosure, the facilities at Folkestone are more than adequate. The stands command a good view of the racing; the paddock, although small, is pretty: there is a large goldfish pond which may amuse children and console hapless punters.

## FIXTURES 1992

| JANUARY | MAY | SEPTEMBER |
|---|---|---|
| 14 (Tue) NH | 12 (Tue evening) NH | 10 (Thu) Flat |
| FEBRUARY | JUNE | 21 (Mon) Flat |
| 12 (Wed) NH | 2 (Tue) Flat | OCTOBER |
| 19 (Wed) NH | 30 (Tue) Flat | 6 (Tue) Flat |
| MARCH | JULY | 19 (Mon) Flat |
| 4 (Wed) NH | 14 (Tue) Flat | NOVEMBER |
| 23 (Mon) Flat | 21 (Tue) Flat | 9 (Mon) Flat |
| 30 (Mon) Flat | AUGUST | 23 (Mon) NH |
| APRIL | 14 (Fri) Flat | DECEMBER |
| 22 (Wed) Flat | 18 (Tue) Flat | 15 (Tue) NH |
| | | 31 (Thu) NH |

# *Fontwell Park*

## NATIONAL HUNT

ADDRESS Fontwell Park Racecourse, nr Arundel, West Sussex BN18 0SX

TELEPHONE 0243 543335 (racedays); 0444 441111 (Clerk of the Course)

LOCATION Fontwell is 6 miles west of Chichester and 6 miles north of Bognor Regis; the racecourse is south of the village at the junction of the A27 (Brighton-Chichester road) and A29

NEAREST STATION Barham (Brighton-Portsmouth line); 2 miles from course: free bus service on racedays

ENCLOSURES Club, Tattersalls, Silver Ring

CLERK OF THE COURSE C. E. Griggs

A compact figure-of eight, the chasing circuit at Fontwell Park provides one of the best viewing tracks in the land: the horses are never very far away from the spectators and, unlike at some figure-of-eight courses, they are always easy to identify. The hurdle course is a left-handed oval which runs outside the chase track. The ideal Fontwell horse is nippy and adaptable, and the same goes for racegoers here: to get the true flavour of chasing close up, position yourself near the crossroads of the figure-of-eight and experience the unparalleled sight of jump racing in the raw. Well appointed and well maintained buildings offer the racegoer fine facilities. Enjoy them: Fontwell is not a place to take racing too seriously.

## FIXTURES 1992

JANUARY
  13  (Mon) NH
FEBRUARY
   3  (Mon) NH
  17  (Mon) NH
MARCH
  17  (Tue) NH
APRIL
  14  (Tue) NH
MAY
   4  (Mon Bank Holiday) NH
  25  (Mon Bank Holiday) NH

AUGUST
  11  (Tue) NH
SEPTEMBER
   2  (Wed) NH
  28  (Mon) NH
OCTOBER
  12  (Mon) NH
  28  (Wed) NH
DECEMBER
   1  (Tue) NH
  30  (Wed) NH

# *Goodwood*

## FLAT

ADDRESS Goodwood Racecourse Ltd, Goodwood, Chichester, West
    Sussex BN18 0SX
TELEPHONE 0243 774107 or 774838 on racedays
LOCATION Goodwood is 4 miles north of Chichester between the A286
    (Midhurst road) and the A285 (Petworth road); access from the A27
NEAREST STATION Chichester (Brighton-Portsmouth line)
FAMILY FACILITIES supervised crèche (at July and August meetings),
    playground
ENCLOSURES Members (Richmond Enclosure), Gordon Enclosure,
    Public Enclosure
CLERK OF THE COURSE R. N. Fabricius

GOODWOOD is a spectacular racecourse set high up on the Sussex downlands above Chichester. The course itself is fairly sharp and undulates considerably, favouring the handy, good actioned horse. Races up to a mile tend to be fast (the 5 furlong sprint is one of the quickest in the country).

With its impressive new stand the facilities at Goodwood are excellent, well laid-out and efficiently run, although crowding at the July meeting does occur.

## FIXTURES 1992

MAY
- 19 (Tue) Flat (A. R. Dennis Predominate Stakes)
- 20 (Wed) Flat (Lupe Stakes)
- 21 (Thu) Flat (SIS Live Action Stakes (Pensioners Day))
- 29 (Fri evening) Flat (Chichester Arun Business Racenight)

JUNE
- 5 (Fri evening) Flat (Charity Racenight)
- 12 (Fri evening) Flat (BBC Radio/TV Racenight)
- 26 (Fri evening) Flat (Mid Summer Racenight)

JULY
- 28 (Tue) Flat (William Hill Stewards Cup)
- 29 (Wed) Flat (Scottish Equitable Richmond Stakes, Sussex Stakes)

- 30 (Thu) Flat (Dickins & Jones Goodwood Cup, Schweppes Golden Mile)
- 31 (Fri) Flat (Leslie & Godwin Spitfire Handicap)

AUGUST
- 1 (Sat) Flat (Vodafone Nassau Stakes)
- 28 (Fri) Flat (Prestige Stakes)
- 29 (Sat) Flat (Beefeater Gin Celebration Mile (Family Day))

SEPTEMBER
- 11 (Fri) Flat (Abtrust Select Stakes)
- 12 (Sat) Flat (Ladbroke Racing Sprint Trophy (Pubs & Clubs Day))

OCTOBER
- 2 (Fri) Flat (City of Portsmouth Supreme Stakes)
- 3 (Sat) Flat (Priory Park Stakes)

# *Hamilton Park*

## FLAT

ADDRESS Hamilton Park Racecourse Company Ltd, Bothwell Road, Hamilton, Lanarkshire ML3 0DZ

TELEPHONE 0698 283 806

LOCATION Hamilton is 12 miles south-east of Glasgow; the racecourse is just north of the town between junctions 5 and 6 of the M74

NEAREST STATION Hamilton West (from Glasgow)

FAMILY FACILITIES supervised playground

ENCLOSURES Club, Grandstand and Paddock

CLERK OF THE COURSE Major T. R. Riley

HAMILTON PARK consists of a straight 6 furlongs with a pear-shaped loop attached, and runners over the longer distances race away from the stands round the left-handed loop before straightening up for home with 5 furlongs to run. The course is extremely undulating, with a stiff uphill climb to the finish, and favours a horse who can see out the trip. The standard of racing at Hamilton tends to be fairly ordinary, though plenty of Newmarket trainers send their lesser charges on the long trip here.

---

## FIXTURES 1992

APRIL
  1  (Wed) Flat
  9  (Thu) Flat
MAY
  1  (Fri) Flat
 11  (Mon) Flat
 16  (Sat evening) Flat
 29  (Fri) Flat
JUNE
 10  (Wed evening) Flat
 11  (Thu) Flat
 29  (Mon evening) Flat

JULY
 16  (Thu evening) Flat
 17  (Fri evening) Flat
 22  (Wed evening) Flat
 23  (Thu evening) Flat
AUGUST
 17  (Mon) Flat
SEPTEMBER
  7  (Mon) Flat
 28  (Mon) Flat
NOVEMBER
  3  (Tue) Flat

# Haydock Park

## FLAT AND NATIONAL HUNT

ADDRESS Haydock Park Racecourse Company Ltd, Newton-le-Willows, Merseyside WA12 0HQ
TELEPHONE 0942 725963
LOCATION Haydock Park lies mid-way between Liverpool and Manchester alongside the A49, under a mile from junction 23 of the M6
NEAREST STATION Wigan or Warrington Bank Quay (from London Euston)
FAMILY FACILITIES children's playground
ENCLOSURES County Stand, Tattersalls, Newton Stand
CLERK OF THE COURSE Maj. P. W. F. Arkwright

HAYDOCK PARK is a left-handed oval about 15 furlongs round; it is a good galloping track which, except for the slight rise throughout the straight, is pretty well flat. The hurdles course (which is on the inside) tends to be sharper than the flat and steeplechase courses which provide a searching test of stamina. Good jumping is essential: the fences are stiff and have large drops to them. It is the only racecourse in Britain where the horses may be saddled in the stables, a useful ploy with a nervous filly.

The facilities at Haydock are extremely good, the stands offer a fine view of the racing, the course is spacious and pleasant and the crowd enthusiastic.

## FIXTURES 1992

JANUARY
  4  (Sat) NH (Newton Pattern Chase)
 18  (Sat) NH (Peter Marsh Chase)
FEBRUARY
 28  (Fri) NH
 29  (Sat) NH (Greenalls Gold Cup,
       Timeform Chase)
APRIL
 18  (Sat) Flat (Field Marshal Stakes)
MAY
  2  (Sat) Flat (Fairey Spring Trophy)
  4  (Mon Bank Holiday) Mixed
       (Swinton Insurance Trophy)
 22  (Fri) Flat
 23  (Sat) Flat (Tote Credit Silver Bowl
       Handicap)
JUNE
  5  (Fri evening) Flat
  6  (Sat) Flat (John of Gaunt Stakes)
JULY
  2  (Thu evening) Flat
  3  (Fri) Flat
  4  (Sat) Flat (Lancashire Oaks, Old
       Newton Cup)

AUGUST
  7  (Fri evening) Flat
  8  (Sat) Flat (Burtonwood Rose of
       Lancaster Stakes)
 14  (Fri evening) Flat
SEPTEMBER
  4  (Fri) Flat
  5  (Sat) Flat (Sprint Cup)
 25  (Fri) Flat
 26  (Sat) Flat
OCTOBER
  7  (Wed) Flat
  8  (Thu) Flat
NOVEMBER
 11  (Wed) NH
 18  (Wed) NH (Edward Hammer
       Memorial Trophy)
 19  (Thu) NH
DECEMBER
  9  (Wed) NH (Waterloo Southern
       Hurdle, Tommy Whittle Chase)
 10  (Thu) NH

# *Hereford*
## NATIONAL HUNT

ADDRESS Hereford Racecourse, Roman Road, Holmer, Hereford
   HR4 9QU
TELEPHONE 0432 273560
LOCATION the racecourse is 1 mile north-west of the city on the A49
   (Hereford-Leominster road)
NEAREST STATION Hereford (from Oxford, Birmingham, South Wales)
FAMILY FACILITIES children under 16 free of charge
ENCLOSURES Club, Tattersalls, Course
CLERK OF THE COURSE J. Williams

HEREFORD is almost square in shape and just under a mile and a half round; it is a good galloping track and, with its easy bends and fall into the home straight, not a stiff course.

There is a strong local following at Hereford races, which have been in existence for over 200 years. Viewing from the stands is good and, while the facilities are not extravagant, they are perfectly adequate. With a large area of grass between the stands and the running rail it is a good racecourse for children.

## FIXTURES 1992

FEBRUARY
  10  (Mon) NH
  29  (Sat) NH
APRIL
   4  (Sat) NH
  20  (Mon Bank Holiday) NH
MAY
   2  (Sat evening) NH
  13  (Wed) NH
  25  (Mon Bank Holiday) NH
AUGUST
  22  (Sat evening) NH

  29  (Sat evening) NH
SEPTEMBER
  25  (Fri) NH
OCTOBER
  23  (Fri) NH
NOVEMBER
   3  (Tue) NH
  25  (Wed) NH
DECEMBER
   4  (Fri) NH
  22  (Tue) NH

# *Hexham*

## NATIONAL HUNT

ADDRESS Hexham Racecourse, High Yarridge, Hexham, Northumberland NE46 2JP

TELEPHONE 0434 603738

LOCATION Hexham is about 20 miles west of Newcastle-upon-Tyne; the racecourse is 2 miles south-west of the town on the B6035, to which access is signed from the A69

NEAREST STATION Hexham (Newcastle-Carlisle line): free bus service to course

FAMILY FACILITIES children's play area

ENCLOSURES Club, Paddock

CLERK OF THE COURSE S. C. Enderby

ALTHOUGH Hexham's sobriquet, the 'Heart of all England', may be geographically dubious (it is only a few miles south of Hadrian's Wall) it is certainly one of the most impressive and attractive racecourses in the country. Set 800 feet above sea level in unspoiled Northumberland countryside, Hexham is a small yet beautiful racecourse well worth visiting. With its height and openness it is advisable to take very warm clothing!

At 12 furlongs round, the left-handed track, with its steep climb at the end of the back straight and up the home straight, is extremely testing. Horses not only need to possess plenty of stamina, but need to be well balanced in order to cope with the long downslope in the back straight which, particularly in soft conditions, is difficult to handle.

## FIXTURES 1992

MARCH
12  (Thu) NH
21  (Sat) NH
23  (Mon) NH
APRIL
25  (Sat) NH
27  (Mon evening) NH
MAY
 2  (Sat evening) NH
23  (Sat) NH
25  (Mon Bank Holiday evening) NH

AUGUST
24  (Mon) NH
OCTOBER
 2  (Fri) NH
15  (Thu) NH
NOVEMBER
 6  (Fri) NH
25  (Wed) NH
DECEMBER
11  (Fri) NH

# Huntingdon
## NATIONAL HUNT

ADDRESS The Racecourse, Brampton, Huntingdon, Cambridgeshire
    PE18 8NN
TELEPHONE 0480 453373 or 454610
LOCATION Huntingdon is 19 miles north-west of Cambridge and 19 miles
    south of Peterborough; the racecourse is 1 mile east of the A1/A604
    intersection, ensuring easy access, and 2 miles west of the town
NEAREST STATION Huntingdon (from London King's Cross)
ENCLOSURES Members, Tattersalls, Centre Enclosure
CLERK OF THE COURSE H. P. C. Bevan

HUNTINGDON, set in flat fenland, provides a fast right-handed galloping track 11 furlongs round. Oval in shape and with easy bends, the course is suited to horses with plenty of speed.

The facilities have been progressively upgraded and the race meetings regularly attract a large and enthusiastic crowd: the open ditch in front of the stands adds to the spectacle.

## FIXTURES 1992

JANUARY
23 (Thu) NH
FEBRUARY
6 (Thu) NH (Sidney Banks Memorial
Chase)
18 (Tue) NH
APRIL
13 (Mon) NH
20 (Mon Bank Holiday) NH
MAY
14 (Thu evening) NH
25 (Mon Bank Holiday) NH
AUGUST
31 (Mon Bank Holiday) NH

SEPTEMBER
18 (Fri) NH
OCTOBER
24 (Sat) NH
NOVEMBER
13 (Fri) NH (Macer Gifford Memorial
Chase)
24 (Tue) NH (Peterborough Chase)
DECEMBER
2 (Wed) NH
26 (Sat) NH

# *Kelso*

## NATIONAL HUNT

ADDRESS Kelso Racecourse, Kelso, Roxburghshire
TELEPHONE 0573 24767 (racecourse) 0668 81611 (enquiries not
raceday)
LOCATION Kelso is 25 miles south-west of Berwick-upon-Tweed; the
racecourse is 1 mile north of the town on the B6461 (Berwick road)
NEAREST STATION Berwick (bus service Berwick-Kelso)
FAMILY FACILITIES television room for small children
ENCLOSURES Club, Tattersalls
CLERK OF THE COURSE J. E. Fenwicke-Clennell

KELSO, set in the heart of the glorious Border Country, is a
wonderful racecourse, with a very strong local feel but plenty of
good horses taking part: the Morebattle Hurdle in February often attracts
Champion Hurdle hopefuls. The tone of the place – small but friendly –
is set by the old grandstand, built in 1822 and still going strong, though
now surrounded by buildings of considerably less architectural distinction. The warmth of the fires on a cold winter's day is matched by the
warmth of the local welcome, and win or lose, Kelso is the place to come
racing. The left-handed chase course goes further from the stands than
the hurdle, and features a demanding run-in of a quarter of a mile. The
hurdle course is tight – a little over a mile round – and needs a nifty sort
of horse.

## FIXTURES 1992

JANUARY
8  (Wed) NH (Tote Novice Chase)
31  (Fri) NH (Bollinger Rutherford
     Chase)
FEBRUARY
21  (Fri) NH (ICP Morebattle Hurdle)
MARCH
18  (Wed) NH (KOSB Challenge Cup)
APRIL
6  (Mon) NH (Horse and Hound
     Buccleuch Hunter Chase)
29  (Wed) NH (Teachers Haddington
     Jubilee Cup)
OCTOBER
3  (Sat) NH (The Christian Salvesen
     Quaich)

17  (Sat) NH (Greenmantle Ale
     Anthony Marshall Chase)
NOVEMBER
4  (Wed) NH (Middlemas Juvenile
     Trophy)
12  (Thu) NH (Edinburgh Woollen Mill
     Reg Tweedie Chase)
30  (Mon) NH (Mason Organisation
     Champion Chase)
DECEMBER
17  (Thu) NH (Glassedin Novice
     Chase)

# Kempton Park

## FLAT AND NATIONAL HUNT

ADDRESS Kempton Park Racecourse, Sunbury-on-Thames, Middlesex
    TW16 5AQ
TELEPHONE 0932 782292
LOCATION the racecourse is 1 mile north-east of Sunbury-on-Thames,
    and is only half a mile from junction 1 of the M3, making access, via
    the A308, very easy
NEAREST STATION Kempton Park (from London Waterloo)
FAMILY FACILITIES supervised crèche
ENCLOSURES Members, Grandstand and Paddock, Silver Ring
CLERK OF THE COURSE Major R. M. O. Webster
RACECOURSE MANAGER A. J. Cooper

NO longer is Kempton Park the poor relation of Sandown and Epsom
in the United Racecourses family. It may not have a Group One race
on the Flat (nor, for that matter, a Group Two), but the quality of the
jump racing here is excellent, and over the last few years the facilities for
racegoers have been significantly improved. The parade ring and unsaddling enclosure area is particularly successful, with plenty of viewing from
terraces above the paddock, and really came into its own when Desert
Orchid returned to be greeted by his adoring public after yet another
Kempton virtuoso performance. Kempton is a user-friendly course:

unlike its sibling Epsom, you don't have much of a trek between paddock and stand, and all the facilities are readily to hand.

The track is basically a right-handed triangle, with a straight 6 furlongs cutting across the middle and a spur for 10-furlong races. It is quite flat. For jumpers the course puts the emphasis on speed and fast, accurate jumping rather than the grinding stamina required at Cheltenham, and the two big races at the Christmas meeting – the King George VI Chase and the Christmas Hurdle – offer fascinating comparisons with their National Hunt Festival counterparts.

## FIXTURES 1992

JANUARY
17  (Fri) NH
18  (Sat) NH (Bic Razor Lanzarote Hurdle)
FEBRUARY
21  (Fri) NH
22  (Sat) NH (Racing Post Chase)
APRIL
3  (Fri) Flat
18  (Sat) Flat (BonusPrint Easter Stakes)
20  (Mon Bank Holiday) Flat (Rosebery Handicap)
MAY
4  (Mon Bank Holiday) Flat (Jubilee Handicap)
13  (Wed evening) Flat
23  (Sat) Flat
JUNE
10  (Wed evening) Flat

24  (Wed evening) Flat
JULY
8  (Wed evening) Flat
AUGUST
5  (Wed evening) Flat
19  (Wed evening) Flat
SEPTEMBER
4  (Fri) Flat
5  (Sat) Flat (BonusPrint September Stakes)
22  (Tue) Flat
OCTOBER
17  (Sat) NH (Charisma Gold Cup)
29  (Thu) NH
NOVEMBER
18  (Wed) NH
DECEMBER
26  (Sat) NH (King George VI Chase)
28  (Mon Bank Holiday) NH (Christmas Hurdle)

# *Leicester*

## FLAT AND NATIONAL HUNT

ADDRESS Leicester Racecourse, Leicester LE2 4AL
TELEPHONE 0533 716515
LOCATION the racecourse is 2½ miles south-east of the city off the A6 (Market Harborough road), subject to easy access from the M69 and M1 (junction 21) intersection
NEAREST STATION Leicester (from London St Pancras)
FAMILY FACILITIES Silver Ring picnic car park overlooks track
ENCLOSURES Members, Tattersalls, Silver Ring
CLERK OF THE COURSE Capt. N. E. S. Lees

A T just under 14 furlongs round, Leicester is a good right-handed galloping, oval-shaped track that provides a strong test of stamina. There is also a straight mile which runs sharply downhill almost to halfway, from where it climbs steadily to the winning post. The course undulates throughout before joining the straight 4½ furlongs from home. The going can get very heavy in winter as it stands on clay and limestone, but generally the groundstaff do an excellent job of providing good ground in the driest of summers.

## FIXTURES 1992

JANUARY
1   (Wed Bank Holiday) NH
7   (Tue) NH
20  (Mon) NH
28  (Tue) NH
FEBRUARY
13  (Thu) NH
24  (Mon) NH
MARCH
2   (Mon) NH
24  (Tue) Flat
31  (Tue) Flat
APRIL
25  (Sat) Flat (Leicestershire Stakes)
MAY
25  (Mon Bank Holiday) Flat
26  (Tue) Flat
JUNE
1   (Mon) Flat
6   (Sat evening) Flat

JULY
6   (Mon) Flat
14  (Tue evening) Flat
28  (Tue evening) Flat
AUGUST
10  (Mon evening) Flat
SEPTEMBER
8   (Tue) Flat
14  (Mon) Flat
OCTOBER
12  (Mon) Flat
13  (Tue) Flat
26  (Mon) Flat
27  (Tue) Flat
NOVEMBER
16  (Mon) NH
20  (Fri) NH
DECEMBER
31  (Thu) NH (Leicestershire Silver Fox Handicap Chase)

# Lingfield Park
## FLAT, NATIONAL HUNT AND ALL-WEATHER

ADDRESS Lingfield Park Racecourse, Lingfield, Surrey RH7 6PQ

TELEPHONE 0342 834800

LOCATION Lingfield is 3 miles north of East Grinstead and 10 miles north-east of Crawley; the racecourse is 1 mile south-east of the town on the B2028, with easy access from the M23 (junction 10) and the M25 (junction 6)

NEAREST STATION Lingfield (from London Victoria and London Bridge)

FAMILY FACILITIES crèche facilities and playground in summer

ENCLOSURES Members, Grandstand

CLERK OF THE COURSE G. R. Stickels

LINGFIELD racecourse was completely restructured two years ago when the new 10-furlong all-weather track was installed. The old turf course remains pretty much as it was and is regarded as being a useful preparation for Epsom. Horses run up to the top of the hill, about 6 furlongs from home, and then face a sharp, left-handed descent into the straight course under 4 furlongs from home. The fast straight course caters for races up to 7 furlongs and 140 yards. Situated on clay, the ground tends to get very firm in summer and heavy in winter.

The decidedly sharp all-weather track, which is constituted of Equi-track, stages meetings throughout the year and is used for both National Hunt and Flat races.

During the summer Lingfield Park lives up to its name with an attractive paddock set amongst trees and with green lawns and flower-beds everywhere. There is a wide variety of excellent bars and restaurants and plenty of atmosphere. Unfortunately, the all-weather meetings through the winter have failed to catch the imagination of racegoers and can be rather dismal affairs.

## FIXTURES 1992

JANUARY
2  (Thu) NH AW
4  (Sat) Flat AW
6  (Mon) NH
7  (Tue) NH AW
9  (Thu) NH AW
11 (Sat) Flat AW
14 (Tue) NH AW
16 (Thu) NH AW
18 (Sat) Flat AW
20 (Mon) NH
21 (Tue) Flat AW
23 (Thu) NH AW
25 (Sat) Flat AW
28 (Tue) NH AW
30 (Thu) NH AW
31 (Fri) NH
FEBRUARY
1  (Sat) Flat AW
4  (Tue) Flat AW
6  (Thu) NH AW
8  (Sat) Flat AW
11 (Tue) NH AW
13 (Thu) NH AW
15 (Sat) Flat AW
18 (Tue) Flat AW
20 (Thu) NH AW
22 (Sat) Flat AW

25 (Tue) NH AW
27 (Thu) NH AW
29 (Sat) Flat AW
MARCH
3  (Tue) Flat AW
5  (Thu) NH AW
7  (Sat) Flat AW
10 (Tue) Flat AW
13 (Fri) NH (Farmers Club Day)
14 (Sat) NH
21 (Sat) Flat AW
APRIL
4  (Sat) Flat AW and Turf
MAY
8  (Fri) Flat
9  (Sat) Flat (Derby Trial, Oaks Trial)
16 (Sat evening) Flat
23 (Sat evening) Flat
30 (Sat) Flat (*Daily Mail* Leisure Stakes)
JUNE
13 (Sat evening) Flat
20 (Sat evening) Flat
26 (Fri) Flat
27 (Sat evening) Flat
JULY
10 (Fri) Flat
11 (Sat) Flat (Silver Trophy)

18  (Sat evening) Flat
27  (Mon) Flat
AUGUST
8  (Sat evening) Flat
15  (Sat evening) Flat
27  (Thu) Flat
SEPTEMBER
8  (Tue) Flat
17  (Thu) Flat
OCTOBER
1  (Thu) Flat
26  (Mon) Flat (Burr Stakes)

NOVEMBER
5  (Thu) Flat AW
14  (Sat) Flat AW
28  (Sat) Flat AW
DECEMBER
3  (Thu) Flat AW
12  (Sat) NH
16  (Wed) Flat AW
19  (Sat) Flat AW
21  (Mon) NH
22  (Tue) Flat AW
31  (Thu) Flat AW

# Liverpool

## NATIONAL HUNT

ADDRESS Aintree Racecourse, Aintree, Liverpool, Lancashire L9 5AS
TELEPHONE 051 523 2600
LOCATION Aintree is in the north of the city, 1 mile south of the M57
    and M58 intersection
NEAREST STATION Aintree (local Liverpool service; Liverpool from
    London Euston)
FAMILY FACILITIES special prices for children on 2 and 3 April
ENCLOSURES County Enclosure, Paddock; several course enclosures
CLERK OF THE COURSE J. Parrett

HOME of the Grand National, Liverpool has two left-handed
courses: the Mildmay Course, a normal Park course, and the
National course. The former is a fair, flat, oval track, 12 furlongs round
and fairly fast in nature. The latter is unique. It is a triangular circuit 2
miles 2 furlongs round and, with its renowned 16 fir fences, provides the
toughest test of jumping in the country.

The three-day Grand National meeting is one of the most atmospheric
and popular fixtures of the season. The horses running are top-class and
the racing, particularly over the National course, very exciting. It is
difficult, though, to see much of the National itself unless one pays heftily
for entrance to the best stands, and consequently large crowds gather
around the famous fences such as Becher's Brook and the Canal Turn.

## FIXTURES 1992

APRIL

2  (Thu) NH (John Hughes Chase, Martell Cup)

3  (Fri) NH (Glenlivet Melling Chase)

4  (Sat) NH (Martell Grand National)

NOVEMBER

21  (Sat) NH

# Ludlow

## NATIONAL HUNT

ADDRESS Ludlow Race Club Ltd, The Racecourse, Bromfield, Ludlow, Shropshire

TELEPHONE 058 477 221 Racedays only; 0981 250 436 (Secretary/ Clerk of Course)

LOCATION Ludlow is about 30 miles south of Shrewsbury; the race-course is 2 miles north-west of the town, off the A49 (Shrewsbury road)

NEAREST STATION Ludlow (Hereford-Shrewsbury line)

ENCLOSURES Members, Tattersalls, Course

CLERK OF THE COURSE B. R. Davies

WITH the finest meat pie to be had anywhere in the kingdom, a 1904 grandstand which still gives off a whiff of Edwardian elegance, an enthusiastic and knowledgeable local crowd and usually competitive (if not very high-class) racing, Ludlow is the quintessence of the small jumping tracks – the 'gaffs' – which add so much to the unique variety of British racing. The right-handed track is set in superb Shropshire countryside and runs through a golf course (which mercifully is not used on racedays). The hurdle course goes further away from the stands than the chase course, and the difference between the two back straights has caused all sorts of shenanigans through riders going the wrong way – most recently early in the 1991/92 season. The circuit, which is about 1½ miles round, is mostly flat.

## FIXTURES 1992

JANUARY

15  (Wed) NH

FEBRUARY

5  (Wed) NH

27  (Thu) NH (Forbra Gold Cup)

MARCH

20  (Fri) NH (Banks' Brewery Day)

APRIL

8  (Wed) NH

22  (Wed evening) NH

MAY

4  (Mon Bank Holiday) NH

OCTOBER

8  (Thu) NH

16  (Fri) NH

NOVEMBER

19  (Thu) NH (Prince and Princess of Wales Handicap Chase)

DECEMBER

2  (Wed) NH

14  (Mon) NH

# Market Rasen
## NATIONAL HUNT

ADDRESS Market Rasen Racecourse, Legsby Road, Market Rasen,
Lincolnshire LN8 3EA
TELEPHONE 0673 843434
LOCATION Market Rasen is 16 miles north-east of Lincoln on the A46;
the racecourse is 1 mile east of the town on the A631
NEAREST STATION Market Rasen
FAMILY FACILITIES unsupervised playground
ENCLOSURES Members, Tattersalls, Silver Ring
CLERK OF THE COURSE C. L. Moore

W ITH its minor undulations and tightish bends, Market Rasen's
right-handed track is quite sharp, 10 furlongs round and oval in
shape; it favours the handy and nippy type of horse.

Since the closure of Lincoln, Market Rasen is the one remaining
course in Lincolnshire. Set in the sparsely populated, flat terrain of this
county, it has survived and progressed extremely well. The facilities are
very good, the stands quite modern, large and give an excellent view of the
racing, and the catering is first-class. It is a warm and friendly racecourse
that is a credit to its management.

## FIXTURES 1992

JANUARY
4   (Sat) NH
11  (Sat) NH
FEBRUARY
29  (Sat) NH
MARCH
6   (Fri) NH
APRIL
20  (Mon Bank Holiday) NH
25  (Sat) NH
MAY
9   (Sat evening) NH
30  (Sat evening) NH

AUGUST
1   (Sat evening) NH
15  (Sat evening) NH
SEPTEMBER
19  (Sat) NH
26  (Sat) NH
OCTOBER
9   (Fri) NH
NOVEMBER
6   (Fri) NH
21  (Sat) NH
DECEMBER
26  (Sat) NH

# Newbury
## FLAT AND NATIONAL HUNT

ADDRESS The Racecourse, Newbury, Berks RG14 7NZ
TELEPHONE 0635 40015
LOCATION the racecourse is a quarter of a mile east of the town, only 3
   miles from the M4 (junction 13) via the A34
NEAREST STATION Newbury Racecourse (London Paddington)
FAMILY FACILITIES supervised playground, crèche
ENCLOSURES Members, Tattersalls, Silver Ring
CLERK OF THE COURSE Capt. C. B. Toller

NEWBURY is considered by many to be one of the finest courses in
the country. It is just under 15 furlongs in length, flat, wide and,
with two long straights and easy bends, provides a very fair test for horses
at all distances in both Flat and National Hunt races. Long striding,
galloping horses are comfortable here.

With the completion of the new Members' stand the facilities should
be first-class. All the stands command a good view of the racing, and the
paddock is spacious and flanked by concrete standing areas. Newbury
attracts top-class horses, particularly at the Spring Meeting (Flat) and the
Hennessy Meeting (NH). It is also a popular course on which to educate
two-year-olds.

## FIXTURES 1992

FEBRUARY
   7  (Fri) NH
   8  (Sat) NH (Tote Gold Trophy)
  28  (Fri) NH (Berkshire Hurdle)
  29  (Sat) NH
MARCH
  20  (Fri) NH
  21  (Sat) NH
APRIL
  10  (Fri) Flat (Gainsborough Stud Fred
       Darling Stakes)
  11  (Sat) Flat (Singer and Friedlander
       Greenham Stakes)
MAY
  15  (Fri) Flat (Juddmonte Lockinge
       Stakes)
  16  (Sat) Flat
JUNE
   2  (Tue evening) Flat
  11  (Thu) Flat

  23  (Tue evening) Flat
JULY
  17  (Fri) Flat
  18  (Sat) Flat
AUGUST
  14  (Fri) Flat (Forte Hungerford Stakes)
  15  (Sat) Flat (Ibn Bey Geoffrey Freer
       Stakes)
SEPTEMBER
  18  (Fri) Flat
  19  (Sat) Flat (Courage Stakes)
OCTOBER
  22  (Thu) Flat (Vodafone Horris Hill
       Stakes)
  23  (Fri) NH
  24  (Sat) Flat (St Simon Stakes)
NOVEMBER
   4  (Wed) NH
  27  (Fri) NH
  28  (Sat) NH (Hennessy Gold Cup)

# Newcastle
FLAT AND NATIONAL HUNT

ADDRESS High Gosforth Park, Newcastle upon Tyne NE3 5HP
TELEPHONE 091 236 2020
LOCATION the racecourse is 5 miles north of the city on the B1322
between the A189 and the A6125; access can be gained from the A1
and A19
NEAREST STATION Newcastle Central
ENCLOSURES Club, Tattersalls, Silver Ring (Easter Monday, Plate
Meeting and August Monday only)
CLERK OF THE COURSE D. G. Parmley

HOME of the Northumberland Plate, Newcastle is a course with a great tradition, but in recent years has been experiencing difficulty in attracting the level of local support it needs. This is a great pity, as the Gosforth Park track is one of the fairest courses in the country, a gentle triangle with no sharp turns or severe contours. The left-handed $1\frac{3}{4}$ mile circuit is ideal for the big, long-striding animal, and really comes into its own with its major National Hunt races such as the Eider Chase, often the supplier of useful clues to the Grand National, and the Fighting Fifth Hurdle.

## FIXTURES 1992

JANUARY
11 (Sat) NH
FEBRUARY
15 (Sat) NH (Tote Eider Handicap
Chase)
MARCH
14 (Sat) NH
16 (Mon) NH
30 (Mon) Flat
APRIL
18 (Sat) Flat
20 (Mon Bank Holiday) Flat
MAY
4 (Mon Bank Holiday) NH
9 (Sat evening) NH
29 (Fri) Flat
JUNE
26 (Fri evening) Flat
27 (Sat) Flat (Newcastle 'Brown Ale'
Northumberland Plate)

JULY
25 (Sat) Flat
27 (Mon) Flat (Federation Brewery
Beeswing Stakes)
AUGUST
29 (Sat) Flat
31 (Mon Bank Holiday) Flat
SEPTEMBER
29 (Tue) Flat
OCTOBER
21 (Wed) NH
NOVEMBER
2 (Mon) Flat
7 (Sat) NH
28 (Sat) NH (Bellway 'Fighting Fifth'
Hurdle)
DECEMBER
1 (Tue) NH
19 (Sat) NH (Northumberland Gold
Cup)

# Newmarket
## FLAT

ADDRESS Westfield House, The Links, Newmarket, Suffolk CB8 0TG
TELEPHONE Rowley Mile Course 0638 662762; July Course 0638
    662752; office on non racedays 0638 663482
LOCATION Newmarket is 12 miles east of Cambridge; the July Course
    and the Rowley Mile Course are adjacent to one another on the
    A1304, and both have easy access from the M11 (junction 9)
NEAREST STATION Cambridge (from London Liverpool Street; there is
    an infrequent local service to Newmarket, but Cambus operate a
    special bus service from Cambridge Station direct to the racecourse,
    with a return trip departing half an hour after the last race)
FAMILY FACILITIES supervised playgrounds (July Course and Rowley
    Mile Course)
ENCLOSURES Members, Tattersalls, Silver Ring (Rowley Mile);
    Members, Tattersalls, Family Enclosure (July Course)
CLERK OF THE COURSE Capt. N. E. S. Lees

THERE are two racecourses in Newmarket, and they are completely
separate, apart from sharing a portion of track in the early stages of
long-distance races. The Rowley Mile, used in the spring and autumn
and the home of the One Thousand and Two Thousand Guineas, the
Cheveley Park, the Middle Park, the Dewhurst and the Champion
Stakes, as well as big handicaps in the Cambridgeshire and Cesarewitch,
is quite straight for races up to 10 furlongs. Longer races turn right-
handed into the straight 11 furlongs from home. The runners race
downhill into the Dip about a furlong out, then uphill to the line. The July
Course, the highlight of whose year is the July Meeting featuring the July
Cup, is similar in shape but has a straight of about a mile. The fierce
uphill finish makes for wonderfully exciting racing.

Newmarket racegoers can freeze at the early and late meetings and be
dry-roasted at the July Meeting, but they are well catered for at both
courses, especially now that the new parade ring and weighing room
complex at the Rowley Mile and the Dante Bar on the July Course have
been completed. A particularly popular feature of midsummer evening
meetings at the July course has been the entertainment put on after
racing.

## FIXTURES 1992

*Rowley Mile Course*
APRIL
14 (Tue) Flat (Shadwell Stud Nell Gwyn Stakes)
15 (Wed) Flat (Earl of Sefton EBF Stakes, European Free Handicap)
16 (Thu) Flat (Craven Stakes)
30 (Thu) Flat (General Accident One Thousand Guineas)
MAY
1 (Fri) Flat (General Accident Jockey Club Stakes)
2 (Sat) Flat (General Accident Two Thousand Guineas)
15 (Fri) Flat (King Charles II Stakes)
16 (Sat) Flat (Coral Handicap)

*July Course*
JUNE
19 (Fri evening) Flat
26 (Fri) Flat
27 (Sat) Flat (Van Geest Criterion Stakes)
JULY
7 (Tue) Flat (Princess of Wales's Stakes, Hillsdown Cherry Hinton Stakes)
8 (Wed) Flat (Anglia Television July Stakes, Falmouth Stakes)
9 (Thu) Flat (July Cup, Ladbroke Bunbury Cup)

17 (Fri evening) Flat
18 (Sat) Flat
31 (Fri evening) Flat
AUGUST
1 (Sat) Flat (Colmans of Norwich Nursery Handicap)
7 (Fri evening) Flat
8 (Sat) Flat (Brierley Group New Zealand Handicap)
28 (Fri) Flat (Hopeful Stakes)
29 (Sat) Flat (Philip Cornes Nursery Handicap)

*Rowley Mile Course*
SEPTEMBER
30 (Wed) Flat (Tattersalls Cheveley Park Stakes)
OCTOBER
1 (Thu) Flat (Newgate Stud Middle Park Stakes)
2 (Fri) Flat (Somerville Tattersall Stakes)
3 (Sat) Flat (William Hill Cambridgeshire, Cheveley Park Stud Sun Chariot Stakes)
15 (Thu) Flat (Challenge Stakes)
16 (Fri) Flat (Dewhurst Stakes)
17 (Sat) Flat (Tote Cesarewitch, Dubai Champion Stakes)
30 (Fri) Flat (James Seymour Stakes)
31 (Sat) Flat (Ladbroke Autumn Handicap, Zetland Stakes)

# *Newton Abbot*

## NATIONAL HUNT

ADDRESS Newton Abbot Races Ltd, Kinsteignton Road, Newton Abbot, Devon

TELEPHONE 0626 53235

LOCATION Newton Abbot is 16 miles south of Exeter and 6 miles north-west of Torbay; the racecourse is north of the town on the A380 (Exeter road) which is 13 miles from junction 31 of the M5

NEAREST STATION Newton Abbot (from London Paddington)

ENCLOSURES Tattersalls, Course

CLERK OF THE COURSE I. S. G. Lang

GENERAL MANAGER P. G Masterson

NEWTON ABBOT racecourse, situated on the outskirts of the town alongside the River Teign, traditionally stages most of its meetings at the beginning and end of the National Hunt season. The course has a problem with poor drainage so that the ground here tends to be either very firm or bottomless. The left-handed track is not one of the jockey's favourites: it has very sharp bends and is just over a mile round. Newton Abbot is an easy course that does not place a premium on stamina and it is suited to handy, well-made types who are able to cope with the tightness of the track.

The facilities are adequate and, as is the case with all the West Country racecourses, the catering is very good. A large and enthusiastic crowd is usually in evidence.

## FIXTURES 1992

JANUARY
3 (Fri) NH
23 (Thu) NH
FEBRUARY
11 (Tue) NH
MARCH
11 (Wed) NH
APRIL
18 (Sat) NH
20 (Mon Bank Holiday) NH
MAY
1 (Fri) NH
12 (Tue) NH
13 (Wed evening) NH
AUGUST
1 (Sat) NH

3 (Mon) NH
13 (Thu) NH
31 (Mon Bank Holiday) NH
SEPTEMBER
1 (Tue) NH
2 (Wed) NH
10 (Thu) NH
OCTOBER
6 (Tue) NH
27 (Tue) NH
NOVEMBER
17 (Tue) NH
DECEMBER
14 (Mon) NH
26 (Sat) NH

# *Nottingham*
## FLAT AND NATIONAL HUNT

ADDRESS Nottingham Racecourse, Colwick Park, Nottingham NG2 4BE
TELEPHONE 0602 580620
LOCATION the racecourse is 2 miles east of the city off the B686
  (Colwick road), with easy access from the M1 (junctions 24 and 25)
NEAREST STATION Nottingham (from London St Pancras)
FAMILY FACILITIES unsupervised playground
ENCLOSURES Centenary Stand Members, Grandstand, Silver Ring

CLERK OF THE COURSE Major C. L. Moore
MANAGER T. Hiscocks

NOTTINGHAM is popular with trainers; many top-class horses have made their debuts here, such as Henry Cecil's Oh So Sharp. Lester Piggott made his first farewell appearance at Colwick Park, and Stan Mellor rode his thousandth winner here.

The course is 12 furlongs round and oval in shape with a 6 furlong straight for flat sprints. It is a good galloping track and a very fair test of a horse. The adjacent river Trent ensures that good going can be provided in the summer, and the ground dries well in the winter.

## FIXTURES 1992

JANUARY
  2  (Thu) NH
 21  (Tue) NH
 29  (Wed) NH
FEBRUARY
 15  (Sat) NH (City Trial Hurdle, Nottinghamshire Novices Chase)
 25  (Tue) NH
MARCH
 17  (Tue) NH
APRIL
 13  (Mon) Flat
 20  (Mon Bank Holiday) Flat
 28  (Tue) Flat
MAY
 29  (Fri) Flat
JUNE
  8  (Mon) Flat
 13  (Sat evening) Flat (Family Night)
 22  (Mon) Flat (Veterans' Raceday)
JULY
  4  (Sat evening) Flat (Ladies' Night)

 20  (Mon evening) Flat
AUGUST
  3  (Mon evening) Flat (Miners' Welfare Night)
  4  (Tue evening) Flat (European Night)
 24  (Mon) Flat
SEPTEMBER
 21  (Mon) Flat
 22  (Tue) Flat
OCTOBER
 19  (Mon) Flat
 29  (Thu) Flat
NOVEMBER
 14  (Sat) NH (Christmas Fair)
 26  (Thu) NH
DECEMBER
  4  (Fri) NH
 19  (Sat) NH (Christmas Lights Meeting)

# *Perth*

## NATIONAL HUNT

ADDRESS Perth Racecourse, Scone Palace Park, Perth PH2 6BB
TELEPHONE 0683 20131 or 0738 51597 (racedays)
LOCATION the racecourse is 4 miles north of the town off the A93 (Blairgowrie road), with easy access from the M90 (junction 10) and M89 (junction 1)

NEAREST STATION Perth (from Dundee)
ENCLOSURES Club, Paddock, Course
CLERK OF THE COURSE S. Morshead

PERTH, the most northerly of Britain's racecourses, is set in the beautiful Scone Park alongside the River Tay. It is an attractive course, with fine facilities and a friendly atmosphere. Although the horses are at times obscured by trees, views from the old stands are pretty good. It is often quite dry in this part of Scotland which can cause the ground to dry up and harden.

The right-handed circuit is 10 furlongs round and oval in shape. Two of the bends are quite easy but the other two are pretty tight, making this flat and easy course fairly sharp in nature.

---

FIXTURES 1992

| APRIL | | AUGUST | |
|---|---|---|---|
| 22 | (Wed) NH | 20 | (Wed evening) NH |
| 23 | (Thu) NH | 21 | (Fri) NH |
| 24 | (Fri) NH | 22 | (Sat) NH |
| MAY | | SEPTEMBER | |
| 13 | (Wed evening) NH | 23 | (Wed) NH |
| 14 | (Thu) NH | 24 | (Thu) NH |

# *Plumpton*
## NATIONAL HUNT

---

ADDRESS Plumpton Racecourse Ltd, Plumpton, Sussex
TELEPHONE 0273 890383
LOCATION Plumpton is about 10 miles north-east of Brighton; the racecourse is 2 miles north of the B2116 (Lewes-Keymer road)
NEAREST STATION Plumpton, adjoining course (from London Victoria)
ENCLOSURES Club, Tattersalls and Paddock, Course
CLERK OF THE COURSE C. E. Griggs

PLUMPTON may not have quite the charm of some of the other 'gaff' tracks, but the racing is usually competitive, and the nature of the course favours the 'horses for courses' theory. A 9-furlong circuit with tight bends and a frighteningly steep downhill back straight, Plumpton has a stiff uphill climb from the home turn and favours the quick-jumping, nifty horse.

## FIXTURES 1992

JANUARY
  8  (Wed) NH
27  (Mon) NH
FEBRUARY
10  (Mon) NH
26  (Wed) NH
MARCH
  9  (Mon) NH
27  (Fri) NH
APRIL
18  (Sat) NH
20  (Mon Bank Holiday) NH

AUGUST
  7  (Fri) NH
31  (Mon Bank Holiday) NH
SEPTEMBER
14  (Mon) NH
OCTOBER
20  (Tue) NH
NOVEMBER
  2  (Mon) NH
25  (Wed) NH
DECEMBER
  8  (Tue) NH
29  (Tue) NH

# *Pontefract*

## FLAT

ADDRESS Pontefract Park Race Club Ltd, The Park, Pontefract, West
    Yorkshire
TELEPHONE 0977 702210 (racedays only) or 703224
LOCATION Pontefract is about 15 miles south-east of Leeds; the
    racecourse is 1 mile north-west of the town with easy access from the
    M62 (junction 32)
NEAREST STATION Pontefract (Baghill) (Sheffield-York line)
FAMILY FACILITIES unsupervised playground
ENCLOSURES Club, Paddock, Silver Ring, Third Ring
CLERK OF THE COURSE J. N. Gundhill

SURROUNDED by collieries, Ferrybridge power station, the railway
and the M62, Pontefract can hardly be described as an attractive
course. It is however, a popular track with both trainers and the public. It
was, along with Stockton, one of only two northern racecourses allowed to
race during World War II. The facilities have been improved over the
years and are now good.

    The track itself is left-handed, 2 miles round, oval in shape and
undulates considerably throughout, which prevents it from being described as a galloping track – although stamina, particularly in sprints, is
very important. The emphasis on stamina is largely due to the punishing
finish, with the last three furlongs on the rise; there is a sharp home bend
and short 2-furlong run-in.

## FIXTURES 1992

APRIL
  7  (Tue) Flat
 15  (Wed) Flat
 27  (Mon) Flat
MAY
  4  (Mon Bank Holiday) Flat (FROM
     DONCASTER)
 22  (Fri evening) Flat
JUNE
  8  (Mon) Flat
  9  (Tue) Flat
 29  (Mon) Flat

JULY
  7  (Tue) Flat
 24  (Fri evening) Flat
AUGUST
  5  (Wed) Flat
  6  (Thu) Flat
 25  (Tue) Flat
SEPTEMBER
 21  (Mon) Flat
OCTOBER
  5  (Mon) Flat
 22  (Thu) Flat

# Redcar

## FLAT

ADDRESS Redcar Racecourse, Redcar, Cleveland TS10 2BY
TELEPHONE 0642 484068
LOCATION Redcar is 9 miles north-east of Middlesbrough; the
  racecourse is in the town off the A1085 (Middlesbrough road)
NEAREST STATION Redcar, half a mile from course (Darlington-
  Saltburn line)
FAMILY FACILITIES supervised playground
ENCLOSURES Club, Grandstand and Paddock, Course
CLERK OF THE COURSE J. G. Cleverly

IN spite of its proximity to the sea (originally the races were run on the
beach), the approach to Redcar racecourse today must be the most
unattractive in the country. Yet the course itself is a green oasis in the
midst of industrial surroundings and provides excellent racing throughout
the summer.

The left-handed course is 14 furlongs round and flat. It provides a true
test and is well suited to long-striding horses with scope. The straight
mile joins the round course 5 furlongs from home and can accommodate
fields of up to thirty. When the going is soft there is usually a strip of
better ground up the middle.

The facilities are good, the flower beds attractive and the new stable
block excellent.

## FIXTURES 1992

APRIL
30  (Thu) Flat
MAY
25  (Mon Bank Holiday) Flat (Zetland
    Gold Cup)
26  (Tue) Flat
JUNE
 1  (Mon) Flat
19  (Fri) Flat
20  (Sat) Flat
JULY
 8  (Wed evening) Flat
 9  (Thu) Flat

22  (Wed evening) Flat
AUGUST
 4  (Tue) Flat
 7  (Fri) Flat
 8  (Sat) Flat
26  (Wed) Flat
SEPTEMBER
25  (Fri) Flat
26  (Sat) Flat
OCTOBER
 6  (Tue) Flat
14  (Wed) Flat
27  (Tue) Flat (Racecall Gold Trophy)

# *Ripon*
## FLAT

ADDRESS Boroughbridge Road, Ripon, North Yorkshire
TELEPHONE 0765 3696
LOCATION Ripon is 10 miles north of Harrogate; the racecourse is 2
   miles south-east of the town on the B6265 (Boroughbridge road), with
   easy access from the A1
NEAREST STATIONS Harrogate (Leeds-York line) and Thirsk (York-
   Darlington line)
ENCLOSURES Club, Tattersalls, Silver Ring, Course
CLERK OF THE COURSE J. M. Hutchinson

RIPON is a narrow, right-handed oval, 13 furlongs round with a 6
furlong straight course. It is nearly flat but there is a pronounced dip
a furlong out and, on account of its tightish bends and mild undulations,
the course is considered rather sharp in nature. The going here tends to
be better than at many of the other Yorkshire tracks since it is only 5 feet
above the water table (being wedged between the river Ure and the canal)
and the drainage is fairly good.

The course itself is extremely pretty; the parade ring and its surroundings are full of well tended and colourful flower beds, trees and lawns; the
buildings are aesthetically appealing; viewing from the stands is pretty
good and the atmosphere is lively.

## FIXTURES 1992

APRIL
 8 (Wed) Flat
 16 (Thu) Flat
 25 (Sat) Flat
MAY
 27 (Wed evening) Flat
JUNE
 17 (Wed) Flat
 18 (Thu) Flat

JULY
 6 (Mon evening) Flat
 18 (Sat) Flat
AUGUST
 3 (Mon) Flat
 15 (Sat) Flat
 22 (Sat) Flat
 31 (Mon Bank Holiday) Flat
SEPTEMBER
 1 (Tue) Flat

# Salisbury

## FLAT

ADDRESS Salisbury Racecourse, Netherhampton, Salisbury, Wiltshire
 SP2 8PN
TELEPHONE 0722 326461 or 327327
LOCATION the racecourse is 3 miles west of the city, just off the A3094 at
 Netherhampton, between the A30 and the A354
NEAREST STATION Salisbury (from London Waterloo)
ENCLOSURES Members, Tattersalls, Course
CLERK OF THE COURSE R. I. Renton

SALISBURY has always been a popular course on which to educate
two-year-olds: the turf is generally good and the straight course rises
all the way from the mile start. All races over a mile involve the loop which
requires more adroitness, for the course runs downhill all the way to the
first tight right-handed bend from where it rises to the equally tight home
bend. Nevertheless, Salisbury is very much a stiff, galloping track.

## FIXTURES 1992

APRIL
 30 (Thu) Flat
MAY
 6 (Wed) Flat
 22 (Fri) Flat
JUNE
 9 (Tue) Flat
 24 (Wed) Flat
 25 (Thu) Flat (Veuve Clicquot
 Champagne Stakes)

JULY
 11 (Sat) Flat
 30 (Thu evening) Flat
AUGUST
 12 (Wed) Flat
 13 (Thu) Flat
 20 (Thu evening) Flat
SEPTEMBER
 3 (Thu) Flat
 30 (Wed) Flat

# Sandown Park
## FLAT AND NATIONAL HUNT

ADDRESS Sandown Park Racecourse, Esher, Surrey KT10 9AJ
TELEPHONE 0372 463072 or 464348
LOCATION Sandown Park is in Esher, 4 miles south-west of Kingston
    upon Thames with easy access from the M25 (junction 10) via the A3
NEAREST STATION Esher (from London Waterloo)
FAMILY FACILITIES playground area in centre of course; crèche planned
    for 1992
ENCLOSURES Members, Grandstand, Silver Ring
CLERK OF THE COURSE A. N. Cheyne

S ANDOWN PARK is the ideal starting place for anyone who has not
been racing and wishes to sample its delights. It is also ideal for
anyone who simply wants to enjoy a day at the races. It provides high-class
sport under both codes throughout the year, has a stiff uphill home
stretch which guarantees exciting finishes, and looks after its patrons well.
Viewing at the course, from the modern stand on the hill overlooking the
track, is superb, and there are few sights in racing to match that of a field
of chasers going down the Railway straight. Another of the joys of
Sandown is the closeness between horses and spectators, best seen on the
Rhododendron Walk along which the runners progress to and from the
track itself: racegoers can stand literally within touching distance (though
touching is not advised) of their fancies. Sandown also has one of the very
best pre-parade rings for watching the runners before they are saddled
up. And the unsaddling enclosure allows everyone a good view of post-
race events.

The right-handed track itself is about 1 mile, 5 furlongs round, with a
downhill run from just past the stands, a flat back straight, and a steady
climb from the home turn. The 5 furlong course cuts across the middle of
the main course.

## FIXTURES 1992

JANUARY
 4 (Sat) NH (Anthony Mildmay, Peter
    Cazalet Memorial Handicap Chase,
    Baring Securities Tolworth Hurdle)
FEBRUARY
 1 (Sat) NH (Agfa Diamond Chase)
13 (Fri) NH

14 (Sat) NH
MARCH
 6 (Fri) NH (Grand Military Meeting)
 7 (Sat) NH (Sunderland Imperial Cup
    Hurdle)
24 (Tue) NH (Royal Artillery Meeting)

APRIL
24 (Fri) Flat (Forte Mile)
25 (Sat) Mixed (Whitbread Gold Cup, Thresher Classic Trial)
MAY
5 (Tue evening) Flat
25 (Mon Bank Holiday) Flat (UB Group Temple Stakes, Cementone Beaver Henry II Stakes)
26 (Tue evening) Flat (Charles Heidsieck National Stakes, Brigadier Gerard Stakes)
JUNE
12 (Fri) Flat
13 (Sat) Flat (Baker Lorenz Day)
JULY
3 (Fri) Flat (Hong Kong Day)
4 (Sat) Flat (Coral-Eclipse Stakes)

15 (Wed evening) Flat (Sloane Ranger Evening)
16 (Thu) Flat (Milcars Stakes)
22 (Wed evening) Flat
AUGUST
21 (Fri) Flat (Solario Stakes)
22 (Sat) Flat (Variety Club Day)
SEPTEMBER
15 (Tue) Flat (Reference Point Stakes)
16 (Wed) Flat
OCTOBER
31 (Sat) NH
DECEMBER
4 (Fri) NH (Crowngap Winter Hurdle)
5 (Sat) NH (William Hill Handicap Hurdle)

# *Sedgefield*
## NATIONAL HUNT

ADDRESS Sedgefield Steeplechase Company (1927) Ltd, 23A The Green, Billingham, Cleveland TS23 1ES
TELEPHONE 0642 557081 or 559050
LOCATION Sedgefield is 9 miles north-west of Stockton-on-Tees, 9 miles north of Darlington and 11 miles south-east of Durham; the racecourse is three-quarters of a mile south-west of the town near the junction of the A689 and A177, and has easy access from the A1(M)
NEAREST STATIONS Stockton, Darlington and Durham
ENCLOSURES Paddock, Course
CLERK OF THE COURSE J. G. Cleverly

SEDGEFIELD, with its alluring setting in the Durham countryside, typifies the small British racecourse; although the facilities have aged and are somewhat limited, there is a great deal of character and charm to Sedgefield that makes a visit well worth while.

The left-handed track undulates considerably and, with its sharp bends, is essentially sharp in character, although staying races tend to provide a stern test of stamina. The ground is usually pretty good. At 525 yards the steeplechase run-in is one of the longest in the country.

## FIXTURES 1992

JANUARY
14    (Tue) NH
22    (Wed) NH
28    (Tue) NH
FEBRUARY
7    (Fri) NH
18    (Tue) NH
MARCH
3    (Tue) NH
10    (Tue) NH
31    (Tue) NH
APRIL
14    (Tue) NH
28    (Tue evening) NH

MAY
5    (Tue evening) NH
SEPTEMBER
4    (Fri) NH
15    (Tue) NH
30    (Wed) NH
OCTOBER
13    (Tue) NH
28    (Wed) NH
NOVEMBER
10    (Tue) NH
20    (Fri) NH
DECEMBER
8    (Tue) NH
26    (Sat) NH

# Southwell

## FLAT, NATIONAL HUNT AND ALL-WEATHER

ADDRESS Southwell Racecourse. Rolleston, Newark, Nottinghamshire NG25 0TS

TELEPHONE 0636 814481

LOCATION Southwell is 5 miles west of Newark-on-Trent and 10 miles north-east of Nottingham; the racecourse is 3 miles south-east of the town at Rolleston

NEAREST STATIONS Rolleston (Nottingham-Newark line), Fiskerton

FAMILY FACILITIES supervised playground, amusement arcade

ENCLOSURES Members, Tattersalls

CLERK OF THE COURSE Mrs J. Groves

SOUTHWELL is one of only two racecourses in Britain with an all-weather as well as a turf track; the left-handed course is sharp, 10 furlongs round and pretty flat. Southwell is suited to well-made, handy horses rather than the more rangy, long-striding type. The facilities are good, up-to-date and make up for the lack of usual racecourse atmosphere.

## FIXTURES 1992

JANUARY
1    (Wed Bank Holiday) Flat AW
3    (Fri) Flat AW
6    (Mon) NH AW
8    (Wed) NH AW

10    (Fri) Flat AW
13    (Mon) NH AW
15    (Wed) Flat AW
17    (Fri) Flat AW
20    (Mon) NH AW

22 (Wed) NH AW
24 (Fri) Flat AW
27 (Mon) NH AW
29 (Wed) Flat AW
31 (Fri) Flat AW

FEBRUARY
3 (Mon) NH AW
5 (Wed) NH AW
7 (Fri) Flat AW
10 (Mon) NH AW
12 (Wed) Flat AW
14 (Fri) Flat AW
17 (Mon) NH AW
19 (Wed) NH AW
21 (Fri) Flat AW
24 (Mon) NH AW
26 (Wed) Flat AW
28 (Fri) Flat AW

MARCH
2 (Mon) NH AW
4 (Wed) NH AW
6 (Fri) Flat AW
9 (Mon) NH AW
14 (Sat) Flat AW
18 (Wed) Flat AW
28 (Sat) NH

APRIL
7 (Tue) NH
18 (Sat) NH

MAY
4 (Mon Bank Holiday) NH
16 (Sat evening) Flat
23 (Sat evening) Flat

JUNE
5 (Fri) Flat
10 (Wed) Flat
12 (Fri) Flat
20 (Sat evening) Flat

JULY
3 (Fri) Flat
11 (Sat evening) Flat
15 (Wed) Flat
17 (Fri) Flat
25 (Sat evening) Flat
29 (Wed evening) Flat

AUGUST
8 (Sat evening) Flat
14 (Fri) Flat
31 (Mon Bank Holiday) NH

SEPTEMBER
18 (Fri) Flat
23 (Wed) NH

OCTOBER
5 (Mon) NH
10 (Sat) NH
17 (Sat) NH

NOVEMBER
10 (Tue) Flat AW
17 (Tue) Flat AW
27 (Fri) Flat AW

DECEMBER
2 (Wed) Flat AW
10 (Thu) Flat AW
15 (Tue) Flat AW
28 (Mon Bank Holiday) Flat AW

# Stratford-upon-Avon
## NATIONAL HUNT

ADDRESS Stratford Racecourse, Luddington Road, Stratford-upon-Avon, Warwickshire CV37 9SE

TELEPHONE 0789 67949

LOCATION the racecourse is 1 mile south-west of the town just off the A439 (Evesham road)

NEAREST STATION Stratford (from Birmingham Moor St)

FAMILY FACILITIES supervised children's play area and crèche available at certain meetings (please enquire for details)

ENCLOSURES Club, Tattersalls, Course

CLERK OF THE COURSE J. W. Ford

STRATFORD-UPON-AVON is a tight course, another which makes 'horses for courses' high on the list of essentials when considering the form. Sharp, flat and left-handed, it can provide exciting sport but favours the compact sort of horse – like old Gambling Prince, who won here seven times. The best sport at Stratford is to be had towards the end of the season, culminating in 1992 in the *Horse and Hound* Cup for hunter chasers on 30 May, the final day of term. One hint: always avoid the town centre when driving to the races!

## FIXTURES 1992

FEBRUARY
   1   (Sat) NH
  22   (Sat) NH
MARCH
   5   (Thu) NH
APRIL
  11   (Sat) NH
MAY
   8   (Fri evening) NH (Roddy Baker
       Gold Cup)
  15   (Fri evening) NH
  29   (Fri evening) NH (John Corbet
       Cup)

  30   (Sat) NH (*Horse and Hound* Cup
       Final Champion Hunters'
       Chase)
SEPTEMBER
   5   (Sat) NH
  26   (Sat) NH
OCTOBER
  17   (Sat) NH
  29   (Thu) NH
NOVEMBER
  24   (Tue) NH
DECEMBER
  29   (Tue) NH

# *Taunton*

## NATIONAL HUNT

ADDRESS Taunton Racecourse, Orchard Portman, Taunton, Somerset
   TA3 7BL
TELEPHONE 0823 337172
LOCATION the racecourse is 2 miles south of the town on the B3170
   (Honiton road), with easy access from the M5 (junction 25) or from
   the A303 via the A358
NEAREST STATION Taunton (from London Paddington)
ENCLOSURES Club, Paddock, Course
CLERK OF THE COURSE A. G. M. Shewen

SET amid the rolling hills of Somerset, yet conveniently close to the M5, Taunton offers cheerful racing in attractive surroundings. The course is 10 furlongs round, oval in shape and sharp in character. Unfortunately there is clay underneath and the going tends to be very firm in summer and very soft in winter. The bends are not unduly tight but have presented problems when rain falls on firm ground and the surface becomes slippery.

The facilities for the public are good, the views from the stands excellent and there is usually a good and enthusiastic crowd in evidence.

## FIXTURES 1992

JANUARY
16 (Thu) NH
FEBRUARY
13 (Thu) NH
MARCH
9 (Mon) NH
26 (Thu) NH
APRIL
9 (Thu) NH
24 (Fri evening) NH

SEPTEMBER
24 (Thu) NH
OCTOBER
15 (Thu) NH
NOVEMBER
12 (Thu) NH
26 (Thu) NH
DECEMBER
10 (Thu) NH
30 (Wed) NH

# *Thirsk*

## FLAT

ADDRESS Thirsk Racecourse Ltd, Station Road, Thirsk, North Yorkshire YO7 1QL
TELEPHONE 0845 522276
LOCATION Thirsk is 23 miles north-west of York and 9 miles south-east of Northallerton; the racecourse is west of the town on the A61, with easy access from the A1
NEAREST STATION Thirsk, 6 furlongs from the course (York-Newcastle line)
FAMILY FACILITIES baby changing facilities
ENCLOSURES Club, Tattersalls, Silver Ring, No. 3 Ring
CLERK OF THE COURSE J. L. Smith

SET only 8 miles from the famous training centre of Hambleton, the 10 furlong, left-handed circuit at Thirsk, with its easy bends and minor undulations, is yet another fine Yorkshire racecourse. Although on the sharp side, the track provides a fair test for horses and is blessed with good drainage and turf.

An attractive racecourse with improved facilities and amenities, Thirsk is popular with the public and well worth a visit.

## FIXTURES 1992

**APRIL**
10   (Fri) Flat
11   (Sat) Flat
**MAY**
2   (Sat) Flat (Thirsk Hunt Cup)
15   (Fri) Flat
16   (Sat) Flat
**JUNE**
16   (Tue) Flat

**JULY**
17   (Fri) Flat
31   (Fri) Flat
**AUGUST**
1   (Sat) Flat
10   (Mon evening) Flat
28   (Fri) Flat
**SEPTEMBER**
5   (Sat) Flat

# *Towcester*

## NATIONAL HUNT

ADDRESS Estate Office, Easton Neston, Towcester, Northamptonshire
NN12 7HS
TELEPHONE 0327 53414
LOCATION Towcester is 8 miles south-west of Northampton; the
racecourse is half a mile south-east of the town on the A5 (London
Road) with easy access from the M1 (junction 15A)
NEAREST STATIONS Northampton, Milton Keynes
FAMILY FACILITIES playground at Festival Meetings (phone for details)
ENCLOSURES Members, Tattersalls, Course
CLERK OF THE COURSE H. P. C. Bevan

TOWCESTER is a very testing, right-handed track, 14 furlongs
round. From the winning post the course rises to the first bend and
then descends steeply into the back-straight which is itself level. From the
turn out of the back straight it rises steadily all the way to the finish, fully
testing a horse's stamina. The ground is often on the soft side since the
clay subsoil makes drainage poor.

Towcester is an extremely attractive racecourse that was laid out by
Lord Hesketh on his impressive estate in 1928. The stands provide
excellent views of the racing, and the facilities are typical of the small
jumping tracks – simple but highly enjoyable.

## FIXTURES 1992

**JANUARY**
17   (Fri) NH
30   (Thu) NH
**FEBRUARY**
11   (Tue) NH

**MARCH**
19   (Thu) NH
**APRIL**
18   (Sat) NH
20   (Mon Bank Holiday) NH

| MAY | NOVEMBER |
|---|---|
| 4 (Mon Bank Holiday) NH | 12 (Thu) NH |
| 12 (Tue evening) NH | 21 (Sat) NH |
| 22 (Fri) NH | DECEMBER |
| OCTOBER | 5 (Sat) NH |
| 7 (Wed) NH | 17 (Thu) NH |

# *Uttoxeter*
## NATIONAL HUNT

ADDRESS The Racecourse, Wood Lane, Uttoxeter, Staffordshire
 ST14 8BD
TELEPHONE 0889 562561
LOCATION Uttoxeter is 14 miles north-east of Stafford and about 20
 miles west of Derby; the racecourse is to the south-east of the town off
 the B5017 (Marchington road), with access from the M6 (junctions 14
 and 15)
NEAREST STATION Uttoxeter, adjoining course (Derby-Crewe line)
ENCLOSURES Club, Tattersalls, Silver Ring, Course
CLERK OF THE COURSE D. McAllister

IN recent years Uttoxeter has shown the benefits of an enterprising
management. Channel Four Racing visited the course for the first time
in March 1991, and the standard of racing here has gradually improved.
The Midlands National is the course's best known race, but it also has a
race rated Grade Two under the new National Hunt pattern – the
Staffordshire Hurdle. Long favoured by jump jockeys as one of the fairest
of the small tracks, Uttoxeter has a gently undulating 10-furlong circuit
with easy bends (mostly left-handed, but with a right-handed kink in the
back straight) and a flat run for home. It thus favours the resolute galloper
– like Bonanza Boy, who ran away with the Ansells National in 1991.

## FIXTURES 1992

| JANUARY | 21 (Tue) NH | OCTOBER |
|---|---|---|
| 24 (Fri) NH | MAY | 3 (Sat) NH |
| FEBRUARY | 2 (Sat) NH (St Modwen | 15 (Thu) NH |
| 8 (Sat) NH | Staffordshire Hurdle) | NOVEMBER |
| MARCH | 7 (Thu evening) NH | 5 (Thu) NH |
| 14 (Sat) NH (Ansells | 25 (Mon Bank Holiday) | DECEMBER |
| Midlands National) | NH | 3 (Thu) NH |
| APRIL | 26 (Tue evening) NH | 18 (Fri) NH |
| 20 (Mon Bank Holiday) | SEPTEMBER | 19 (Sat) NH |
| NH | 17 (Thu) NH | |

# *Warwick*
## FLAT AND NATIONAL HUNT

ADDRESS Warwick Racecourse, Hampton Street, Warwick CV34 6HN
TELEPHONE 0926 491553
LOCATION the racecourse is a quarter of a mile to the west of the town,
    with easy access from the M40 (junction 15)
NEAREST STATION Warwick (from Birmingham Snow Hill)
FAMILY FACILITIES supervised playground
ENCLOSURES Club, Tattersalls, Course
CLERK OF THE COURSE E. W. Gillespie
MANAGER P. R. McNeile

R ACES from 5 furlongs to a mile on the Flat at Warwick are very
sharp, largely because of the tight left-handed bend into the 2½
furlong long straight. However, the course sets a very fair test in longer
Flat and National Hunt races, being 14 furlongs round and flat, apart
from the run to the turn into the back straight where the ground rises and
falls sharply.

The stands are quite small and the runners are obscured for a while by
the hump in the middle of the course, but there is a new stand alongside
the paddock which signals a distinct improvement.

## FIXTURES 1992

JANUARY
  11  (Sat) NH
  18  (Sat) NH (Racephone National
      Steeplechase)
FEBRUARY
  4  (Tue) NH
  19  (Wed) NH (Pertemps Group
      Regency Hurdle)
MARCH
  3  (Tue) NH
  28  (Sat) Flat
APRIL
  20  (Mon Bank Holiday) Flat
  21  (Tue) Flat
MAY
  4  (Mon Bank Holiday) Flat
  9  (Sat evening) NH (Kingmaker
      Novices' Chase)
  16  (Sat evening) NH (Warwickshire
      Countrysports Evening)

  23  (Sat evening) Flat
JUNE
  20  (Sat evening) Flat (Warwick Oaks)
  27  (Sat evening) Flat (Warwick Vase)
JULY
  1  (Wed) Flat
  10  (Fri) Flat
  25  (Sat evening) Flat
AUGUST
  31  (Mon Bank Holiday) Flat
OCTOBER
  5  (Mon) Flat
  6  (Tue) Flat
  31  (Sat) NH
NOVEMBER
  17  (Tue) NH
  28  (Sat) NH (St Mary's Trial Hurdle)
DECEMBER
  7  (Mon) NH
  30  (Wed) NH

# *Wetherby*

## NATIONAL HUNT

ADDRESS Wetherby Steeplechase Committee Ltd, The Racecourse,
York Road, Wetherby, West Yorkshire LS22 5EJ
TELEPHONE 0937 582035
LOCATION Wetherby is 12 miles north-east of Leeds and 12 miles west
of York; the racecourse is east of the town just off the B1224 (York
road), with easy access from the A1
NEAREST STATIONS Harrogate, Leeds, York
FAMILY FACILITIES children's playground; accompanied children under
16 admitted free
ENCLOSURES Club, Tattersalls, Course
CLERK OF THE COURSE P. B. Firth

THE only track in Yorkshire to stage National Hunt racing alone,
Wetherby attracts top horses and puts on some very good racing.
The track is very fair, a left-handed oval 12 furlongs round and, with its
easy bends, long straights and gentle undulations, suited to free-running,
galloping types of horses. There is a premium on both good jumping and
stamina here.

## FIXTURES 1992

JANUARY
10 (Fri) NH
FEBRUARY
1 (Sat) NH (Marston Moor Chase)
26 (Wed) NH
APRIL
20 (Mon Bank Holiday) NH (Wetherby
Chase)
21 (Tue) NH
MAY
6 (Wed evening) NH
25 (Mon Bank Holiday) NH

OCTOBER
14 (Wed) NH
30 (Fri) NH
31 (Sat) NH (Charlie Hall Chase, West
Yorkshire Hurdle)
NOVEMBER
17 (Tue) NH
DECEMBER
5 (Sat) NH (Tetley Bitter Handicap
Chase)
26 (Sat) NH (Rowland Meyrick
Handicap Chase)
28 (Mon Bank Holiday) NH
(Castleford Chase)

# *Wincanton*

## NATIONAL HUNT

ADDRESS Wincanton Racecourse, Wincanton, Somerset BA9 8BJ
TELEPHONE 0963 32344

LOCATION Wincanton is 10 miles west of Shaftesbury; the racecourse is
1 mile north of the town on the A3081 (Shepton Mallet road); access
from A303

NEAREST STATION Gillingham (London Waterloo)

ENCLOSURES Members, Tattersalls, Public Enclosure

CLERK OF THE COURSE R. I. Renton

WINCANTON has a faithful following, and in the spring takes on an
added significance as a final trial ground for Cheltenham hopefuls
in races such as the Kingwell Hurdle and the Jim Ford Chase. It also has
the distinction of hosting the first race named after Desert Orchid – the
Desert Orchid South Western Pattern Chase, in which the grey finished
second to Sabin du Loir on his seasonal debut in October 1991. Wincanton is a galloping and very fair course, with easy right-hand bends, no
trappy undulations, and well-made obstacles. It's also a good place for
fans: several new buildings in recent years have improved the lot of
racegoers, and the viewing is excellent.

## FIXTURES 1992

JANUARY
9  (Thu) NH
24  (Fri) NH
FEBRUARY
6  (Thu) NH
20  (Thu) NH (Kingwell Pattern
Hurdle, Jim Ford Chase)
MARCH
5  (Thu) NH
27  (Fri) NH
APRIL
20  (Mon Bank Holiday) NH

MAY
8  (Fri evening) NH
OCTOBER
8  (Thu) NH
22  (Thu) NH (Desert Orchid South
Western Pattern Chase)
NOVEMBER
5  (Thu) NH (Badger Beer Chase)
19  (Thu) NH
DECEMBER
26  (Sat) NH

# *Windsor*
## FLAT AND NATIONAL HUNT

ADDRESS Royal Windsor Racecourse, Windsor, Berkshire SL4 5JJ

TELEPHONE 0753 865234 or 864726

LOCATION the racecourse is 1 mile north-west of the town on the A308
(Maidenhead road), with easy access from the M4 (junction 6)

NEAREST STATION Windsor Riverside (London Waterloo) or Windsor
Central (from London Paddington via Slough)

FAMILY FACILITIES crèche and playground

ENCLOSURES Club, Tattersalls and Paddock, Silver Ring
CLERK OF THE COURSE H. P. C. Bevan

SITUATED alongside the river Thames, Windsor is an easy track, 12 furlongs round and dead flat. It is also pretty sharp because, being a figure-of-eight, the horses are on the turn for much of the time. Excellent drainage usually ensures good going and the turf flourishes in the rich alluvial soil. The National Hunt course, also both sharp and easy, runs on the outside of the first loop and on the inside of the second.

The facilities at Windsor are reasonable, but at the immensely popular evening meetings crowding is often a problem. On a fine summer's evening a very pleasurable way of getting to the course is by the Thames river boats which set off from the Windsor/Eton bridge.

## FIXTURES 1992

JANUARY
  1  (Wed Bank Holiday) NH (New Year's Day Hurdle)
 15  (Wed) NH
 29  (Wed) NH
FEBRUARY
 15  (Sat) NH (Fairlawne Chase)
MARCH
  2  (Mon) NH
APRIL
 27  (Mon evening) Flat
MAY
 11  (Mon evening) Flat (St John Ambulance Raceday)
JUNE
 15  (Mon evening) Flat
 22  (Mon evening) Flat (MOUF Leukaemia Research Raceday)
 29  (Mon evening) Flat

JULY
  6  (Mon evening) Flat
 13  (Mon evening) Flat
 20  (Mon evening) Flat (Cancer Relief Macmillan Fund Raceday)
 27  (Mon evening) Flat (Family Welfare Association Raceday)
AUGUST
  1  (Sat evening) Flat (Courage Beer Company Raceday)
 10  (Mon) Flat
 17  (Mon) Flat
 29  (Sat evening) Flat
NOVEMBER
  7  (Sat) NH
 16  (Mon) NH
DECEMBER
  3  (Thu) NH

# *Wolverhampton*
## FLAT AND NATIONAL HUNT

ADDRESS Wolverhampton Racecourse, Gorsebrook Road, Wolverhampton WV6 0PE
TELEPHONE 0902 24481
LOCATION the racecourse is 1 mile north of the town off the A449 (Stafford road), with easy access from the M54 (junction 2)

NEAREST STATION Wolverhampton (from London Euston)
ENCLOSURES Members, Tattersalls
CLERK OF THE COURSE Mrs J. Groves

RECENTLY purchased by Ron Muddle, who has ambitious plans to install an all-weather track and institute night-racing under floodlights, Wolverhampton is at present a fair and galloping track, left-handed, 12 furlongs round, with a straight 5-furlong course which runs slightly downhill and is decidedly sharp. The course drains particularly well and the going on the chase course remains comparatively fast throughout the NH season.

## FIXTURES 1992

| | |
|---|---|
| JANUARY | 29  (Mon) Flat |
| 6  (Mon) NH | JULY |
| 22  (Wed) NH | 13  (Mon) Flat |
| FEBRUARY | 18  (Sat evening) Flat |
| 3  (Mon) NH | 27  (Mon evening) Flat |
| 17  (Mon) NH | AUGUST |
| MARCH | 7  (Fri) Flat |
| 13  (Fri) NH | 15  (Sat evening) Flat |
| 16  (Mon) NH | 31  (Mon Bank Holiday) Flat |
| 26  (Thu) Flat | SEPTEMBER |
| APRIL | 7  (Mon) Flat |
| 6  (Mon) Flat | 28  (Mon) Flat |
| 27  (Mon) Flat | NOVEMBER |
| MAY | 2  (Mon) NH |
| 11  (Mon) Flat | 9  (Mon) NH |
| 30  (Sat evening) Flat | 23  (Mon) NH |
| JUNE | DECEMBER |
| 13  (Sat evening) Flat | 26  (Sat) NH |
| 22  (Mon evening) Flat | 28  (Mon Bank Holiday) NH |

# *Worcester*

## NATIONAL HUNT

ADDRESS Worcester Racecourse, Pitchcroft, Worcester WR1 3EJ
TELEPHONE 0905 25364 or 23936
LOCATION the racecourse is in the west of the city off the A449 (Kidderminster road), with easy access from the M5 (junctions 5 and 6)
NEAREST STATION Worcester Foregate St (from London Paddington) half a mile from course

ENCLOSURES Members, Tattersalls, Centre Enclosure
CLERK OF THE COURSE H. P. C. Bevan

WORCESTER Situated near the centre of the city hard by the banks of the Severn (which makes it susceptible to flooding), Worcester regularly provides highly enjoyable sport in the second division. The course is flat and consists of two long straights joined at each end by fairly easy left-handed turns – thus a good track for big, galloping types – but the bend beyond the winning post cannot be viewed properly from the stands: the grandstand was wrongly sited. That apart, Worcester is a good venue for the racegoer: compact, casual and friendly.

## FIXTURES 1992

| | |
|---|---|
| FEBRUARY | 10 (Mon) NH |
| 12 (Wed) NH | 27 (Thu) NH |
| 26 (Wed) NH | SEPTEMBER |
| MARCH | 11 (Fri) NH |
| 18 (Wed) NH | 12 (Sat) NH |
| 25 (Wed) NH | 19 (Sat) NH |
| APRIL | OCTOBER |
| 1 (Wed) NH | 10 (Sat) NH |
| 25 (Sat evening) NH | 24 (Sat) NH |
| MAY | NOVEMBER |
| 6 (Wed evening) NH | 11 (Wed) NH |
| 20 (Wed) NH | 30 (Mon) NH |
| AUGUST | DECEMBER |
| 8 (Sat evening) NH | 9 (Wed) NH |

# *Yarmouth*

FLAT

ADDRESS Great Yarmouth Racecourse, Jellicoe Road, Great Yarmouth, Norfolk NR30 4AU
TELEPHONE 0493 842527
LOCATION the racecourse is 2 miles north of the town on the A149 (Caister road); access from the A47
NEAREST STATION Yarmouth (from Norwich)
FAMILY FACILITIES unsupervised playground in family enclosure and supervised playground in east side of course
ENCLOSURES Club, Tattersalls, Course and Family Enclosure
CLERK OF THE COURSE P. B. Firth

YARMOUTH is a thriving seaside racecourse that is very popular with holiday crowds to such an extent that the facilities, although good enough in themselves, are barely able to cope with the throng.

The track is left-handed, nearly flat, oval in shape, 13 furlongs round and very much suited to long-striding, galloping types. The straight course caters for races up to a mile and attracts some very useful two-year-olds from Newmarket out for their first run.

---

## FIXTURES 1992

JUNE
2   (Tue) Flat
3   (Wed) Flat
23   (Tue) Flat
JULY
1   (Wed) Flat
2   (Thu) Flat
15   (Wed evening) Flat
22   (Wed) Flat
23   (Thu) Flat
24   (Fri) Flat

30   (Thu) Flat
AUGUST
11   (Tue) Flat
19   (Wed) Flat
20   (Thu) Flat
SEPTEMBER
15   (Tue) Flat
16   (Wed) Flat
17   (Thu) Flat
OCTOBER
28   (Wed) Flat

# *York*

## FLAT

ADDRESS York Race Committee, The Racecourse, York YO2 1EX
TELEPHONE 0904 620911
LOCATION the racecourse is 1 mile south of the city on the A1036 (Tadcaster road); from the South or West use the A64 (access from A1), from the North and North East use the northern by-pass linking the A19
NEAREST STATION York (London King's Cross)
FAMILY FACILITIES children under 16 admitted to all enclosures free (except Members in May/August) provided they are accompanied by an adult
ENCLOSURES Club, Tattersalls, Silver Ring, Course Enclosure
CLERK OF THE COURSE J. L. Smith

YORK is the venue of two of the great meetings of the year – the August Meeting, with the International Stakes, Yorkshire Oaks, Ebor and Nunthorpe outstanding in three days of the highest-class Flat racing imaginable, and the much quieter but always highly informative May

Meeting, featuring the Dante Stakes, Musidora Stakes and Yorkshire Cup.

For many people – not only fiercely loyal Yorkshire folk – the course on the vast common land of the Knavesmire, just outside the city centre, is the finest in the country. The stands and facilities are superb, and the course itself could hardly be bettered. It is flat and wide with a gradual left-handed bend from the back straight towards home following an easier bend about 10 furlongs out; races over less than a mile start on spurs off the main course.

To go racing at York – either in the stands or in the excellent enclosure inside the course – is to experience the Flat at its best.

## FIXTURES 1992

MAY

12 (Tue) Flat (Tattersalls Musidora Stakes)
13 (Wed) Flat (Dante Stakes)
14 (Thu) Flat (Polo Mints Yorkshire Cup)

JUNE

12 (Fri) Flat (Innovative Marketing Sprint)
13 (Sat) Flat (William Hill Golden Spurs Trophy)

JULY

10 (Fri) Flat (A. F. Budge Handicap)
11 (Sat) Flat (John Smith's Magnet Cup)

AUGUST

18 (Tue) Flat (Juddmonte International Stakes, Great Voltigeur Stakes)

19 (Wed) Flat (Aston Upthorpe Yorkshire Oaks, Scottish Equitable Gimcrack Stakes, Tote Ebor)
20 (Thu) Flat (Bradford and Bingley Handicap, Keeneland Nunthorpe Stakes)

SEPTEMBER

2 (Wed) Flat (Batleys Cash and Carry Day)
3 (Thu) Flat (Sun Life of Canada Garrowby Stakes)

OCTOBER

7 (Wed) Flat (Charles Heidsieck Stakes)
8 (Thu) Flat (Allied Dunbar Handicap)
10 (Sat) Flat (Rockingham Stakes)

# CHAMPION JOCKEYS AND TRAINERS IN GREAT BRITAIN SINCE 1946

## CHAMPION JOCKEYS (FLAT)

| | | RACES WON | | | RACES WON |
|---|---|---|---|---|---|
| 1946 | G. Richards | 212 | 1969 | L. Piggott | 163 |
| 1947 | G. Richards | 269 | 1970 | L. Piggott | 162 |
| 1948 | G. Richards | 224 | 1971 | L. Piggott | 162 |
| 1949 | G. Richards | 261 | 1972 | W. Carson | 132 |
| 1950 | G. Richards | 201 | 1973 | W. Carson | 164 |
| 1951 | G. Richards | 227 | 1974 | Pat Eddery | 148 |
| 1952 | G. Richards | 231 | 1975 | Pat Eddery | 164 |
| 1953 | G. Richards | 191 | 1976 | Pat Eddery | 162 |
| 1954 | D. Smith | 129 | 1977 | Pat Eddery | 176 |
| 1955 | D. Smith | 168 | 1978 | W. Carson | 182 |
| 1956 | D. Smith | 155 | 1979 | J. Mercer | 164 |
| 1957 | A. Breasley | 173 | 1980 | W. Carson | 166 |
| 1958 | D. Smith | 165 | 1981 | L. Piggott | 179 |
| 1959 | D. Smith | 157 | 1982 | L. Piggott | 188 |
| 1960 | L. Piggott | 170 | 1983 | W. Carson | 159 |
| 1961 | A. Breasley | 171 | 1984 | S. Cauthen | 130 |
| 1962 | A. Breasley | 179 | 1985 | S. Cauthen | 195 |
| 1963 | A. Breasley | 176 | 1986 | Pat Eddery | 176 |
| 1964 | L. Piggott | 140 | 1987 | S. Cauthen | 197 |
| 1965 | L. Piggott | 160 | 1988 | Pat Eddery | 183 |
| 1966 | L. Piggott | 191 | 1989 | Pat Eddery | 171 |
| 1967 | L. Piggott | 117 | 1990 | Pat Eddery | 209 |
| 1968 | L. Piggott | 139 | 1991 | Pat Eddery | 165 |

## CHAMPION APPRENTICES (FLAT)

| | | RACES WON | | | RACES WON |
|---|---|---|---|---|---|
| 1946 | J. Sime | 40 | 1949 | W. Snaith | 31 |
| 1947 | D. Buckle | 20 | 1950 | L. Piggott | 52 |
| 1948 | D. Buckle | 25 | 1951 | L. Piggott | 51 |

## CHAMPION APPRENTICES (FLAT) *continued*

| | | RACES WON | | | | RACES WON |
|---|---|---|---|---|---|---|
| 1952 | J. Mercer | 26 | | 1972 | R. Edmondson | 45 |
| 1953 | J. Mercer | 61 | | 1973 | S. Perks | 41 |
| 1954 | E. Hide | 53 | | 1974 | A. Bond | 40 |
| 1955 | P. Robinson | 46 | | 1975 | A. Bond | 66 |
| 1956 | E. Hide | 75 | | 1976 | D. Dineley | 54 |
| 1957 | G. Starkey | 45 | | 1977 | J. Bleasdale | 67 |
| 1958 | P. Boothman | 37 | | 1978 | K. Darley | 70 |
| 1959 | R. Elliott | 27 | | 1979 | P. Robinson | 51 |
| 1960 | R. Elliott | 39 | | 1980 | P. Robinson | 59 |
| 1961 | B. Lee | 52 | | 1981 | B. Crossley | 45 |
| 1962 | B. Raymond | 13 | | 1982 | W. Newnes | 57 |
| 1963 | D. Yates | 24 | | 1983 | M. Hills | 39 |
| 1964 | P. Cook | 46 | | 1984 | T. Quinn | 62 |
| 1965 | P. Cook | 62 | | 1985 | G. Carter, W. Ryan | 37 |
| 1966 | A. Barclay | 71 | | 1986 | G. Carter | 34 |
| 1967 | E. Johnson | 39 | | 1987 | G. Bardwell | 27 |
| 1968 | D. Coates, R. Dicey | 40 | | 1988 | G. Bardwell | 39 |
| 1969 | C. Eccleston | 41 | | 1989 | L. Dettori | 75 |
| 1970 | P. Waldron | 59 | | 1990 | J. Fortune | 47 |
| 1971 | Pat Eddery | 71 | | 1991 | D. Holland | 83 |

## LEADING TRAINERS (FLAT)

| | | £ | RACES WON | | | | £ | RACES WON |
|---|---|---|---|---|---|---|---|---|
| 1946 | F. Butters | 56,140 | 60 | | 1966 | M. V. O'Brien (Ire) | 123,848 | 8 |
| 1947 | F. Darling | 65,313 | 56 | | 1967 | N. Murless | 256,899 | 60 |
| 1948 | N. Murless | 66,542 | 63 | | 1968 | N. Murless | 141,508 | 47 |
| 1949 | F. Butters | 71,721 | 42 | | 1969 | A. Budgett | 105,349 | 35 |
| 1950 | C. Semblat (Fr) | 57,044 | 11 | | 1970 | N. Murless | 199,524 | 53 |
| 1951 | J. Jarvis | 56,397 | 62 | | 1971 | I. Balding | 157,488 | 45 |
| 1952 | M. Marsh | 92,093 | 30 | | 1972 | W. R. Hern | 206,767 | 42 |
| 1953 | J. Jarvis | 71,546 | 60 | | 1973 | N. Murless | 132,984 | 34 |
| 1954 | C. Boyd-Rochfort | 65,326 | 39 | | 1974 | P. Walwyn | 206,445 | 96 |
| 1955 | C. Boyd-Rochfort | 74,424 | 38 | | 1975 | P. Walwyn | 382,527 | 121 |
| 1956 | C. Elsey | 61,621 | 83 | | 1976 | H. Cecil | 261,301 | 52 |
| 1957 | N. Murless | 116,898 | 48 | | 1977 | M. V. O'Brien (Ire) | 439,124 | 18 |
| 1958 | C. Boyd-Rochfort | 84,186 | 37 | | 1978 | H. Cecil | 382,812 | 109 |
| 1959 | N. Murless | 145,727 | 63 | | 1979 | H. Cecil | 683,971 | 128 |
| 1960 | N. Murless | 118,327 | 42 | | 1980 | W. R. Hern | 831,964 | 65 |
| 1961 | N. Murless | 95,972 | 36 | | 1981 | M. Stoute | 723,786 | 95 |
| 1962 | W. R. Hern | 70,206 | 39 | | 1982 | H. Cecil | 872,614 | 111 |
| 1963 | P. Prendergast (Ire) | 125,294 | 19 | | 1983 | W. R. Hern | 549,598 | 57 |
| 1964 | P. Prendergast (Ire) | 128,102 | 17 | | 1984 | H. Cecil | 551,939 | 108 |
| 1965 | P. Prendergast (Ire) | 75,323 | 11 | | 1985 | H. Cecil | 1,148,206 | 132 |

## LEADING TRAINERS (FLAT) *continued*

| | | £ | RACES WON | | | £ | RACES WON |
|---|---|---|---|---|---|---|---|
| 1986 | M. Stoute | 1,269,820 | 76 | 1989 | M. Stoute | 1,469,158 | 117 |
| 1987 | H. Cecil | 1,882,359 | 180 | 1990 | H. Cecil | 1,520,092 | 111 |
| 1988 | H. Cecil | 1,186,083 | 112 | 1991 | P. Cole | 1,520,617 | 73 |

## CHAMPION JOCKEYS (NATIONAL HUNT)

| | | RACES WON | | | RACES WON |
|---|---|---|---|---|---|
| 1945/46 | F. Rimell | 54 | 1969/70 | B. Davies | 91 |
| 1946/47 | J. Dowdeswell | 58 | 1970/71 | G. Thorner | 74 |
| 1947/48 | B. Marshall | 66 | 1971/72 | B. Davies | 89 |
| 1948/49 | T. Molony | 60 | 1972/73 | R. Barry | 125 |
| 1949/50 | T. Molony | 95 | 1973/74 | R. Barry | 94 |
| 1950/51 | T. Molony | 83 | 1974/75 | T. Stack | 82 |
| 1951/52 | T. Molony | 99 | 1975/76 | J. Francome | 96 |
| 1952/53 | F. Winter | 121 | 1976/77 | T. Stack | 97 |
| 1953/54 | R. Francis | 76 | 1977/78 | J. J. O'Neill | 149 |
| 1954/55 | T. Molony | 67 | 1978/79 | J. Francome | 95 |
| 1955/56 | F. Winter | 74 | 1979/80 | J. J. O'Neill | 115 |
| 1956/57 | F. Winter | 80 | 1980/81 | J. Francome | 105 |
| 1957/58 | F. Winter | 82 | 1981/82 | { J. Francome | 120 |
| 1958/59 | T. Brookshaw | 83 | | { P. Scudamore | 120 |
| 1959/60 | S. Mellor | 68 | 1982/83 | J. Francome | 106 |
| 1960/61 | S. Mellor | 118 | 1983/84 | J. Francome | 131 |
| 1961/62 | S. Mellor | 80 | 1984/85 | J. Francome | 101 |
| 1962/63 | J. Gifford | 70 | 1985/86 | P. Scudamore | 91 |
| 1963/64 | J. Gifford | 94 | 1986/87 | P. Scudamore | 123 |
| 1964/65 | T. Biddlecombe | 114 | 1987/88 | P. Scudamore | 132 |
| 1965/66 | T. Biddlecombe | 102 | 1988/89 | P. Scudamore | 221 |
| 1966/67 | J. Gifford | 122 | 1989/90 | P. Scudamore | 170 |
| 1967/68 | J. Gifford | 82 | 1990/91 | P. Scudamore | 141 |
| 1968/69 | { B. Davies | 77 | | | |
| | { T. Biddlecombe | 77 | | | |

## LEADING TRAINERS (NATIONAL HUNT)

| | | £ | RACES WON | | | £ | RACES WON |
|---|---|---|---|---|---|---|---|
| 1945/46 | T. Rayson | 9,933 | 5 | 1949/50 | P. Cazalet | 18,427 | 75 |
| 1946/47 | F. Walwyn | 11,115 | 60 | 1950/51 | F. Rimell | 18,381 | 60 |
| 1947/48 | F. Walwyn | 16,790 | 75 | 1951/52 | N. Crump | 19,357 | 41 |
| 1948/49 | F. Walwyn | 15,563 | 64 | 1952/53 | M. V. O'Brien (Ire) | 15,515 | 5 |

## LEADING TRAINERS (NATIONAL HUNT) *continued*

| | | £ | RACES WON | | | £ | RACES WON |
|---|---|---|---|---|---|---|---|
| 1953/54 | M. V. O'Brien (Ire) | 14,274 | 8 | 1972/73 | F. Winter | 79,066 | 85 |
| 1954/55 | H. R. Price | 13,888 | 47 | 1973/74 | F. Winter | 101,782 | 89 |
| 1955/56 | W. Hall | 15,807 | 41 | 1974/75 | F. Winter | 74,205 | 81 |
| 1956/57 | N. Crump | 18,495 | 39 | 1975/76 | F. Rimell | 111,740 | 49 |
| 1957/58 | F. Walwyn | 23,013 | 35 | 1976/77 | F. Winter | 85,202 | 75 |
| 1958/59 | H. R. Price | 26,550 | 52 | 1977/78 | F. Winter | 145,915 | 90 |
| 1959/60 | P. Cazalet | 22,270 | 58 | 1978/79 | M. H. Easterby | 150,746 | 56 |
| 1960/61 | F. Rimell | 34,811 | 58 | 1979/80 | M. H. Easterby | 218,258 | 75 |
| 1961/62 | H. R. Price | 40,950 | 64 | 1980/81 | M. H. Easterby | 235,867 | 71 |
| 1962/63 | K. Piggott | 23,091 | 6 | 1981/82 | M. Dickinson | 296,028 | 84 |
| 1963/64 | F. Walwyn | 67,129 | 59 | 1982/83 | M. Dickinson | 358,837 | 120 |
| 1964/65 | P. Cazalet | 36,153 | 82 | 1983/84 | M. Dickinson | 266,146 | 86 |
| 1965/66 | H. R. Price | 42,276 | 65 | 1984/85 | F. Winter | 218,978 | 85 |
| 1966/67 | H. R. Price | 41,222 | 73 | 1985/86 | N. Henderson | 168,234 | 46 |
| 1967/68 | D. Smith | 37,944 | 55 | 1986/87 | N. Henderson | 222,924 | 67 |
| 1968/69 | F. Rimell | 38,344 | 62 | 1987/88 | D. Elsworth | 341,717 | 47 |
| 1969/70 | F. Rimell | 61,864 | 77 | 1988/89 | M. Pipe | 589,379 | 208 |
| 1970/71 | F. Winter | 60,739 | 73 | 1989/90 | M. Pipe | 668,606 | 224 |
| 1971/72 | F. Winter | 62,396 | 72 | 1990/91 | M. Pipe | 956,635 | 230 |

# A RACING GLOSSARY

**added money**  money contributed towards the value of a race by sponsors or the racecourse in addition to entry fees

**All-Weather**  racing on an artificial surface; currently at Lingfield (Equitrack) and Southwell (Fibresand)

**apprentice jockey**  young (16–24) Flat jockey tied by annually renewed contract to a licensed trainer, under whom he will learn the skills of race-riding; may claim an allowance of 3, 5 or 7lb until he/she has won 75, 50 or 10 races respectively

**auction race**  race for horses which were bought as yearlings at public auction; weight allowances are given to horses bought for lower sums

**backward**  describes a horse still needing time to mature

**ballot**  method by which numbers of runners in non-handicap races are reduced to the official safety level

**bay**  all shades of brown with the points (muzzle, mane, tail and extremities of the legs) black

**blinkers**  hood fitted to a horse's head to prevent backward vision and thus increase its concentration

**box-walker**  horse which expends nervous energy by walking round its stable

**break down**  to rupture severely tendons in the leg

**breeze-up**  horses coming a nice pace together, hence the Breeze-Up Sales of two-year-olds where prospective purchasers can see horses work together before the sale

**brood-mare**  mare used for breeding

**'bumper'**  NH Flat race

**'change legs'**  when galloping a horse extends one foreleg further than the other; when changing the leading leg from left to right or vice versa, it is said to 'change legs'

**claiming race**  race in which any runner can be claimed for the advertised sum or more

**Clerk of the Course**    official responsible to the Stewards for the general arrangements of a race meeting

**Clerk of the Scales**    official responsible for the weighing in and out of the jockeys, for the number board and for reporting, to the *Racing Calendar*, the day's events (e.g. decisions of the Stewards, overweights, etc.)

**colt**    male, ungelded horse below the age of five

**conditional jockey**    NH equivalent to apprentice; may claim an allowance of 7, 5 or 3lb until he/she has won 15, 25 or 40 races respectively

**dam**    mother of a horse

**distance, a**    more than 30 lengths between two finishers of a race

**distance, the**    240 yards from the winning post

**distances, the**    margins between finishers of a race

**doer**    a 'good doer' is a horse that eats well

**draw, the**    the order in which horses in a flat race line up at the start, numbering from left to right as they face out of the stalls

**entire**    ungelded horse

**eye-shield**    similar to blinkers but with one eye of defective vision completely covered

**field, the**    all the runners of a race

**filly**    female horse below the age of five

**firing**    method of treating tendon strains by the application of red-hot irons to the skin around the affected area

**foal**    colt, filly or gelding from the time of its birth until 31 December of the same year

**furlong**    220 yds

**gelding**    castrated horse

**going**    the condition of the ground; there are seven official descriptions: hard, firm, good to firm, good, good to soft, soft and heavy

**gone in its coat**    describes a horse which has started to grow its winter coat

**graduation race**    race designed to develop the capabilities of horses with limited experience

**green**    decribes an inexperienced horse, whose education in racing is incomplete

**hand**    4 inches, the unit in which a horse's height is measured

**handicap**    race in which every runner is allotted a weight in order to give all of them (in theory) an equal chance of winning

**handicapper, the**    official responsible for formulating and adjusting the weights carried by the horses in handicaps

**'Headquarters'**    Newmarket, the home of horse-racing

**hood**    similar to blinkers but leaves the eyes clear and covers the ears

**hunter chase**    steeplechase for horses which have been regularly hunted during the current season

**hurdle**    jump made of gorse and birch woven into a wooden frame impaled in the ground; it must be at least 3ft 6in from top to bottom

**Jockey Club, The**    controlling body of racing *c.* 1760

**Judge**    official responsible for declaring the finishers of a race and the distances between them

**Levy, The**    tax collected from punters through the bookmakers and distributed by the Horse-race Betting Levy Board (Levy Board) for the good of horse-racing

**long handicap, the**    allotted weights of all the horses entered for a particular race; these weights may go below the minimum weight set to be carried: horses with such weights are said to be 'out of the handicap'

**maiden race**    flat race for horses which have not won at starting

**mare**    female horse aged 5 or more

**National Hunt Flat Race**    flat races for four-, five- and six-year-olds who have not run under the Rules of Racing except in NH Flat Races; riders must be either amateurs or conditionals

**not off**    not trying to win

**nomination**    right to send a mare to be mated with a stallion in any one season

**novices' race**    a novice hurdle or steeplechase is a race for horses which have not won a hurdle or steeplechase respectively before the current season

**nursery**    handicap race for two-year-olds

**objection**    objection by jockey to another horse which he/she feels interferred with his/her mount during the race

**on the bit**    describes a horse going well within itself without being pushed along by the jockey, as opposed to 'off the bit'

**on the leg**   describes a horse that is too long in the leg in relation to its body

**open ditch**   plain fence with a ditch on the take-off side

**over the top**   describes a horse deemed to have passed its peak as a result of too much racing

**pacemaker**   a horse which leads and ensures a strong pace is set for a more fancied runner from the same connections

**Pattern, the**   Pattern races are the elite contests of both Flat and NH racing; flat races in the Pattern are graded: Groups one, two, three and Listed; NH races: Grades one, two and three (see pages 230–3)

**penalty**   weight added to the allotted handicap weight of a horse which has won since the weights were published

**penalty value**   total sum of money won by the winners' connections of a particular race, before mandatory deductions

**permit holder**   person entitled to train horses which are either his/her own property or his/her immediate family's property for steeplechases, hurdle or NH Flat races

**photo finish**   finish of a race that is decided by the Judge studying a photograph of the finish; called for by the Judge when the first two or more horses finish within a half-length of each other

**pin-hook**   practice of buying foals at the sales and then reselling them at the yearling sales

**plain fence**   jump no lower than 4ft 6in, usually made of birch with a gorse apron

**Racecourse Technical Services (RTS)**   body which provides the technology at race meetings (e.g. photo-finish equipment, electrical timing facilities, etc.)

*Racing Calendar, The*   weekly publication from Weatherbys listing official information relating to the organisation of racing (e.g. accounts of stewards' enquiries , big-race entries, etc.)

**retainer**   contract under which a jockey is retained to ride for a particular trainer or owner

**rig**   horse imperfectly gelded or in which only one testicle has descended; often difficult to train

**ring, the**   area where on-course bookmakers operate

**ringer**   horse of superior ability but similar appearance which is run in the place of another horse to deceive the public and bookmakers

**roaring**   harsh rasping noise made by horse's heavy breathing when galloping; caused by paralysis of the larynx

**run free**    describes a horse which goes too fast in the early part of a race

**run up light**    describes a horse which has lost condition of muscle through racing too much

**Satellite Information Services (SIS)**    body providing live television coverage of horse and greyhound races to betting shops and a few private subscribers

**schooled**    trained to jump

**selling race**    race where the winner is offered for sale at auction after the race, and in which the other runners may be claimed for the advertised sum or more

**Silver Ring, the**    racecourse enclosure so named because it was in silver (rather than notes) that people bet

**sire**    father of a horse

**soft palate disease**    when the junction between the larynx and the soft palate becomes unsealed causing the passage of air to be obstructed: the horse tends to 'swallow its tongue'.

**sore shins**    inflammation of the shins caused by fast work or racing on hard ground; prevalent in young horses

**spread a plate**    describes the incident when a horseshoe has come off or moved on the horse's foot; necessitates reshoeing

**stallion**    entire horse used for breeding

**Starter**    official responsible for starting a race, making sure all the horses have arrived at the start of a race, etc.

**Steward**    unpaid official responsible for seeing that the Rules of Racing are adhered to at every race meeting

**Stewards' Enquiry**    enquiry, by the Stewards, into the running of a race to ascertain whether any interference occurred

**Stewards' Secretary**    (colloq. 'stipe') official responsible for providing professional advice to the stewards

**supplement**    enter a horse in a race that has already closed by paying a large sum of money

**syndication**    the dividing of the ownership of a stallion into shares (usually forty) of equal value

**Tattersalls Sales**    yearling sales held at Newmarket in October by the famous bloodstock auctioneers

**teaser**    stallion used to gauge a brood mare's sexual response and to prepare her for the stallion with whom she is to mate

**Tote**    body that runs totalisator system of betting; the pooled money is shared out between those who have won and running costs, which include contributions to the Levy Board and racecourses

**Timeform squiggle** sign used by Timeform to denote an unreliable or difficult horse

**tucked up** describes a horse which is tightly drawn-up round the abdomen; suggests that the horse has been overworked, is ill, or has not been well looked after

**tubing** operation whereby a hole is made in a horse's neck and a metal tube is inserted in order to bypass a defective larynx

**valet** person who takes care of a jockey's equipment (clothes, saddle, etc.) during and after racing

**virus** varieties of equine flu

**visor** pair of blinkers with a slit or hole cut in each of the shields to allow a small amount of lateral vision

**walk-over** race with only one runner; this horse must weigh in and out and must cross the finishing line, although it does not have to run the entire distance of the race

**water jump** small plain fence with water on landing side

**Weatherbys** racing's civil service, responsible for the day-to-day running

**weaver** a horse which expends nervous energy by swinging his head from side to side

**weigh in/out** weighing of jockey before and after a race to ensure that the horse carries the correct weight

**weight-for-age race** any race that is not a handicap

**weight-for-age scale** scale devised by Admiral Henry John Rous to allot weights to horses of different ages to compensate for the immaturity of younger horses

**whistler** a horse which makes a wind noise indicating a defective larynx

**yearling** a colt, filly or gelding from 1 January to 31 December of the year following its birth

# A BETTING GLOSSARY

**accumulator**   bet involving several horses where the returns from each successive winning selection are invested on the next

**across the card**   used of races run at the same time at different meetings

**ante-post**   betting prior to the day of the race, and for some big races many months in advance

**any to come**   term instructing the whole or part of the returns of one bet to be automatically reinvested on another

**bar**   term concerning the lowest odds of those horses not quoted in a betting show – so '33–1 bar' means that the horses not quoted in the show are at 33–1 or longer

**beeswax**   betting tax

**blower**   telephone line through which off-course bookmakers put money into the on-course market

**board price**   price available in betting shops during the pre-race exchanges and displayed on the screen or board, which the punter has the option of taking regardless of the horse's starting price

**bogey**   the biggest loser in a bookmaker's book

**bottle**   2–1

**Burlington Bertie**   100–30

**Canadian**   five selections combined as ten doubles, ten trebles, five fourfolds and one fivefold – twenty-six bets: a £1 Canadian (also known as a Super Yankee) would cost £26

**carpet**   3–1

**century**   £100

**computer straight forecast (CSF)**   bet involving the prediction of the first two home in a race in the correct finishing order

**double**   bet involving two selections in different races, where the win-

nings and stake from the first, if that horse is successful, go on to the
second
**double carpet**   33–1

**each way**   one bet on the horse to win and another on it to be placed
**ear 'ole**   6–4

**face**   5–2
**faces**   especially well-informed punters, whose faces are familiar to the
bookmakers
**fiddlers**   bookies who will lay only small bets
**flimping**   giving under the odds
**forecast**   naming the first two horse in the race in correct order (straight
forecast) or either order (dual forecast)

**Goliath**   bet involving 247 combinations with 8 selections in separate
events: 28 doubles, 56 trebles, 70 fourfolds, 56 fivefolds, 28 sixfolds, 8
sevenfolds and one eightfold
**grand**   £1000

**hand**   5–1
**Heinz**   bet combining six selections in different races in 57 bets: 15
doubles, 20 trebles, 15 fourfolds, 6 fivefolds, and one sixfold

**jolly**   the favourite

**kite**   cheque

**laying off**   a bookmaker reducing his liability on a horse by himself
backing it with other bookmakers
**levels**   evens
**Lucky 15**   fifteen-bet wager consisting of a Yankee (six doubles, four
trebles and one four-horse acccumulator) plus singles on each of the
four selections; if only one of the selections wins the odds of that
winner are doubled

**monkey**   £500

**nap**   newspaper correspondent's best bet of the day
**net**   10–1
**neves**   7–1

**on the shoulders**    9–2

**over-broke**    betting without a profit margin for the bookmaker

**over-round**    betting with a profit margin for the bookmaker

**Patent**    bet combining three horses in different races in seven separate wagers: 3 singles, 3 doubles and one treble

**pony**    £25

**rag**    rank outsider

**rick**    error

**rouf**    4–1 (pronounced 'rofe')

**Rule 4**    the betting rule which stipulates how much money is to be deducted from winning bets when a horse is withdrawn from a race too late for a new market to be formed

**score**    £20

**shoulder**    7–4

**skinner**    a horse not backed

**sleeper**    uncollected winnings

**steamer**    horse whose odds shorten significantly on the morning of race following heavy support

**Super Heinz**    bet combining seven selections in different races in 120 bets: 21 doubles, 35 trebles, 35 fourfolds, 21 fivefolds, 7 sixfolds and one sevenfold

**super yankee**    see 'Canadian'

**tic-tac**    sign language through which on-course bookmakers communicate with each other

**tips**    11–10

**tissue**    course bookmakers' forecast of how the betting will open

**ton**    £100

**top of the head**    9–4

**treble**    a bet combining three horses in three different races

**tricast**    a bet selecting the first three in correct order in handicaps of eight or more declared runners and no fewer than six actual runners

**Trixie**    multiple bet involving three selections in different events – three doubles and one treble

**up the arm**    11–8

**with the thumb**    raising the thumb in tic-tac to indicate that the price quoted is being taken by the punters

**wrist**  5–4

**Yankee**  bet combining four horses in seperate events in eleven bets –
six doubles, four trebles and one four-horse accumulator

# WINNERS
# OF BIG RACES

This section lists the winners of major races since the Second World War. It includes all Group One events on the Flat in Britain, along with other significant weight-for-age races and the most famous handicaps; the high points of the National Hunt season; and the races in Ireland, France and the USA which command most interest from British racing fans.

For the five English Classics, Champion Hurdle, Cheltenham Gold Cup, Grand National and Prix de l'Arc de Triomphe, winners are listed since 1900 or the first running of the race, whichever is the earlier.

# THE FLAT
## Lincoln Handicap

DONCASTER                         I MILE                    FIRST RUN 1849

| Year | Horse | Trainer | Jockey | SP | RAN |
|------|-------|---------|--------|----|----|
| 1946 | LANGTON ABBOT | C. Elsey | T. Weston | 7/1 | 37 |
| 1947 | JOCKEY TREBLE | W. Smallwood | E. Mercer | 100/1 | 46 |
| 1948 | COMMISSAR | A. Budgett | W. Rickaby | 33/1 | 58 |
| 1949 | FAIR JUDGEMENT | J. Jarvis | E. Smith | 6/1 | 43 |
| 1950 | DRAMATIC | G. Todd | G. Richards | 7/1 | 40 |
| 1951 | BARNES PARK | G. Boyd | J. Sime | 33/1 | 35 |
| 1952 | PHARIZA | J. Powell | D. Forte | 33/1 | 40 |
| 1953 | SAILING LIGHT | G. Armstrong | A. Roberts | 100/8 | 41 |
| 1954 | NAHAR | A. Head | J. Massard | 100/7 | 32 |
| 1955 | MILITARY COURT | H. Wragg | E. Mercer | 8/1 | 29 |
| 1956 | THREE STAR II | H. Davison | D. Morris | 40/1 | 41 |
| 1957 | BABUR | C. Elsey | E. Hide | 25/1 | 32 |
| 1958 | BABUR | C. Elsey | E. Britt | 25/1 | 37 |
| 1959 | MARSHALL PIL | S. Hall | P. Robinson | 15/2 | 32 |
| 1960 | MUSTAVON | S. Hall | N. McIntosh | 8/1 | 31 |
| 1961 | JOHNS COURT | E. Cousins | B. Lee | 25/1 | 37 |
| 1962 | HILL ROYAL | E. Cousins | J. Sime | 50/1 | 40 |
| 1963 | MONAWIN | R. Mason | J. Sime | 25/1 | 40 |
| 1964 | MIGHTY GURKHA | E. Lambton | P. Robinson | 33/1 | 45 |

| Year | Horse | Trainer | Jockey | SP | RAN |
|------|-------|---------|--------|-----|-----|
| 1965 | OLD TOM | M.H. Easterby | A. Breasley | 22/1 | 38 |
| 1966 | RIOT ACT | F. Armstrong | A. Breasley | 8/1 | 49 |
| 1967 | BEN NOVUS | W. Hide | P. Robinson | 22/1 | 24 |
| 1968 | FRANKINCENSE | J. Oxley | G. Starkey | 100/8 | 31 |
| 1969 | FOGGY BELL | D. Smith | A. Barclay | 20/1 | 25 |
| 1970 | NEW CHAPTER | F. Armstrong | A. Barclay | 100/9 | 23 |
| 1971 | DOUBLE CREAM | W. Elsey | E. Hide | 30/1 | 26 |
| 1972 | SOVEREIGN BILL | P. Robinson | E. Hide | 9/2 | 21 |
| 1973 | BRONZE HILL | M.H. Easterby | M. Birch | 50/1 | 26 |
| 1974 | QUIZAIR | R. Jarvis | M. Thomas | 28/1 | 26 |
| 1975 | SOUTHWARK STAR | G. Peter-Hoblyn | R. Fox | 33/1 | 24 |
| 1976 | THE HERTFORD | B. Swift | G. Lewis | 20/1 | 26 |
| 1977 | BLUSTERY | M. Smyly | D. McKay | 20/1 | 26 |
| 1978 | CAPTAIN'S WINGS | R. Boss | M. Wigham | 13/2 | 25 |
| 1979 | FAIR SEASON | I. Balding | G. Starkey | 8/1 | 23 |
| 1980 | KING'S RIDE | W. Wightman | G. Baxter | 10/1 | 18 |
| 1981 | SAHER | R. Sheather | R. Cochrane | 14/1 | 19 |
| 1982 | KING'S GLORY | P. Mitchell | B. Crossley | 11/1 | 26 |
| 1983 | MIGHTY FLY | D. Elsworth | S. Cauthen | 14/1 | 26 |
| 1984 | SAVING MERCY | D. Weld | W. R. Swinburn | 14/1 | 26 |
| 1985 | CATALDI | G. Harwood | G. Starkey | 10/1 | 26 |
| 1986 | K-BATTERY | C. Elsey | J. Lowe | 25/1 | 25 |
| 1987 | STAR OF A GUNNER | R. Holder | J. Reid | 9/1 | 25 |
| 1988 | CUVEE CHARLIE | H. Collingridge | M. Rimmer | 33/1 | 25 |
| 1989 | FACT FINDER | R. Akehurst | T. Williams | 20/1 | 25 |
| 1990 | EVICHSTAR | J. FitzGerald | A. Munro | 33/1 | 24 |
| 1991 | AMENABLE | T.D. Barron | Alex Greaves | 22/1 | 25 |

## *Nell Gwyn Stakes*

NEWMARKET            7 FURLONGS            FIRST RUN 1962

| Year | Horse | Trainer | Jockey | SP | RAN |
|------|-------|---------|--------|-----|-----|
| 1962 | WEST SIDE STORY | T. Leader | E. Smith | 5/4 | 6 |
| 1963 | AMICABLE | C. Boyd-Rochfort | W. Carr | 100/7 | 12 |
| 1964 | ALBORADA | J. Oxley | G. Starkey | 9/4 | 6 |
| 1965 | GENTLY | G. Richards | A. Breasley | 7/4 | 4 |
| 1966 | HIDING PLACE | J. Clayton | A. Breasley | 4/1 | 11 |
| 1967 | CRANBERRY SAUCE | N. Murless | G. Moore | 7/4 | 9 |
| 1968 | ABBIE WEST | N. Murless | A. Barclay | 10/11 | 4 |
| 1969 | ANCHOR | J. Oxley | G. Starkey | 7/4 | 7 |
| 1970 | OBELISK | N. Murless | A. Barclay | 6/1 | 13 |
| 1971 | SUPER HONEY | H. R. Price | L. Piggott | 3/1 | 4 |
| 1972 | CAREZZA | B. van Cutsem | W. Carson | 4/5 | 5 |
| 1973 | CASPIAN | H. Cecil | G. Starkey | 4/7 | 7 |

| YEAR | HORSE | TRAINER | JOCKEY | SP | RAN |
|------|-------|---------|--------|-----|-----|
| 1974 | ANGELS TWO | W. Elsey | E. Hide | 11/1 | 7 |
| 1975 | ROSE BOWL | R.F. J. Houghton | L. Piggott | 7/4 | 10 |
| 1976 | FLYING WATER | A. Penna | Y. Saint-Martin | 15/8 | 10 |
| 1977 | FREEZE THE SECRET | L. Cumani | G. Dettori | 11/2 | 12 |
| 1978 | SERAPHIMA | P. Walwyn | P. Eddery | 9/2 | 9 |
| 1979 | ONE IN A MILLION | H. Cecil | J. Mercer | 8/13 | 8 |
| 1980 | EVITA | H. Cecil | J. Mercer | 7/2 | 11 |
| 1981 | FAIRY FOOTSTEPS | H. Cecil | L. Piggott | 4/6 | 9 |
| 1982 | CHALON | H. Cecil | L. Piggott | 8/1 | 12 |
| 1983 | FAVORIDGE | G. Wragg | P. Eddery | 13/8 | 9 |
| 1984 | PEBBLES | C. Brittain | P. Robinson | 7/1 | 9 |
| 1985 | OH SO SHARP | H. Cecil | S. Cauthen | 8/13 | 8 |
| 1986 | SONIC LADY | M. Stoute | W. R. Swinburn | 13/8 | 9 |
| 1987 | MARTHA STEVENS | H. Cecil | S. Cauthen | 4/1 | 6 |
| 1988 | GHARIBA | A. Stewart | M. Roberts | 11/2 | 10 |
| 1989 | ENSCONSE | L. Cumani | R. Cochrane | 2/1 | 8 |
| 1990 | HEART OF JOY | M. Stoute | W. R. Swinburn | 5/6 | 6 |
| 1991 | CRYSTAL GAZING | L. Cumani | L. Dettori | 6/4 | 5 |

## Craven Stakes

NEWMARKET                 I MILE                 FIRST RUN 1878

| YEAR | HORSE | TRAINER | JOCKEY | SP | RAN |
|------|-------|---------|--------|-----|-----|
| 1946 | GULF STREAM | W. Earl | H. Wragg | 1/8 | 8 |
| 1947 | MIGOLI | F. Butters | D. Smith | 4/11 | 6 |
| 1948 | MY BABU | F. Armstrong | C. Smirke | 4/7 | 9 |
| 1949 | MOONDUST | F. Butters | D. Smith | 7/1 | 8 |
| 1950 | RISING FLAME | C. Elsey | G. Littlewood | 100/30 | 6 |
| 1951 | CLAUDIUS | R. Warden | D. Page | 20/1 | 13 |
| 1952 | KARA TEPE | G. Colling | E. Mercer | 6/1 | 11 |
| 1953 | OLEANDRIN | H. Leader | G. Richards | 4/1 | 7 |
| 1954 | AMBLER II | C. Boyd-Rochfort | W. Carr | 6/1 | 8 |
| 1955 | TRUE CAVALIER | H. Leader | R. Fawdon | 8/1 | 9 |
| 1956 | PIRATE KING | H. Cottrill | W. Snaith | 100/8 | 15 |
| 1957 | SHEARWATER | N. Murless | L. Piggott | 10/1 | 7 |
| 1958 | BALD EAGLE | C. Boyd-Rochfort | W. Carr | 7/2 | 6 |
| 1959 | PINDARI | N. Murless | L. Piggott | 6/1 | 7 |
| 1960 | TUDORICH | G. Richards | A. Breasley | 11/4 | 13 |
| 1961 | AURELIUS | N. Murless | L. Piggott | 8/1 | 6 |
| 1962 | HIGH NOON | W. Elsey | E. Hide | 5/2 | 7 |
| 1963 | CROCKET | G. Brooke | D. Smith | 4/11 | 5 |
| 1964 | YOUNG CHRISTOPHER | F. Maxwell | R. Sheather | 100/7 | 12 |
| 1965 | CORIFI | S. Ingham | G. Lewis | 20/1 | 7 |
| 1966 | SALVO | H. Wragg | F. Durr | 3/1 | 11 |

# THE RACING YEAR 1991

An unruffled Generous after the Ever Ready Derby.

The Guineas. *Above* Willie Carson pushes Shadayid clear of Lester Piggott and Kooyonga in the General Accident One Thousand Guineas. The Two Thousand Guineas (*below*) is a much closer affair, with Mystiko (Michael Roberts, rails) holding off Lycius (Steve Cauthen) by a head. On the extreme left is Generous (Richard Quinn), who finished fourth.

A shock in the Gold Seal Oaks (*above*) as Christy Roche brings the 50–1
'rag' Jet Ski Lady storming home. But the Coalite St Leger (*below*) goes
to the favourite: Pat Eddery and Toulon (left) wear down John Reid and
Saddlers' Hall in the closing stages.

Early on in the Whitbread Gold Cup, the Grand National winner Seagram (Nigel Hawke) leads Docklands Express (Anthony Tory) and Cahervillahow (Charlie Swan).

Star turns in the two great European middle-distance races: Alan Munro
celebrates a breathtaking surge from Generous in the King George VI
and Queen Elizabeth Diamond Stakes at Ascot (*above*),
and Cash Asmussen steers Suave Dancer home to a no less impressive
victory over Magic Night (Alain Badel) in the Ciga Prix
de l'Arc de Triomphe (*below*).

The Breeders' Cup at Churchill Downs, Kentucky: Sheikh Albadou and Pat Eddery (*above*) turn the Sprint into a procession, and four races later Arazi (Pat Valenzuela) produces one of the all-time great performances in the Juvenile (*below*).

Suave Dancer after the Prix du Jockey-Club Lancia at Chantilly.

| YEAR | HORSE | TRAINER | JOCKEY | SP | RAN |
|------|-------|---------|--------|----|----|
| 1967 | SLOOP | J. Oxley | G. Starkey | 7/1 | 11 |
| 1968 | PETINGO | F. Armstrong | J. Mercer | 2/5 | 4 |
| 1969 | PADDY'S PROGRESS | N. Murless | A. Barclay | 13/2 | 8 |
| 1970 | TAMIL | B. van Cutsem | W. Carson | 11/10 | 9 |
| 1971 | LEVANTER | H. R. Price | A. Murray | 9/2 | 6 |
| 1972 | LEICESTER | N. Murless | G. Lewis | 8/1 | 5 |
| 1973 | MY DRIFTER | J. Sutcliffe, jr | E. Eldin | 25/1 | 14 |
| 1974 | NUMA | P. Walwyn | P. Eddery | 9/4 | 12 |
| 1975 | NO ALIMONY | P. Walwyn | P. Eddery | 6/5 | 10 |
| 1976 | MALINOWSKI | M. V. O'Brien | L. Piggott | 8/15 | 7 |
| 1977 | LIMONE | G. Harwood | G. Starkey | 10/1 | 9 |
| 1978 | ADMIRAL'S LAUNCH | W. R. Hern | W. Carson | 2/1 | 10 |
| 1979 | LYPHARD'S WISH | H. Cecil | J. Mercer | 11/2 | 3 |
| 1980 | TYRNAVOS | B. Hobbs | E. Hide | 5/1 | 9 |
| 1981 | KIND OF HUSH | B. Hills | S. Cauthen | 25/1 | 9 |
| 1982 | SILVER HAWK | M. Albina | A. Murray | 11/2 | 9 |
| 1983 | MUSCATITE | J. Hindley | B. Taylor | 7/2 | 5 |
| 1984 | LEAR FAN | G. Harwood | G. Starkey | 5/6 | 5 |
| 1985 | SHADEED | M. Stoute | W. R. Swinburn | 9/4 | 6 |
| 1986 | DANCING BRAVE | G. Harwood | G. Starkey | 11/8 | 11 |
| 1987 | AJDAL | M. Stoute | W. R. Swinburn | 6/5 | 6 |
| 1988 | DOYOUN | M. Stoute | W. R. Swinburn | 100/30 | 5 |
| 1989 | SHAADI | M. Stoute | W. R. Swinburn | 5/2 | 5 |
| 1990 | TIROL | R. Hannon | P. Eddery | 9/2 | 6 |
| 1991 | MARJU | J. Dunlop | W. Carson | 11/2 | 8 |

## Forte Mile

SANDOWN PARK      1 MILE      FIRST RUN 1985

| YEAR | HORSE | TRAINER | JOCKEY | SP | RAN |
|------|-------|---------|--------|----|----|
| 1985 | PEBBLES | C. Brittain | S. Cauthen | 11/8 | 7 |
| 1986 | FIELD HAND | B. Hills | B. Thomson | 11/2 | 7 |
| 1987 | VERTIGE | P. Biancone | A. Cruz | 8/1 | 8 |
| 1988 | SOVIET STAR | A. Fabre | C. Asmussen | 5/4 | 6 |
| 1989 | REPRIMAND | H. Cecil | S. Cauthen | 7/4 | 5 |
| 1990 | MARKOFDISTINCTION | L. Cumani | L. Dettori | 9/2 | 7 |
| 1991 | IN THE GROOVE | D. Elsworth | S. Cauthen | 15/8 | 5 |

## Classic Trial

SANDOWN PARK      1 MILE 2 FURLONGS      FIRST RUN 1953

| YEAR | HORSE | TRAINER | JOCKEY | SP | RAN |
|------|-------|---------|--------|-----|-----|
| 1953 | MOUNTAIN KING | J. Waugh | E. Smith | 8/1 | 9 |
| 1954 | TAW VALLEY | G. Barling | E. Smith | 20/1 | 5 |
| 1955 | PETER AEGUS | J. Jarvis | W. Rickaby | 10/1 | 8 |
| 1956 | PEARL ORAMA | S. Ingham | A. Breasley | 8/1 | 13 |
| 1957 | SUN CHARGER | N. Murless | L. Piggott | 7/1 | 9 |
| 1958 | SNOW CAT | N. Murless | L. Piggott | 11/2 | 7 |
| 1959 | CASQUE | H. Blagrave | A. Breasley | 20/1 | 7 |
| 1960 | MARENGO | M. Marsh | R. Fawdon | 6/1 | 13 |
| 1961 | JUST GREAT | S. Ingham | G. Lewis | 7/2 | 11 |
| 1962 | FERNELEY | N. Murless | L. Piggott | 4/1 | 8 |
| 1963 | RAISE YOU TEN | C. Boyd-Rochfort | W. Carr | 100/8 | 7 |
| 1964 | ONCIDIUM | J. Waugh | E. Smith | 7/2 | 14 |
| 1965 | NEARSIDE | W. R. Hern | J. Mercer | 11/8 | 7 |
| 1966 | MEHARI | J. Winter | D. Smith | 10/1 | 13 |
| 1967 | SUN ROCK | N. Murless | L. Piggott | 9/4 | 7 |
| 1968 | SAFETY MARCH | J. Oxley | G. Starkey | 100/8 | 7 |
| 1969 | SHOEMAKER | P. Walwyn | D. Keith | 11/2 | 12 |
| 1970 | CRY BABY | N. Murless | A. Barclay | 9/1 | 5 |
| 1971 | L'APACHE | T. Gosling | A. Murray | 33/1 | 10 |
| 1972 | PENTLAND FIRTH | G. Barling | P. Eddery | 5/2 | 9 |
| 1973 | KSAR | B. van Cutsem | W. Carson | 8/15 | 6 |
| 1974 | BUSTINO | W. R. Hern | J. Mercer | 5/2 | 9 |
| 1975 | CONSOL | P. Walwyn | P. Eddery | 10/11 | 9 |
| 1976 | RIBOBOY | W. R. Hern | J. Mercer | 9/2 | 7 |
| 1977 | ARTAIUS | M. V. O'Brien | L. Piggott | evens | 5 |
| 1978 | WHITSTEAD | H. R. Price | B. Taylor | 9/2 | 8 |
| 1979 | TROY | W. R. Hern | W. Carson | 4/7 | 5 |
| 1980 | HENBIT | W. R. Hern | W. Carson | 9/4 | 6 |
| 1981 | SHERGAR | M. Stoute | W. R. Swinburn | evens | 9 |
| 1982 | PEACETIME | J. Tree | P. Eddery | 9/2 | 11 |
| 1983 | GORDIAN | G. Harwood | G. Starkey | 10/1 | 7 |
| 1984 | ALPHABATIM | G. Harwood | B. Rouse | 4/1 | 8 |
| 1985 | DAMISTER | J. Tree | S. Cauthen | 10/11 | 4 |
| 1986 | SHAHRASTANI | M. Stoute | W. R. Swinburn | 2/1 | 4 |
| 1987 | GULF KING | P. Kelleway | P. Cook | 25/1 | 8 |
| 1988 | GALITZIN | C. Brittain | R. Cochrane | 11/2 | 5 |
| 1989 | OLD VIC | H. Cecil | S. Cauthen | 4/9 | 3 |
| 1990 | DEFENSIVE PLAY | G. Harwood | P. Eddery | 7/4 | 6 |
| 1991 | HAILSHAM | C. Brittain | M. Roberts | 3/1 | 5 |

# One Thousand Guineas

| YEAR | HORSE | TRAINER | JOCKEY | SP | RAN |
|------|-------|---------|--------|-----|-----|
| 1900 | WINIFREDA | T. Jennings, jr | S. Loates | 11/2 | 10 |
| 1901 | AÏDA | G. Blackwell | D. Maher | 13/8 | 15 |
| 1902 | SCEPTRE | R. Sievier | H. Randall | 1/2 | 15 |
| 1903 | QUINTESSENCE | J. Chandler | H. Randall | 4/1 | 12 |
| 1904 | PRETTY POLLY | P. Gilpin | W. Lane | 1/4 | 7 |
| 1905 | CHERRY LASS | W. Robinson | G. McCall | 5/4 | 19 |
| 1906 | FLAIR | P. Gilpin | B. Dillon | 11/10 | 12 |
| 1907 | WITCH ELM | W. Robinson | B. Lynham | 4/1 | 17 |
| 1908 | RHODORA | J. Allen | L. Lyne | 100/8 | 19 |
| 1909 | ELECTRA | P. Gilpin | B. Dillon | 9/1 | 10 |
| 1910 | WINKIPOP | W. Waugh | B. Lynham | 5/2 | 13 |
| 1911 | ATMAH | F. Pratt | F. Fox | 7/1 | 16 |
| 1912 | TAGALIE | D. Waugh | L. Hewitt | 20/1 | 13 |
| 1913 | JEST | C. Morton | F. Rickaby, jr | 9/1 | 22 |
| 1914 | PRINCESS DORRIE | C. Morton | W. Huxley | 100/9 | 13 |
| 1915 | VAUCLUSE | F. Hartigan | F. Rickaby, jr | 5/2 | 15 |
| 1916 | CANYON | G. Lambton | F. Rickaby, jr | 9/2 | 10 |
| 1917 | DIADEM | G. Lambton | F. Rickaby, jr | 6/4 | 14 |
| 1918 | FERRY | G. Lambton | B. Carslake | 50/1 | 8 |
| 1919 | ROSEWAY | F. Hartigan | A. Whalley | 2/1 | 15 |
| 1920 | CINNA | R. Waugh | W. Griggs | 4/1 | 21 |
| 1921 | BETTINA | P. Linton | G. Bellhouse | 33/1 | 24 |
| 1922 | SILVER URN | H. Persse | B. Carslake | 10/1 | 20 |
| 1923 | TRANQUIL | G. Lambton | E. Gardner | 5/2 | 16 |
| 1924 | PLACK | J. Jarvis | C. Elliott | 8/1 | 16 |
| 1925 | SAUCY SUE | A. Taylor, jr | F. Bullock | 1/4 | 11 |
| 1926 | PILLION | J. Watson | R. Perryman | 25/1 | 29 |
| 1927 | CRESTA RUN | P. Gilpin | A. Balding | 10/1 | 28 |
| 1928 | SCUTTLE | W. Jarvis | J. Childs | 15/8 | 14 |
| 1929 | TAJ MAH | J. Torterolo | W. Sibbritt | 33/1 | 19 |
| 1930 | FAIR ISLE | F. Butters | T. Weston | 7/4 | 19 |
| 1931 | FOUR COURSE | F. Darling | C. Elliott | 100/9 | 20 |
| 1932 | KANDY | F. Carter | C. Elliott | 33/1 | 19 |
| 1933 | BROWN BETTY | C. Boyd-Rochfort | J. Childs | 8/1 | 22 |
| 1934 | CAMPANULA | J. Jarvis | H. Wragg | 2/5 | 10 |
| 1935 | MESA | A. Swann | W. Johnstone | 8/1 | 22 |
| 1936 | TIDE-WAY | C. Leader | R. Perryman | 100/30 | 22 |
| 1937 | EXHIBITIONIST | J. Lawson | S. Donoghue | 10/1 | 20 |
| 1938 | ROCKFEL | O. Bell | S. Wragg | 8/1 | 20 |
| 1939 | GALATEA | J. Lawson | R. Jones | 6/1 | 18 |
| 1940 | GODIVA | W. Jarvis | D. Marks | 10/1 | 11 |
| 1941 | DANCING TIME | J. Lawson | R. Perryman | 100/8 | 13 |
| 1942 | SUN CHARIOT | F. Darling | G. Richards | evens | 18 |
| 1943 | HERRINGBONE | W. Earl | H. Wragg | 15/2 | 12 |
| 1944 | PICTURE PLAY | J. Watts | C. Elliott | 15/2 | 11 |
| 1945 | SUN STREAM | W. Earl | H. Wragg | 5/2 | 14 |

| YEAR | HORSE | TRAINER | JOCKEY | SP | RAN |
|------|-------|---------|--------|-----|-----|
| 1946 | HYPERICUM | C. Boyd-Rochfort | D. Smith | 100/6 | 13 |
| 1947 | IMPRUDENCE | J. Lieux | W. Johnstone | 4/1 | 20 |
| 1948 | QUEENPOT | N. Murless | G. Richards | 6/1 | 22 |
| 1949 | MUSIDORA | C. Elsey | E. Britt | 100/8 | 18 |
| 1950 | CAMARÉE | A. Lieux | W. Johnstone | 10/1 | 17 |
| 1951 | BELLE OF ALL | N. Bertie | G. Richards | 4/1 | 18 |
| 1952 | ZABARA | V. Smyth | K. Gethin | 7/1 | 20 |
| 1953 | HAPPY LAUGHTER | J. Jarvis | E. Mercer | 10/1 | 14 |
| 1954 | FESTOON | N. Cannon | A. Breasley | 9/2 | 12 |
| 1955 | MELD | C. Boyd-Rochfort | W. Carr | 11/4 | 12 |
| 1956 | HONEYLIGHT | C. Elsey | E. Britt | 100/6 | 19 |
| 1957 | ROSE ROYALE | A. Head | C. Smirke | 6/1 | 20 |
| 1958 | BELLA PAOLA | F. Mathet | S. Boullenger | 8/11 | 11 |
| 1959 | PETITE ETOILE | N. Murless | D. Smith | 8/1 | 14 |
| 1960 | NEVER TOO LATE | E. Pollet | R. Poincelet | 8/11 | 14 |
| 1961 | SWEET SOLERA | R. Day | W. Rickaby | 4/1 | 14 |
| 1962 | ABERMAID | H. Wragg | W. Williamson | 100/6 | 14 |
| 1963 | HULA DANCER | E. Pollet | R. Poincelet | 1/2 | 12 |
| 1964 | POURPARLER | P. Prendergast | G. Bougoure | 11/2 | 18 |
| 1965 | NIGHT OFF | W. Wharton | W. Williamson | 9/2 | 16 |
| 1966 | GLAD RAGS | M. V. O'Brien | P. Cook | 100/6 | 21 |
| 1967 | FLEET | N. Murless | G. Moore | 11/2 | 16 |
| 1968 | CAERGWRLE | N. Murless | A. Barclay | 4/1 | 19 |
| 1969 | FULL DRESS II | H. Wragg | R. Hutchinson | 7/1 | 13 |
| 1970 | HUMBLE DUTY | P. Walwyn | L. Piggott | 3/1 | 12 |
| 1971 | ALTESSE ROYALE | N. Murless | Y. Saint-Martin | 25/1 | 10 |
| 1972 | WATERLOO | J. Watts | E. Hide | 8/1 | 18 |
| 1973 | MYSTERIOUS | N. Murless | G. Lewis | 11/1 | 14 |
| 1974 | HIGHCLERE | W. R. Hern | J. Mercer | 12/1 | 15 |
| 1975 | NOCTURNAL SPREE | H. Murless | J. Roe | 14/1 | 16 |
| 1976 | FLYING WATER | A. Penna | Y. Saint-Martin | 2/1 | 25 |
| 1977 | MRS McARDY | M. W. Easterby | E. Hide | 16/1 | 18 |
| 1978 | ENSTONE SPARK | B. Hills | E. Johnson | 35/1 | 16 |
| 1979 | ONE IN A MILLION | H. Cecil | J. Mercer | evens | 17 |
| 1980 | QUICK AS LIGHTNING | J. Dunlop | B. Rouse | 12/1 | 23 |
| 1981 | FAIRY FOOTSTEPS | H. Cecil | L. Piggott | 6/4 | 14 |
| 1982 | ON THE HOUSE | H. Wragg | J. Reid | 33/1 | 15 |
| 1983 | MA BICHE | Mme C. Head | F. Head | 5/2 | 18 |
| 1984 | PEBBLES | C. Brittain | P. Robinson | 8/1 | 15 |
| 1985 | OH SO SHARP | H. Cecil | S. Cauthen | 2/1 | 17 |
| 1986 | MIDWAY LADY | B. Hanbury | R. Cochrane | 10/1 | 15 |
| 1987 | MIESQUE | F. Boutin | F. Head | 15/8 | 14 |
| 1988 | RAVINELLA | Mme C. Head | G. Moore | 4/5 | 12 |
| 1989 | MUSICAL BLISS | M. Stoute | W. R. Swinburn | 7/2 | 7 |
| 1990 | SALSABIL | J. Dunlop | W. Carson | 6/4 | 10 |
| 1991 | SHADAYID | J. Dunlop | W. Carson | 4/6 | 14 |

# Two Thousand Guineas

NEWMARKET       1 MILE       FIRST RUN 1809

| YEAR | HORSE | TRAINER | JOCKEY | SP | RAN |
|------|-------|---------|--------|-----|-----|
| 1900 | DIAMOND JUBILEE | R. Marsh | H. Jones | 11/4 | 10 |
| 1901 | HANDICAPPER | F. Day | W. Halsey | 33/1 | 17 |
| 1902 | SCEPTRE | R. Sievier | H. Randall | 4/1 | 14 |
| 1903 | ROCK SAND | G. Blackwell | J. Martin | 6/4 | 11 |
| 1904 | ST AMANT | A. Hayhoe | K. Cannon | 11/4 | 14 |
| 1905 | VEDAS | W. Robinson | H. Jones | 11/2 | 13 |
| 1906 | GORGOS | R. Marsh | H. Jones | 20/1 | 12 |
| 1907 | SLIEVE GALLION | S. Darling | W. Higgs | 4/11 | 10 |
| 1908 | NORMAN | J. Watson | O. Madden | 25/1 | 17 |
| 1909 | MINORU | R. Marsh | H. Jones | 4/1 | 11 |
| 1910 | NEIL GOW | P. Peck | D. Maher | 2/1 | 13 |
| 1911 | SUNSTAR | C. Morton | G. Stern | 5/1 | 14 |
| 1912 | SWEEPER | H. Persse | D. Maher | 6/1 | 14 |
| 1913 | LOUVOIS | D. Waugh | J. Reiff | 25/1 | 15 |
| 1914 | KENNYMORE | A. Taylor, jr | G. Stern | 2/1 | 18 |
| 1915 | POMMERN | C. Peck | S. Donoghue | 2/1 | 16 |
| 1916 | CLARISSIMUS | W. Waugh | J. Clark | 100/7 | 17 |
| 1917 | GAY CRUSADER | A. Taylor, jr | S. Donoghue | 9/4 | 14 |
| 1918 | GAINSBOROUGH | A. Taylor, jr | J. Childs | 4/1 | 13 |
| 1919 | THE PANTHER | G. Manser | R. Cooper | 10/1 | 12 |
| 1920 | TETRATEMA | H. Persse | B. Carslake | 2/1 | 17 |
| 1921 | CRAIG AN ERAN | A. Taylor, jr | J. Brennan | 100/6 | 26 |
| 1922 | ST LOUIS | P. Gilpin | G. Archibald | 6/1 | 22 |
| 1923 | ELLANGOWAN | J. Jarvis | C. Elliott | 7/1 | 18 |
| 1924 | DIOPHON | R. Dawson | G. Hulme | 11/2 | 20 |
| 1925 | MANNA | F. Darling | S. Donoghue | 100/8 | 13 |
| 1926 | COLORADO | G. Lambton | T. Weston | 100/8 | 19 |
| 1927 | ADAM'S APPLE | H. Cottrill | J. Leach | 20/1 | 23 |
| 1928 | FLAMINGO | J. Jarvis | C. Elliott | 5/1 | 17 |
| 1929 | MR JINKS | H. Persse | H. Beasley | 5/2 | 22 |
| 1930 | DIOLITE | F. Templeman | F. Fox | 10/1 | 28 |
| 1931 | CAMERONIAN | F. Darling | J. Childs | 100/8 | 24 |
| 1932 | ORWELL | J. Lawson | R. Jones | evens | 11 |
| 1933 | RODOSTO | H. Count | R. Brethès | 9/1 | 27 |
| 1934 | COLOMBO | T. Hogg | W. Johnstone | 2/7 | 12 |
| 1935 | BAHRAM | F. Butters | F. Fox | 7/2 | 16 |
| 1936 | PAY UP | J. Lawson | R. Dick | 11/2 | 19 |
| 1937 | LE KSAR | F. Carter | C. Semblat | 20/1 | 18 |
| 1938 | PASCH | F. Darling | G. Richards | 5/2 | 18 |
| 1939 | BLUE PETER | J. Jarvis | E. Smith | 5/1 | 25 |
| 1940 | DJEBEL | A. Swann | C. Elliott | 9/4 | 21 |
| 1941 | LAMBERT SIMNEL | F. Templeman | C. Elliott | 10/1 | 19 |
| 1942 | BIG GAME | F. Darling | G. Richards | 8/11 | 14 |
| 1943 | KINGSWAY | J. Lawson | S. Wragg | 18/1 | 19 |
| 1944 | GARDEN PATH | W. Earl | H. Wragg | 5/1 | 26 |
| 1945 | COURT MARTIAL | J. Lawson | C. Richards | 13/2 | 20 |

| Year | Horse | Trainer | Jockey | SP | RAN |
|------|-------|---------|--------|-----|-----|
| 1946 | HAPPY KNIGHT | H. Jelliss | T. Weston | 28/1 | 13 |
| 1947 | TUDOR MINSTREL | F. Darling | G. Richards | 8/11 | 15 |
| 1948 | MY BABU | F. Armstrong | C. Smirke | 2/1 | 18 |
| 1949 | NIMBUS | G. Colling | C. Elliott | 10/1 | 13 |
| 1950 | PALESTINE | M. Marsh | C. Smirke | 4/1 | 19 |
| 1951 | KI MING | M. Beary | A. Breasley | 100/8 | 27 |
| 1952 | THUNDERHEAD | E. Pollet | R. Poincelet | 100/7 | 26 |
| 1953 | NEARULA | C. Elsey | E. Britt | 2/1 | 16 |
| 1954 | DARIUS | H. Wragg | E. Mercer | 8/1 | 19 |
| 1955 | OUR BABU | G. Brooke | D. Smith | 13/2 | 23 |
| 1956 | GILLES DE RETZ | Mrs G. Johnson-Houghton | F. Barlow | 50/1 | 19 |
| 1957 | CREPELLO | N. Murless | L. Piggott | 7/2 | 14 |
| 1958 | PALL MALL | C. Boyd-Rochfort | D. Smith | 20/1 | 14 |
| 1959 | TABOUN | A. Head | G. Moore | 5/2 | 13 |
| 1960 | MARTIAL | P. Prendergast | R. Hutchinson | 18/1 | 17 |
| 1961 | ROCKAVON | G. Boyd | N. Stirk | 66/1 | 22 |
| 1962 | PRIVY COUNCILLOR | T. Waugh | W. Rickaby | 100/6 | 19 |
| 1963 | ONLY FOR LIFE | J. Tree | J. Lindley | 33/1 | 21 |
| 1964 | BALDRIC | E. Fellows | W. Pyers | 20/1 | 27 |
| 1965 | NIKSAR | W. Nightingall | D. Keith | 100/8 | 22 |
| 1966 | KASHMIR II | C. Bartholomew | J. Lindley | 7/1 | 25 |
| 1967 | ROYAL PALACE | N. Murless | G. Moore | 100/30 | 18 |
| 1968 | SIR IVOR | M. V. O'Brien | L. Piggott | 11/8 | 10 |
| 1969 | RIGHT TACK | W. R. Hern | G. Lewis | 15/2 | 13 |
| 1970 | NIJINSKY | M. V. O'Brien | L. Piggott | 4/7 | 14 |
| 1971 | BRIGADIER GERARD | W. R. Hern | J. Mercer | 11/2 | 6 |
| 1972 | HIGH TOP | B. van Cutsem | W. Carson | 85/40 | 12 |
| 1973 | MON FILS | R. Hannon | F. Durr | 50/1 | 18 |
| 1974 | NONOALCO | F. Boutin | Y. Saint-Martin | 19/2 | 12 |
| 1975 | BOLKONSKI | H. Cecil | G. Dettori | 33/1 | 24 |
| 1976 | WOLLOW | H. Cecil | G. Dettori | evens | 17 |
| 1977 | NEBBIOLO | K. Prendergast | G. Curran | 20/1 | 18 |
| 1978 | ROLAND GARDENS | D. Sasse | F. Durr | 28/1 | 19 |
| 1979 | TAP ON WOOD | B. Hills | S. Cauthen | 20/1 | 20 |
| 1980 | KNOWN FACT* | J. Tree | W. Carson | 14/1 | 14 |
| 1981 | TO-AGORI-MOU | G. Harwood | G. Starkey | 5/2 | 19 |
| 1982 | ZINO | F. Boutin | F. Head | 8/1 | 26 |
| 1983 | LOMOND | M. V. O'Brien | P. Eddery | 9/1 | 16 |
| 1984 | EL GRAN SENOR | M. V. O'Brien | P. Eddery | 15/8 | 9 |
| 1985 | SHADEED | M. Stoute | L. Piggott | 4/5 | 14 |
| 1986 | DANCING BRAVE | G. Harwood | G. Starkey | 15/8 | 15 |
| 1987 | DON'T FORGET ME | R. Hannon | W. Carson | 9/1 | 14 |
| 1988 | DOYOUN | M. Stoute | W. R. Swinburn | 4/5 | 9 |
| 1989 | NASHWAN | W. R. Hern | W. Carson | 3/1 | 14 |
| 1990 | TIROL | R. Hannon | M. Kinane | 9/1 | 14 |
| 1991 | MYSTIKO | C. Brittain | M. Roberts | 13/2 | 14 |

* 1980: Nureyev finished first but was disqualified

# *Chester Vase*

CHESTER      I MILE 4 FURLONGS 65 YARDS     FIRST RUN 1907

| YEAR | HORSE | TRAINER | JOCKEY | SP | RAN |
|------|-------|---------|--------|-----|-----|
| 1946 | SKY HIGH | W. Earl | T. Weston | 9/4 | 5 |
| 1947 | EDWARD TUDOR | F. Darling | G. Richards | 5/6 | 3 |
| 1948 | VALOGNES | M. Marsh | E. Britt | 4/1 | 8 |
| 1949 | SWALLOW TAIL | W. Earl | D. Smith | 2/5 | 4 |
| 1950 | CASTLE ROCK | J. Jarvis | D. Smith | 1/3 | 6 |
| 1951 | SUPREME COURT | E. Williams | W. Johnstone | 9/4 | 8 |
| 1952 | SUMMER RAIN | J. Jarvis | E. Mercer | 7/4 | 5 |
| 1953 | EMPIRE HONEY | J. Jarvis | E. Mercer | 11/10 | 4 |
| 1954 | BLUE ROD | H. Leader | D. Greening | 33/1 | 7 |
| 1955 | DAEMON | P. Prendergast | J. Wilson | 10/11 | 5 |
| 1956 | ARTICULATE | W. Stephenson | D. Ryan | 5/1 | 7 |
| 1957 | KING BABAR | P. Prendergast | P. Robinson | 9/2 | 5 |
| 1958 | ALCIDE | C. Boyd-Rochfort | W. Snaith | 15/8 | 7 |
| 1959 | FIDALGO | H. Wragg | S. Calyton | 10/1 | 9 |
| 1960 | MR HIGGINS | H. Cottrill | W. Carr | 10/1 | 6 |
| 1961 | SOVRANGO | H. Wragg | J. Mercer | 7/1 | 10 |
| 1962 | SILVER CLOUD | J. Jarvis | R. Hutchinson | 5/1 | 6 |
| 1963 | CHRISTMAS ISLAND | P. Prendergast | L. Piggott | 100/8 | 7 |
| 1964 | INDIANA | J. Watts | J. Mercer | 11/4 | 8 |
| 1965 | GULF PEARL | J. Tree | J. Lindley | 7/1 | 6 |
| 1966 | GENERAL GORDON | J. Jarvis | P. Cook | 6/1 | 9 |
| 1967 | GREAT HOST | P. Prendergast | D. Lake | 2/1 | 7 |
| 1968 | REMAND | W. R. Hern | J. Mercer | 4/11 | 4 |
| 1969 | *Abandoned – waterlogged* | | | | |
| 1970 | POLITICO | N. Murless | A. Barclay | 5/2 | 6 |
| 1971 | LINDEN TREE | P. Walwyn | D. Keith | 11/2 | 5 |
| 1972 | ORMINDO | H. Wragg | B. Taylor | 12/1 | 6 |
| 1973 | PROVERB | B. Hills | E. Johnson | 33/1 | 7 |
| 1974 | JUPITER PLUVIUS | B. Hobbs | J. Gorton | 11/2 | 8 |
| 1975 | SHANTALLAH | H. Wragg | B. Taylor | 15/2 | 7 |
| 1976 | OLD BILL | H. Wragg | B. Taylor | 33/1 | 6 |
| 1977 | HOT GROVE | R. F. J. Houghton | L. Piggott | 100/30 | 6 |
| 1978 | ICELANDIC | P. Prendergast | C. Roche | 8/1 | 4 |
| 1979 | CRACAVAL | B. Hills | S. Cauthen | 4/1 | 6 |
| 1980 | HENBIT | W. R. Hern | W. Carson | evens | 5 |
| 1981 | SHERGAR | M. Stoute | W. R. Swinburn | 4/11 | 10 |
| 1982 | SUPER SUNRISE | G. Hunter | P. Cook | 10/1 | 8 |
| 1983 | *Abandoned – waterlogged* | | | | |
| 1984 | KAYTU | W. R. Hern | W. Carson | 11/2 | 7 |
| 1985 | LAW SOCIETY | M. V. O'Brien | P. Eddery | 5/2 | 5 |
| 1986 | NOMROOD | P. Cole | T. Quinn | 11/2 | 7 |
| 1987 | DRY DOCK | W. R. Hern | W. Carson | 11/2 | 8 |
| 1988 | UNFUWAIN | W. R. Hern | W. Carson | 1/3 | 4 |
| 1989 | OLD VIC | H. Cecil | S. Cauthen | 6/4 | 5 |
| 1990 | BELMEZ | H. Cecil | S. Cauthen | 8/13 | 3 |
| 1991 | TOULON | A. Fabre | P. Eddery | 9/4 | 5 |

# Dante Stakes

YORK        1 MILE 2½ FURLONGS        FIRST RUN 1958

| YEAR | HORSE | TRAINER | JOCKEY | SP | RAN |
|------|-------|---------|--------|-----|-----|
| 1958 | BALD EAGLE | C. Boyd-Rochfort | W. Carr | 11/10 | 7 |
| 1959 | DICKENS | C. Boyd-Rochfort | W. Carr | 100/8 | 9 |
| 1960 | ST PADDY | N. Murless | L. Piggott | 8/11 | 10 |
| 1961 | GALLANT KNIGHT | T. Leader | E. Smith | 3/1 | 5 |
| 1962 | LUCKY BRIEF | W. Gray | B. Connorton | 9/2 | 5 |
| 1963 | MERCHANT VENTURER | J. Oxley | G. Starkey | 9/2 | 6 |
| 1964 | SWEET MOSS | N. Murless | L. Piggott | 3/1 | 9 |
| 1965 | BALLYMARAIS | W. Gray | W. Pyers | 10/1 | 11 |
| 1966 | HERMES | J. Oxley | G. Starkey | 3/1 | 9 |
| 1967 | GAY GARLAND | H. Wragg | R. Hutchinson | 100/7 | 5 |
| 1968 | LUCKY FINISH | H. Leader | B. Taylor | 10/1 | 10 |
| 1969 | ACTIVATOR | G. Barling | M. Thomas | 6/1 | 15 |
| 1970 | APPROVAL | H. Cecil | G. Starkey | 9/4 | 8 |
| 1971 | FAIR WORLD | G. Todd | J. Lindley | 6/1 | 8 |
| 1972 | RHEINGOLD | B. Hills | E. Johnson | 4/1 | 9 |
| 1973 | OWEN DUDLEY | N. Murless | G. Lewis | 5/4 | 10 |
| 1974 | HONOURED GUEST | N. Murless | G. Lewis | 7/1 | 6 |
| 1975 | HOBNOB | H. Wragg | W. Carson | 15/2 | 9 |
| 1976 | TRASI'S SON | M. Tate | E. Hide | 50/1 | 11 |
| 1977 | LUCKY SOVEREIGN | H. Wragg | M. Thomas | 20/1 | 15 |
| 1978 | SHIRLEY HEIGHTS | J. Dunlop | G. Starkey | 10/1 | 9 |
| 1979 | LYPHARD'S WISH | H. Cecil | J. Mercer | 100/30 | 14 |
| 1980 | HELLO GORGEOUS | H. Cecil | J. Mercer | 4/1 | 8 |
| 1981 | BELDALE FLUTTER | M. Jarvis | P. Eddery | 11/1 | 6 |
| 1982 | SIMPLY GREAT | H. Cecil | L. Piggott | 11/10 | 6 |
| 1983 | HOT TOUCH | G. Wragg | P. Eddery | 11/1 | 9 |
| 1984 | CLAUDE MONET | H. Cecil | S. Cauthen | 2/1 | 15 |
| 1985 | DAMISTER | J. Tree | P. Eddery | 5/1 | 5 |
| 1986 | SHAHRASTANI | M. Stoute | W. R. Swinburn | 10/11 | 7 |
| 1987 | REFERENCE POINT | H. Cecil | S. Cauthen | 13/8 | 8 |
| 1988 | RED GLOW | G. Wragg | P. Eddery | 7/1 | 7 |
| 1989 | TORJOUN | L. Cumani | R. Cochrane | 6/1 | 7 |
| 1990 | SANGLAMORE | R. Charlton | P. Eddery | 11/2 | 7 |
| 1991 | ENVIRONMENT FRIEND | J. Fanshawe | G. Duffield | 20/1 | 8 |

## *Musidora Stakes*

| Year | Horse | Trainer | Jockey | SP | RAN |
|------|-------|---------|--------|-----|-----|
| 1961 | AMBERGRIS | H. Wragg | L. Piggott | 4/9 | 8 |
| 1962 | FOOL'S GOLD | C. Boyd-Rochfort | W. Carr | 8/11 | 6 |
| 1963 | NOBLESSE | P. Prendergast | G. Bougoure | evens | 8 |
| 1964 | ELA MARITA | P. Prendergast | G. Bougoure | 20/21 | 9 |
| 1965 | ARCTIC MELODY | P. Prendergast | G. Bougoure | 5/4 | 5 |
| 1966 | ORABELLA II | H. Leader | B. Taylor | 8/1 | 9 |
| 1967 | PALATCH | H. Leader | B. Taylor | 9/1 | 7 |
| 1968 | EXCHANGE | H. Leader | B. Taylor | 11/4 | 7 |
| 1969 | LOVERS LANE | N. Murless | A. Barclay | 9/2 | 10 |
| 1970 | WHITEFOOT | H. Wragg | J. Lindley | 7/4 | 4 |
| 1971 | CATHERINE WHEEL | B. Hobbs | J. Gorton | 10/11 | 5 |
| 1972 | JAKOMIMA | P. Walwyn | D. Keith | 4/1 | 10 |
| 1973 | WHERE YOU LEAD | M. V. O'Brien | E. Hide | 10/1 | 6 |
| 1974 | ESCORIAL | I. Balding | L. Piggott | 4/5 | 6 |
| 1975 | MOONLIGHT NIGHT | N. Murless | G. Lewis | 9/1 | 10 |
| 1976 | EVERYTHING NICE | B. Hobbs | G. Lewis | 9/4 | 8 |
| 1977 | TRIPLE FIRST | M. Stoute | E. Hide | 9/1 | 9 |
| 1978 | PRINCESS OF MAN | B. Hills | E. Johnson | 8/1 | 9 |
| 1979 | ROMOSA'S PET | M. Stoute | G. Starkey | 7/2 | 10 |
| 1980 | BIREME | W. R. Hern | W. Carson | 5/1 | 9 |
| 1981 | CONDESSA | J. Bolger | D. Gillespie | 16/1 | 5 |
| 1982 | LAST FEATHER | B. Hills | S. Cauthen | 7/4 | 5 |
| 1983 | GIVE THANKS | J. Bolger | D. Gillespie | 13/8 | 8 |
| 1984 | OPTIMISTIC LASS | M. Stoute | W. R. Swinburn | 9/1 | 9 |
| 1985 | FATAH FLARE | H. Cecil | S. Cauthen | 10/1 | 9 |
| 1986 | REJUVENATE | B. Hills | B. Thomson | 9/2 | 7 |
| 1987 | INDIAN SKIMMER | H. Cecil | S. Cauthen | 1/2 | 3 |
| 1988 | DIMINUENDO | H. Cecil | S. Cauthen | 8/13 | 6 |
| 1989 | SNOW BRIDE | H. Cecil | S. Cauthen | 4/1 | 6 |
| 1990 | IN THE GROOVE | D. Elsworth | R. Cochrane | 15/2 | 5 |
| 1991 | GUSSY MARLOWE | C. Brittain | M. Roberts | 7/1 | 5 |

## *Derby Stakes*

| Year | Horse | Trainer | Jockey | SP | RAN |
|------|-------|---------|--------|-----|-----|
| 1900 | DIAMOND JUBILEE | R. Marsh | H. Jones | 6/4 | 14 |
| 1901 | VOLODYOVSKI | J. Huggins | L. Reiff | 5/2 | 25 |
| 1902 | ARD PATRICK | S. Darling | J. Martin | 100/14 | 18 |
| 1903 | ROCK SAND | G. Blackwell | D. Maher | 4/6 | 7 |

| YEAR | HORSE | TRAINER | JOCKEY | SP | RAN |
|------|-------|---------|--------|-----|-----|
| 1904 | ST AMANT | A. Hayhoe | K. Cannon | 5/1 | 8 |
| 1905 | CICERO | P. Peck | D. Maher | 4/11 | 9 |
| 1906 | SPEARMINT | P. Gilpin | D. Maher | 6/1 | 22 |
| 1907 | ORBY | F. MacCabe | J. Reiff | 100/9 | 9 |
| 1908 | SIGNORINETTA | Chev. E. Ginistrelli | W. Bullock | 100/1 | 18 |
| 1909 | MINORU | R. Marsh | H. Jones | 7/2 | 15 |
| 1910 | LEMBERG | A. Taylor | B. Dillon | 7/4 | 15 |
| 1911 | SUNSTAR | C. Morton | G. Stern | 13/8 | 26 |
| 1912 | TAGALIE | D. Waugh | J. Reiff | 100/8 | 20 |
| 1913 | ABOYEUR* | T. Lewis | E. Piper | 100/1 | 15 |
| 1914 | DURBAR II | T. Murphy | M. MacGee | 20/1 | 30 |
| 1915 | POMMERN | C. Peck | S. Donoghue | 10/11 | 17 |
| 1916 | FIFINELLA | R. Dawson | J. Childs | 11/2 | 10 |
| 1917 | GAY CRUSADER | A. Taylor, jr | S. Donoghue | 7/4 | 12 |
| 1918 | GAINSBOROUGH | A. Taylor, jr | J. Childs | 8/13 | 13 |
| 1919 | GRAND PARADE | F. Barling | F. Templeman | 33/1 | 13 |
| 1920 | SPION KOP | P. Gilpin | F. O'Neill | 100/6 | 19 |
| 1921 | HUMORIST | C. Morton | S. Donoghue | 6/1 | 23 |
| 1922 | CAPTAIN CUTTLE | F. Darling | S. Donoghue | 10/1 | 30 |
| 1923 | PAPYRUS | B. Jarvis | S. Donoghue | 100/15 | 19 |
| 1924 | SANSOVINO | G. Lambton | T. Weston | 9/2 | 27 |
| 1925 | MANNA | F. Darling | S. Donoghue | 9/1 | 27 |
| 1926 | CORONACH | F. Darling | J. Childs | 11/2 | 19 |
| 1927 | CALL BOY | J. Watts | E. Elliott | 4/1 | 23 |
| 1928 | FELSTEAD | O. Bell | H. Wragg | 33/1 | 19 |
| 1929 | TRIGO | R. Dawson | J. Marshall | 33/1 | 26 |
| 1930 | BLENHEIM | R. Dawson | H. Wragg | 18/1 | 17 |
| 1931 | CAMERONIAN | F. Darling | F. Fox | 7/2 | 25 |
| 1932 | APRIL THE FIFTH | T. Walls | F. Lane | 100/6 | 21 |
| 1933 | HYPERION | G. Lambton | T. Weston | 6/1 | 24 |
| 1934 | WINDSOR LAD | M. Marsh | C. Smirke | 15/2 | 19 |
| 1935 | BAHRAM | F. Butters | F. Fox | 5/4 | 16 |
| 1936 | MAHMOUD | F. Butters | C. Smirke | 100/8 | 22 |
| 1937 | MID-DAY SUN | Fred. Butters | M. Beary | 100/7 | 21 |
| 1938 | BOIS ROUSSEL | F. Darling | E. Elliott | 20/1 | 22 |
| 1939 | BLUE PETER | J. Jarvis | E. Smith | 7/2 | 27 |
| 1940 | PONT L'EVÊQUE | F. Darling | S. Wragg | 10/1 | 16 |
| 1941 | OWEN TUDOR | F. Darling | W. Nevett | 25/1 | 20 |
| 1942 | WATLING STREET | W. Earl | H. Wragg | 6/1 | 13 |
| 1943 | STRAIGHT DEAL | W. Nightingall | T. Carey | 100/6 | 23 |
| 1944 | OCEAN SWELL | J. Jarvis | W. Nevett | 28/1 | 20 |
| 1945 | DANTE | M. Peacock | W. Nevett | 100/30 | 27 |
| 1946 | AIRBORNE | R. Perryman | T. Lowrey | 50/1 | 17 |
| 1947 | PEARL DIVER | W. Halsey | G. Bridgland | 40/1 | 15 |
| 1948 | MY LOVE | R. Carver | W. Johnston | 100/9 | 32 |
| 1949 | NIMBUS | G. Colling | E. Elliott | 7/1 | 32 |
| 1950 | GALCADOR | C. Semblat | W. Johnstone | 100/9 | 25 |
| 1951 | ARCTIC PRINCE | W. Stephenson | C. Spares | 28/1 | 33 |
| 1952 | TULYAR | M. Marsh | C. Smirke | 11/2 | 33 |
| 1953 | PINZA | N. Bertie | G. Richards | 5/1 | 27 |

| YEAR | HORSE | TRAINER | JOCKEY | SP | RAN |
|------|-------|---------|--------|-----|-----|
| 1954 | NEVER SAY DIE | J. Lawson | L. Piggott | 33/1 | 22 |
| 1955 | PHIL DRAKE | F. Mathet | F. Palmer | 100/8 | 23 |
| 1956 | LAVANDIN | A. Head | W. Johnstone | 7/1 | 27 |
| 1957 | CREPELLO | N. Murless | L. Piggott | 6/4 | 22 |
| 1958 | HARD RIDDEN | J. Rogers | C. Smirke | 18/1 | 20 |
| 1959 | PARTHIA | C. Boyd-Rochfort | W. Carr | 10/1 | 20 |
| 1960 | ST PADDY | N. Murless | L. Piggott | 7/1 | 17 |
| 1961 | PSIDIUM | H. Wragg | R. Poincelet | 66/1 | 28 |
| 1962 | LARKSPUR | M. V. O'Brien | N. Sellwood | 22/1 | 26 |
| 1963 | RELKO | F. Mathet | Y. Saint-Martin | 5/1 | 26 |
| 1964 | SANTA CLAUS | J. Rogers | A. Breasley | 15/8 | 17 |
| 1965 | SEA BIRD II | E. Pollet | T. Glennon | 7/4 | 22 |
| 1966 | CHARLOTTOWN | G. Smyth | A. Breasley | 5/1 | 25 |
| 1967 | ROYAL PALACE | N. Murless | G. Moore | 7/4 | 22 |
| 1968 | SIR IVOR | M. V. O'Brien | L. Piggott | 4/5 | 13 |
| 1969 | BLAKENEY | A. Budgett | E. Johnson | 15/2 | 26 |
| 1970 | NIJINSKY | M. V. O'Brien | L. Piggott | 11/8 | 11 |
| 1971 | MILL REEF | I. Balding | G. Lewis | 100/30 | 21 |
| 1972 | ROBERTO | M. V. O'Brien | L. Piggott | 3/1 | 22 |
| 1973 | MORSTON | A. Budgett | E. Hide | 25/1 | 25 |
| 1974 | SNOW KNIGHT | P. Nelson | B. Taylor | 50/1 | 18 |
| 1975 | GRUNDY | P. Walwyn | P. Eddery | 5/1 | 18 |
| 1976 | EMPERY | M. Zilber | L. Piggott | 10/1 | 23 |
| 1977 | THE MINSTREL | M. V. O'Brien | L. Piggott | 5/1 | 22 |
| 1978 | SHIRLEY HEIGHTS | J. Dunlop | G. Starkey | 8/1 | 25 |
| 1979 | TROY | W. R. Hern | W. Carson | 6/1 | 23 |
| 1980 | HENBIT | W. R. Hern | W. Carson | 7/1 | 24 |
| 1981 | SHERGAR | M. Stoute | W. R. Swinburn | 10/11 | 18 |
| 1982 | GOLDEN FLEECE | M. V. O'Brien | P. Eddery | 3/1 | 18 |
| 1983 | TEENOSO | G. Wragg | L. Piggott | 9/2 | 21 |
| 1984 | SECRETO | D. O'Brien | C. Roche | 14/1 | 17 |
| 1985 | SLIP ANCHOR | H. Cecil | S. Cauthen | 9/4 | 14 |
| 1986 | SHAHRASTANI | M. Stoute | W. R. Swinburn | 11/2 | 17 |
| 1987 | REFERENCE POINT | H. Cecil | S. Cauthen | 6/4 | 19 |
| 1988 | KAHYASI | L. Cumani | R. Cochrane | 11/1 | 14 |
| 1989 | NASHWAN | W. R. Hern | W. Carson | 5/4 | 12 |
| 1990 | QUEST FOR FAME | R. Charlton | P. Eddery | 7/1 | 18 |
| 1991 | GENEROUS | P. Cole | A. Munro | 9/1 | 13 |

\* 1913: Craganour finished first but was disqualified

# Coronation Cup

| YEAR | HORSE | TRAINER | JOCKEY | SP | RAN |
|------|-------|---------|--------|-----|-----|
| 1946 | ARDAN | C. Semblat | C. Elliott | 5/6 | 3 |
| 1947 | CHANTEUR II | H. Count | R. Brethes | 1/3 | 5 |
| 1948 | GOYAMA | C. Semblat | C. Elliott | 5/2 | 5 |
| 1949 | BEAU SABREUR | C. Brabazon | W. Cook | 9/4 | 3 |
| 1950 | AMOUR DRAKE | R. Carver | R. Poincelet | 15/8 | 6 |
| 1951 | TANTIÈME | F. Mathet | J. Doyasbère | 2/7 | 5 |
| 1952 | NUCCIO | A. Head | R. Poincelet | 3/1 | 5 |
| 1953 | ZUCCHERO | W. Payne | L. Piggott | 100/7 | 10 |
| 1954 | AUREOLE | C. Boyd-Rochfort | E. Smith | 5/2 | 8 |
| 1955 | NARRATOR | H. Cottrill | F. Barlow | 100/30 | 6 |
| 1956 | TROPIQUE | G. Watson | P. Blanc | 13/8 | 6 |
| 1957 | FRIC | P. Callie | J. Deforge | 7/2 | 8 |
| 1958 | BALLYMOSS | M. V. O'Brien | A. Breasley | evens | 5 |
| 1959 | NAGAMI | H. Wragg | L. Piggott | 5/4 | 3 |
| 1960 | PETITE ETOILE | N. Murless | L. Piggott | 1/3 | 3 |
| 1961 | PETITE ETOILE | N. Murless | L. Piggott | 2/5 | 5 |
| 1962 | DICTA DRAKE | F. Mathet | Y. Saint-Martin | 2/1 | 7 |
| 1963 | EXBURY | G. Watson | J. Deforge | 11/8 | 9 |
| 1964 | RELKO | F. Mathet | Y. Saint-Martin | 4/6 | 7 |
| 1965 | ONCIDIUM | G. Todd | A. Breasley | 11/2 | 10 |
| 1966 | I SAY | W. Nightingall | D. Keith | 10/1 | 7 |
| 1967 | CHARLOTTOWN | G. Smyth | J. Lindley | 11/8 | 7 |
| 1968 | ROYAL PALACE | N. Murless | A. Barclay | 4/9 | 4 |
| 1969 | PARK TOP | B. van Cutsem | L. Piggott | 11/4 | 7 |
| 1970 | CALIBAN | N. Murless | A. Barclay | 8/1 | 4 |
| 1971 | LUPE | N. Murless | G. Lewis | 5/2 | 6 |
| 1972 | MILL REEF | I. Balding | G. Lewis | 2/15 | 4 |
| 1973 | ROBERTO | M. V. O'Brien | L. Piggott | 4/9 | 5 |
| 1974 | BUOY | W. R. Hern | J. Mercer | 4/1 | 5 |
| 1975 | BUSTINO | W. R. Hern | J. Mercer | 11/10 | 6 |
| 1976 | QUIET FLING | J. Tree | L. Piggott | 5/2 | 6 |
| 1977 | EXCELLER | F. Mathet | G. Dubroeucq | 13/8 | 6 |
| 1978 | CROW | P. Walwyn | P. Eddery | 9/4 | 5 |
| 1979 | ILE DE BOURBON | R. F. J. Houghton | J. Reid | 4/6 | 4 |
| 1980 | SEA CHIMES | J. Dunlop | L. Piggott | 5/4 | 4 |
| 1981 | MASTER WILLIE | H. Candy | P. Waldron | 1/2 | 5 |
| 1982 | EASTER SUN | M. Jarvis | B. Raymond | 20/1 | 8 |
| 1983 | BE MY NATIVE | R. Armstrong | L. Piggott | 8/1 | 6 |
| 1984 | TIME CHARTER | H. Candy | S. Cauthen | 100/30 | 6 |
| 1985 | RAINBOW QUEST | J. Tree | P. Eddery | 8/15 | 7 |
| 1986 | SAINT ESTEPHE | A. Fabre | P. Eddery | 20/1 | 10 |
| 1987 | TRIPTYCH | P. Biancone | A. Cruz | 4/5 | 5 |
| 1988 | TRIPTYCH | P. Biancone | S. Cauthen | 11/8 | 4 |
| 1989 | SHERIFF'S STAR | Lady Herries | R. Cochrane | 11/4 | 9 |
| 1990 | IN THE WINGS | A. Fabre | C. Asmussen | 15/8 | 6 |
| 1991 | IN THE GROOVE | D. Elsworth | S. Cauthen | 7/2 | 7 |

# *Oaks Stakes*

EPSOM                     1 MILE 4 FURLONGS            FIRST RUN 1779

| YEAR | HORSE | TRAINER | JOCKEY | SP | RAN |
|------|-------|---------|--------|-----|-----|
| 1900 | LA ROCHE | J. Porter | M. Cannon | 5/1 | 14 |
| 1901 | CAP AND BELLS | S. Darling | M. Henry | 9/4 | 21 |
| 1902 | SCEPTRE | R. Sievier | H. Randall | 5/2 | 14 |
| 1903 | OUR LASSIE | C. Morton | M. Cannon | 6/1 | 10 |
| 1904 | PRETTY POLLY | P. Gilpin | W. Lane | 8/100 | 4 |
| 1905 | CHERRY LASS | W. Robinson | H. Jones | 4/5 | 12 |
| 1906 | KEYSTONE | G. Lambton | D. Maher | 5/2 | 12 |
| 1907 | GLASS DOLL | C. Morton | H. Randall | 25/1 | 14 |
| 1908 | SIGNORINETTA | O. Ginistrelli | W. Bullock | 3/1 | 13 |
| 1909 | PEROLA | G. Davies | F. Wootton | 5/1 | 14 |
| 1910 | ROSEDROP | A. Taylor, jr | C. Trigg | 7/1 | 11 |
| 1911 | CHERIMOYA | C. Marsh | F. Winter | 25/1 | 21 |
| 1912 | MIRSKA | T. Jennings, jr | J. Childs | 33/1 | 14 |
| 1913 | JEST | C. Morton | F. Rickaby, jr | 8/1 | 12 |
| 1914 | PRINCESS DORRIE | C. Morton | W. Huxley | 11/4 | 21 |
| 1915 | SNOW MARTEN | P. Gilpin | W. Griggs | 20/1 | 11 |
| 1916 | FIFINELLA | R. Dawson | J. Childs | 8/13 | 7 |
| 1917 | SUNNY JANE | A. Taylor, jr | O. Madden | 4/1 | 11 |
| 1918 | MY DEAR* | A. Taylor, jr | S. Donoghue | 3/1 | 15 |
| 1919 | BAYUDA | A. Taylor, jr | J. Childs | 100/7 | 10 |
| 1920 | CHARLEBELLE | H. Braime | A. Whalley | 7/2 | 17 |
| 1921 | LOVE IN IDLENESS | A. Taylor, jr | J. Childs | 5/1 | 22 |
| 1922 | POGROM | A. Taylor, jr | E. Gardner | 5/4 | 11 |
| 1923 | BROWNHYLDA | R. Dawson | V. Smyth | 10/1 | 12 |
| 1924 | STRAITLACE | D. Waugh | F. O'Neill | 100/30 | 12 |
| 1925 | SAUCY SUE | A. Taylor, jr | F. Bullock | 30/100 | 12 |
| 1926 | SHORT STORY | A. Taylor, jr | R. Jones | 5/1 | 16 |
| 1927 | BEAM | F. Butters | T. Weston | 4/1 | 16 |
| 1928 | TOBOGGAN | F. Butters | T. Weston | 100/15 | 13 |
| 1929 | PENNYCOMEQUICK | J. Lawson | H. Jelliss | 11/10 | 13 |
| 1930 | ROSE OF ENGLAND | T. Hogg | G. Richards | 7/1 | 15 |
| 1931 | BRULETTE | F. Carter | C. Elliott | 7/2 | 15 |
| 1932 | UDAIPUR | F. Butters | M. Beary | 10/1 | 12 |
| 1933 | CHÂTELAINE | F. Templeman | S. Wragg | 25/1 | 14 |
| 1934 | LIGHT BROCADE | F. Butters | B. Carslake | 7/4 | 8 |
| 1935 | QUASHED | C. Leader | H. Jelliss | 33/1 | 17 |
| 1936 | LOVELY ROSA | H. Cottrill | T. Weston | 33/1 | 17 |
| 1937 | EXHIBITIONIST | J. Lawson | S. Donoghue | 3/1 | 13 |
| 1938 | ROCKFEL | O. Bell | H. Wragg | 3/1 | 14 |
| 1939 | GALATEA | J. Lawson | R. Jones | 10/11 | 21 |
| 1940 | GODIVA | W. Jarvis | D. Marks | 7/4 | 14 |
| 1941 | COMMOTION | F. Darling | H. Wragg | 8/1 | 12 |
| 1942 | SUN CHARIOT | F. Darling | G. Richards | 1/4 | 12 |
| 1943 | WHY HURRY | N. Cannon | C. Elliott | 7/1 | 13 |

* 1918: Stony Ford finished first but was disqualified

| Year | Horse | Trainer | Jockey | SP | RAN |
|------|-------|---------|--------|----|----|
| 1944 | HYCILLA | C. Boyd-Rochfort | G. Bridgland | 8/1 | 16 |
| 1945 | SUN STREAM | W. Earl | H. Wragg | 6/4 | 16 |
| 1946 | STEADY AIM | F. Butters | H. Wragg | 7/1 | 10 |
| 1947 | IMPRUDENCE | J. Lieux | W. Johnstone | 7/4 | 11 |
| 1948 | MASAKA | F. Butters | W. Nevett | 7/1 | 25 |
| 1949 | MUSIDORA | C. Elsey | E. Britt | 4/1 | 17 |
| 1950 | ASMENA | C. Semblat | W. Johnstone | 5/1 | 19 |
| 1951 | NEASHAM BELLE | G. Brooke | S. Clayton | 33/1 | 16 |
| 1952 | FRIEZE | C. Elsey | E. Britt | 100/7 | 19 |
| 1953 | AMBIGUITY | J. Colling | J. Mercer | 18/1 | 21 |
| 1954 | SUN CAP | R. Carver | W. Johnstone | 100/8 | 21 |
| 1955 | MELD | C. Boyd-Rochfort | W. Carr | 7/4 | 13 |
| 1956 | SICARELLE | F. Mathet | F. Palmer | 3/1 | 14 |
| 1957 | CARROZZA | N. Murless | L. Piggott | 100/8 | 11 |
| 1958 | BELLA PAOLA | F. Mathet | M. Garcia | 6/4 | 17 |
| 1959 | PETITE ETOILE | N. Murless | L. Piggott | 11/2 | 11 |
| 1960 | NEVER TOO LATE | E. Pollet | R. Poincelet | 6/5 | 10 |
| 1961 | SWEET SOLERA | R. Day | W. Rickaby | 11/4 | 12 |
| 1962 | MONADE | J. Lieux | Y. Saint-Martin | 7/1 | 18 |
| 1963 | NOBLESSE | P. Prendergast | G. Bougoure | 4/11 | 9 |
| 1964 | HOMEWARD BOUND | J. Oxley | G. Starkey | 100/7 | 18 |
| 1965 | LONG LOOK | M. V. O'Brien | J. Purtell | 100/7 | 18 |
| 1966 | VALORIS | M. V. O'Brien | L. Piggott | 11/10 | 13 |
| 1967 | PIA | C. Elsey | E. Hide | 100/7 | 12 |
| 1968 | LA LAGUNE | F. Boutin | J. Thiboeuf | 11/8 | 14 |
| 1969 | SLEEPING PARTNER | D. Smith | J. Gorton | 100/6 | 15 |
| 1970 | LUPE | N. Murless | A. Barclay | 100/30 | 16 |
| 1971 | ALTESSE ROYALE | N. Murless | G. Lewis | 6/4 | 11 |
| 1972 | GINEVRA | H. R. Price | A. Murray | 8/1 | 17 |
| 1973 | MYSTERIOUS | N. Murless | G. Lewis | 13/8 | 10 |
| 1974 | POLYGAMY | P. Walwyn | P. Eddery | 3/1 | 15 |
| 1975 | JULIETTE MARNY | J. Tree | L. Piggott | 12/1 | 12 |
| 1976 | PAWNEESE | A. Penna | Y. Saint-Martin | 6/5 | 14 |
| 1977 | DUNFERMLINE | W. R. Hern | W. Carson | 6/1 | 13 |
| 1978 | FAIR SALINIA | M. Stoute | G. Starkey | 8/1 | 15 |
| 1979 | SCINTILLATE | J. Tree | P. Eddery | 20/1 | 14 |
| 1980 | BIREME | W. R. Hern | W. Carson | 9/2 | 11 |
| 1981 | BLUE WIND | D. Weld | L. Piggott | 3/1 | 12 |
| 1982 | TIME CHARTER | H. Candy | W. Newnes | 12/1 | 13 |
| 1983 | SUN PRINCESS | W. R. Hern | W. Carson | 6/1 | 15 |
| 1984 | CIRCUS PLUME | J. Dunlop | L. Piggott | 4/1 | 16 |
| 1985 | OH SO SHARP | H. Cecil | S. Cauthen | 6/4 | 12 |
| 1986 | MIDWAY LADY | B. Hanbury | R. Cochrane | 15/8 | 15 |
| 1987 | UNITE | M. Stoute | W. R. Swinburn | 11/1 | 11 |
| 1988 | DIMINUENDO | H. Cecil | S. Cauthen | 7/4 | 11 |
| 1989 | SNOW BRIDE* | H. Cecil | S. Cauthen | 13/2 | 9 |
| 1990 | SALSABIL | J. Dunlop | W. Carson | 2/1 | 8 |
| 1991 | JET SKI LADY | J. Bolger | C. Roche | 50/1 | 9 |

* 1989: Aliysa finished first but was subsequently disqualified for failing the drugs test

# St James's Palace Stakes

ROYAL ASCOT       I MILE       FIRST RUN 1825

| YEAR | HORSE | TRAINER | JOCKEY | SP | RAN |
|------|-------|---------|--------|-----|-----|
| 1946 | KHALED | F. Butters | G. Richards | 2/1 | 5 |
| 1947 | TUDOR MINSTREL | F. Darling | G. Richards | 6/100 | 3 |
| 1948 | BLACK TARQUIN | C. Boyd-Rochfort | E. Britt | 5/1 | 5 |
| 1949 | FAUX TIRAGE | N. Murless | G. Richards | 11/10 | 8 |
| 1950 | PALESTINE | M. Marsh | C. Smirke | 4/7 | 4 |
| 1951 | TURCO II | C. Boyd-Rochfort | W. Carr | 7/1 | 10 |
| 1952 | KING'S BENCH | M. Feakes | G. Richards | 3/1 | 7 |
| 1953 | NEARULA | C. Elsey | E. Britt | 4/6 | 6 |
| 1954 | DARIUS | H. Wragg | E. Mercer | evens | 7 |
| 1955 | TAMERLANE | N. Bertie | A. Breasley | 8/11 | 5 |
| 1956 | PIRATE KING | H. Cottrill | D. Smith | 6/1 | 6 |
| 1957 | CHEVASTRID | S. McGrath | J. Eddery | 8/1 | 5 |
| 1958 | MAJOR PORTION | T. Leader | E. Smith | evens | 5 |
| 1959 | ABOVE SUSPICION | C. Boyd-Rochfort | W. Carr | 9/4 | 5 |
| 1960 | VENTURE VII | A. Head | G. Moore | 1/33 | 2 |
| 1961 | TUDOR TREASURE | J. Watts | D. Smith | 11/4 | 9 |
| 1962 | COURT SENTENCE | T. Leader | E. Smith | 100/8 | 8 |
| 1963 | CROCKET | G. Brooke | D. Smith | 9/2 | 10 |
| 1964 | ROAN ROCKET | G. Todd | L. Piggott | 5/4 | 8 |
| 1965 | SILLY SEASON | I. Balding | G. Lewis | 5/1 | 12 |
| 1966 | TRACK SPARE | R. Mason | J. Lindley | 100/9 | 7 |
| 1967 | REFORM | G. Richards | A. Breasley | 4/6 | 5 |
| 1968 | PETINGO | F. Armstrong | L. Piggott | 10/11 | 3 |
| 1969 | RIGHT TACK | J. Sutcliffe, jr | G. Lewis | 4/6 | 4 |
| 1970 | SAINTLY SONG | N. Murless | A. Barclay | 11/10 | 6 |
| 1971 | BRIGADIER GERARD | W. R. Hern | J. Mercer | 4/11 | 4 |
| 1972 | SUN PRINCE | W. R. Hern | J. Lindley | 7/4 | 5 |
| 1973 | THATCH | M. V. O'Brien | L. Piggott | evens | 2 |
| 1974 | AVEROF | C. Brittain | B. Taylor | 7/4 | 7 |
| 1975 | BOLKONSKI | H. Cecil | G. Dettori | 4/5 | 8 |
| 1976 | RADETZKY* | C. Brittain | P. Eddery | 16/1 | 8 |
| 1977 | DON | W. Elsey | E. Hide | 11/2 | 7 |
| 1978 | JAAZEIRO | M. V. O'Brien | L. Piggott | 5/2 | 8 |
| 1979 | KRIS | H. Cecil | J. Mercer | 11/10 | 5 |
| 1980 | POSSE | J. Dunlop | P. Eddery | 11/2 | 8 |
| 1981 | TO-AGORI-MOU | G. Harwood | G. Starkey | 2/1 | 8 |
| 1982 | DARA MONARCH | L. Browne | J. Kinane | 7/2 | 9 |
| 1983 | HORAGE | M. McCormack | S. Cauthen | 18/1 | 7 |
| 1984 | CHIEF SINGER | R. Sheather | R. Cochrane | 85/40 | 8 |
| 1985 | BAIRN | L. Cumani | L. Piggott | 6/4 | 8 |
| 1986 | SURE BLADE | B. Hills | B. Thomson | 9/2 | 7 |
| 1987 | HALF A YEAR | L. Cumani | R. Cochrane | 11/2 | 5 |
| 1988 | PERSIAN HEIGHTS | G. Huffer | P. Eddery | 9/2 | 7 |
| 1989 | SHAADI | M. Stoute | W. R. Swinburn | 6/4 | 5 |
| 1990 | SHAVIAN | H. Cecil | S. Cauthen | 11/1 | 8 |
| 1991 | MARJU | J. Dunlop | W. Carson | 7/4 | 7 |

* 1976: Patris dead-heated for first but was disqualified

# Coronation Stakes

ROYAL ASCOT                    I MILE                    FIRST RUN 1870

| YEAR | HORSE | TRAINER | JOCKEY | SP | RAN |
|------|-------|---------|--------|-----|-----|
| 1946 | NEOLIGHT | F. Darling | G. Richards | 15/8 | 7 |
| 1947 | SAUCY SAL | H. Blagrave | W. Johnstone | 20/1 | 9 |
| 1948 | FORTUITY | M. Marsh | E. Britt | 20/1 | 8 |
| 1949 | AVILA | C. Boyd-Rochfort | M. Beary | 11/2 | 15 |
| 1950 | TAMBARA | M. Marsh | C. Smirke | 6/5 | 7 |
| 1951 | BELLE OF ALL | N. Bertie | G. Richards | 15/8 | 11 |
| 1952 | ZABARA | V. Smyth | K. Gethin | 6/5 | 7 |
| 1953 | HAPPY LAUGHTER | J. Jarvis | W. Rickaby | 7/4 | 7 |
| 1954 | FESTOON | N. Cannon | J. Mercer | 11/8 | 6 |
| 1955 | MELD | C. Boyd-Rochfort | W. Carr | 4/9 | 5 |
| 1956 | MIDGET II | A. Head | W. Johnstone | 5/6 | 7 |
| 1957 | TORO | A. Head | J. Massard | 3/1 | 11 |
| 1958 | ST LUCIA | P. Hastings-Bass | G. Lewis | 100/8 | 8 |
| 1959 | ROSALBA | J. Colling | J. Mercer | 11/8 | 8 |
| 1960 | BARBARESQUE | W. Clout | G. Moore | 9/2 | 6 |
| 1961 | AIMING HIGH | N. Murless | L. Piggott | 100/8 | 6 |
| 1962 | DISPLAY | P. Prendergast | G. Bougoure | 3/1 | 8 |
| 1963 | FIJI | J. Oxley | G. Starkey | 7/2 | 7 |
| 1964 | OCEAN | J. Oxley | G. Starkey | 7/1 | 6 |
| 1965 | GREENGAGE | G. Richards | A. Breasley | 5/4 | 8 |
| 1966 | HAYMAKING | R. F. J. Houghton | J. Mercer | 100/7 | 8 |
| 1967 | FLEET | N. Murless | G. Moore | 15/8 | 8 |
| 1968 | SOVEREIGN | H. Wragg | R. Hutchinson | 3/1 | 6 |
| 1969 | LUCYROWE | P. Walwyn | D. Keith | 15/8 | 10 |
| 1970 | HUMBLE DUTY | P. Walwyn | D. Keith | 4/6 | 3 |
| 1971 | MAGIC FLUTE | N. Murless | G. Lewis | 85/40 | 4 |
| 1972 | CALVE | P. Prendergast | L. Piggott | 12/1 | 7 |
| 1973 | JACINTH | B. Hobbs | J. Gorton | 15/8 | 9 |
| 1974 | LISADELL | M. V. O'Brien | L. Piggott | 7/2 | 8 |
| 1975 | ROUSSALKA | H. Cecil | L. Piggott | 9/1 | 11 |
| 1976 | KESAR QUEEN | A. Breasley | Y. Saint-Martin | 7/2 | 8 |
| 1977 | ORCHESTRATION | A. Maxwell | P. Eddery | 12/1 | 10 |
| 1978 | SUTTON PLACE | D. Weld | W. Swinburn | 14/1 | 14 |
| 1979 | ONE IN A MILLION | H. Cecil | J. Mercer | 10/11 | 13 |
| 1980 | CAIRN ROUGE | M. Cunningham | A. Murray | 6/5 | 8 |
| 1981 | TOLMI | B. Hobbs | E. Hide | 4/1 | 10 |
| 1982 | CHALON | H. Cecil | L. Piggott | 9/4 | 8 |
| 1983 | FLAME OF TARA | J. Bolger | D. Gillespie | 11/2 | 6 |
| 1984 | KATIES | M. Ryan | P. Robinson | 11/2 | 10 |
| 1985 | AL BAHATHRI | H. T. Jones | A. Murray | 4/6 | 7 |
| 1986 | SONIC LADY | M. Stoute | W. R. Swinburn | 8/15 | 7 |
| 1987 | MILLIGRAM | M. Stoute | W. R. Swinburn | 4/5 | 6 |
| 1988 | MAGIC OF LIFE | J. Tree | P. Eddery | 16/1 | 8 |
| 1989 | GOLDEN OPINION | A. Fabre | C. Asmussen | 7/2 | 8 |
| 1990 | CHIMES OF FREEDOM | H. Cecil | S. Cauthen | 11/2 | 7 |
| 1991 | KOOYONGA | M. Kauntze | W. O'Connor | 3/1 | 8 |

# *Royal Hunt Cup*

ROYAL ASCOT                    I MILE                    FIRST RUN 1843

| YEAR | HORSE | TRAINER | JOCKEY | SP | RAN |
|------|-------|---------|--------|-----|-----|
| 1946 | FRIAR'S FANCY | T. Leader | E. Smith | 15/2 | 16 |
| 1947 | MASTER VOTE | H. Blagrave | T. Sidebotham | 25/1 | 28 |
| 1948 | MASTER VOTE | H. Blagrave | W. Johnstone | 100/7 | 27 |
| 1949 | STEROPE | P. Beasley | J. Caldwell | 100/6 | 29 |
| 1950 | HYPERBOLE | N. Cannon | A. Breasley | 10/1 | 20 |
| 1951 | VAL D'ASSA | H. Persse | N. Sellwood | 100/6 | 23 |
| 1952 | QUEEN OF SHEBA | H. Persse | F. Barlow | 100/7 | 29 |
| 1953 | CHOIR BOY | C. Boyd-Rochfort | D. Smith | 100/6 | 21 |
| 1954 | CHIVALRY | F. Rimell | D. Forte | 33/1 | 26 |
| 1955 | NICHOLAS NICKLEBY | F. Armstrong | W. Snaith | 50/1 | 22 |
| 1956 | ALEXANDER | C. Boyd-Rochfort | W. Carr | 13/2 | 27 |
| 1957 | RETRIAL | C. Boyd-Rochfort | P. Robinson | 100/7 | 18 |
| 1958 | AMOS | S. Mercer | P. Boothman | 20/1 | 17 |
| 1959 | FAULTLESS SPEECH | H. Wallington | G. Lewis | 8/1 | 23 |
| 1960 | SMALL SLAM | G. Barling | R. Elliott | 28/1 | 26 |
| 1961 | KING'S TROOP | P. Hastings-Bass | G. Lewis | 100/7 | 39 |
| 1962 | SMARTIE | R. Mason | J. Sime | 22/1 | 31 |
| 1963 | SPANIARDS CLOSE | F. Winter | L. Piggott | 25/1 | 38 |
| 1964 | ZALEUCUS | G. Brooke | D. Smith | 100/7 | 30 |
| 1965 | CASABIANCA | N. Murless | L. Piggott | 100/9 | 26 |
| 1966 | CONTINUATION | S. McGrath | J. Roe | 25/1 | 30 |
| 1967 | REGAL LIGHT | S. Hall | G. Sexton | 100/9 | 15 |
| 1968 | GOLDEN MEAN | D. Smith | F. Durr | 28/1 | 26 |
| 1969 | KAMUNDU | F. Carr | L. Piggott | 7/1 | 24 |
| 1970 | CALPURNIUS | J. Watts | G. Duffield | 33/1 | 18 |
| 1971 | PICTURE BOY | G. Todd | J. Wilson | 11/1 | 18 |
| 1972 | TEMPEST BOY | J. Sutcliffe, jr | R. Hutchinson | 20/1 | 20 |
| 1973 | CAMOUFLAGE | J. Dunlop | D. Cullen | 14/1 | 20 |
| 1974 | OLD LUCKY | B. van Cutsem | W. Carson | 8/1 | 30 |
| 1975 | ARDOON | G. Pritchard-Gordon | D. Maitland | 9/1 | 18 |
| 1976 | JUMPING HILL | N. Murless | L. Piggott | 6/1 | 16 |
| 1977 | MY HUSSAR | J. Sutcliffe | W. Carson | 10/1 | 15 |
| 1978 | FEAR NAUGHT | J. Etherington | M. Wigham | 12/1 | 19 |
| 1979 | PIPEDREAMER | H. Candy | P. Waldron | 12/1 | 24 |
| 1980 | TENDER HEART | J. Sutcliffe | J. Mercer | 13/2 | 22 |
| 1981 | TEAMWORK | G. Harwood | G. Starkey | 8/1 | 20 |
| 1982 | BUZZARDS BAY | H. Collingridge | J. Mercer | 14/1 | 20 |
| 1983 | MIGHTY FLY | D. Elsworth | S. Cauthen | 12/1 | 31 |
| 1984 | HAWKLEY | P. Haslam | T. Williams | 10/1 | 18 |
| 1985 | COME ON THE BLUES | C. Brittain | C. Rutter | 14/1 | 27 |
| 1986 | PATRIARCH | J. Dunlop | T. Quinn | 20/1 | 32 |
| 1987 | VAGUE SHOT | R. Casey | S. Cauthen | 10/1 | 25 |
| 1988 | GOVERNORSHIP | C. Nelson | J. Reid | 33/1 | 26 |
| 1989 | TRUE PANACHE | J. Tree | P. Eddery | 25/1 | 29 |
| 1990 | PONTENUOVO | D. Elsworth | G. Bardwell | 50/1 | 32 |
| 1991 | EUROLINK THE LAD | J. Dunlop | J. Reid | 25/1 | 29 |

# Gold Cup

ASCOT                    2 MILES 4 FURLONGS                    FIRST RUN 1807

| YEAR | HORSE | TRAINER | JOCKEY | SP | RAN |
|------|-------|---------|--------|-----|-----|
| 1946 | CARACALLA II | C. Semblat | C. Elliott | 4/9 | 7 |
| 1947 | SOUVERAIN | H. Delavaud | M. Lollierou | 6/4 | 6 |
| 1948 | ARBAR | C. Semblat | C. Elliott | 4/6 | 8 |
| 1949 | ALYCIDON | W. Earl | D. Smith | 5/4 | 7 |
| 1950 | SUPERTELLO | J. Waugh | D. Smith | 10/1 | 13 |
| 1951 | PAN II | E. Pollet | R. Poincelet | 100/8 | 11 |
| 1952 | AQUINO II | F. Armstrong | G. Richards | 4/1 | 6 |
| 1953 | SOUEPI | G. Digby | C. Elliott | 11/2 | 10 |
| 1954 | ELPENOR | C. Elliott | J. Doyasbère | 100/8 | 11 |
| 1955 | BOTTICELLI | M. della Rochetta | E. Camici | 9/4 | 6 |
| 1956 | MACIP | C. Elliott | S. Boullenger | 6/1 | 10 |
| 1957 | ZARATHUSTRA | C. Boyd-Rochfort | L. Piggott | 6/1 | 9 |
| 1958 | GLADNESS | M. V. O'Brien | L. Piggott | 3/1 | 8 |
| 1959 | WALLABY II | P. Carter | F. Palmer | 9/4 | 6 |
| 1960 | SHESHOON | A. Head | G. Moore | 7/4 | 6 |
| 1961 | PANDOFELL | F. Maxwell | L. Piggott | 100/8 | 10 |
| 1962 | BALTO | M. Bonaventure | F. Palmer | 7/4 | 7 |
| 1963 | TWILIGHT ALLEY | N. Murless | L. Piggott | 100/30 | 7 |
| 1964 | *Abandoned – waterlogged* | | | | |
| 1965 | FIGHTING CHARLIE | F. Maxwell | L. Piggott | 6/1 | 7 |
| 1966 | FIGHTING CHARLIE | F. Maxwell | G. Starkey | 15/8 | 7 |
| 1967 | PARBURY | D. Candy | J. Mercer | 7/1 | 7 |
| 1968 | PARDALLO II | C. Bartholomew | W. Pyers | 13/2 | 9 |
| 1969 | LEVMOSS | S. McGrath | W. Williamson | 15/8 | 6 |
| 1970 | PRECIPICE WOOD | Mrs R. Lomax | J. Lindley | 5/1 | 6 |
| 1971 | RANDOM SHOT* | A. Budgett | G. Lewis | 11/1 | 10 |
| 1972 | ERIMO HAWK† | G. Barling | P. Eddery | 10/1 | 8 |
| 1973 | LASSALLE | R. Carver | J. Lindley | 2/1 | 7 |
| 1974 | RAGSTONE | J. Dunlop | R. Hutchinson | 6/4 | 6 |
| 1975 | SAGARO | F. Boutin | L. Piggott | 7/4 | 8 |
| 1976 | SAGARO | F. Boutin | L. Piggott | 8/15 | 7 |
| 1977 | SAGARO | F. Boutin | L. Piggott | 9/4 | 6 |
| 1978 | SHANGAMUZO | M. Stoute | G. Starkey | 13/2 | 10 |
| 1979 | LE MOSS | H. Cecil | L. Piggott | 7/4 | 6 |
| 1980 | LE MOSS | H. Cecil | J. Mercer | 3/1 | 8 |
| 1981 | ARDROSS | H. Cecil | L. Piggott | 3/10 | 4 |
| 1982 | ARDROSS | H. Cecil | L. Piggott | 1/5 | 5 |
| 1983 | LITTLE WOLF | W. R. Hern | W. Carson | 4/1 | 12 |
| 1984 | GILDORAN | B. Hills | S. Cauthen | 10/1 | 9 |
| 1985 | GILDORAN | B. Hills | B. Thomson | 5/2 | 12 |
| 1986 | LONGBOAT | W. R. Hern | W. Carson | evens | 11 |
| 1987 | PAEAN | H. Cecil | S. Cauthen | 6/1 | 8 |
| 1988 | SADEEM‡ | G. Harwood | G. Starkey | 7/2 | 13 |
| 1989 | SADEEM | G. Harwood | W. Carson | 8/11 | 8 |
| 1990 | ASHAL | H. T. Jones | R. Hills | 14/1 | 11 |
| 1991 | INDIAN QUEEN | Lord Huntingdon | W. R. Swinburn | 25/1 | 12 |

\* 1971 and † 1972: Rock Roi finished first but was disqualified
‡ 1988: Royal Gait finished first but was disqualified

# Eclipse Stakes

SANDOWN PARK            1 MILE 2 FURLONGS            FIRST RUN 1886

| Year | Horse | Trainer | Jockey | SP | Ran |
|------|-------|---------|--------|-----|-----|
| 1946 | GULF STREAM | W. Earl | H. Wragg | 8/13 | 5 |
| 1947 | MIGOLI | F. Butters | C. Smirke | 1/2 | 5 |
| 1948 | PETITION | F. Butters | K. Gethin | 8/1 | 8 |
| 1949 | DJEDDAH | C. Semblat | C. Elliott | 6/4 | 7 |
| 1950 | FLOCON | P. Carter | F. Palmer | 100/9 | 6 |
| 1951 | MYSTERY IX | P. Carter | L. Piggott | 100/8 | 8 |
| 1952 | TULYAR | M. Marsh | C. Smirke | 1/3 | 7 |
| 1953 | ARGUR | J. Glym | C. Elliott | 100/9 | 7 |
| 1954 | KING OF THE TUDORS | W. Stephenson | K. Gethin | 9/2 | 6 |
| 1955 | DARIUS | H. Wragg | L. Piggott | 11/10 | 7 |
| 1956 | TROPIQUE | G. Watson | P. Blanc | 3/1 | 8 |
| 1957 | ARCTIC EXPLORER | N. Murless | L. Piggott | 100/30 | 5 |
| 1958 | BALLYMOSS | M. V. O'Brien | A. Breasley | 8/11 | 7 |
| 1959 | SAINT CRESPIN III | A. Head | G. Moore | 5/2 | 9 |
| 1960 | JAVELOT | P. Carter | F. Palmer | 4/1 | 9 |
| 1961 | ST PADDY | N. Murless | L. Piggott | 2/13 | 7 |
| 1962 | HENRY THE SEVENTH | W. Elsey | E. Hide | 8/11 | 7 |
| 1963 | KHALKIS | P. Prendergast | G. Bougoure | 7/4 | 9 |
| 1964 | RAGUSA | P. Prendergast | G. Bougoure | 4/6 | 11 |
| 1965 | CANISBAY | C. Boyd-Rochfort | S. Clayton | 20/1 | 8 |
| 1966 | PIECES OF EIGHT | M. V. O'Brien | L. Piggott | 15/2 | 10 |
| 1967 | BUSTED | N. Murless | W. Rickaby | 8/1 | 9 |
| 1968 | ROYAL PALACE | N. Murless | A. Barclay | 9/4 | 5 |
| 1969 | WOLVER HOLLOW | H. Cecil | L. Piggott | 8/1 | 7 |
| 1970 | CONNAUGHT | N. Murless | A. Barclay | 5/4 | 3 |
| 1971 | MILL REEF | I. Balding | G. Lewis | 5/4 | 6 |
| 1972 | BRIGADIER GERARD | W. R. Hern | J. Mercer | 4/11 | 6 |
| 1973 | SCOTTISH RIFLE | J. Dunlop | R. Hutchinson | 15/8 | 6 |
| 1974 | COUP DE FEU | D. Sasse | P. Eddery | 33/1 | 12 |
| 1975 | STAR APPEAL | T. Grieper | G. Starkey | 20/1 | 16 |
| 1976 | WOLLOW* | H. Cecil | G. Dettori | 9/4 | 9 |
| 1977 | ARTAIUS | M. V. O'Brien | L. Piggott | 9/2 | 10 |
| 1978 | GUNNER B | H. Cecil | J. Mercer | 7/4 | 9 |
| 1979 | DICKENS HILL | M. O'Toole | A. Murray | 7/4 | 7 |
| 1980 | ELA-MANA-MOU | W. R. Hern | W. Carson | 85/40 | 6 |
| 1981 | MASTER WILLIE | H. Candy | P. Waldron | 6/4 | 7 |
| 1982 | KALAGLOW | G. Harwood | G. Starkey | 11/10 | 9 |
| 1983 | SOLFORD | M. V. O'Brien | P. Eddery | 3/1 | 9 |
| 1984 | SADLER'S WELLS | M. V. O'Brien | P. Eddery | 11/4 | 9 |
| 1985 | PEBBLES | C. Brittain | S. Cauthen | 7/2 | 4 |
| 1986 | DANCING BRAVE | G. Harwood | G. Starkey | 4/9 | 8 |
| 1987 | MTOTO | A. Stewart | M. Roberts | 6/1 | 8 |
| 1988 | MTOTO | A. Stewart | M. Roberts | 6/4 | 8 |
| 1989 | NASHWAN | W. R. Hern | W. Carson | 2/5 | 6 |
| 1990 | ELMAAMUL | W. R. Hern | W. Carson | 13/2 | 7 |
| 1991 | ENVIRONMENT FRIEND | J. Fanshawe | G. Duffield | 28/1 | 7 |

\* 1976: Trepan finished first but was disqualified

## July Cup

NEWMARKET                     6 FURLONGS                     FIRST RUN 1876

| Year | Horse | Trainer | Jockey | SP | Ran |
|------|-------|---------|--------|-----|-----|
| 1946 | THE BUG | H. Wellesley | C. Smirke | 8/11 | 3 |
| 1947 | FALLS OF CLYDE | E. Williams | S. Wragg | 100/30 | 5 |
| 1948 | PALM VISTA | P. Beasley | E. Smith | 13/8 | 9 |
| 1949 | ABERNANT | N. Murless | G. Richards | 2/11 | 3 |
| 1950 | ABERNANT | N. Murless | G. Richards | 8/13 | 6 |
| 1951 | HARD SAUCE | N. Bertie | G. Richards | 8/1 | 6 |
| 1952 | SET FAIR | W. Nightingall | E. Smith | 15/8 | 4 |
| 1953 | DEVON VINTAGE | J. Colling | G. Richards | 11/4 | 5 |
| 1954 | VILMORAY | B. Bullock | W. Snaith | 6/4 | 4 |
| 1955 | PAPPA FOURWAY | W. Dutton | W. Carr | 1/6 | 3 |
| 1956 | MATADOR | J. Waugh | W. Rickaby | 11/2 | 5 |
| 1957 | VIGO | W. Dutton | L. Piggott | 7/2 | 4 |
| 1958 | RIGHT BOY | W. Dutton | L. Piggott | 4/5 | 4 |
| 1959 | RIGHT BOY | P. Rohan | L. Piggott | 11/10 | 6 |
| 1960 | TIN WHISTLE | P. Rohan | L. Piggott | — | w.o |
| 1961 | GALIVANTER | W. R. Hern | W. Carr | 9/2 | 3 |
| 1962 | MARSOLVE | R. Day | W. Rickaby | 5/1 | 4 |
| 1963 | SECRET STEP | P. Hastings-Bass | G. Lewis | 2/1 | 8 |
| 1964 | DAYLIGHT ROBBERY | A. Budgett | A. Breasley | 100/9 | 7 |
| 1965 | MERRY MADCAP | F. Maxwell | R. Hutchinson | 100/8 | 14 |
| 1966 | LUCASLAND | J. Waugh | E. Eldin | 100/6 | 18 |
| 1967 | FORLORN RIVER | W. Stephenson | B. Raymond | 8/1 | 9 |
| 1968 | SO BLESSED | M. Jarvis | F. Durr | 7/2 | 7 |
| 1969 | TUDOR MUSIC | M. Jarvis | F. Durr | 4/5 | 3 |
| 1970 | HUNTERCOMBE | A. Budgett | A. Barclay | 8/13 | 4 |
| 1971 | REALM | J. Winter | B. Taylor | 11/2 | 8 |
| 1972 | PARSIMONY | R. F. J. Houghton | R. Hutchinson | 16/1 | 5 |
| 1973 | THATCH | M. V. O'Brien | L. Piggott | 4/5 | 6 |
| 1974 | SARITAMER | M. V. O'Brien | L. Piggott | 11/4 | 9 |
| 1975 | LIANGA | A. Penna | Y. Saint-Martin | 10/1 | 13 |
| 1976 | LOCHNAGER | M. W. Easterby | E. Hide | 3/1 | 10 |
| 1977 | GENTILHOMBRE* | N. Adam | P. Cook | 10/1 | 8 |
| 1978 | SOLINUS | M. V. O'Brien | L. Piggott | 4/7 | 14 |
| 1979 | THATCHING | M. V. O'Brien | L. Piggott | 2/1 | 11 |
| 1980 | MOORESTYLE | R. Armstrong | L. Piggott | 3/1 | 14 |
| 1981 | MARWELL | M. Stoute | W. R. Swinburn | 13/8 | 14 |
| 1982 | SHARPO | J. Tree | P. Eddery | 13/2 | 16 |
| 1983 | HABIBTI | J. Dunlop | W. Carson | 8/1 | 15 |
| 1984 | CHIEF SINGER | R. Sheather | R. Cochrane | 15/8 | 9 |
| 1985 | NEVER SO BOLD | R. Armstrong | S. Cauthen | 5/4 | 9 |
| 1986 | GREEN DESERT | M. Stoute | W. R. Swinburn | 7/4 | 5 |
| 1987 | AJDAL | M. Stoute | W. R. Swinburn | 9/2 | 11 |
| 1988 | SOVIET STAR | A. Fabre | C. Asmussen | 15/8 | 9 |
| 1989 | CADEAUX GENEREUX | A. Scott | Paul Eddery | 10/1 | 11 |
| 1990 | ROYAL ACADEMY | M. V. O'Brien | J. Reid | 7/1 | 9 |
| 1991 | POLISH PATRIOT | G. Harwood | R. Cochrane | 6/1 | 8 |

* 1977: Marinsky finished first but was disqualified

# *King George VI & Queen Elizabeth Diamond Stakes*

ASCOT          1 MILE 4 FURLONGS          FIRST RUN 1951

| YEAR | HORSE | TRAINER | JOCKEY | SP | RAN |
|------|-------|---------|--------|-----|-----|
| 1951 | SUPREME COURT | E. Williams | C. Elliott | 100/9 | 19 |
| 1952 | TULYAR | M. Marsh | C. Smirke | 3/1 | 15 |
| 1953 | PINZA | N. Bertie | G. Richards | 2/1 | 13 |
| 1954 | AUREOLE | C. Boyd-Rochfort | E. Smith | 9/2 | 17 |
| 1955 | VIMY | A. Head | R. Poincelet | 10/1 | 10 |
| 1956 | RIBOT | U. Penco | E. Camici | 2/5 | 9 |
| 1957 | MONTAVAL | G. Bridgland | F. Palmer | 20/1 | 12 |
| 1958 | BALLYMOSS | M. V. O'Brien | A. Breasley | 7/4 | 8 |
| 1959 | ALCIDE | C. Boyd-Rochfort | W. Carr | 2/1 | 11 |
| 1960 | AGGRESSOR | J. Gosden | J. Lindley | 100/8 | 8 |
| 1961 | RIGHT ROYAL V | E. Pollet | R. Poincelet | 6/4 | 4 |
| 1962 | MATCH III | F. Mathet | Y. Saint-Martin | 9/2 | 11 |
| 1963 | RAGUSA | P. Prendergast | G. Bougoure | 4/1 | 10 |
| 1964 | NASRAM II | E. Fellows | W. Pyers | 100/7 | 4 |
| 1965 | MEADOW COURT | P. Prendergast | L. Piggott | 6/5 | 12 |
| 1966 | AUNT EDITH | N. Murless | L. Piggott | 7/2 | 5 |
| 1967 | BUSTED | N. Murless | G. Moore | 4/1 | 9 |
| 1968 | ROYAL PALACE | N. Murless | A. Barclay | 7/4 | 7 |
| 1969 | PARK TOP | B. van Cutsem | L. Piggott | 9/4 | 9 |
| 1970 | NIJINSKY | M. V. O'Brien | L. Piggott | 40/85 | 6 |
| 1971 | MILL REEF | I. Balding | G. Lewis | 8/13 | 10 |
| 1972 | BRIGADIER GERARD | W. R. Hern | J. Mercer | 8/13 | 9 |
| 1973 | DAHLIA | M. Zilber | W. Pyers | 10/1 | 12 |
| 1974 | DAHLIA | M. Zilber | L. Piggott | 15/8 | 10 |
| 1975 | GRUNDY | P. Walwyn | P. Eddery | 4/5 | 11 |
| 1976 | PAWNEESE | A. Penna | Y. Saint-Martin | 9/4 | 10 |
| 1977 | THE MINSTREL | M. V. O'Brien | L. Piggott | 7/4 | 11 |
| 1978 | ILE DE BOURBON | R. F. J. Houghton | J. Reid | 12/1 | 14 |
| 1979 | TROY | W. R. Hern | W. Carson | 2/5 | 7 |
| 1980 | ELA-MANA-MOU | W. R. Hern | W. Carson | 11/4 | 10 |
| 1981 | SHERGAR | M. Stoute | W. R. Swinburn | 2/5 | 7 |
| 1982 | KALAGLOW | G. Harwood | G. Starkey | 13/2 | 9 |
| 1983 | TIME CHARTER | H. Candy | J. Mercer | 5/1 | 9 |
| 1984 | TEENOSO | G. Wragg | L. Piggott | 13/2 | 13 |
| 1985 | PETOSKI | W. R. Hern | W. Carson | 12/1 | 12 |
| 1986 | DANCING BRAVE | G. Harwood | P. Eddery | 6/4 | 9 |
| 1987 | REFERENCE POINT | H. Cecil | S. Cauthen | 11/10 | 9 |
| 1988 | MTOTO | A. Stewart | M. Roberts | 4/1 | 10 |
| 1989 | NASHWAN | W. R. Hern | W. Carson | 2/9 | 7 |
| 1990 | BELMEZ | H. Cecil | M. Kinane | 15/2 | 11 |
| 1991 | GENEROUS | P. Cole | A. Munro | 4/6 | 9 |

# Stewards' Cup

GOODWOOD                    6 FURLONGS              FIRST RUN 1840

| Year | Horse | Trainer | Jockey | SP | Ran |
|------|-------|---------|--------|-----|-----|
| 1946 | COMMISSAR | E. Stedall | A. Richardson | 10/1 | 15 |
| 1947 | CLOSEBURN | N. Murless | G. Richards | 100/7 | 19 |
| 1948 | DRAMATIC | G. Todd | E. Smith | 9/1 | 16 |
| 1949 | THE BITE | J. Wood | H. Packham | 33/1 | 21 |
| 1950 | FIRST CONSUL | F. Armstrong | E. Britt | 100/9 | 21 |
| 1951 | SUGAR BOWL | F. Armstrong | W. Snaith | 100/6 | 21 |
| 1952 | SMOKEY EYES | R. Jarvis | C. Smirke | 100/7 | 18 |
| 1953 | PALPITATE | F. Armstrong | W. Snaith | 5/1 | 22 |
| 1954 | ASHURST WONDER | L. Hall | A. Shrive | 50/1 | 28 |
| 1955 | KING BRUCE | P. Hastings-Bass | W. Rickaby | 100/6 | 26 |
| 1956 | MATADOR | J. Waugh | E. Smith | 100/8 | 24 |
| 1957 | ARCANDY | G. Beeby | T. Gosling | 100/7 | 16 |
| 1958 | EPAULETTE | W. O'Gorman | F. Durr | 33/1 | 20 |
| 1959 | TUDOR MONARCH | W. Nightingall | G. Lewis | 25/1 | 21 |
| 1960 | MONET | J. Tree | J. Lindley | 20/1 | 18 |
| 1961 | SKYMASTER | G. Smyth | A. Breasley | 100/7 | 22 |
| 1962 | VICTORINA | P. Nelson | W. Williamson | 10/1 | 26 |
| 1963 | CREOLE | J. Jarvis | S. Smith | 20/1 | 25 |
| 1964 | DUNME | R. Read | P. Cook | 9/1 | 20 |
| 1965 | POTIER | J. Jarvis | R. Hutchinson | 100/7 | 20 |
| 1966 | PATIENT CONSTABLE | R. Smyth | R. Reader | 33/1 | 25 |
| 1967 | SKY DIVER | P. Payne Gallwey | D. Cullen | 20/1 | 31 |
| 1968 | SKY DIVER | P. Payne Gallwey | T. Sturrock | 100/6 | 18 |
| 1969 | ROYAL SMOKE | W. O'Gorman | M. Thomas | 100/7 | 15 |
| 1970 | JUKEBOX | H. Wallington | L. Piggott | 100/6 | 24 |
| 1971 | APOLLO NINE | P. Nelson | J. Lindley | 14/1 | 26 |
| 1972 | TOUCH PAPER | B. Hobbs | P. Cook | 25/1 | 22 |
| 1973 | ALPHADAMUS | M. Stoute | P. Cook | 16/1 | 27 |
| 1974 | RED ALERT | D. Weld | J. Roe | 16/1 | 25 |
| 1975 | IMPORT | W. Wightman | M. Thomas | 14/1 | 21 |
| 1976 | JIMMY THE SINGER | B. Lunness | E. Johnson | 15/1 | 17 |
| 1977 | CALIBINA | P. Cole | G. Baxter | 8/1 | 24 |
| 1978 | AHONOORA | B. Swift | P. Waldron | 50/1 | 23 |
| 1979 | STANDAAM | C. Brittain | P. Bradwell | 5/1 | 16 |
| 1980 | REPETITIOUS | G. Harwood | A. Clark | 15/1 | 28 |
| 1981 | CREWS HILL | F. Durr | G. Starkey | 11/1 | 30 |
| 1982 | SOBA | D. Chapman | D. Nicholls | 18/1 | 30 |
| 1983 | AUTUMN SUNSET | M. Stoute | W. Carson | 6/1 | 23 |
| 1984 | PETONG | M. Jarvis | B. Raymond | 8/1 | 26 |
| 1985 | AL TRUI | S. Mellor | M. Wigham | 9/1 | 28 |
| 1986 | GREEN RUBY | G. Balding | J. Williams | 20/1 | 24 |
| 1987 | MADRACO | P. Calver | P. Hill | 50/1 | 30 |
| 1988 | ROTHERFIELD GREYS | C. Wall | N. Day | 14/1 | 28 |
| 1989 | VERY ADJACENT | G. Lewis | D. Gibson | 12/1 | 22 |
| 1990 | KNIGHT OF MERCY | R. Hannon | B. Raymond | 14/1 | 30 |
| 1991 | NOTLEY | R. Hannon | R. Perham | 14/1 | 29 |

# *Sussex Stakes*

GOODWOOD                    I MILE                FIRST RUN 1841

| YEAR | HORSE | TRAINER | JOCKEY | SP | RAN |
|------|-------|---------|--------|-----|-----|
| 1946 | RADIOTHERAPY | F. Templeman | G. Richards | 7/4 | 6 |
| 1947 | COMBAT | F. Darling | G. Richards | — | 2 |
| 1948 | MY BABU | F. Armstrong | C. Smirke | 1/3 | 2 |
| 1949 | KRAKATOA | N. Murless | G. Richards | 2/11 | 2 |
| 1950 | PALESTINE | M. Marsh | C. Smirke | 1/2 | 4 |
| 1951 | LE SAGE | T. Carey | G. Richards | 6/4 | 7 |
| 1952 | AGITATOR | N. Murless | G. Richards | 8/15 | 5 |
| 1953 | KING OF THE TUDORS | W. Stephenson | C. Spares | 11/10 | 4 |
| 1954 | LANDAU | N. Murless | W. Snaith | 6/4 | 4 |
| 1955 | MY KINGDOM | W. Nightingall | D. Smith | 13/2 | 5 |
| 1956 | LUCERO | H. Wragg | E. Mercer | 8/1 | 6 |
| 1957 | QUORUM | W. Lyde | A. Russell | 10/11 | 4 |
| 1958 | MAJOR PORTION | T. Leader | E. Smith | 8/11 | 5 |
| 1959 | PETITE ETOILE | N. Murless | L. Piggott | 1/10 | 6 |
| 1960 | VENTURE VII | A. Head | G. Moore | 13/8 | 6 |
| 1961 | LE LEVANSTELL | S. McGrath | W. Williamson | 100/7 | 11 |
| 1962 | ROMULUS | R. F. J. Houghton | W. Swinburn | 9/1 | 8 |
| 1963 | QUEEN'S HUSSAR | T. Corbett | R. Hutchinson | 25/1 | 10 |
| 1964 | ROAN ROCKET | G. Todd | L. Piggott | 4/6 | 8 |
| 1965 | CARLEMONT | P. Prendergast | R. Hutchinson | 7/2 | 11 |
| 1966 | PAVEH | T. Ainsworth | R. Hutchinson | 5/1 | 7 |
| 1967 | REFORM | Sir G. Richards | A. Breasley | evens | 10 |
| 1968 | PETINGO | F. Armstrong | L. Piggott | 6/4 | 6 |
| 1969 | JIMMY REPPIN | J. Sutcliffe, jr | G. Lewis | 7/4 | 5 |
| 1970 | HUMBLE DUTY | P. Walwyn | D. Keith | 11/8 | 5 |
| 1971 | BRIGADIER GERARD | W. R. Hern | J. Mercer | 4/6 | 5 |
| 1972 | SALLUST | W. R. Hern | J. Mercer | 9/2 | 3 |
| 1973 | THATCH | M. V. O'Brien | L. Piggott | 4/5 | 7 |
| 1974 | ACE OF ACES | M. Zilber | J. Lindley | 8/1 | 10 |
| 1975 | BOLKONSKI | H. Cecil | G. Dettori | 1/2 | 9 |
| 1976 | WOLLOW | H. Cecil | G. Dettori | 10/11 | 9 |
| 1977 | ARTAIUS | M. V. O'Brien | L. Piggott | 6/4 | 11 |
| 1978 | JAAZEIRO | M. V. O'Brien | L. Piggott | 8/13 | 6 |
| 1979 | KRIS | H. Cecil | J. Mercer | 4/5 | 7 |
| 1980 | POSSE | J. Dunlop | P. Eddery | 8/13 | 9 |
| 1981 | KINGS LAKE | M. V. O'Brien | P. Eddery | 5/2 | 9 |
| 1982 | ON THE HOUSE | H. Wragg | J. Reid | 14/1 | 13 |
| 1983 | NOALCOHOLIC | G. Pritchard-Gordon | G. Duffield | 18/1 | 11 |
| 1984 | CHIEF SINGER | R. Sheather | R. Cochrane | 4/7 | 5 |
| 1985 | ROUSILLON | G. Harwood | G. Starkey | 2/1 | 10 |
| 1986 | SONIC LADY | M. Stoute | W. R. Swinburn | 5/6 | 5 |
| 1987 | SOVIET STAR | A. Fabre | G. Starkey | 3/1 | 7 |
| 1988 | WARNING | G. Harwood | P. Eddery | 11/10 | 9 |
| 1989 | ZILZAL | M. Stoute | W. R. Swinburn | 5/2 | 8 |
| 1990 | DISTANT RELATIVE | B. Hills | W. Carson | 4/1 | 7 |
| 1991 | SECOND SET | L. Cumani | L. Dettori | 5/1 | 8 |

## International Stakes

YORK                    1 MILE 2½ FURLONGS          FIRST RUN 1972

| Year | Horse | Trainer | Jockey | SP | Ran |
|------|-------|---------|--------|-----|-----|
| 1972 | ROBERTO | M. V. O'Brien | B. Baeza | 12/1 | 5 |
| 1973 | MOULTON | H. Wragg | G. Lewis | 14/1 | 8 |
| 1974 | DAHLIA | M. Zilber | L. Piggott | 8/15 | 9 |
| 1975 | DAHLIA | M. Zilber | L. Piggott | 7/2 | 6 |
| 1976 | WOLLOW | H. Cecil | G. Dettori | 9/4 | 7 |
| 1977 | RELKINO | W. R. Hern | W. Carson | 33/1 | 8 |
| 1978 | HAWAIIAN SOUND | B. Hills | L. Piggott | 2/1 | 10 |
| 1979 | TROY | W. R. Hern | W. Carson | 1/2 | 10 |
| 1980 | MASTER WILLIE | H. Candy | P. Waldron | 13/2 | 12 |
| 1981 | BELDALE FLUTTER | M. Jarvis | P. Eddery | 9/1 | 9 |
| 1982 | ASSERT | D. O'Brien | P. Eddery | 4/5 | 7 |
| 1983 | CAERLEON | M. V. O'Brien | P. Eddery | 100/30 | 9 |
| 1984 | CORMORANT WOOD | B. Hills | S. Cauthen | 15/1 | 9 |
| 1985 | COMMANCHE RUN | L. Cumani | L. Piggott | 5/1 | 6 |
| 1986 | SHARDARI | M. Stoute | W. R. Swinburn | 13/8 | 12 |
| 1987 | TRIPTYCH | P. Biancone | S. Cauthen | 13/8 | 10 |
| 1988 | SHADY HEIGHTS* | R. Armstrong | W. Carson | 7/2 | 6 |
| 1989 | ILE DE CHYPRE | G. Harwood | A. Clark | 16/1 | 7 |
| 1990 | IN THE GROOVE | D. Elsworth | S. Cauthen | 4/1 | 9 |
| 1991 | TERIMON | C. Brittain | M. Roberts | 16/1 | 6 |

* 1988: Persian Heights finished first but was relegated to third

# *Yorkshire Oaks*

YORK                    I MILE 4 FURLONGS              FIRST RUN 1849

| YEAR | HORSE | TRAINER | JOCKEY | SP | RAN |
|------|-------|---------|--------|-----|-----|
| 1946 | LIVE LETTERS | N. Cannon | T. Weston | 8/1 | 11 |
| 1947 | LADYCROSS | C. Boyd-Rochfort | W. Carr | 2/1 | 6 |
| 1948 | ANGELOLA | C. Boyd-Rochfort | E. Britt | 4/1 | 9 |
| 1949 | UNKNOWN QUALITY | J. Jarvis | W. Rickaby | 3/1 | 6 |
| 1950 | ABOVE BOARD | C. Boyd-Rochfort | E. Smith | 100/30 | 5 |
| 1951 | SEA PARROT | N. Murless | G. Richards | 13/2 | 8 |
| 1952 | FRIEZE | C. Elsey | E. Britt | 5/4 | 4 |
| 1953 | KERKEB | M. Marsh | G. Richards | 7/4 | 8 |
| 1954 | FEEVAGH | W. Stephenson | K. Gethin | 20/1 | 10 |
| 1955 | ARK ROYAL | G. Colling | E. Mercer | evens | 5 |
| 1956 | INDIAN TWILIGHT | J. Colling | J. Mercer | 13/2 | 9 |
| 1957 | ALMERIA | C. Boyd-Rochfort | W. Carr | 11/10 | 7 |
| 1958 | NONE NICER | W. R. Hern | S. Clayton | 4/1 | 8 |
| 1959 | PETITE ETOILE | N. Murless | L. Piggott | 2/15 | 3 |
| 1960 | LYNCHRIS | J. Oxx | W. Williamson | 5/4 | 7 |
| 1961 | TENACITY | G. Richards | A. Breasley | 7/1 | 7 |
| 1962 | WEST SIDE STORY | T. Leader | E. Smith | 2/1 | 5 |
| 1963 | OUTCROP | G. Barling | E. Smith | 9/1 | 11 |
| 1964 | HOMEWARD BOUND | J. Oxley | G. Starkey | 2/1 | 7 |
| 1965 | MABEL | P. Walwyn | J. Mercer | 7/4 | 5 |
| 1966 | PARTHIAN GLANCE | G. Todd | L. Piggott | 3/1 | 8 |
| 1967 | PALATCH | H. Leader | B. Taylor | 7/1 | 6 |
| 1968 | EXCHANGE | H. Leader | B. Taylor | 7/2 | 8 |
| 1969 | FRONTIER GODDESS | P. Walwyn | D. Keith | 3/1 | 4 |
| 1970 | LUPE | N. Murless | A. Barclay | 4/6 | 3 |
| 1971 | FLEET WAHINE | H. T. Jones | G. Lewis | 9/4 | 6 |
| 1972 | ATTICA MELI | N. Murless | G. Lewis | 13/2 | 6 |
| 1973 | MYSTERIOUS | N. Murless | G. Lewis | 4/6 | 5 |
| 1974 | DIBIDALE | B. Hills | W. Carson | 1/3 | 3 |
| 1975 | MAY HILL | P. Walwyn | P. Eddery | 4/1 | 5 |
| 1976 | SARAH SIDDONS | P. Prendergast | C. Roche | 100/30 | 13 |
| 1977 | BUSACA | P. Walwyn | P. Eddery | 5/1 | 8 |
| 1978 | FAIR SALINIA | M. Stoute | G. Starkey | 5/1 | 10 |
| 1979 | CONNAUGHT BRIDGE | H. Cecil | J. Mercer | 9/2 | 5 |
| 1980 | SHOOT A LINE | W. R. Hern | L. Piggott | 13/8 | 7 |
| 1981 | CONDESSA | J. Bolger | D. Gillespie | 5/1 | 11 |
| 1982 | AWAASIF | J. Dunlop | L. Piggott | 11/4 | 7 |
| 1983 | SUN PRINCESS | W. R. Hern | W. Carson | 6/5 | 6 |
| 1984 | CIRCUS PLUME | J. Dunlop | W. Carson | 5/6 | 5 |
| 1985 | SALLY BROWN | M. Stoute | W. R. Swinburn | 6/1 | 7 |
| 1986 | UNTOLD | M. Stoute | G. Starkey | 5/1 | 11 |
| 1987 | BINT PASHA | P. Cole | T. Quinn | 5/1 | 9 |
| 1988 | DIMINUENDO | H. Cecil | S. Cauthen | 30/100 | 6 |
| 1989 | ROSEATE TERN | W. R. Hern | W. Carson | 11/2 | 5 |
| 1990 | HELLENIC | M. Stoute | W. Carson | 100/30 | 6 |
| 1991 | MAGNIFICENT STAR | M. Moubarak | A. Cruz | 16/1 | 7 |

# Ebor Handicap

YORK　　　　　　　1 MILE 5 FURLONGS　　　　FIRST RUN 1903

| Year | Horse | Trainer | Jockey | SP | RAN |
|------|-------|---------|--------|-----|-----|
| 1946 | FOXTROT | E. Lambton | E. Britt | 3/1 | 13 |
| 1947 | PROCNE | C. Elsey | J. Sime | 8/1 | 11 |
| 1948 | DONINO | A. Cooper | J. Sime | 100/7 | 20 |
| 1949 | MIRACULOUS ATOM | S. Hall | W. Nevett | 100/7 | 16 |
| 1950 | CADZOW OAK | G. Thwaites | J. Thompson | 100/8 | 21 |
| 1951 | BOB | C. Elsey | E. Carter | 8/1 | 25 |
| 1952 | SIGNIFICATION | J. Peace | H. Jones | 10/1 | 15 |
| 1953 | NOROOZ | M. Marsh | R. Fawdon | 100/9 | 21 |
| 1954 | BY THUNDER! | F. Armstrong | W. Swinburn | 7/1 | 22 |
| 1955 | HYPERION KID | H. Wragg | P. Robinson | 100/8 | 25 |
| 1956 | DONALD | J. Jarvis | D. Smith | 5/1 | 17 |
| 1957 | MORECAMBE | S. Hall | J. Sime | 100/8 | 30 |
| 1958 | GLADNESS | M. V. O'Brien | L. Piggott | 5/1 | 25 |
| 1959 | PRIMERA | N. Murless | L. Piggott | 6/1 | 21 |
| 1960 | PERSIAN ROAD | J. Tree | G. Moore | 18/1 | 21 |
| 1961 | DIE HARD | M. V. O'Brien | L. Piggott | 11/2 | 21 |
| 1962 | SOSTENUTO | W. Elsey | D. Morris | 9/1 | 18 |
| 1963 | PARTHOLON | T. Shaw | J. Sime | 100/6 | 22 |
| 1964 | PROPER PRIDE | W. Wharton | D. Smith | 28/1 | 20 |
| 1965 | TWELFTH MAN | H. Wragg | P. Cook | 6/1 | 25 |
| 1966 | LOMOND | R. Jarvis | E. Eldin | 100/8 | 23 |
| 1967 | OVALTINE | J. Watts | E. Johnson | 100/8 | 22 |
| 1968 | ALIGNMENT | W. Elsey | E. Johnson | 9/1 | 20 |
| 1969 | BIG HAT | D. Hanley | R. Still | 40/1 | 19 |
| 1970 | TINTAGEL II | R. Sturdy | L. Piggott | 6/1 | 21 |
| 1971 | KNOTTY PINE | M. Jarvis | F. Durr | 9/2 | 21 |
| 1972 | CRAZY RHYTHM | S. Ingham | F. Durr | 19/2 | 21 |
| 1973 | BONNE NOEL | P. Prendergast | C. Roche | 4/1 | 20 |
| 1974 | ANJI | J. Sutcliffe, jr | T. McKeown | 20/1 | 18 |
| 1975 | DAKOTA | S. Hall | A. Barclay | 7/1 | 18 |
| 1976 | SIR MONTAGU | H. R. Price | W. Carson | 11/4 | 15 |
| 1977 | MOVE OFF | J. Calvert | J. Bleasdale | 9/1 | 14 |
| 1978 | TOTOWAH | M. Jarvis | P. Cook | 20/1 | 22 |
| 1979 | SEA PIGEON | M. H. Easterby | J. J. O'Neill | 18/1 | 17 |
| 1980 | SHAFTESBURY | M. Stoute | G. Starkey | 12/1 | 16 |
| 1981 | PROTECTION RACKET | J. Hindley | M. Birch | 15/2 | 22 |
| 1982 | ANOTHER SAM | R. Hannon | B. Rouse | 16/1 | 15 |
| 1983 | JUPITER ISLAND | C. Brittain | L. Piggott | 9/1 | 16 |
| 1984 | CRAZY | G. Harwood | W. R. Swinburn | 10/1 | 14 |
| 1985 | WESTERN DANCER | C. Horgan | P. Cook | 20/1 | 19 |
| 1986 | PRIMARY | G. Harwood | G. Starkey | 6/1 | 22 |
| 1987 | DAARKOM | A. Stewart | M. Roberts | 13/2 | 15 |
| 1988 | KNELLER | H. Cecil | Paul Eddery | 9/1 | 21 |
| 1989 | SAPIENCE | J. FitzGerald | P. Eddery | 15/2 | 18 |
| 1990 | FURTHER FLIGHT | B. Hills | M. Hills | 7/1 | 22 |
| 1991 | DEPOSKI | M. Stoute | F. Norton | 12/1 | 22 |

# Nunthorpe Stakes

YORK        5 FURLONGS        FIRST RUN 1903

| YEAR | HORSE | TRAINER | JOCKEY | SP | RAN |
|------|-------|---------|--------|-----|-----|
| 1946 | THE BUG | M. Marsh | C. Smirke | 4/6 | 4 |
| 1947 | COMO | G. Armstrong | W. Carr | 3/1 | 6 |
| 1948 | CARELESS NORA | J. Dines | C. Elliott | 6/4 | 6 |
| 1949 | ABERNANT | N. Murless | G. Richards | 2/11 | 4 |
| 1950 | ABERNANT | N. Murless | G. Richards | 7/100 | 3 |
| 1951 | ROYAL SERENADE | H. Wragg | C. Elliott | 4/1 | 6 |
| 1952 | ROYAL SERENADE | H. Wragg | G. Richards | 4/6 | 5 |
| 1953 | HIGH TREASON | T. Leader | D. Greening | 9/4 | 8 |
| 1954 | MY BEAU | P. Prendergast | T. Carter | 7/1 | 11 |
| 1955 | ROYAL PALM | F. Armstrong | W. Snaith | 11/10 | 4 |
| 1956 | ENNIS | W. Nightingall | P. Tulk | 11/2 | 5 |
| 1957 | GRATITUDE | H. Cottrill | W. Snaith | 7/2 | 5 |
| 1958 | RIGHT BOY | W. Dutton | L. Piggott | 8/100 | 3 |
| 1959 | RIGHT BOY | P. Rohan | L. Piggott | 4/9 | 6 |
| 1960 | BLEEP-BLEEP | H. Cottrill | W. Carr | 9/2 | 7 |
| 1961 | FLORIBUNDA | P. Prendergast | R. Hutchinson | 4/1 | 6 |
| 1962 | GAY MAIRI | H. Whiteman | A. Breasley | 100/8 | 9 |
| 1963 | MATATINA | F. Armstrong | L. Piggott | 7/2 | 6 |
| 1964 | ALTHREY DON | P. Rohan | R. Maddock | 3/1 | 10 |
| 1965 | POLYFOTO | E. Reavey | J. Wilson | 20/1 | 8 |
| 1966 | CATERINA | F. Armstrong | L. Piggott | 13/2 | 11 |
| 1967 | FORLORN RIVER | W. Stephenson | B. Raymond | 6/1 | 12 |
| 1968 | SO BLESSED | M. Jarvis | F. Durr | 4/6 | 5 |
| 1969 | TOWER WALK | G. Barling | L. Piggott | 7/1 | 6 |
| 1970 | HUNTERCOMBE | A. Budgett | A. Barclay | 5/4 | 3 |
| 1971 | SWING EASY* | J. Tree | L. Piggott | 2/1 | 9 |
| 1972 | DEEP DIVER | P. Davey | W. Williamson | 100/30 | 7 |
| 1973 | SANDFORD LAD | H. R. Price | A. Murray | 4/1 | 8 |
| 1974 | BLUE CASHMERE | M. Stoute | E. Hide | 18/1 | 12 |
| 1975 | BAY EXPRESS | P. Nelson | W. Carson | 100/30 | 10 |
| 1976 | LOCHNAGER | M. W. Easterby | E. Hide | 4/5 | 11 |
| 1977 | HAVEROID | N. Adam | E. Hide | 10/1 | 8 |
| 1978 | SOLINUS | M. V. O'Brien | L. Piggott | 1/2 | 9 |
| 1979 | AHONOORA | F. Durr | G. Starkey | 3/1 | 9 |
| 1980 | SHARPO | J. Tree | P. Eddery | 3/1 | 11 |
| 1981 | SHARPO | J. Tree | P. Eddery | 14/1 | 9 |
| 1982 | SHARPO | J. Tree | S. Cauthen | 13/1 | 11 |
| 1983 | HABIBTI | J. Dunlop | W. Carson | 13/8 | 10 |
| 1984 | COMMITTED | D. Weld | B. Thomson | 5/1 | 8 |
| 1985 | NEVER SO BOLD | R. Armstrong | S. Cauthen | 4/6 | 7 |
| 1986 | LAST TYCOON | R. Collet | Y. Saint-Martin | 7/2 | 8 |
| 1987 | AJDAL | M. Stoute | W. R. Swinburn | 2/1 | 11 |
| 1988 | HANDSOME SAILOR | B. Hills | M. Hills | 5/2 | 12 |
| 1989 | CADEAUX GENEREUX | A. Scott | P. Eddery | 11/10 | 11 |
| 1990 | DAYJUR | W. R. Hern | W. Carson | 8/11 | 9 |
| 1991 | SHEIKH ALBADOU | A. Scott | P. Eddery | 6/1 | 9 |

* 1971: Green God finished first but was disqualified and placed 2nd

# Sprint Cup

HAYDOCK PARK  6 FURLONGS  FIRST RUN 1966

| Year | Horse | Trainer | Jockey | SP | Ran |
|------|-------|---------|--------|----|----|
| 1966 | BE FRIENDLY | C. Mitchell | C. Williams | 15/2 | 15 |
| 1967 | BE FRIENDLY | C. Mitchell | A. Breasley | 2/1 | 9 |
| 1968 | *Abandoned – fog* | | | | |
| 1969 | TUDOR MUSIC | M. Jarvis | F. Durr | 11/4 | 11 |
| 1970 | GOLDEN ORANGE | K. Cundell | J. Lindley | 10/1 | 5 |
| 1971 | GREEN GOD | M. Jarvis | L. Piggott | 7/4 | 7 |
| 1972 | ABERGWAUN | M. V. O'Brien | L. Piggott | 11/10 | 10 |
| 1973 | THE BLUES | W. Marshall | R. Marshall | 10/1 | 8 |
| 1974 | PRINCELY SON | K. Cundell | J. Seagrave | 8/1 | 9 |
| 1975 | LIANGA | A. Penna | Y. Saint-Martin | 2/1 | 7 |
| 1976 | RECORD TOKEN | P. Walwyn | P. Eddery | 3/1 | 8 |
| 1977 | BOLDBOY | W. R. Hern | W. Carson | evens | 8 |
| 1978 | ABSALOM | R. Jarvis | M. Thomas | 20/1 | 14 |
| 1979 | DOUBLE FORM | R. F. J. Houghton | G. Lewis | 11/4 | 8 |
| 1980 | MOORESTYLE | R. Armstrong | L. Piggott | 8/13 | 8 |
| 1981 | RUNNETT | J. Dunlop | B. Raymond | 6/1 | 6 |
| 1982 | INDIAN KING | G. Harwood | G. Starkey | 3/1 | 9 |
| 1983 | HABIBTI | J. Dunlop | W. Carson | 8/13 | 6 |
| 1984 | PETONG | M. Jarvis | B. Raymond | 11/1 | 9 |
| 1985 | OROJOYA | J. Hindley | B. Thomson | 11/1 | 8 |
| 1986 | GREEN DESERT | M. Stoute | W. R. Swinburn | 5/4 | 8 |
| 1987 | AJDAL | M. Stoute | W. R. Swinburn | 8/11 | 8 |
| 1988 | DOWSING | J. Tree | P. Eddery | 15/2 | 10 |
| 1989 | DANEHILL | J. Tree | P. Eddery | 3/1 | 9 |
| 1990 | DAYJUR | W. R. Hern | W. Carson | 1/2 | 9 |
| 1991 | POLAR FALCON | J. Hammond | C. Asmussen | 13/2 | 6 |

# St Leger Stakes

DONCASTER      1 MILE 6 FURLONGS 132 YARDS   FIRST RUN 1776

| YEAR | HORSE | TRAINER | JOCKEY | SP | RAN |
|------|-------|---------|--------|-----|-----|
| 1900 | DIAMOND JUBILEE | R. Marsh | H. Jones | 2/7 | 11 |
| 1901 | DORICLES | A. Hayhoe | K. Cannon | 40/1 | 13 |
| 1902 | SCEPTRE | R. Sievier | F. Hardy | 100/30 | 12 |
| 1903 | ROCK SAND | G. Blackwell | D. Maher | 2/5 | 5 |
| 1904 | PRETTY POLLY | P. Gilpin | W. Lane | 2/5 | 6 |
| 1905 | CHALLACOMBE | A. Taylor, jr | O. Madden | 100/6 | 8 |
| 1906 | TROUTBECK | W. Waugh | G. Stern | 5/1 | 12 |
| 1907 | WOOL WINDER | H. Enoch | W. Halsey | 11/10 | 12 |
| 1908 | YOUR MAJESTY | C. Morton | W. Griggs | 11/8 | 10 |
| 1909 | BAYARDO | A. Taylor | D. Maher | 10/11 | 7 |
| 1910 | SWYNFORD | G. Lambton | F. Wootton | 9/2 | 11 |
| 1911 | PRINCE PALATINE | H. Beardsley | F. O'Neill | 100/30 | 8 |
| 1912 | TRACERY | J. Watson | G. Bellhouse | 8/1 | 14 |
| 1913 | NIGHT HAWK | W. Robinson | E. Wheatley | 50/1 | 12 |
| 1914 | BLACK JESTER | C. Morton | W. Griggs | 10/1 | 18 |
| 1915 | POMMERN | C. Peck | S. Donoghue | 1/3 | 7 |
| 1916 | HURRY ON | F. Darling | C. Childs | 11/10 | 5 |
| 1917 | GAY CRUSADER | A. Taylor, jr | S. Donoghue | 2/11 | 3 |
| 1918 | GAINSBOROUGH | A. Taylor, jr | J. Childs | 4/11 | 5 |
| 1919 | KEYSOE | G. Lambton | B. Carslake | 100/8 | 10 |
| 1920 | CALIGULA | H. Leader | A. Smith | 100/6 | 14 |
| 1921 | POLEMARCH | T. Green | J. Childs | 50/1 | 9 |
| 1922 | ROYAL LANCER | A. Sadler, jr | R. Jones | 33/1 | 24 |
| 1923 | TRANQUIL | C. Morton | T. Weston | 100/9 | 13 |
| 1924 | SALMON-TROUT | R. Dawson | B. Carslake | 6/1 | 17 |
| 1925 | SOLARIO | R. Day | J. Childs | 7/2 | 15 |
| 1926 | CORONACH | F. Darling | J. Childs | 8/15 | 12 |
| 1927 | BOOK LAW | A. Taylor, jr | H. Jelliss | 7/4 | 16 |
| 1928 | FAIRWAY | F. Butters | T. Weston | 7/4 | 13 |
| 1929 | TRIGO | R. Dawson | M. Beary | 5/1 | 14 |
| 1930 | SINGAPORE | T. Hogg | G. Richards | 4/1 | 13 |
| 1931 | SANDWICH | J. Jarvis | H. Wragg | 9/1 | 10 |
| 1932 | FIRDAUSSI | F. Butters | F. Fox | 20/1 | 19 |
| 1933 | HYPERION | G. Lambton | T. Weston | 6/4 | 14 |
| 1934 | WINDSOR LAD | M. Marsh | C. Smirke | 4/9 | 10 |
| 1935 | BAHRAM | F. Butters | C. Smirke | 4/11 | 8 |
| 1936 | BOSWELL | C. Boyd-Rochfort | P. Beasley | 20/1 | 13 |
| 1937 | CHULMLEIGH | T. Hogg | G. Richards | 18/1 | 15 |
| 1938 | SCOTTISH UNION | N. Cannon | B. Carslake | 7/1 | 9 |
| 1939 | *No race* | | | | |
| 1940 | TURKHAN | F. Butters | G. Richards | 4/1 | 6 |
| 1941 | SUN CASTLE | C. Boyd-Rochfort | G. Bridgland | 10/1 | 16 |
| 1942 | SUN CHARIOT | F. Darling | G. Richards | 9/4 | 8 |
| 1943 | HERRINGBONE | W. Earl | H. Wragg | 100/6 | 12 |
| 1944 | TEHRAN | F. Butters | G. Richards | 9/2 | 17 |
| 1945 | CHAMOSSAIRE | R. Perryman | T. Lowrey | 11/2 | 10 |

| Year | Horse | Trainer | Jockey | SP | RAN |
|------|-------|---------|--------|-----|-----|
| 1946 | AIRBORNE | R. Perryman | T. Lowrey | 3/1 | 11 |
| 1947 | SAYAJIRAO | F. Armstrong | E. Britt | 9/2 | 11 |
| 1948 | BLACK TARQUIN | C. Boyd-Rochfort | E. Britt | 15/2 | 14 |
| 1949 | RIDGE WOOD | N. Murless | M. Beary | 100/7 | 16 |
| 1950 | SCRATCH | C. Semblat | W. Johnstone | 9/2 | 15 |
| 1951 | TALMA | C. Semblat | W. Johnstone | 7/1 | 18 |
| 1952 | TULYAR | M. Marsh | C. Smirke | 10/11 | 12 |
| 1953 | PREMONITION | C. Boyd-Rochfort | E. Smith | 10/1 | 11 |
| 1954 | NEVER SAY DIE | J. Lawson | C. Smirke | 100/30 | 16 |
| 1955 | MELD | C. Boyd-Rochfort | W. Carr | 10/11 | 8 |
| 1956 | CAMBREMER | G. Bridgland | F. Palmer | 8/1 | 13 |
| 1957 | BALLYMOSS | M. V. O'Brien | T. Burns | 8/1 | 16 |
| 1958 | ALCIDE | C. Boyd-Rochfort | W. Carr | 4/9 | 8 |
| 1959 | CANTELO | C. Elsey | E. Hide | 100/7 | 11 |
| 1960 | ST PADDY | N. Murless | L. Piggott | 4/6 | 9 |
| 1961 | AURELIUS | N. Murless | L. Piggott | 9/2 | 13 |
| 1962 | HETHERSETT | W. R. Hern | W. Carr | 100/8 | 15 |
| 1963 | RAGUSA | P. Prendergast | G. Bougoure | 2/5 | 7 |
| 1964 | INDIANA | J. Watts | J. Lindley | 100/7 | 15 |
| 1965 | PROVOKE | W. R. Hern | J. Mercer | 28/1 | 11 |
| 1966 | SODIUM | G. Todd | F. Durr | 7/1 | 9 |
| 1967 | RIBOCCO | R. F. J. Houghton | L. Piggott | 7/2 | 9 |
| 1968 | RIBERO | R. F. J. Houghton | L. Piggott | 100/30 | 8 |
| 1969 | INTERMEZZO | H. Wragg | R. Hutchinson | 7/1 | 11 |
| 1970 | NIJINSKY | M. V. O'Brien | L. Piggott | 2/7 | 9 |
| 1971 | ATHENS WOOD | H. T. Jones | L. Piggott | 5/2 | 8 |
| 1972 | BOUCHER | M. V. O'Brien | L. Piggott | 3/1 | 7 |
| 1973 | PELEID | C. Elsey | F. Durr | 28/1 | 13 |
| 1974 | BUSTINO | W. R. Hern | J. Mercer | 11/10 | 10 |
| 1975 | BRUNI | H. R. Price | A. Murray | 9/1 | 12 |
| 1976 | CROW | A. Penna | Y. Saint-Martin | 6/1 | 15 |
| 1977 | DUNFERMLINE | W. R. Hern | W. Carson | 10/1 | 13 |
| 1978 | JULIO MARINER | C. Brittain | E. Hide | 28/1 | 14 |
| 1979 | SON OF LOVE | R. Collet | A. Lequeux | 20/1 | 17 |
| 1980 | LIGHT CAVALRY | H. Cecil | J. Mercer | 3/1 | 7 |
| 1981 | CUT ABOVE | W. R. Hern | J. Mercer | 28/1 | 7 |
| 1982 | TOUCHING WOOD | H. T. Jones | P. Cook | 7/1 | 15 |
| 1983 | SUN PRINCESS | W. R. Hern | W. Carson | 11/8 | 10 |
| 1984 | COMMANCHE RUN | L. Cumani | L. Piggott | 7/4 | 11 |
| 1985 | OH SO SHARP | H. Cecil | S. Cauthen | 8/11 | 6 |
| 1986 | MOON MADNESS | J. Dunlop | P. Eddery | 9/2 | 8 |
| 1987 | REFERENCE POINT | H. Cecil | S. Cauthen | 4/11 | 7 |
| 1988 | MINSTER SON | N. Graham | W. Carson | 15/2 | 6 |
| 1989 | MICHELOZZO | H. Cecil | S. Cauthen | 6/4 | 8 |
| 1990 | SNURGE | P. Cole | T. Quinn | 7/2 | 8 |
| 1991 | TOULON | A. Fabre | P. Eddery | 5/2 | 10 |

# *Ayr Gold Cup*

AYR                          6 FURLONGS                    FIRST RUN 1804

| YEAR | HORSE | TRAINER | JOCKEY | SP | RAN |
|------|-------|---------|--------|-----|-----|
| 1946 | ROYAL CHARGER | J. Jarvis | E. Smith | 2/1 | 9 |
| 1947 | KILBELIN | B. Bullock | W. Carr | 6/1 | 12 |
| 1948 | COMO | G. Armstrong | J. Marshall | 10/1 | 9 |
| 1949 | IRISH DANCE | H. Whiteman | E. Britt | 4/1 | 16 |
| 1950 | FIRST CONSUL | F. Armstrong | C. Smirke | 2/1 | 17 |
| 1951 | FAIR SELLER | E. Davey | R. Sheather | 10/1 | 15 |
| 1952 | VATELLUS | J. Pearce | H. Jones | 10/1 | 13 |
| 1953 | BLUE BUTTERFLY | H. Wragg | E. Mercer | 11/2 | 16 |
| 1954 | ORTHOPAEDIC | J. Gosden | J. Lindley | 11/2 | 18 |
| 1955 | HOOK MONEY | A. Budgett | W. Elliott | 4/1 | 10 |
| 1956 | PRECIOUS HEATHER | J. Gosden | E. Hide | 5/1 | 16 |
| 1957 | JACINTHA | W. Lyde | E. Larkin | 100/7 | 17 |
| 1958 | RHYTHMIC | W. Dutton | F. Durr | 20/1 | 22 |
| 1959 | WHISTLING VICTOR | G. Laurence | J. Sime | 7/1 | 16 |
| 1960 | DAWN WATCH | E. Cousins | L. Parkes | 100/9 | 23 |
| 1961 | KLONDYKE BILL | C. Benstead | E. Smith | 100/8 | 17 |
| 1962 | JANEAT | A. Vasey | B. Henry | 25/1 | 25 |
| 1963 | EGUALITA | S. Hall | F. Durr | 10/1 | 18 |
| 1964 | COMPENSATION | E. Lambton | P. Robinson | 10/1 | 18 |
| 1965 | KAMUNDU | E. Cousins | G. Cadwaladr | 100/8 | 20 |
| 1966 | MILESIUS | G. Boyd | N. McIntosh | 25/1 | 24 |
| 1967 | BE FRIENDLY | C. Mitchell | G. Lewis | 100/8 | 33 |
| 1968 | PETITE PATH | R. Mason | J. Higgins | 100/7 | 21 |
| 1969 | BRIEF STAR | E. Cousins | L. Parkes | 10/1 | 23 |
| 1970 | JOHN SPLENDID | J. Dunlop | R. Hutchinson | 10/1 | 19 |
| 1971 | ROYBEN | A. Breasley | W. Williamson | 9/1 | 28 |
| 1972 | SWINGING JUNIOR | N. Angus | R. Hutchinson | 14/1 | 20 |
| 1973 | BLUE CASHMERE | M. Stoute | E. Johnson | 7/1 | 19 |
| 1974 | SOMERSWAY | W. Wightman | D. Cullen | 16/1 | 23 |
| 1975 | ROMAN WARRIOR | N. Angus | J. Seagrave | 8/1 | 23 |
| 1976 | LAST TANGO | J. Sutcliffe | L. Charnock | 6/1 | 18 |
| 1977 | JON GEORGE | M. W. Easterby | B. Raymond | 22/1 | 26 |
| 1978 | VAIGLY GREAT | M. Stoute | G. Starkey | 5/1 | 24 |
| 1979 | PRIMULA BOY | W. Bentley | W. Higgins | 40/1 | 22 |
| 1980 | SPARKLING BOY | P. Kelleway | J. Lowe | 15/1 | 24 |
| 1981 | FIRST MOVEMENT | G. Huffer | M. Miller | 14/1 | 21 |
| 1982 | FAMOUS STAR | M. Albina | Paul Eddery | 13/2 | 14 |
| 1983 | POLLY'S BROTHER | M. H. Easterby | K. Hodgson | 11/1 | 28 |
| 1984 | ABLE ALBERT | M. H. Easterby | M. Birch | 9/1 | 29 |
| 1985 | CAMPS HEATH | F. Durr | W. Woods | 14/1 | 25 |
| 1986 | GREEN RUBY | G. Balding | J. Williams | 25/1 | 29 |
| 1987 | NOT SO SILLY | A. Bailey | G. Bardwell | 12/1 | 29 |
| 1988 | SO CAREFUL | J. Berry | N. Carlisle | 33/1 | 29 |
| 1989 | JOVEWORTH | M. O'Neill | J. Fortune | 50/1 | 29 |
| 1990 | FINAL SHOT | M. H. Easterby | J. Lowe | 12/1 | 29 |
| 1991 | SARCITA | D. Elsworth | B. Doyle | 14/1 | 28 |

# Fillies' Mile

ASCOT                          I MILE                    FIRST RUN 1973

| Year | Horse | Trainer | Jockey | SP | Ran |
|------|-------|---------|--------|-----|-----|
| 1973 | ESCORIAL | I. Balding | L. Piggott | 7/4 | 11 |
| 1974 | *Abandoned – waterlogged* | | | | |
| 1975 | ICING | P. Prendergast | C. Roche | 5/1 | 6 |
| 1976 | MISS PINKIE | N. Murless | L. Piggott | 5/1 | 8 |
| 1977 | CHERRY HINTON | H. Wragg | L. Piggott | 10/11 | 8 |
| 1978 | FORMULATE | H. Cecil | J. Mercer | 5/4 | 9 |
| 1979 | QUICK AS LIGHTNING | J. Dunlop | W. Carson | 9/1 | 9 |
| 1980 | LEAP LIVELY | I. Balding | J. Matthias | 9/2 | 7 |
| 1981 | HEIGHT OF FASHION | W. R. Hern | J. Mercer | 15/8 | 8 |
| 1982 | ACCLIMATISE | B. Hobbs | A. Murray | 3/1 | 8 |
| 1983 | NEPULA | G. Huffer | B. Crossley | 3/1 | 8 |
| 1984 | OH SO SHARP | H. Cecil | L. Piggott | 6/5 | 8 |
| 1985 | UNTOLD | M. Stoute | W. R. Swinburn | 6/4 | 9 |
| 1986 | INVITED GUEST | R. Armstrong | S. Cauthen | 8/11 | 12 |
| 1987 | DIMINUENDO | H. Cecil | S. Cauthen | 2/1 | 7 |
| 1988 | TESSLA | H. Cecil | P. Eddery | 5/2 | 8 |
| 1989 | SILK SLIPPERS | B. Hills | M. Hills | 10/1 | 8 |
| 1990 | SHAMSHIR | L. Cumani | L. Dettori | 11/2 | 12 |
| 1991 | CULTURE VULTURE* | P. Cole | T. Quinn | 5/2 | 7 |

* 1991: Midnight Air finished first but was disqualified

Desert Orchid and Richard Dunwoody in full flight – at the last fence of the
Agfa Diamond Chase at Sandown Park in February 1991.

One of the fifty best-dressed men in Britain doing his homework on Cesarewitch day at Newmarket. In the foreground are the remains of a prawn curry.

And one for McCririck's album: 'The Cuddly One' Jenny Pitman with
her 1991 Cheltenham Gold Cup winner Garrison Savannah, ridden by
son Mark.

Brough Scott on Royal Phoebe (no. 1) and John Lawrence (now Lord Oaksey) on Cham at the last in the Horse and Hound Cup at Stratford-upon-Avon in 1967. Cham won by one and a half lengths.

After the Shadwell Estates Private Sweepstakes at Ascot in September 1991, John Oaksey receives his memento from sponsor Sheikh Hamdan Al Maktoum. The other jockeys are (left to right): John Francome, Robin Gray, Bill Smith, Joe Mercer and Brough Scott.

# *Queen Elizabeth II Stakes*

ASCOT                                          I MILE                                    FIRST RUN 1955

| YEAR | HORSE | TRAINER | JOCKEY | SP | RAN |
|------|-------|---------|--------|-----|-----|
| 1955 | HAFIZ II | A. Head | R. Poincelet | 9/4 | 8 |
| 1956 | CIGALON | M. d'Okhuysen | S. Boullenger | 8/1 | 11 |
| 1957 | MIDGET II | A. Head | A. Breasley | 5/6 | 7 |
| 1958 | MAJOR PORTION | T. Leader | E. Smith | 1/3 | 4 |
| 1959 | ROSALBA | J. Colling | J. Mercer | 5/2 | 6 |
| 1960 | SOVEREIGN PATH | R. Mason | W. Carr | 13/8 | 4 |
| 1961 | LE LEVANSTELL | S. McGrath | W. Williamson | 20/1 | 6 |
| 1962 | ROMULUS | R. F. J. Houghton | W. Swinburn | 7/4 | 7 |
| 1963 | THE CREDITOR | N. Murless | L. Piggott | 5/4 | 9 |
| 1964 | LINACRE | P. Prendergast | L. Piggott | 11/10 | 5 |
| 1965 | DERRING-DO | A. Budgett | A. Breasley | 9/4 | 6 |
| 1966 | HILL RISE | N. Murless | L. Piggott | 7/2 | 6 |
| 1967 | REFORM | Sir G. Richards | A. Breasley | 6/5 | 4 |
| 1968 | WORLD CUP | P. Prendergast | W. Williamson | 7/2 | 5 |
| 1969 | JIMMY REPPIN | J. Sutcliffe, jr | G. Lewis | 13/8 | 6 |
| 1970 | WELSH PAGEANT | N. Murless | A. Barclay | 100/30 | 5 |
| 1971 | BRIGADIER GERARD | W. R. Hern | J. Mercer | 2/11 | 3 |
| 1972 | BRIGADIER GERARD | W. R. Hern | J. Mercer | 4/11 | 4 |
| 1973 | JAN EKELS | G. Harwood | J. Lindley | 5/1 | 5 |
| 1974 | *Abandoned – waterlogged* | | | | |
| 1975 | ROSE BOWL | R. F. J. Houghton | W. Carson | 9/2 | 5 |
| 1976 | ROSE BOWL | R. F. J. Houghton | W. Carson | 13/8 | 8 |
| 1977 | TRUSTED | J. Dunlop | W. Carson | 20/1 | 7 |
| 1978 | HOMING | W. R. Hern | W. Carson | 9/2 | 11 |
| 1979 | KRIS | H. Cecil | J. Mercer | 8/11 | 7 |
| 1980 | KNOWN FACT | J. Tree | W. Carson | 3/1 | 7 |
| 1981 | TO-AGORI-MOU | G. Harwood | L. Piggott | 5/4 | 6 |
| 1982 | BUZZARDS BAY | H. Collingridge | W. R. Swinburn | 50/1 | 10 |
| 1983 | SACKFORD | G. Harwood | G. Starkey | 11/2 | 9 |
| 1984 | TELEPROMPTER | J. Watts | W. Carson | 11/2 | 6 |
| 1985 | SHADEED | M. Stoute | W. R. Swinburn | 9/4 | 7 |
| 1986 | SURE BLADE | B. Hills | B. Thomson | 6/5 | 7 |
| 1987 | MILLIGRAM | M. Stoute | P. Eddery | 6/1 | 5 |
| 1988 | WARNING | G. Harwood | P. Eddery | 9/4 | 8 |
| 1989 | ZILZAL | M. Stoute | W. R. Swinburn | evens | 5 |
| 1990 | MARKOFDISTINCTION | L. Cumani | L. Dettori | 6/1 | 10 |
| 1991 | SELKIRK | I. Balding | R. Cochrane | 10/1 | 9 |

# Cheveley Park Stakes

NEWMARKET                          6 FURLONGS                    FIRST RUN 1870

| Year | Horse | Trainer | Jockey | SP | Ran |
|------|-------|---------|--------|-----|-----|
| 1946 | DJERBA | C. Semblat | C. Elliott | 9/2 | 6 |
| 1947 | ASH BLONDE | J. Colling | P. Evans | 100/8 | 7 |
| 1948 | PAMBIDIAN | W. Nightingall | G. Richards | 100/6 | 7 |
| 1949 | COREJADA | C. Semblat | C. Elliott | 9/4 | 3 |
| 1950 | BELLE OF ALL | N. Bertie | G. Richards | 5/4 | 8 |
| 1951 | ZABARA | V. Smyth | G. Richards | 10/11 | 5 |
| 1952 | BEBE GRANDE | F. Armstrong | G. Richards | 1/2 | 6 |
| 1953 | SIXPENCE | P. Prendergast | G. Richards | 4/1 | 6 |
| 1954 | GLORIA NICKY | N. Bertie | A. Breasley | 10/1 | 10 |
| 1955 | MIDGET II | A. Head | R. Poincelet | evens | 8 |
| 1956 | SARCELLE | N. Cannon | A. Breasley | 4/6 | 7 |
| 1957 | RICH AND RARE | J. Jarvis | E. Mercer | 5/1 | 8 |
| 1958 | LINDSAY | R. Peacock | E. Mercer | 100/8 | 15 |
| 1959 | QUEENSBERRY | J. Warr | E. Smith | 2/5 | 6 |
| 1960 | OPALINE II | A. Head | G. Moore | 11/10 | 6 |
| 1961 | DISPLAY | P. Prendergast | R. Hutchinson | 8/11 | 10 |
| 1962 | MY GOODNESS ME | G. Brooke | E. Smith | 100/8 | 10 |
| 1963 | CRIMEA II | C. Boyd-Rochfort | W. Carr | 9/1 | 12 |
| 1964 | NIGHT OFF | W. Wharton | J. Mercer | 20/1 | 6 |
| 1965 | BERKELEY SPRINGS | I. Balding | G. Lewis | 100/8 | 11 |
| 1966 | FLEET | N. Murless | L. Piggott | 5/2 | 8 |
| 1967 | LALIBELA | M. V. O'Brien | L. Piggott | 5/1 | 5 |
| 1968 | MIGE | A. Head | J. Taillard | 5/2 | 18 |
| 1969 | HUMBLE DUTY | P. Walwyn | D. Keith | 11/4 | 8 |
| 1970 | MAGIC FLUTE | N. Murless | A. Barclay | 13/8 | 11 |
| 1971 | WATERLOO | J. Watts | E. Hide | 100/30 | 17 |
| 1972 | JACINTH | B. Hobbs | J. Gorton | 9/2 | 13 |
| 1973 | GENTLE THOUGHTS | T. Curtin | W. Pyers | 9/1 | 14 |
| 1974 | CRY OF TRUTH | B. Hobbs | J. Gorton | 4/1 | 15 |
| 1975 | PASTY | P. Walwyn | P. Eddery | 9/1 | 14 |
| 1976 | DURTAL | B. Hills | L. Piggott | 5/1 | 15 |
| 1977 | SOOKERA | D. Weld | W. Swinburn | 3/1 | 10 |
| 1978 | DEVON DITTY | H. T. Jones | G. Starkey | 11/8 | 7 |
| 1979 | MRS PENNY | I. Balding | J. Matthias | 7/1 | 12 |
| 1980 | MARWELL | M. Stoute | L. Piggott | 4/9 | 8 |
| 1981 | WOODSTREAM | M. V. O'Brien | P. Eddery | 5/2 | 13 |
| 1982 | MA BICHE | Mme C. Head | F. Head | 11/4 | 9 |
| 1983 | DESIRABLE | B. Hills | S. Cauthen | 12/1 | 12 |
| 1984 | PARK APPEAL | J. Bolger | D. Gillespie | 4/1 | 13 |
| 1985 | EMBLA | L. Cumani | A. Cordero | 20/1 | 14 |
| 1986 | MINSTRELLA* | C. Nelson | J. Reid | 11/10 | 5 |
| 1987 | RAVINELLA | Mme C. Head | G. Moore | 9/2 | 8 |
| 1988 | PASS THE PEACE | P. Cole | T. Quinn | 5/1 | 7 |
| 1989 | DEAD CERTAIN | D. Elsworth | C. Asmussen | 11/2 | 11 |
| 1990 | CAPRICCIOSA | M. V. O'Brien | J. Reid | 7/1 | 11 |
| 1991 | MARLING | G. Wragg | W. R. Swinburn | 15/8 | 9 |

* 1986: Forest Flower finished first but was disqualified

# Middle Park Stakes

NEWMARKET                    6 FURLONGS                  FIRST RUN 1866

| YEAR | HORSE | TRAINER | JOCKEY | SP | RAN |
|------|-------|---------|--------|----|----|
| 1946 | SARAVAN | F. Butters | C. Elliott | 100/8 | 8 |
| 1947 | THE COBBLER | F. Darling | G. Richards | 8/11 | 4 |
| 1948 | ABERNANT | N. Murless | G. Richards | 1/7 | 3 |
| 1949 | MASKED LIGHT | N. Scobie | D. Smith | 7/2 | 5 |
| 1950 | BIG DIPPER | C. Boyd-Rochfort | W. Carr | 2/5 | 5 |
| 1951 | KING'S BENCH | M. Feakes | C. Elliott | 7/2 | 8 |
| 1952 | NEARULA | C. Elsey | E. Britt | 13/2 | 9 |
| 1953 | ROYAL CHALLENGER | P. Beasley | G. Richards | 4/1 | 5 |
| 1954 | OUR BABU | G. Brooke | D. Smith | 6/1 | 10 |
| 1955 | BUISSON ARDENT | A. Head | D. Smith | 9/2 | 6 |
| 1956 | PIPE OF PEACE | G. Richards | A. Breasley | 8/1 | 8 |
| 1957 | MAJOR PORTION | T. Leader | E. Smith | 11/2 | 7 |
| 1958 | MASHAM | G. Brooke | D. Smith | 2/1 | 5 |
| 1959 | VENTURE VII | A. Head | G. Moore | 1/4 | 5 |
| 1960 | SKYMASTER | W. Smyth | A. Breasley | 100/30 | 4 |
| 1961 | GUSTAV | J. Tree | J. Lindley | 100/6 | 7 |
| 1962 | CROCKET | G. Brooke | E. Smith | 5/4 | 4 |
| 1963 | SHOWDOWN | F. Winter | D. Smith | 100/30 | 11 |
| 1964 | SPANISH EXPRESS | L. Hall | J. Mercer | 9/1 | 4 |
| 1965 | TRACK SPARE | R. Mason | J. Lindley | 10/1 | 9 |
| 1966 | BOLD LAD | P. Prendergast | D. Lake | 2/7 | 5 |
| 1967 | PETINGO | F. Armstrong | L. Piggott | 1/4 | 3 |
| 1968 | RIGHT TACK | J. Sutcliffe, jr | G. Lewis | 11/2 | 7 |
| 1969 | HUNTERCOMBE | A. Budgett | E. Johnson | 3/1 | 7 |
| 1970 | BRIGADIER GERARD | W. R. Hern | J. Mercer | 9/2 | 5 |
| 1971 | SHARPEN UP | B. van Cutsem | W. Carson | 5/6 | 5 |
| 1972 | TUDENHAM | Denys Smith | J. Lindley | 4/1 | 7 |
| 1973 | HABAT | P. Walwyn | P. Eddery | 4/6 | 7 |
| 1974 | STEEL HEART | D. Weld | L. Piggott | 10/11 | 8 |
| 1975 | HITTITE GLORY | A. Breasley | F. Durr | 9/2 | 8 |
| 1976 | TACHYPOUS | B. Hobbs | G. Lewis | 5/1 | 11 |
| 1977 | FORMIDABLE | P. Walwyn | P. Eddery | 15/8 | 7 |
| 1978 | JUNIUS | M. V. O'Brien | L. Piggott | 7/1 | 10 |
| 1979 | KNOWN FACT | J. Tree | W. Carson | 10/1 | 7 |
| 1980 | MATTABOY | R. Armstrong | L. Piggott | 7/1 | 9 |
| 1981 | CAJUN | H. Cecil | L. Piggott | 20/1 | 13 |
| 1982 | DIESIS | H. Cecil | L. Piggott | 10/11 | 5 |
| 1983 | CREAG AN SGOR | C. Nelson | S. Cauthen | 50/1 | 9 |
| 1984 | BASSENTHWAITE | J. Tree | P. Eddery | 7/2 | 8 |
| 1985 | STALKER | P. Walwyn | J. Mercer | 9/2 | 6 |
| 1986 | MISTER MAJESTIC | R. Williams | R. Cochrane | 33/1 | 7 |
| 1987 | GALLIC LEAGUE | B. Hills | S. Cauthen | 6/4 | 5 |
| 1988 | MON TRESOR | R. Boss | M. Roberts | 8/1 | 6 |
| 1989 | BALLA COVE | R. Boss | S. Cauthen | 20/1 | 6 |
| 1990 | LYCIUS | A. Fabre | C. Asmussen | 13/8 | 9 |
| 1991 | RODRIGO DE TRIANO | P. Chapple-Hyam | W. Carson | evens | 6 |

# Cambridgeshire Handicap

NEWMARKET　　　　1 MILE 1 FURLONG　　　FIRST RUN 1839

| YEAR | HORSE | TRAINER | JOCKEY | SP | RAN |
|------|-------|---------|--------|-----|-----|
| 1946 | SAYANI | J. Lieux | W. Johnstone | 25/1 | 34 |
| 1947 | FAIREY FULMAR | O. Bell | T. Gosling | 28/1 | 39 |
| 1948 | STEROPE | P. Beasley | D. Schofield | 25/1 | 32 |
| 1949 | STEROPE | P. Beasley | C. Elliott | 25/1 | 39 |
| 1950 | KELLING | A. Waugh | D. Smith | 100/7 | 31 |
| 1951 | FLEETING MOMENT | T. Bartlam | A. Breasley | 28/1 | 45 |
| 1952 | RICHER | S. Ingham | K. Gethin | 100/6 | 42 |
| 1953 | JUPITER | P. Beasley | G. Richards | 100/6 | 29 |
| 1954 | MINSTREL | J. Jarvis | C. Gaston | 66/1 | 36 |
| 1955 | RETRIAL | C. Boyd-Rochfort | P. Robinson | 18/1 | 40 |
| 1956 | LOPPYLUGS | J. Beary | E. Smith | 100/7 | 34 |
| 1957 | STEPHANOTIS | J. Rogers | W. Carr | 100/6 | 38 |
| 1958 | LONDON CRY | G. Richards | A. Breasley | 22/1 | 33 |
| 1959 | REXEQUUS | G. Boyd | N. Stirk | 25/1 | 36 |
| 1960 | MIDSUMMER NIGHT | P. Hastings-Bass | D. Keith | 40/1 | 40 |
| 1961 | HENRY THE SEVENTH | H. Wragg | E. Hide | 100/8 | 27 |
| 1962 | HIDDEN MEANING | H. Leader | A. Breasley | 7/1 | 46 |
| 1963 | COMMANDER IN CHIEF | E. Cousins | F. Durr | 100/7 | 23 |
| 1964 | HASTY CLOUD | H. Wallington | J. Wilson | 100/8 | 43 |
| 1965 | TAROOGAN | S. McGrath | W. Williamson | 100/8 | 30 |
| 1966 | DITES | H. Leader | D. Maitland | 33/1 | 34 |
| 1967 | LACQUER | H. Wragg | R. Hutchinson | 20/1 | 34 |
| 1968 | EMERILO | P. Allden | M. Thomas | 20/1 | 35 |
| 1969 | PRINCE DE GALLES | P. Robinson | F. Durr | 5/2 | 26 |
| 1970 | PRINCE DE GALLES | P. Robinson | F. Durr | 6/1 | 27 |
| 1971 | KING MIDAS | D. Candy | D. Cullen | 10/1 | 29 |
| 1972 | NEGUS | D. Candy | P. Waldron | 16/1 | 35 |
| 1973 | SILICIANA | I. Balding | G. Lewis | 14/1 | 37 |
| 1974 | FLYING NELLY | W. Wightman | L. Maitland | 22/1 | 39 |
| 1975 | LOTTOGIFT | D. Hanley | R. Wernham | 33/1 | 36 |
| 1976 | INTERMISSION | M. Stoute | G. Starkey | 14/1 | 29 |
| 1977 | SIN TIMON | J. Hindley | A. Kimberley | 18/1 | 27 |
| 1978 | BARONET | C. Benstead | B. Rouse | 12/1 | 18 |
| 1979 | SMARTSET | R. F. J. Houghton | J. Reid | 33/1 | 24 |
| 1980 | BARONET | C. Benstead | B. Rouse | 22/1 | 19 |
| 1981 | BRAUGHING | C. Brittain | S. Cauthen | 50/1 | 28 |
| 1982 | CENTURY CITY | L. Cumani | J. Mercer | 20/1 | 29 |
| 1983 | SAGAMORE | F. Durr | M. Thomas | 35/1 | 30 |
| 1984 | LEYSH | S. Norton | J. Lowe | 33/1 | 34 |
| 1985 | TREMBLANT | R. Smyth | P. Eddery | 16/1 | 31 |
| 1986 | DALLAS | L. Cumani | R. Cochrane | 10/1 | 31 |
| 1987 | BALTHUS | J. Glover | D. McKeown | 50/1 | 31 |
| 1988 | QUINLAN TERRY | Sir M. Prescott | G. Duffield | 11/1 | 29 |
| 1989 | RAMBO'S HALL | J. Glover | D. McKeown | 15/1 | 34 |
| 1990 | RISEN MOON | B. Hills | S. Cauthen | 7/1 | 40 |
| 1991 | MELLOTTIE | Mrs G. Reveley | J. Lowe | 10/1 | 29 |

# *Dewhurst Stakes*

NEWMARKET 7 FURLONGS FIRST RUN 1875

| YEAR | HORSE | TRAINER | JOCKEY | SP | RAN |
|------|-------|---------|--------|-----|-----|
| 1946 | MIGOLI | F. Butters | G. Richards | 5/1 | 8 |
| 1947 | PRIDE OF INDIA | J. Watts | J. Sime | 5/2 | 11 |
| 1948 | ROYAL FOREST | N. Murless | G. Richards | 5/4 | 11 |
| 1949 | EMPEROR II | C. Semblat | C. Elliott | 7/2 | 7 |
| 1950 | TURCO II | C. Boyd-Rochfort | W. Carr | 11/8 | 6 |
| 1951 | MARSYAD | C. Semblat | W. Johnstone | 7/1 | 11 |
| 1952 | PINZA | N. Bertie | G. Richards | evens | 9 |
| 1953 | INFATUATION | V. Smyth | K. Gethin | 11/8 | 5 |
| 1954 | MY SMOKEY | J. Watts | D. Smith | 7/2 | 9 |
| 1955 | DACIAN | H. Cottrill | W. Snaith | 7/1 | 10 |
| 1956 | CREPELLO | N. Murless | L. Piggott | 1/2 | 4 |
| 1957 | TORBELLA III | W. Clout | A. Breasley | 9/4 | 7 |
| 1958 | BILLUM | C. Elsey | E. Hide | 6/1 | 8 |
| 1959 | ANCIENT LIGHTS | T. Leader | E. Smith | 100/7 | 12 |
| 1960 | BOUNTEOUS | P. Beasley | J. Sime | 2/1 | 7 |
| 1961 | RIVER CHANTER | G. Todd | J. Mercer | 100/30 | 8 |
| 1962 | FOLLOW SUIT | N. Murless | L. Piggott | 10/1 | 10 |
| 1963 | KING'S LANE | S. Hall | J. Sime | 10/1 | 9 |
| 1964 | SILLY SEASON | I. Balding | G. Lewis | 13/2 | 11 |
| 1965 | PRETENDRE | J. Jarvis | R. Hutchinson | 11/2 | 11 |
| 1966 | DART BOARD | G. Richards | D. Smith | 10/1 | 13 |
| 1967 | HAMETUS | W. Nightingall | F. Durr | 100/9 | 7 |
| 1968 | RIBOFILIO | R. F. J. Houghton | L. Piggott | 8/11 | 11 |
| 1969 | NIJINSKY | M. V. O'Brien | L. Piggott | 1/3 | 6 |
| 1970 | MILL REEF | I. Balding | G. Lewis | 4/7 | 3 |
| 1971 | CROWNED PRINCE | B. van Cutsem | L. Piggot | 4/9 | 11 |
| 1972 | LUNCHTIME | P. Walwyn | P. Eddery | 11/8 | 8 |
| 1973 | CELLINI | M. V. O'Brien | L. Piggott | 40/85 | 7 |
| 1974 | GRUNDY | P. Walwyn | P. Eddery | 6/5 | 8 |
| 1975 | WOLLOW | H. Cecil | G. Dettori | 6/4 | 7 |
| 1976 | THE MINSTREL | M. V. O'Brien | L. Piggott | 6/5 | 11 |
| 1977 | TRY MY BEST | M. V. O'Brien | L. Piggott | 4/6 | 7 |
| 1978 | TROMOS | B. Hobbs | J. Lynch | 11/4 | 6 |
| 1979 | MONTEVERDI | M. V. O'Brien | L. Piggott | 15/8 | 6 |
| 1980 | STORM BIRD | M. V. O'Brien | P. Eddery | 4/5 | 5 |
| 1981 | WIND AND WUTHERING | H. Candy | P. Waldron | 11/1 | 9 |
| 1982 | DIESIS | H. Cecil | L. Piggott | 2/1 | 4 |
| 1983 | EL GRAN SENOR | M. V. O'Brien | P. Eddery | 7/4 | 10 |
| 1984 | KALA DANCER | B. Hanbury | G. Baxter | 20/1 | 11 |
| 1985 | HUNTINGDALE | J. Hindley | M. Hills | 12/1 | 8 |
| 1986 | AJDAL | M. Stoute | W. R. Swinburn | 4/9 | 5 |
| 1987 | *Abandoned – high winds* | | | | |
| 1988 | PRINCE OF DANCE | N. Graham | W. Carson | 6/4 | 6 |
|      | SCENIC | B. Hills | M. Hills | 33/1 | — |
| 1989 | DASHING BLADE | I. Balding | J. Matthias | 8/1 | 7 |
| 1990 | GENEROUS | P. Cole | T. Quinn | 50/1 | 8 |
| 1991 | DR DEVIOUS | P. Chapple-Hyam | W. Carson | 3/1 | 9 |

## Champion Stakes

NEWMARKET                    1 MILE 2 FURLONGS                    FIRST RUN 1877

| YEAR | HORSE | TRAINER | JOCKEY | SP | RAN |
|------|-------|---------|--------|-----|-----|
| 1946 | HONEYWAY | J. Jarvis | E. Smith | 8/1 | 8 |
| 1947 | MIGOLI | F. Butter | G. Richards | evens | 4 |
| 1948 | SOLAR SLIPPER | H. Smyth | E. Smith | 6/1 | 7 |
| 1949 | DJEDDAH | C. Semblat | C. Elliott | 4/6 | 5 |
| 1950 | PETER FLOWER | J. Jarvis | W. Rickaby | 3/1 | 7 |
| 1951 | DYNAMITER | J. Glynn | C. Elliott | 100/8 | 10 |
| 1952 | DYNAMITER | J. Glynn | C. Elliott | 4/5 | 5 |
| 1953 | NEARULA | Capt. C. Elsey | E. Britt | 4/1 | 7 |
| 1954 | NARRATOR | H. Cottrill | F. Barlow | 20/1 | 6 |
| 1955 | HAFIZ II | A. Head | R. Poincelet | 100/30 | 5 |
| 1956 | HUGH LUPUS | N. Murless | W. Johnstone | 3/1 | 11 |
| 1957 | ROSE ROYALE II | A. Head | J. Massard | 5/2 | 7 |
| 1958 | BELLA PAOLA | F. Mathet | A. Lequeux | 4/1 | 7 |
| 1959 | PETITE ETOILE | N. Murless | L. Piggott | 2/11 | 3 |
| 1960 | MARGUERITE VERNAUT | U. Penco | E. Camici | 9/4 | 4 |
| 1961 | BOBAR II | R. Corme | M. Garcia | 100/8 | 8 |
| 1962 | ARCTIC STORM | J. Oxx | W. Williamson | 6/1 | 7 |
| 1963 | HULA DANCER | E. Pollet | J. Deforge | 9/2 | 11 |
| 1964 | BALDRIC II | E. Fellows | W. Pyers | 7/2 | 9 |
| 1965 | SILLY SEASON | I. Balding | G. Lewis | 100/8 | 13 |
| 1966 | PIECES OF EIGHT | M. V. O'Brien | L. Piggott | 5/4 | 8 |
| 1967 | REFORM | Sir G. Richards | A. Breasley | 100/30 | 7 |
| 1968 | SIR IVOR | M. V. O'Brien | L. Piggott | 8/11 | 6 |
| 1969 | FLOSSY | F. Boutin | J. Deforge | 100/7 | 9 |
| 1970 | LORENZACCIO | N. Murless | G. Lewis | 100/7 | 8 |
| 1971 | BRIGADIER GERARD | W. R. Hern | J. Mercer | 1/2 | 10 |
| 1972 | BRIGADIER GERARD | W. R. Hern | J. Mercer | 1/3 | 9 |
| 1973 | HURRY HARRIET | P. Mullins | J. Cruguet | 33/1 | 16 |
| 1974 | GIACOMETTI | H. R. Price | L. Piggott | 4/1 | 14 |
| 1975 | ROSE BOWL | R. F. J. Houghton | W. Carson | 11/2 | 9 |
| 1976 | VITIGES | P. Walwyn | P. Eddery | 22/1 | 19 |
| 1977 | FLYING WATER | A. Penna | Y. Saint-Martin | 9/1 | 8 |
| 1978 | SWISS MAID | P. Kelleway | G. Starkey | 9/1 | 10 |
| 1979 | NORTHERN BABY | F. Boutin | P. Paquet | 9/1 | 14 |
| 1980 | CAIRN ROUGE | M. Cunningham | A. Murray | 6/1 | 13 |
| 1981 | VAYRANN | F. Mathet | Y. Saint-Martin | 15/2 | 16 |
| 1982 | TIME CHARTER | H. Candy | W. Newnes | 9/2 | 14 |
| 1983 | CORMORANT WOOD | B. Hills | S. Cauthen | 18/1 | 19 |
| 1984 | PALACE MUSIC | P. Biancone | Y. Saint-Martin | 18/1 | 15 |
| 1985 | PEBBLES | C. Brittain | P. Eddery | 9/2 | 10 |
| 1986 | TRIPTYCH | P. Biancone | A. Cruz | 4/1 | 11 |
| 1987 | TRIPTYCH | P. Biancone | A. Cruz | 6/5 | 11 |
| 1988 | INDIAN SKIMMER | H. Cecil | M. Roberts | 8/15 | 5 |
| 1989 | LEGAL CASE | L. Cumani | R. Cochrane | 5/1 | 11 |
| 1990 | IN THE GROOVE | D. Elsworth | S. Cauthen | 9/2 | 10 |
| 1991 | TEL QUEL | A. Fabre | T. Jarnet | 16/1 | 12 |

# Cesarewitch Handicap

NEWMARKET      2 MILES 2 FURLONGS      FIRST RUN 1839

| YEAR | HORSE | TRAINER | JOCKEY | SP | RAN |
|------|-------|---------|--------|-----|-----|
| 1946 | MONSIEUR L'AMIRAL | E. Charlier | H. Wragg | 33/1 | 27 |
| 1947 | WHITEWAY | W. Pratt | W. Evans | 100/8 | 22 |
| 1948 | WOODBURN | C. Elsey | E. Britt | 100/9 | 32 |
| 1949 | STRATHSPEY | N. Cannon | E. Smith | 25/1 | 37 |
| 1950 | ABOVE BOARD | C. Boyd-Rochfort | E. Smith | 18/1 | 38 |
| 1951 | THREE CHEERS | P. Thrale | E. Mercer | 17/2 | 30 |
| 1952 | FLUSH ROYAL | J. Fawcus | W. Nevett | 33/1 | 36 |
| 1953 | CHANTRY | S. Ingham | K. Gethin | 4/1 | 24 |
| 1954 | FRENCH DESIGN | G. Todd | D. Smith | 100/6 | 31 |
| 1955 | CURRY | F. Armstrong | P. Tulk | 100/6 | 21 |
| 1956 | PRELONE | W. Hide | E. Hide | 20/1 | 19 |
| 1957 | SANDIACRE | W. Dutton | D. Smith | 100/8 | 24 |
| 1958 | MORECAMBE | S. Hall | J. Sime | 15/2 | 30 |
| 1959 | COME TO DADDY | W. Lyde | D. Smith | 6/1 | 17 |
| 1960 | ALCOVE | J. Watts | D. Smith | 100/30 | 20 |
| 1961 | AVON'S PRIDE | W. R. Hern | E. Smith | 100/8 | 27 |
| 1962 | GOLDEN FIRE | D. Marks | D. Yates | 25/1 | 25 |
| 1963 | UTRILLO | H. R. Price | J. Sime | 100/8 | 25 |
| 1964 | GREY OF FALLODEN | W. R. Hern | J. Mercer | 20/1 | 26 |
| 1965 | MINTMASTER | A. Cooper | J. Sime | 13/2 | 18 |
| 1966 | PERSIAN LANCER | H. R. Price | D. Smith | 100/7 | 24 |
| 1967 | BOISMOSS | M. W. Easterby | E. Johnson | 13/1 | 23 |
| 1968 | MAJOR ROSE | H. R. Price | L. Piggott | 9/1 | 33 |
| 1969 | FLORIDIAN | L. Shedden | D. McKay | 20/1 | 23 |
| 1970 | SCORIA | C. Crossley | D. McKay | 33/1 | 21 |
| 1971 | OROSIO | H. Cecil | G. Lewis | 5/1 | 18 |
| 1972 | CIDER WITH ROSIE | S. Ingham | M. Thomas | 14/1 | 21 |
| 1973 | FLASH IMP | R. Smyth | T. Cain | 25/1 | 29 |
| 1974 | OCEAN KING | A. Pitt | T. Carter | 25/1 | 27 |
| 1975 | SHANTALLAH | H. Wragg | B. Taylor | 7/1 | 17 |
| 1976 | JOHN CHERRY | J. Tree | L. Piggott | 13/2 | 14 |
| 1977 | ASSURED | H. Candy | P. Waldron | 10/1 | 11 |
| 1978 | CENTURION | I. Balding | J. Matthias | 9/2 | 17 |
| 1979 | SIR MICHAEL | G. Huffer | M. Rimmer | 10/1 | 11 |
| 1980 | POPSI'S JOY | M. Haynes | L. Piggott | 10/1 | 27 |
| 1981 | HALSBURY | P. Walwyn | J. Mercer | 14/1 | 30 |
| 1982 | MOUNTAIN LODGE | J. Dunlop | W. Carson | 9/1 | 28 |
| 1983 | BAJAN SUNSHINE | R. Simpson | B. Rouse | 7/1 | 28 |
| 1984 | TOM SHARP | W. Wharton | S. Dawson | 40/1 | 26 |
| 1985 | KAYUDEE | J. FitzGerald | A. Murray | 7/1 | 21 |
| 1986 | ORANGE HILL | J. Tree | R. Fox | 20/1 | 25 |
| 1987 | PRIVATE AUDITION | M. Tompkins | G. Carter | 50/1 | 28 |
| 1988 | NOMADIC WAY | B. Hills | W. Carson | 6/1 | 24 |
| 1989 | DOUBLE DUTCH | Miss B. Sanders | W. Newnes | 15/2 | 22 |
| 1990 | TRAINGLOT | J. FitzGerald | W. Carson | 13/2 | 25 |
| 1991 | GO SOUTH | J. Jenkins | N. Carlisle | 33/1 | 22 |

# Racing Post Trophy

DONCASTER                     I MILE                    FIRST RUN 1961

| YEAR | HORSE | TRAINER | JOCKEY | SP | RAN |
|------|-------|---------|--------|-----|-----|
| 1961 | MIRALGO | H. Wragg | W. Williamson | 10/1 | 13 |
| 1962 | NOBLESSE | P. Prendergast | G. Bougoure | 11/10 | 12 |
| 1963 | PUSHFUL | S. Meaney | W. Carr | 100/6 | 10 |
| 1964 | HARDICANUTE | P. Prendergast | W. Williamson | 13/8 | 11 |
| 1965 | PRETENDRE | J. Jarvis | R. Hutchinson | 6/1 | 13 |
| 1966 | RIBOCCO | R. F. J. Houghton | L. Piggott | 4/9 | 11 |
| 1967 | VAGUELY NOBLE | W. Wharton | W. Williamson | 8/1 | 8 |
| 1968 | THE ELK | J. Tree | W. Pyers | 10/1 | 11 |
| 1969 | APPROVAL | H. Cecil | D. Keith | 5/1 | 9 |
| 1970 | LINDEN TREE | P. Walwyn | D. Keith | 25/1 | 9 |
| 1971 | HIGH TOP | B. van Cutsem | W. Carson | 11/2 | 13 |
| 1972 | NOBLE DECREE | B. van Cutsem | L. Piggott | 8/1 | 10 |
| 1973 | APALACHEE | M. V. O'Brien | L. Piggott | evens | 10 |
| 1974 | GREEN DANCER | A. Head | F. Head | 7/2 | 10 |
| 1975 | TAKE YOUR PLACE | H. Cecil | G. Dettori | 4/1 | 11 |
| 1976 | SPORTING YANKEE | P. Walwyn | P. Eddery | 9/2 | 6 |
| 1977 | DACTYLOGRAPHER | P. Walwyn | P. Eddery | 100/30 | 12 |
| 1978 | SANDY CREEK | C. Collins | C. Roche | 15/1 | 11 |
| 1979 | HELLO GORGEOUS | H. Cecil | J. Mercer | 11/8 | 7 |
| 1980 | BELDALE FLUTTER | M. Jarvis | P. Eddery | 14/1 | 7 |
| 1981 | COUNT PAHLEN | B. Hobbs | G. Baxter | 25/1 | 13 |
| 1982 | DUNBEATH | H. Cecil | L. Piggott | 4/7 | 8 |
| 1983 | ALPHABATIM | G. Harwood | G. Starkey | 9/2 | 9 |
| 1984 | LANFRANCO | H. Cecil | L. Piggott | 100/30 | 10 |
| 1985 | BAKHAROFF | G. Harwood | G. Starkey | 2/1 | 9 |
| 1986 | REFERENCE POINT | H. Cecil | P. Eddery | 4/1 | 10 |
| 1987 | EMMSON | W. R. Hern | W. Carson | 7/1 | 6 |
| 1988 | AL HAREB | N. Graham | W. Carson | 100/30 | 8 |
| 1989 | BE MY CHIEF | H. Cecil | S. Cauthen | 4/7 | 5 |
| 1990 | PETER DAVIES | H. Cecil | S. Cauthen | 2/1 | 4 |
| 1991 | SEATTLE RHYME | D. Elsworth | C. Asmussen | 2/1 | 8 |

# *November Handicap*

DONCASTER      I MILE 4 FURLONGS      FIRST RUN 1876

| YEAR | HORSE | TRAINER | JOCKEY | SP | RAN |
|------|-------|---------|--------|-----|-----|
| 1946 | LAS VEGAS | G. Boyd | H. Wragg | 20/1 | 23 |
| 1947 | REGRET | P. Vasey | J. Walker | 66/1 | 34 |
| 1948 | SPORTS MASTER | J. Beary | D. Greening | 20/1 | 40 |
| 1949 | FIDONIA | E. Parker | W. Carr | 40/1 | 41 |
| 1950 | COLTBRIDGE | S. Hall | J. Sime | 100/6 | 37 |
| 1951 | GOOD TASTE | S. Hall | W. Nevett | 28/1 | 31 |
| 1952 | SUMMER RAIN | J. Jarvis | P. Evans | 100/6 | 24 |
| 1953 | TORCH SINGER | N. Scobie | D. Ward | 40/1 | 25 |
| 1954 | *Abandoned – waterlogged* | | | | |
| 1955 | TEARAWAY | S. Hall | W. Bentley | 40/1 | 38 |
| 1956 | TRENTHAM BOY | J. Gosden | J. Gifford | 100/6 | 26 |
| 1957 | CHIEF BARKER | H. R. Price | D. Ward | 33/1 | 40 |
| 1958 | PAUL JONES | A. Budgett | J. Mercer | 100/7 | 30 |
| 1959 | OPERATIC SOCIETY | J. Benstead | K. Gethin | 18/1 | 49 |
| 1960 | DALNAMEIN | S. Hall | H. Greenaway | 28/1 | 30 |
| 1961 | HENRY'S CHOICE | P. Beasley | E. Hide | 100/8 | 29 |
| 1962 | DAMREDUB | J. Gosden | M. Germon | 20/1 | 35 |
| 1963 | BEST SONG | J. Gosden | J. Lindley | 100/7 | 31 |
| 1964 | OSIER | B. van Cutsem | D. Smith | 20/1 | 28 |
| 1965 | CONCEALDEM | J. Gosden | R. Hutchinson | 100/8 | 18 |
| 1966 | POLISH WARRIOR | A. Budgett | A. Barclay | 100/6 | 26 |
| 1967 | BUGLE BOY | A. Budgett | A. Barclay | 22/1 | 25 |
| 1968 | ZARDIA | A. Vasey | R. Still | 25/1 | 29 |
| 1969 | TINTAGEL II | R. Sturdy | L. Piggott | 15/2 | 21 |
| 1970 | SARACENO | H. Wragg | G. Sexton | 15/2 | 21 |
| 1971 | MISTY LIGHT | F. Armstrong | J. Mercer | 25/1 | 20 |
| 1972 | KING TOP | J. Oxley | W. Carson | 6/1 | 16 |
| 1973 | ONLY FOR JO | R. Smyth | I. Jenkinson | 13/1 | 22 |
| 1974 | GRITTI PALACE | P. Robinson | R. Fox | 7/2 | 21 |
| 1975 | MR BIGMORE | P. Robinson | G. Starkey | 100/30 | 12 |
| 1976 | GALE BRIDGE | H. R. Price | B. Taylor | 10/1 | 14 |
| 1977 | SAILCLOTH | W. Hastings-Bass | M. Thomas | 13/2 | 20 |
| 1978 | EASTERN SPRING | L. Cumani | M. Wigham | 17/2 | 21 |
| 1979 | MORSE CODE | J. Dunlop | P. Cook | 11/2 | 14 |
| 1980 | PATH OF PEACE | C. Thornton | J. Bleasdale | 14/1 | 22 |
| 1981 | LAFONTAINE | C. Brittain | G. Duffield | 16/1 | 20 |
| 1982 | DOUBLE SHUFFLE | G. Pritchard-Gordon | G. Duffield | 12/1 | 17 |
| | TURKOMAN | D. Sasse | D. McKay | 20/1 | — |
| 1983 | ASIR | G. Harwood | G. Starkey | 10/1 | 25 |
| 1984 | ABU KADRA | M. Stoute | W. R. Swinburn | 25/1 | 23 |
| 1985 | BOLD REX | J. Dunlop | J. Mercer | 20/1 | 24 |
| 1986 | BEIJING | P. Cole | T. Quinn | 16/1 | 25 |
| 1987 | SWINGIT GUNNER | C. Tinkler | M. Birch | 9/1 | 25 |
| 1988 | YOUNG BENZ | M. H. Easterby | M. Birch | 12/1 | 22 |
| 1989 | FIRELIGHT FIESTA | B. Hanbury | B. Raymond | 9/2 | 19 |
| 1990 | AZZAAM | J. Dunlop | W. Carson | 7/1 | 24 |
| 1991 | HIEROGLYPHIC | J. Gosden | W. Carson | 11/4 | 22 |

# NATIONAL HUNT
## *Mackeson Gold Cup*

CHELTENHAM          2 MILES 4 FURLONGS          FIRST RUN 1960

| YEAR | HORSE | TRAINER | JOCKEY | SP | RAN |
|------|-------|---------|--------|-----|-----|
| 1960 | FORTRIA | T. Dreaper | P. Taaffe | 8/1 | 19 |
| 1961 | SCOTTISH MEMORIES | A. Thomas | C. Finnegan | 9/2 | 17 |
| 1962 | FORTRIA | T. Dreaper | P. Taaffe | 5/1 | 25 |
| 1963 | RICHARD OF BORDEAUX | F. Walwyn | H. Beasley | 20/1 | 20 |
| 1964 | SUPER FLASH | F. Cundell | S. Mellor | 8/1 | 9 |
| 1965 | DUNKIRK | P. Cazalet | W. Rees | 11/10 | 8 |
| 1966 | PAWNBROKER | W. A. Stephenson | P. Broderick | 7/2 | 5 |
| 1967 | CHARLIE WORCESTER | R. Price | J. Gifford | 7/1 | 13 |
| 1968 | JUPITER BOY | F. Rimell | E. Harty | 9/1 | 13 |
| 1969 | GAY TRIP | F. Rimell | T. Biddlecombe | 8/1 | 14 |
| 1970 | CHATHAM | F. Rimell | K. White | 33/1 | 17 |
| 1971 | GAY TRIP | F. Rimell | T. Biddlecombe | 8/1 | 10 |
| 1972 | RED CANDLE | G. Vallance | J. Fox | 20/1 | 11 |
| 1973 | SKYMAS | B. Lusk | T. Murphy | 7/1 | 15 |
| 1974 | BRUSLEE | M. Scudamore | A. Turnell | 2/1 | 11 |
| 1975 | CLEAR CUT | M. Camacho | D. Greaves | 13/2 | 13 |
| 1976 | CANCELLO | N. Crump | D. Atkins | 4/1 | 13 |
| 1977 | BACHELOR'S HALL | P. Cundell | M. O'Halloran | 11/2 | 16 |
| 1978 | BAWNOGUES | M. Tate | C. Smith | 5/1 | 11 |
| 1979 | MAN ALIVE | G. Richards | R. Barry | 6/1 | 11 |
| 1980 | BRIGHT HIGHWAY | M. J. O'Brien | G. Newman | 5/1 | 15 |
| 1981 | HENRY KISSINGER | D. Gandolfo | P. Barton | 5/1 | 11 |
| 1982 | FIFTY DOLLARS MORE | F. Winter | R. Linley | 11/1 | 11 |
| 1983 | POUNENTES | W. McGhie | N. Doughty | 7/1 | 9 |
| 1984 | HALF FREE | F. Winter | R. Linley | 5/2 | 10 |
| 1985 | HALF FREE | F. Winter | R. Linley | 9/2 | 10 |
| 1986 | VERY PROMISING | D. Nicholson | R. Dunwoody | 7/1 | 11 |
| 1987 | BEAU RANGER | M. Pipe | M. Perrett | 13/2 | 14 |
| 1988 | PEGWELL BAY | T. Forster | P. Scudamore | 6/1 | 13 |
| 1989 | JOINT SOVEREIGNTY | P. Hobbs | G. McCourt | 10/1 | 15 |
| 1990 | MULTUM IN PARVO | J. Edwards | N. Williamson | 12/1 | 13 |
| 1991 | ANOTHER CORAL | D. Nicholson | R. Dunwoody | 15/2 | 15 |

# Hennessy Cognac Gold Cup

NEWBURY        3 MILES 2 FURLONGS 82 YARDS   FIRST RUN 1957

| Year | Horse | Trainer | Jockey | SP | Ran |
|------|-------|---------|--------|-----|-----|
| 1957 | MANDARIN | F. Walwyn | P. Madden | 8/1 | 19 |
| 1958 | TAXIDERMIST | F. Walwyn | Mr J. Lawrence | 10/1 | 13 |
| 1959 | KERSTIN | C. Bewicke | S. Hayhurst | 4/1 | 26 |
| 1960 | KNUCKLECRACKER | D. Ancil | D. Ancil | 100/7 | 20 |
| 1961 | MANDARIN | F. Walwyn | G. Robinson | 7/1 | 22 |
| 1962 | SPRINGBOK | N. Crump | G. Scott | 15/2 | 27 |
| 1963 | MILL HOUSE | F. Walwyn | G. Robinson | 15/8 | 10 |
| 1964 | ARKLE | T. Dreaper | P. Taaffe | 5/4 | 9 |
| 1965 | ARKLE | T. Dreaper | P. Taaffe | 1/6 | 8 |
| 1966 | STALBRIDGE COLONIST | K. Cundell | S. Mellor | 25/1 | 6 |
| 1967 | RONDETTO | R. Turnell | J. King | 100/8 | 13 |
| 1968 | MAN OF THE WEST | F. Walwyn | G. Robinson | 20/1 | 11 |
| 1969 | SPANISH STEPS | E. Courage | J. Cook | 7/1 | 15 |
| 1970 | BORDER MASK | P. Cazalet | D. Mould | 7/1 | 12 |
| 1971 | BIGHORN | C. Vernon Miller | D. Cartwright | 7/1 | 13 |
| 1972 | CHARLIE POTHEEN | F. Walwyn | R. Pitman | 10/1 | 13 |
| 1973 | RED CANDLE | C. Vallance | J. Fox | 12/1 | 11 |
| 1974 | ROYAL MARSHALL II | T. Forster | G. Thorner | 11/2 | 13 |
| 1975 | APRIL SEVENTH | R. Turnell | A. Turnell | 11/1 | 13 |
| 1976 | ZETA'S SON | P. Bailey | I. Watkinson | 12/1 | 21 |
| 1977 | BACHELOR'S HALL | P. Cundell | M. O'Halloran | 11/2 | 14 |
| 1978 | APPROACHING | J. Gifford | R. Champion | 3/1 | 8 |
| 1979 | FIGHTING FIT | K. Oliver | R. Linley | 15/2 | 15 |
| 1980 | BRIGHT HIGHWAY | M. J. O'Brien | G. Newman | 2/1 | 14 |
| 1981 | DIAMOND EDGE | F. Walwyn | W. Smith | 9/2 | 14 |
| 1982 | BREGAWN | M. Dickinson | G. Bradley | 9/4 | 11 |
| 1983 | BROWN CHAMBERLIN | F. Winter | J. Francome | 7/2 | 12 |
| 1984 | BURROUGH HILL LAD | Mrs J. Pitman | J. Francome | 100/30 | 13 |
| 1985 | GALWAY BLAZE | J. FitzGerald | M. Dwyer | 11/2 | 15 |
| 1986 | BROADHEATH | D. Barons | P. Nicholls | 6/1 | 15 |
| 1987 | PLAYSCHOOL | D. Barons | P. Nicholls | 6/1 | 12 |
| 1988 | STRANDS OF GOLD | M. Pipe | P. Scudamore | 10/1 | 12 |
| 1989 | GHOFAR | D. Elsworth | H. Davies | 5/1 | 8 |
| 1990 | ARCTIC CALL | O. Sherwood | J. Osborne | 5/1 | 13 |
| 1991 | CHATAM | M. Pipe | P. Scudamore | 10/1 | 15 |

## *Welsh National*

CHEPSTOW       3 MILES 6 FURLONGS       FIRST RUN 1895

| YEAR | HORSE | TRAINER | JOCKEY | SP | RAN |
|------|-------|---------|--------|-----|-----|
| 1948 | BORA'S COTTAGE | H. R. Price | E. Reavey | 100/8 | 16 |
| 1949 | FIGHTING LINE | K. Cundell | R. Francis | 7/1 | 15 |
| 1950 | GALLERY | W. Bissill | A. Mullins | 7/2 | 12 |
| 1951 | SKYREHOLME | N. Crump | A. Thompson | 7/2 | 16 |
| 1952 | DINTON LASS | J. Roberts | A. Mullins | 10/1 | 16 |
| 1953 | STALBRIDGE ROCK | H. Dufosse | R. McCreery | 6/1 | 15 |
| 1954 | BLOW HORN | T. Jarvis | J. Hunter | 100/8 | 17 |
| 1955 | MONALEEN | H. Smith | P. FitzGerald | 20/1 | 17 |
| 1956 | CRUDWELL | F. Cundell | R. Francis | 100/9 | 16 |
| 1957 | CREEOLA II | F. Rimell | M. Scudamore | 3/1 | 11 |
| 1958 | OSCAR WILDE | W. Wightman | B. Lawrence | 20/1 | 14 |
| 1959 | LIMONALI | E. Morel | D. Nicholson | 100/8 | 10 |
| 1960 | CLOVER BUD | G. Llewellin | D. Nicholson | 7/1 | 14 |
| 1961 | LIMONALI | I. Lewis | D. Nicholson | 7/4 | 9 |
| 1962 | FORTY SECRETS | E. Jones | J. Gifford | 6/1 | 15 |
| 1963 | MOTEL | W. Lowe | P. Cowley | 7/1 | 10 |
| 1964 | RAINBOW BATTLE | W. A. Stephenson | P. Broderick | 3/1 | 11 |
| 1965 | NORTHER | D. Jenkins | T. Biddlecombe | 9/2 | 11 |
| 1966 | KILBURN | C. Nesfield | T. Norman | 11/4 | 11 |
| 1967 | HAPPY SPRING | J. Wright | K. White | 6/1 | 6 |
| 1968 | GLENN | F. Rimell | E. Harty | 11/2 | 8 |
| 1969 | *Abandoned – snow* | | | | |
| 1970 | FRENCH EXCUSE | F. Rimell | T. Biddlecombe | 3/1 | 11 |
| 1971 | ROYAL TOSS | H. Handel | P. Cowley | 15/8 | 13 |
| 1972 | CHARLIE II | R. Turnell | J. Haine | 11/2 | 9 |
| 1973 | DEBLIN'S GREEN | G. Yardley | N. Wakley | 20/1 | 16 |
| 1974 | PATTERED | E. Jones | K. White | 25/1 | 24 |
| 1975 | *Abandoned – waterlogged* | | | | |
| 1976 | RAG TRADE | F. Rimell | J. Burke | 17/2 | 17 |
| 1977 | *Abandoned – waterlogged* | | | | |
| 1978 | *Abandoned – frost* | | | | |
| 1979 | (Feb.) *Abandoned – snow* | | | | |
| 1979 | (Dec.) PETER SCOT | D. Gandolfo | P. Barton | 8/1 | 15 |
| 1980 | NARVIK | N. Crump | J. Francome | 15/1 | 18 |
| 1981 | PEATY SANDY | Miss H. Hamilton | Mr T. G. Dun | 3/1 | 23 |
| 1982 | CORBIERE | Mrs J. Pitman | B. de Haan | 12/1 | 10 |
| 1983 | BURROUGH HILL LAD | Mrs J. Pitman | J. Francome | 100/30 | 18 |
| 1984 | RIGHTHAND MAN | Mrs M. Dickinson | G. Bradley | 6/1 | 18 |
| 1985 | RUN AND SKIP | J. Spearing | P. Scudamore | 13/1 | 18 |
| 1986 | STEARSBY | Mrs J. Pitman | G. Bradley | 8/1 | 17 |
| 1987 | PLAYSCHOOL | D. Barons | P. Nicholls | 5/1 | 13 |
| 1988 | BONANZA BOY | M. Pipe | P. Scudamore | 9/4 | 12 |
| 1989 | BONANZA BOY | M. Pipe | P. Scudamore | 15/8 | 12 |
| 1990 | COOL GROUND | R. Akehurst | L. Harvey | 9/2 | 14 |
| 1991 | CARVILL'S HILL | M. Pipe | P. Scudamore | 9/4 | 17 |

# King George VI Chase

KEMPTON PARK                    3 MILES                    FIRST RUN 1937

| YEAR | HORSE | TRAINER | JOCKEY | SP | RAN |
|------|-------|---------|--------|----|----|
| 1947 | ROWLAND ROY | F. Walwyn | B. Marshall | 5/1 | 10 |
| 1948 | COTTAGE RAKE | M. V. O'Brien | A. Brabazon | 13/8 | 9 |
| 1949 | FINNURE | G. Beeby | R. Francis | 9/2 | 4 |
| 1950 | MANICOU | P. Cazalet | B. Marshall | 5/1 | 7 |
| 1951 | STATECRAFT | P. Cazalet | A. Grantham | 100/6 | 6 |
| 1952 | HALLOWEEN | W. Wightman | F. Winter | 7/4 | 6 |
| 1953 | GALLOWAY BRAES | A. Kilpatrick | R. Morrow | 9/4 | 7 |
| 1954 | HALLOWEEN | W. Wightman | F. Winter | 9/2 | 8 |
| 1955 | LIMBER HILL | W. Dutton | J. Power | 3/1 | 8 |
| 1956 | ROSE PARK | P. Cazalet | M. Scudamore | 100/6 | 6 |
| 1957 | MANDARIN | F. Walwyn | P. Madden | 7/1 | 9 |
| 1958 | LOCHROE | P. Cazalet | A. Freeman | 7/2 | 7 |
| 1959 | MANDARIN | F. Walwyn | P. Madden | 5/2 | 9 |
| 1960 | SAFFRON TARTAN | D. Butchers | F. Winter | 5/2 | 10 |
| 1961 | *Abandoned – frost* | | | | |
| 1962 | *Abandoned – frost* | | | | |
| 1963 | MILL HOUSE | F. Walwyn | G. Robinson | 2/7 | 3 |
| 1964 | FRENCHMAN'S COVE | H. Thomson Jones | S. Mellor | 4/11 | 2 |
| 1965 | ARKLE | T. Dreaper | P. Taaffe | 1/7 | 4 |
| 1966 | DORMANT | Mrs D. Wells-Kendrew | J. King | 10/1 | 7 |
| 1967 | *Abandoned – frost* | | | | |
| 1968 | *Abandoned – foot and mouth disease* | | | | |
| 1969 | TITUS OATES | G. Richards | S. Mellor | 100/30 | 5 |
| 1970 | *Abandoned – snow* | | | | |
| 1971 | THE DIKLER | F. Walwyn | B. Brogan | 11/2 | 10 |
| 1972 | PENDIL | F. Winter | R. Pitman | 4/5 | 6 |
| 1973 | PENDIL | F. Winter | R. Pitman | 30/100 | 4 |
| 1974 | CAPTAIN CHRISTY | P. Taaffe | R. Coonan | 5/1 | 6 |
| 1975 | CAPTAIN CHRISTY | P. Taaffe | G. Newman | 11/10 | 7 |
| 1976 | ROYAL MARSHALL II | T. Forster | G. Thorner | 16/1 | 10 |
| 1977 | BACHELOR'S HALL | P. Cundell | M. O'Halloran | 9/2 | 9 |
| 1978 | GAY SPARTAN | A. Dickinson | T. Carmody | 3/1 | 16 |
| 1979 | SILVER BUCK | A. Dickinson | T. Carmody | 3/1 | 11 |
| 1980 | SILVER BUCK | M. Dickinson | T. Carmody | 9/4 | 8 |
| 1981 | *Abandoned – snow and frost* | | | | |
| 1982 | WAYWARD LAD | M. Dickinson | J. Francome | 7/2 | 6 |
| 1983 | WAYWARD LAD | M. Dickinson | R. Earnshaw | 11/8 | 5 |
| 1984 | BURROUGH HILL LAD | Mrs J. Pitman | J. Francome | 1/2 | 3 |
| 1985 | WAYWARD LAD | M. Dickinson | G. Bradley | 12/1 | 5 |
| 1986 | DESERT ORCHID | D. Elsworth | S. Sherwood | 16/1 | 9 |
| 1987 | NUPSALA | F. Doumen | A. Pommier | 25/1 | 9 |
| 1988 | DESERT ORCHID | D. Elsworth | S. Sherwood | 1/2 | 9 |
| 1989 | DESERT ORCHID | D. Elsworth | R. Dunwoody | 4/6 | 6 |
| 1990 | DESERT ORCHID | D. Elsworth | R. Dunwoody | 9/4 | 9 |
| 1991 | THE FELLOW | F. Doumen | A. Kondrat | 10/1 | 8 |

# Christmas Hurdle

KEMPTON PARK               2 MILES               FIRST RUN 1969

| Year | Horse | Trainer | Jockey | SP | RAN |
|------|-------|---------|--------|-----|-----|
| 1969 | CORAL DIVER | F. Rimell | T. Biddlecombe | 9/4 | 6 |
| 1970 | *Abandoned – snow* | | | | |
| 1971 | CORAL DIVER | F. Rimell | T. Biddlecombe | 7/4 | 4 |
| 1972 | CANASTA LAD | P. Bailey | J. King | 4/7 | 6 |
| 1973 | LANZAROTE | F. Winter | R. Pitman | 1/6 | 4 |
| 1974 | TREE TANGLE | R. Turnell | A. Turnell | 30/100 | 5 |
| 1975 | LANZAROTE | F. Winter | J. Francome | evens | 5 |
| 1976 | DRAMATIST | F. Walwyn | W. Smith | 9/1 | 6 |
| 1977 | BEACON LIGHT | R. Turnell | A. Turnell | 5/2 | 3 |
| 1978 | KYBO | R. Champion | J. Gifford | 5/4 | 6 |
| 1979 | BIRD'S NEST | R. Turnell | A. Turnell | 6/4 | 5 |
| 1980 | CELTIC RYDE | P. Cundell | J. Francome | 2/1 | 5 |
| 1981 | *Abandoned – frost* | | | | |
| 1982 | EKBALCO | R. Fisher | J. J. O'Neill | 1/2 | 4 |
| 1983 | DAWN RUN | P. Mullins | J. J. O'Neill | 9/4 | 4 |
| 1984 | BROWNE'S GAZETTE | Mrs M. Dickinson | D. Browne | 11/8 | 7 |
| 1985 | AONOCH | Mrs S. Oliver | J. Duggan | 14/1 | 9 |
| 1986 | NOHALMDUN | M. H. Easterby | P. Scudamore | 15/8 | 7 |
| 1987 | OSRIC | M. Ryan | G. McCourt | 12/1 | 8 |
| 1988 | KRIBENSIS | M. Stoute | R. Dunwoody | 4/9 | 7 |
| 1989 | KRIBENSIS | M. Stoute | R. Dunwoody | 4/6 | 8 |
| 1990 | FIDWAY | T. Thompson Jones | S. Smith Eccles | 100/30 | 8 |
| 1991 | GRAN ALBA | R. Hannon | G. McCourt | 3/1 | 7 |

# Anthony Mildmay, Peter Cazalet Memorial Chase

SANDOWN PARK   3 MILES 5 FURLONGS 18 YARDS   FIRST RUN 1952

| YEAR | HORSE | TRAINER | JOCKEY | SP | RAN |
|------|-------|---------|--------|-----|-----|
| 1952 | CROMWELL | P. Cazalet | B. Marshall | 9/2 | 12 |
| 1953 | WHISPERING STEEL | A. Kilpatrick | R. Emery | 7/1 | 16 |
| 1954 | DOMATA | F. Cundell | A. Corbett | 6/1 | 10 |
| 1955 | *Abandoned – snow and frost* | | | | |
| 1956 | LINWELL | C. Mallon | R. Hamey | 4/1 | 10 |
| 1957 | MUCH OBLIGED | N. Crump | H. East | 100/8 | 20 |
| 1958 | POLAR FLIGHT | G. Spann | G. Slack | 11/2 | 14 |
| 1959 | *Abandoned – snow and frost* | | | | |
| 1960 | TEAM SPIRIT | D. Moore | G. Robinson | 10/1 | 12 |
| 1961 | MAC JOY | K. Bailey | M. Scudamore | 25/1 | 13 |
| 1962 | DUKE OF YORK | J. Tilling | Mr D. Scott | 6/1 | 18 |
| 1963 | *Abandoned – snow and frost* | | | | |
| 1964 | DORMANT | N. Crump | P. Buckley | 11//4 | 9 |
| 1965 | FREDDIE | R. Tweedie | P. McCarron | 2/1 | 12 |
| 1966 | WHAT A MYTH | H. R. Price | P. Kelleway | 4/1 | 5 |
| 1967 | *Abandoned – frost* | | | | |
| 1968 | STALBRIDGE COLONIST | K. Cundell | S. Mellor | 7/1 | 18 |
| 1969 | *Abandoned – fog* | | | | |
| 1970 | LARBAWN | M. Marsh | J. Gifford | 9/1 | 8 |
| 1971 | *Abandoned – frost* | | | | |
| 1972 | ROYAL TOSS | H. Handel | N. Wakley | 5/2 | 9 |
| 1973 | MIDNIGHT FURY | F. Winter | V. Soane | 12/1 | 9 |
| 1974 | HIGH KEN | J. Edwards | B. R. Davies | 16/1 | 10 |
| 1975 | MONEY MARKET | C. Bewicke | J. King | 6/1 | 11 |
| 1976 | MONEY MARKET | C. Bewicke | R. Barry | 3/1 | 9 |
| 1977 | ZETA'S SON | P. Bailey | R. Barry | 11/2 | 12 |
| 1978 | SHIFTING GOLD | K. Bailey | J. Francome | 11/8 | 5 |
| 1979 | *Abandoned – snow and frost* | | | | |
| 1980 | MODESTY FORBIDS | J. Gifford | R. Rowe | 9/1 | 13 |
| 1981 | PETER SCOT | D. Gandolfo | P. Barton | 6/1 | 9 |
| 1982 | *Abandoned – snow and frost* | | | | |
| 1983 | FIFTY DOLLARS MORE* | F. Winter | R. Linley | 4/6 | 5 |
| 1984 | BURROUGH HILL LAD | Mrs J. Pitman | J. Francome | 11/8 | 9 |
| 1985 | WEST TIP | M. Oliver | R. Dunwoody | 11/4 | 5 |
| 1986 | RUN AND SKIP | J. Spearing | P. Scudamore | 7/2 | 8 |
| 1987 | STEARSBY | Mrs J. Pitman | G. McCourt | 11/8 | 7 |
| 1988 | RHYME 'N' REASON | D. Elsworth | C. Brown | 11/8 | 6 |
| 1989 | MR FRISK | K. Bailey | R. Dunwoody | 3/1 | 7 |
| 1990 | COOL GROUND | N. Mitchell | A. Tory | 6/1 | 12 |
| 1991 | COOL GROUND | R. Akehurst | L. Harvey | 6/4 | 8 |

* 1983: Lesley Ann finished first but was disqualified

# Tote Gold Trophy

NEWBURY                    2 MILES 100 YARDS                    FIRST RUN 1963

| Year | Horse | Trainer | Jockey | SP | RAN |
|------|-------|---------|--------|-----|-----|
| 1963 | ROSYTH | H. R. Price | J. Gifford | 20/1 | 41 |
| 1964 | ROSYTH | H. R. Price | J. Gifford | 10/1 | 24 |
| 1965 | ELAN | J. Sutcliffe, jr | D. Nicholson | 9/2 | 21 |
| 1966 | LE VERMONTOIS | H. R. Price | J. Gifford | 15/2 | 28 |
| 1967 | HILL HOUSE | H. R. Price | J. Gifford | 9/1 | 28 |
| 1968 | PERSIAN WAR | C. Davies | J. Uttley | 9/2 | 33 |
| 1969 | *Abandoned – frost* | | | | |
| 1970 | *Abandoned – snow and frost* | | | | |
| 1971 | CALA MESQUIDA | J. Sutcliffe | J. Cook | 33/1 | 23 |
| 1972 | GOOD REVIEW | J. Dreaper | V. O'Brien | 8/1 | 26 |
| 1973 | INDIANAPOLIS | J. Sutcliffe | J. King | 15/2 | 26 |
| 1974 | *Abandoned – waterlogged* | | | | |
| 1975 | TAMMUZ | F. Walwyn | W. Smith | 18/1 | 28 |
| 1976 | IRISH FASHION | M. Cunningham | R. Barry | 16/1 | 29 |
| 1977 | TRUE LAD | W. Swainson | T. Stack | 14/1 | 27 |
| 1978 | *Abandoned – frost* | | | | |
| 1979 | WITHIN THE LAW | M. H. Easterby | A. Brown | 25/1 | 28 |
| 1980 | BOOTLACES | D. Barons | P. Leach | 20/1 | 21 |
| 1981 | *Abandoned – frost* | | | | |
| 1982 | DONEGAL PRINCE | P. Kelleway | J. Francome | 13/1 | 27 |
| 1983 | *Abandoned – snow and frost* | | | | |
| 1984 | RA NOVA | Mrs N. Kennedy | P. Farrell | 16/1 | 26 |
| 1985 | *Abandoned – snow* | | | | |
| 1986 | *Abandoned – snow* | | | | |
| 1987 | NEBLIN | G. Balding | S. Moore | 10/1 | 21 |
| 1988 | JAMESMEAD | D. Elsworth | B. Powell | 11/1 | 19 |
| 1989 | GREY SALUTE | J. Jenkins | R. Dunwoody | 8/1 | 10 |
| 1990 | DEEP SENSATION | J. Gifford | R. Rowe | 7/1 | 17 |
| 1991 | *Abandoned – frost* | | | | |

# *Racing Post Handicap Chase*

| Year | Horse | Trainer | Jockey | SP | RAN |
|------|-------|---------|--------|-----|-----|
| 1949 | ROYAL MOUNT | J. Powell | P. Doyle | 15/8 | 5 |
| 1950 | PRINTERS PIE | G. Wilson | I. Stephens | 4/1 | 7 |
| 1951 | CADAMSTOWN | V. Brunt | J. Dowdeswell | 6/1 | 7 |
| 1952 | MONT TREMBLANT | F. Walwyn | D. Dick | 6/4 | 7 |
| 1953 | WIGBY | F. Cundell | R. Francis | 5/2 | 4 |
| 1954 | CLAUDE DUVAL | P. Thrale | J. Beasty | 7/2 | 5 |
| 1955 | HALLOWEEN | W. Wightman | F. Winter | 11/10 | 5 |
| 1956 | *Abandoned – snow and frost* | | | | |
| 1957 | POINTSMAN | A. Kilpatrick | R. Morrow | 3/1 | 7 |
| 1958 | LOCHROE | P. Cazalet | Mr E. Cazalet | 9/4 | 5 |
| 1959 | STANTON JOHNIE | D. Ancil | R. Hirons | 20/1 | 3 |
| 1960 | DANDY SCOT | H. R. Price | F. Winter | 4/11 | 4 |
| 1961 | POUDING | F. Walwyn | F. Winter | 7/4 | 6 |
| 1962 | FRENCHMAN'S COVE | H. T. Jones | S. Mellor | 4/5 | 4 |
| 1963 | DARK VENETIAN | R. Bassett | D. Bassett | 6/1 | 7 |
| 1964 | *Abandoned – frost* | | | | |
| 1965 | THE RIP | P. Cazalet | D. Dick | 7/4 | 6 |
| 1966 | KAPENO | P. Cazalet | D. Mould | 100/30 | 9 |
| 1967 | MAIGRET | E. Herbert | J. Haine | 9/1 | 5 |
| 1968 | DIFFERENT CLASS | P. Cazalet | D. Mould | 30/100 | 2 |
| 1969 | BASSNET | H. R. Price | J. Gifford | 3/1 | 8 |
| 1970 | TITUS OATES | G. Richards | S. Mellor | 3/1 | 9 |
| 1971 | THE LAIRD | R. Turnell | J. King | 11/8 | 5 |
| 1972 | CRISP | F. Winter | R. Pitman | 9/4 | 5 |
| 1973 | PENDIL | F. Winter | R. Pitman | 1/7 | 3 |
| 1974 | PENDIL | F. Winter | R. Pitman | 1/6 | 3 |
| 1975 | CUCKOLDER | R. Turnell | A. Turnell | 6/1 | 5 |
| 1976 | CANADIUS | G. Richards | J. J. O'Neill | 4/1 | 4 |
| 1977 | DON'T HESITATE | P. Cundell | M. O'Halloran | 20/1 | 7 |
| 1978 | FORT DEVON | F. Walwyn | W. Smith | 10/11 | 5 |
| 1979 | STROMBOLUS | P. Bailey | R. Champion | 16/1 | 14 |
| 1980 | FATHER DELANEY | M. H. Easterby | A. Brown | 9/1 | 10 |
| 1981 | SUGARALLY | G. Fairbairn | P. Scudamore | 9/2 | 8 |
| 1982 | TWO SWALLOWS | R. Armytage | A. Webber | 6/1 | 7 |
| 1983 | MANTON CASTLE | J. Gifford | H. Davies | 15/2 | 10 |
| 1984 | TOM'S LITTLE AL | W. R. Williams | C. Brown | 6/1 | 10 |
| 1985 | *Abandoned – frost* | | | | |
| 1986 | *Abandoned – frost* | | | | |
| 1987 | COMBS DITCH | D. Elsworth | C. Brown | 11/10 | 4 |
| 1988 | RHYME 'N' REASON | D. Elsworth | B. Powell | 7/2 | 12 |
| 1989 | BONANZA BOY | M. Pipe | P. Scudamore | 5/1 | 11 |
| 1990 | DESERT ORCHID | D. Elsworth | R. Dunwoody | 8/11 | 8 |
| 1991 | DOCKLANDS EXPRESS | K. Bailey | A. Tory | 7/2 | 9 |

# Champion Hurdle

CHELTENHAM                    2 MILES                    FIRST RUN 1927

| YEAR | HORSE | TRAINER | JOCKEY | SP | RAN |
|------|-------|---------|--------|-----|-----|
| 1927 | BLARIS | W. Payne | G. Duller | 11/10 | 4 |
| 1928 | BROWN JACK | A. Hastings | L. Rees | 4/1 | 6 |
| 1929 | ROYAL FALCON | R. Gore | F. Rees | 11/2 | 6 |
| 1930 | BROWN TONY | J. Anthony | T. Cullinan | 7/2 | 5 |
| 1931 | *Abandoned* | | | | |
| 1932 | INSURANCE | B. Briscoe | T. Leader | 4/5 | 3 |
| 1933 | INSURANCE | B. Briscoe | W. Stott | 10/11 | 5 |
| 1934 | CHENANGO | I. Anthony | D. Morgan | 4/9 | 5 |
| 1935 | LION COURAGE | F. Brown | G. Wilson | 100/8 | 11 |
| 1936 | VICTOR NORMAN | M. Blair | H. Nicholson | 4/1 | 8 |
| 1937 | FREE FARE | E. Gwilt | G. Pellerin | 2/1 | 7 |
| 1938 | OUR HOPE | R. Gubbins | Capt. P. Harding | 5/1 | 5 |
| 1939 | AFRICAN SISTER | C. Piggott | K. Piggott | 10/1 | 13 |
| 1940 | SOLFORD | O. Anthony | S. Magee | 5/2 | 8 |
| 1941 | SENECA | V. Smyth | R. Smyth | 7/1 | 6 |
| 1942 | FORESTATION | V. Smyth | R. Smyth | 10/1 | 20 |
| 1943–4 | *No race* | | | | |
| 1945 | BRAINS TRUST | G. Wilson | T. Rimell | 9/2 | 16 |
| 1946 | DISTEL | M. Arnott | R. O'Ryan | 4/5 | 8 |
| 1947 | NATIONAL SPIRIT | V. Smyth | D. Morgan | 7/1 | 14 |
| 1948 | NATIONAL SPIRIT | V. Smyth | R. Smyth | 6/4 | 12 |
| 1949 | HATTON'S GRACE | M. V. O'Brien | A. Brabazon | 100/7 | 14 |
| 1950 | HATTON'S GRACE | M. V. O'Brien | A. Brabazon | 5/2 | 12 |
| 1951 | HATTON'S GRACE | M. V. O'Brien | T. Molony | 4/1 | 8 |
| 1952 | SIR KEN | W. Stephenson | T. Molony | 3/1 | 16 |
| 1953 | SIR KEN | W. Stephenson | T. Molony | 2/5 | 7 |
| 1954 | SIR KEN | W. Stephenson | T. Molony | 4/9 | 13 |
| 1955 | CLAIR SOLEIL | H. R. Price | F. Winter | 5/2 | 21 |
| 1956 | DOORKNOCKER | W. Hall | H. Sprague | 100/9 | 14 |
| 1957 | MERRY DEAL | A. Jones | G. Underwood | 28/1 | 16 |
| 1958 | BANDALORE | S. Wright | G. Slack | 20/1 | 18 |
| 1959 | FARE TIME | H. H. R. Price | F. Winter | 13/2 | 14 |
| 1960 | ANOTHER FLASH | P. Sleator | H. Beasley | 11/4 | 12 |
| 1961 | EBORNEEZER | H. H. R. Price | F. Winter | 4/1 | 17 |
| 1962 | ANZIO | F. Walwyn | G. Robinson | 11/2 | 14 |
| 1963 | WINNING FAIR | G. Spencer | Mr A. Lillingston | 100/9 | 21 |
| 1964 | MAGIC COURT | T. Robson | P. McCarron | 100/6 | 24 |
| 1965 | KIRRIEMUIR | F. Walwyn | G. Robinson | 50/1 | 19 |
| 1966 | SALMON SPRAY | R. Turnell | J. Haine | 4/1 | 17 |
| 1967 | SAUCY KIT | M. H. Easterby | R. Edwards | 100/6 | 23 |
| 1968 | PERSIAN WAR | C. Davies | J. Uttley | 4/1 | 16 |
| 1969 | PERSIAN WAR | C. Davies | J. Uttley | 6/4 | 17 |
| 1970 | PERSIAN WAR | C. Davies | J. Uttley | 5/4 | 14 |
| 1971 | BULA | F. Winter | P. Kelleway | 15/8 | 9 |
| 1972 | BULA | F. Winter | P. Kelleway | 8/11 | 12 |
| 1973 | COMEDY OF ERRORS | F. Rimell | W. Smith | 8/1 | 8 |

| YEAR | HORSE | TRAINER | JOCKEY | SP | RAN |
|------|-------|---------|--------|-----|-----|
| 1974 | LANZAROTE | F. Winter | R. Pitman | 7/4 | 7 |
| 1975 | COMEDY OF ERRORS | F. Rimell | K. White | 11/8 | 13 |
| 1976 | NIGHT NURSE | M. H. Easterby | P. Broderick | 2/1 | 8 |
| 1977 | NIGHT NURSE | M. H. Easterby | P. Broderick | 15/2 | 10 |
| 1978 | MONKSFIELD | D. McDonogh | T. Kinane | 11/2 | 13 |
| 1979 | MONKSFIELD | D. McDonogh | D. Hughes | 9/4 | 10 |
| 1980 | SEA PIGEON | M. H. Easterby | J. J. O'Neill | 13/2 | 9 |
| 1981 | SEA PIGEON | M. H. Easterby | J. Francome | 7/4 | 14 |
| 1982 | FOR AUCTION | M. Cunningham | Mr C. Magnier | 40/1 | 14 |
| 1983 | GAYE BRIEF | Mrs M. Rimell | R. Linley | 7/1 | 17 |
| 1984 | DAWN RUN | P. Mullins | J. J. O'Neill | 4/5 | 14 |
| 1985 | SEE YOU THEN | N. Henderson | S. Smith Eccles | 16/1 | 14 |
| 1986 | SEE YOU THEN | N. Henderson | S. Smith Eccles | 5/6 | 23 |
| 1987 | SEE YOU THEN | N. Henderson | S. Smith Eccles | 11/10 | 18 |
| 1988 | CELTIC SHOT | F. Winter | P. Scudamore | 7/1 | 21 |
| 1989 | BEECH ROAD | G. Balding | R. Guest | 50/1 | 15 |
| 1990 | KRIBENSIS | M. Stoute | R. Dunwoody | 95/40 | 19 |
| 1991 | MORLEY STREET | G. Balding | J. Frost | 4/1 | 24 |

# Queen Mother Champion Chase

CHELTENHAM                    2 MILES                    FIRST RUN 1959

| YEAR | HORSE | TRAINER | JOCKEY | SP | RAN |
|------|-------|---------|--------|-----|-----|
| 1959 | QUITA QUE | D. Moore | Mr J. Cox | 4/9 | 9 |
| 1960 | FORTRIA | T. Dreaper | P. Taaffe | 15/8 | 7 |
| 1961 | FORTRIA | T. Dreaper | P. Taaffe | 2/5 | 5 |
| 1962 | PIPERTON | A. Thomlinson | D. Dick | 100/6 | 7 |
| 1963 | SANDY ABBOT | G. Owen | S. Mellor | 5/1 | 5 |
| 1964 | BEN STACK | T. Dreaper | P. Taaffe | 2/1 | 5 |
| 1965 | DUNKIRK | P. Cazalet | D. Dick | 8/1 | 6 |
| 1966 | FLYINGBOLT | T. Dreaper | P. Taaffe | 1/5 | 6 |
| 1967 | DRINNY'S DOUBLE | R. Turnell | F. Nash | 7/2 | 8 |
| 1968 | DRINNY'S DOUBLE | R. Turnell | F. Nash | 6/1 | 5 |
| 1969 | MUIR | T. Dreaper | B. Hannon | 15/2 | 11 |
| 1970 | STRAIGHT FORT | T. Dreaper | P. Taaffe | 7/4 | 6 |
| 1971 | CRISP | F. Winter | P. Kelleway | 3/1 | 8 |
| 1972 | ROYAL RELIEF | E. Courage | W. Smith | 15/8 | 5 |
| 1973 | INKSLINGER | D. Moore | T. Carberry | 6/1 | 6 |
| 1974 | ROYAL RELIEF | E. Courage | W. Smith | 6/1 | 6 |
| 1975 | LOUGH INAGH | J. Dreaper | S. Barker | 100/30 | 8 |
| 1976 | SKYMAS | B. Lusk | M. Morris | 8/1 | 7 |
| 1977 | SKYMAS | B. Lusk | M. Morris | 7/2 | 8 |
| 1978 | HILLY WAY | P. McCreery | T. Carmody | 7/1 | 10 |
| 1979 | HILLY WAY | P. McCreery | Mr T. Walsh | 7/1 | 9 |
| 1980 | ANOTHER DOLLY | F. Rimell | S. Morshead | 33/1 | 7 |
| 1981 | DRUMGORA | A. Moore | F. Berry | 25/1 | 9 |
| 1982 | RATHGORMAN | M. Dickinson | K. Whyte | 100/30 | 9 |
| 1983 | BADSWORTH BOY | M. Dickinson | R. Earnshaw | 2/1 | 6 |
| 1984 | BADSWORTH BOY | M. Dickinson | R. Earnshaw | 8/13 | 10 |
| 1985 | BADSWORTH BOY | Mrs M. Dickinson | R. Earnshaw | 11/8 | 5 |
| 1986 | BUCK HOUSE | M. Morris | T. Carmody | 5/2 | 11 |
| 1987 | PEARLYMAN | J. Edwards | P. Scudamore | 13/8 | 8 |
| 1988 | PEARLYMAN | J. Edwards | T. Morgan | 15/8 | 8 |
| 1989 | BARNBROOK AGAIN | D. Elsworth | S. Sherwood | 7/1 | 8 |
| 1990 | BARNBROOK AGAIN | D. Elsworth | H. Davies | 11/10 | 9 |
| 1991 | KATABATIC | A. Turnell | S. McNeill | 9/1 | 7 |

# *Triumph Hurdle*

CHELTENHAM      2 MILES      FIRST RUN 1950

| YEAR | HORSE | TRAINER | JOCKEY | SP | RAN |
|------|-------|---------|--------|-----|-----|
| 1950 | ABRUPTO | E. Diggle | R. Mantelin | 9/2 | 19 |
| 1951 | BLUE SONG | G. Pelat | F. Thirion | 6/1 | 12 |
| 1952 | HOGGAR | J. Cunnington | R. Triboit | 13/2 | 15 |
| 1953 | CLAIR SOLEIL | H. R. Price | F. Winter | 8/1 | 13 |
| 1954 | PRINCE CHARLEMAGNE | T. Carey | L. Piggott | 11/4 | 12 |
| 1955 | KWANNIN | A. Head | P. Delfarguiel | 2/1 | 12 |
| 1956 | SQUARE DANCE | F. Walwyn | M. Scudamore | 13/2 | 11 |
| 1957 | MERITORIUS | P. Thrale | D. Dillon | 20/1 | 14 |
| 1958 | PUNDIT | S. Ingham | H. Sprague | 5/2 | 14 |
| 1959 | AMAZON'S CHOICE | P. Thrale | J. Gilbert | 7/1 | 13 |
| 1960 | TURPIAL | P. Cazalet | A. Freeman | 7/1 | 13 |
| 1961 | CANTAB | H. R. Price | F. Winter | 4/1 | 15 |
| 1962 | BEAVER II | H. R. Price | J. Gifford | 100/6 | 11 |
| 1963–4 | *No race* | | | | |
| 1965 | BLARNEY BEACON | R. Smyth | G. Ramshaw | 8/1 | 7 |
| 1966 | BLACK ICE | A. Thomas | H. Beasley | 9/2 | 11 |
| 1967 | PERSIAN WAR | B. Swift | J. Uttley | 4/1 | 13 |
| 1968 | ENGLAND'S GLORY | S. Ingham | J. Uttley | 9/2 | 16 |
| 1969 | CORAL DIVER | F. Rimell | T. Biddlecombe | 3/1 | 26 |
| 1970 | VARMA | M. Masson | B. Barker | 100/7 | 31 |
| 1971 | BOXER | R. Smyth | J. Uttley | 100/30 | 18 |
| 1972 | ZARIB | F. Rimell | W. Smith | 16/1 | 16 |
| 1973 | MOONLIGHT BAY | H. R. Price | J. Haine | 85/40 | 18 |
| 1974 | ATTIVO | C. Mitchell | R. Hughes | 4/5 | 21 |
| 1975 | ROYAL EPIC | V. Cross | F. McKenna | 20/1 | 28 |
| 1976 | PETERHOF | M. W. Easterby | J. J. O'Neill | 10/1 | 23 |
| 1977 | MELADON | A. Maxwell | T. Carberry | 6/1 | 30 |
| 1978 | CONNAUGHT RANGER | F. Rimell | J. Burke | 25/1 | 14 |
| 1979 | POLLARDSTOWN | S. Mellor | P. Blacker | 12/1 | 28 |
| 1980 | HEIGHLIN | D. Elsworth | S. Jobar | 40/1 | 26 |
| 1981 | BARON BLAKENEY | M. Pipe | P. Leach | 66/1 | 29 |
| 1982 | SHINY COPPER | Mrs N. Smith | A. Webb | 66/1 | 29 |
| 1983 | SAXON FARM | S. Mellor | M. Perrett | 12/1 | 30 |
| 1984 | NORTHERN GAME | E. O'Grady | T. Ryan | 20/1 | 30 |
| 1985 | FIRST BOUT | N. Henderson | S. Smith Eccles | 5/1 | 27 |
| 1986 | SOLAR CLOUD | D. Nicholson | P. Scudamore | 40/1 | 28 |
| 1987 | ALONE SUCCESS | N. Henderson | S. Smith Eccles | 11/1 | 29 |
| 1988 | KRIBENSIS | M. Stoute | R. Dunwoody | 6/1 | 26 |
| 1989 | IKDAM | R. Holder | N. Coleman | 66/1 | 27 |
| 1990 | RARE HOLIDAY | D. Weld | B. Sheridan | 25/1 | 30 |
| 1991 | OH SO RISKY | D. Elsworth | P. Holley | 14/1 | 27 |

# Cheltenham Gold Cup

CHELTENHAM        3 MILES 2 FURLONGS        FIRST RUN 1924

| YEAR | HORSE | TRAINER | JOCKEY | SP | RAN |
|------|-------|---------|--------|-----|-----|
| 1924 | RED SPLASH | F. Withington | F. Rees | 5/1 | 8 |
| 1925 | BALLINODE | F. Morgan | E. Leader | 3/1 | 4 |
| 1926 | KOKO | A. Bickley | J. Hamey | 10/1 | 8 |
| 1927 | THROWN IN | O. Anthony | H. Grosvenor | 10/1 | 8 |
| 1928 | PATRON SAINT | H. Harrison | F. Rees | 7/2 | 7 |
| 1929 | EASTER HERO | J. Anthony | F. Rees | 7/4 | 10 |
| 1930 | EASTER HERO | J. Anthony | T. Cullinan | 8/11 | 4 |
| 1931 | *Abandoned* | | | | |
| 1932 | GOLDEN MILLER | B. Briscoe | T. Leader | 13/2 | 6 |
| 1933 | GOLDEN MILLER | B. Briscoe | W. Stott | 4/7 | 7 |
| 1934 | GOLDEN MILLER | B. Briscoe | G. Wilson | 6/5 | 7 |
| 1935 | GOLDEN MILLER | B. Briscoe | G. Wilson | 1/2 | 5 |
| 1936 | GOLDEN MILLER | O. Anthony | E. Williams | 20/21 | 6 |
| 1937 | *Abandoned* | | | | |
| 1938 | MORSE CODE | I. Anthony | D. Morgan | 13/2 | 6 |
| 1939 | BRENDAN'S COTTAGE | G. Beeby | G. Owen | 8/1 | 5 |
| 1940 | ROMAN HACKLE | O. Anthony | E. Williams | evens | 7 |
| 1941 | POET PRINCE | I. Anthony | R. Burford | 7/2 | 10 |
| 1942 | MÉDOC | R. Hobbs | H. Nicholson | 9/2 | 12 |
| 1943–4 | *No race* | | | | |
| 1945 | RED ROWER | Lord Stalbridge | D. Jones | 11/4 | 12 |
| 1946 | PRINCE REGENT | T. Dreaper | T. Hyde | 4/7 | 6 |
| 1947 | FORTINA | H. Christie | Mr R. Black | 8/1 | 12 |
| 1948 | COTTAGE RAKE | M. V. O'Brien | A. Brabazon | 10/1 | 12 |
| 1949 | COTTAGE RAKE | M. V. O'Brien | A. Brabazon | 4/6 | 6 |
| 1950 | COTTAGE RAKE | M. V. O'Brien | A. Brabazon | 5/6 | 6 |
| 1951 | SILVER FAME | G. Beeby | M. Molony | 6/4 | 6 |
| 1952 | MONT TREMBLANT | F. Walwyn | D. Dick | 8/1 | 13 |
| 1953 | KNOCK HARD | M. V. O'Brien | T. Molony | 11/2 | 12 |
| 1954 | FOUR TEN | J. Roberts | T. Cusack | 100/6 | 6 |
| 1955 | GAY DONALD | J. Ford | A. Grantham | 33/1 | 9 |
| 1956 | LIMBER HILL | W. Dutton | J. Power | 11/8 | 11 |
| 1957 | LINWELL | C. Mallon | M. Scudamore | 100/9 | 13 |
| 1958 | KERSTIN | C. Bewicke | S. Hayhurst | 7/1 | 9 |
| 1959 | RODDY OWEN | D. Morgan | H. Beasley | 5/1 | 11 |
| 1960 | PAS SEUL | R. Turnell | W. Rees | 6/1 | 12 |
| 1961 | SAFFRON TARTAN | D. Butchers | F. Winter | 2/1 | 11 |
| 1962 | MANDARIN | F. Walwyn | F. Winter | 7/2 | 9 |
| 1963 | MILL HOUSE | F. Walwyn | G. Robinson | 7/2 | 12 |
| 1964 | ARKLE | T. Dreaper | P. Taaffe | 7/4 | 4 |
| 1965 | ARKLE | T. Dreaper | P. Taaffe | 30/100 | 4 |
| 1966 | ARKLE | T. Dreaper | P. Taaffe | 1/10 | 5 |
| 1967 | WOODLAND VENTURE | F. Rimell | T. Biddlecombe | 100/8 | 8 |
| 1968 | FORT LENEY | T. Dreaper | P. Taaffe | 11/2 | 5 |
| 1969 | WHAT A MYTH | H. R. Price | P. Kelleway | 8/1 | 11 |
| 1970 | L'ESCARGOT | D. Moore | T. Carberry | 33/1 | 12 |

| YEAR | HORSE | TRAINER | JOCKEY | SP | RAN |
|------|-------|---------|--------|-----|-----|
| 1971 | L'ESCARGOT | D. Moore | T. Carberry | 7/2 | 8 |
| 1972 | GLENCARAIG LADY | F. Flood | F. Berry | 6/1 | 12 |
| 1973 | THE DIKLER | F. Walwyn | R. Barry | 9/1 | 8 |
| 1974 | CAPTAIN CHRISTY | P. Taaffe | H. Beasley | 7/1 | 7 |
| 1975 | TEN UP | J. Dreaper | T. Carberry | 2/1 | 8 |
| 1976 | ROYAL FROLIC | F. Rimell | J. Burke | 14/1 | 11 |
| 1977 | DAVY LAD | M. O'Toole | D. Hughes | 14/1 | 13 |
| 1978 | MIDNIGHT COURT | F. Winter | J. Francome | 5/2 | 10 |
| 1979 | ALVERTON | M. H. Easterby | J. J. O'Neill | 5/1 | 14 |
| 1980 | MASTER SMUDGE* | A. Barrow | R. Hoare | 14/1 | 15 |
| 1981 | LITTLE OWL | M. H. Easterby | Mr A. J. Wilson | 6/1 | 15 |
| 1982 | SILVER BUCK | M. Dickinson | R. Earnshaw | 8/1 | 22 |
| 1983 | BREGAWN | M. Dickinson | G. Bradley | 100/30 | 11 |
| 1984 | BURROUGH HILL LAD | Mrs J. Pitman | P. Tuck | 7/2 | 12 |
| 1985 | FORGIVE 'N FORGET | J. FitzGerald | M. Dwyer | 7/1 | 15 |
| 1986 | DAWN RUN | P. Mullins | J. J. O'Neill | 15/8 | 11 |
| 1987 | THE THINKER | W. A. Stephenson | R. Lamb | 13/2 | 12 |
| 1988 | CHARTER PARTY | D. Nicholson | R. Dunwoody | 10/1 | 15 |
| 1989 | DESERT ORCHID | D. Elsworth | S. Sherwood | 5/2 | 13 |
| 1990 | NORTON'S COIN | S. Griffiths | G. McCourt | 100/1 | 12 |
| 1991 | GARRISON SAVANNAH | Mrs J. Pitman | M. Pitman | 16/1 | 14 |

* 1980: Tied Cottage finished first but was subsequently disqualified for failing the drugs test

# Grand National

LIVERPOOL                ABOUT 4½ MILES                FIRST RUN 1839

| YEAR | HORSE | TRAINER | JOCKEY | SP | RAN |
|------|-------|---------|--------|-----|-----|
| 1900 | AMBUSH II | A. Anthony | A. Anthony | 4/1 | 16 |
| 1901 | GRUDON | B. Bletsoe | A. Nightingall | 9/1 | 24 |
| 1902 | SHANNON LASS | J. Hackett | D. Read | 20/1 | 21 |
| 1903 | DRUMCREE | Sir C. Nugent | P. Woodland | 13/2 | 23 |
| 1904 | MOIFAA | W. Hickey | A. Birch | 25/1 | 26 |
| 1905 | KIRKLAND | E. Thomas | F. Mason | 6/1 | 27 |
| 1906 | ASCETIC'S SILVER | A. Hastings | A. Hastings | 20/1 | 23 |
| 1907 | EREMON | T. Coulthwaite | A. Newey | 8/1 | 23 |
| 1908 | RUBIO | F. Withington | H. Bletsoe | 66/1 | 24 |
| 1909 | LUTTEUR III | H. Escott | G. Parfrement | 100/9 | 32 |
| 1910 | JENKINSTOWN | T. Coulthwaite | R. Chadwick | 100/8 | 25 |
| 1911 | GLENSIDE | Capt. R. Collis | J. Anthony | 20/1 | 26 |
| 1912 | JERRY M | R. Gore | E. Piggott | 4/1 | 24 |
| 1913 | COVERTCOAT | R. Gore | P. Woodland | 100/9 | 22 |
| 1914 | SUNLOCH | T. Tyler | W. Smith | 100/6 | 20 |
| 1915 | ALLY SLOPER | A. Hastings | Mr J. Anthony | 100/8 | 20 |
| 1916–18 | *No race* | | | | |
| 1919 | POETHLYN | H. Escott | E. Piggott | 11/4 | 22 |
| 1920 | TROYTOWN | A. Anthony | Mr J. Anthony | 6/1 | 24 |
| 1921 | SHAUN SPADAH | G. Poole | F. Rees | 100/9 | 35 |
| 1922 | MUSIC HALL | O. Anthony | L. Rees | 100/9 | 32 |
| 1923 | SERGEANT MURPHY | G. Blackwell | Capt. G. Bennet | 100/6 | 28 |
| 1924 | MASTER ROBERT | A. Hastings | R. Trudgill | 25/1 | 30 |
| 1925 | DOUBLE CHANCE | F. Archer | Maj. J. Wilson | 100/9 | 33 |
| 1926 | JACK HORNER | H. Leader | W. Watkinson | 25/1 | 30 |
| 1927 | SPRIG | T. Leader | T. Leader | 8/1 | 37 |
| 1928 | TIPPERARY TIM | J. Dodd | W. Dutton | 100/1 | 42 |
| 1929 | GREGALACH | T. Leader | R. Everett | 100/1 | 66 |
| 1930 | SHAUN GOILIN | F. Hartigan | T. Cullinan | 100/8 | 41 |
| 1931 | GRAKLE | T. Coulthwaite | R. Lyall | 100/6 | 43 |
| 1932 | FORBRA | T. Rimell | J. Hamey | 50/1 | 36 |
| 1933 | KELLSBORO' JACK | I. Anthony | D. Williams | 25/1 | 34 |
| 1934 | GOLDEN MILLER | B. Briscoe | G. Wilson | 8/1 | 30 |
| 1935 | REYNOLDSTOWN | Maj. N. Furlong | Mr F. Furlong | 22/1 | 27 |
| 1936 | REYNOLDSTOWN | Maj. N. Furlong | Mr F. Walwyn | 10/1 | 35 |
| 1937 | ROYAL MAIL | I. Anthony | E. Williams | 100/6 | 33 |
| 1938 | BATTLESHIP | R. Hobbs | B. Hobbs | 40/1 | 36 |
| 1939 | WORKMAN | J. Ruttle | T. Hyde | 100/8 | 37 |
| 1940 | BOGSKAR | Lord Stalbridge | M. Jones | 25/1 | 30 |
| 1941–5 | *No race* | | | | |
| 1946 | LOVELY COTTAGE | T. Rayson | Capt. R. Petre | 3/1 | 34 |
| 1947 | CAUGHOO | H. McDowell | E. Dempsey | 100/1 | 57 |
| 1948 | SHEILA'S COTTAGE | N. Crump | A. Thompson | 50/1 | 43 |
| 1949 | RUSSIAN HERO | G. Owen | L. McMorrow | 66/1 | 43 |
| 1950 | FREEBOOTER | R. Renton | J. Power | 10/1 | 49 |
| 1951 | NICKEL COIN | J. O'Donaghue | J. Bullock | 40/1 | 36 |

| Year | Horse | Trainer | Jockey | SP | RAN |
|------|-------|---------|--------|-----|-----|
| 1952 | TEAL | N. Crump | A. Thompson | 100/7 | 47 |
| 1953 | EARLY MIST | M. V. O'Brien | B. Marshall | 20/1 | 31 |
| 1954 | ROYAL TAN | M. V. O'Brien | B. Marshall | 8/1 | 29 |
| 1955 | QUARE TIMES | M. V. O'Brien | P. Taaffe | 100/9 | 30 |
| 1956 | E.S.B. | F. Rimell | D. Dick | 100/7 | 29 |
| 1957 | SUNDEW | F. Hudson | F. Winter | 20/1 | 35 |
| 1958 | MR WHAT | T. Taaffe | A. Freeman | 18/1 | 31 |
| 1959 | OXO | W. Stephenson | M. Scudamore | 8/1 | 34 |
| 1960 | MERRYMAN II | N. Crump | G. Scott | 13/2 | 26 |
| 1961 | NICOLAUS SILVER | F. Rimell | H. Beasley | 28/1 | 35 |
| 1962 | KILMORE | H. R. Price | F. Winter | 28/1 | 32 |
| 1963 | AYALA | K. Piggott | P. Buckley | 66/1 | 47 |
| 1964 | TEAM SPIRIT | F. Walwyn | G. Robinson | 18/1 | 33 |
| 1965 | JAY TRUMP | F. Winter | T. Smith | 100/6 | 47 |
| 1966 | ANGLO | F. Winter | T. Norman | 50/1 | 47 |
| 1967 | FOINAVON | J. Kempton | J. Buckingham | 100/1 | 44 |
| 1968 | RED ALLIGATOR | D. Smith | B. Fletcher | 100/7 | 45 |
| 1969 | HIGHLAND WEDDING | G. Balding | E. Harty | 100/9 | 30 |
| 1970 | GAY TRIP | F. Rimell | P. Taaffe | 15/1 | 28 |
| 1971 | SPECIFY | J. Sutcliffe | J. Cook | 28/1 | 38 |
| 1972 | WELL TO DO | T. Forster | G. Thorner | 14/1 | 42 |
| 1973 | RED RUM | D. McCain | B. Fletcher | 9/1 | 38 |
| 1974 | RED RUM | D. McCain | B. Fletcher | 11/1 | 42 |
| 1975 | L'ESCARGOT | D. Moore | T. Carberry | 13/2 | 31 |
| 1976 | RAG TRADE | F. Rimell | J. Burke | 14/1 | 32 |
| 1977 | RED RUM | D. McCain | T. Stack | 9/1 | 42 |
| 1978 | LUCIUS | G. Richards | B. Davies | 14/1 | 37 |
| 1979 | RUBSTIC | J. Leadbetter | M. Barnes | 25/1 | 34 |
| 1980 | BEN NEVIS | T. Forster | Mr C. Fenwick | 40/1 | 30 |
| 1981 | ALDANITI | J. Gifford | R. Champion | 10/1 | 39 |
| 1982 | GRITTAR | F. Gilman | Mr C. Saunders | 7/1 | 39 |
| 1983 | CORBIERE | Mrs J. Pitman | B. de Haan | 13/1 | 41 |
| 1984 | HALLO DANDY | G. Richards | N. Doughty | 13/1 | 40 |
| 1985 | LAST SUSPECT | T. Forster | H. Davies | 50/1 | 40 |
| 1986 | WEST TIP | M. Oliver | R. Dunwoody | 15/2 | 40 |
| 1987 | MAORI VENTURE | A. Turnell | S. Knight | 28/1 | 40 |
| 1988 | RHYME 'N' REASON | D. Elsworth | B. Powell | 10/1 | 40 |
| 1989 | LITTLE POLVEIR | G. Balding | J. Frost | 28/1 | 40 |
| 1990 | MR FRISK | K. Bailey | Mr M. Armytage | 16/1 | 38 |
| 1991 | SEAGRAM | D. Barons | N. Hawke | 12/1 | 40 |

## Scottish National

| AYR | | 4 MILES 120 YARDS | | FIRST RUN 1867 | |
|-----|------|------|------|------|------|
| **YEAR** | **HORSE** | **TRAINER** | **JOCKEY** | **SP** | **RAN** |
| 1947 | ROWLAND ROY | F. Walwyn | Mr R. Black | 6/1 | 15 |
| 1948 | MAGNETIC FIN | W. Hall | L. Vick | 100/8 | 12 |
| 1949 | WOT NO SUN | N. Crump | A. Thompson | 2/1 | 10 |
| 1950 | SANVINA | J. Wight | Mr K. Oliver | 25/1 | 19 |
| 1951 | COURT PAINTER | C. Bewicke | F. Carroll | 20/1 | 13 |
| 1952 | FLAGRANT MAC | R. Renton | J. Power | 100/8 | 17 |
| 1953 | QUEEN'S TASTE | H. Clarkson | T. Robson | 100/6 | 21 |
| 1954 | QUEEN'S TASTE | H. Clarkson | G. Stack | 10/1 | 15 |
| 1955 | BAR POINT | R. Renton | D. Ancil | 20/1 | 18 |
| 1956 | QUEEN'S TASTE | H. Clarkson | R. Curran | 8/1 | 14 |
| 1957 | BREMONTIER | P. Taylor | A. Rossio | 10/1 | 13 |
| 1958 | GAME FIELD | J. Fawcus | J. Boddy | 9/1 | 14 |
| 1959 | MERRYMAN II | N. Crump | G. Scott | 100/8 | 18 |
| 1960 | FINCHAM | J. White | M. Batchelor | 9/4 | 8 |
| 1961 | KINMONT WULLIE | W. A. Stephenson | C. Stobbs | 8/1 | 18 |
| 1962 | SHAM FIGHT | T. Robson | T. Robson | 100/6 | 18 |
| 1963 | PAPPAGENO'S COTTAGE | K. Oliver | T. Brookshaw | 100/8 | 18 |
| 1964 | POPHAM DOWN | F. Walwyn | J. Haine | 8/1 | 14 |
| 1965 | BRASHER | T. Robson | J. FitzGerald | 4/1 | 9 |
| 1966 | AFRICAN PATROL | R. Fairbairn | J. Leech | 10/1 | 17 |
| 1967 | THE FOSSA | F. Rimell | A. Turnell | 8/1 | 18 |
| 1968 | ARCTURUS | N. Crump | P. Buckley | 4/1 | 10 |
| 1969 | PLAYLORD | G. Richards | R. Barry | 9/1 | 17 |
| 1970 | THE SPANIARD | K. Oliver | B. Brogan | 8/1 | 10 |
| 1971 | YOUNG ASH LEAF | K. Oliver | P. Ennis | 12/1 | 21 |
| 1972 | QUICK REPLY | H. Bell | M. Barnes | 11/1 | 17 |
| 1973 | ESBAN | R. Clay | J. Bourke | 16/1 | 21 |
| 1974 | RED RUM | D. McCain | B. Fletcher | 11/8 | 17 |
| 1975 | BARONA | R. Armytage | P. Kelleway | 33/1 | 17 |
| 1976 | BARONA | R. Armytage | P. Kelleway | 12/1 | 23 |
| 1977 | SEBASTIAN V | H. Bell | R. Lamb | 9/2 | 23 |
| 1978 | KING CON | G. Renilson | Mr P. Craggs | 33/1 | 21 |
| 1979 | FIGHTING FIT | K. Oliver | C. Hawkins | 9/1 | 19 |
| 1980 | SALKELD | N. Crump | D. Atkins | 14/1 | 23 |
| 1981 | ASTRAL CHARMER | H. Bell | J. Goulding | 66/1 | 21 |
| 1982 | COCKLE STRAND | K. Oliver | D. Dutton | 9/1 | 15 |
| 1983 | CANTON | N. Crump | K. Whyte | 16/1 | 22 |
| 1984 | ANDROMA | J. FitzGerald | M. Dwyer | 7/1 | 19 |
| 1985 | ANDROMA | J. FitzGerald | M. Dwyer | 11/1 | 18 |
| 1986 | HARDY LAD | B. Wilkinson | M. Hammond | 28/1 | 24 |
| 1987 | LITTLE POLVEIR | J. Edwards | P. Scudamore | 12/1 | 11 |
| 1988 | MIGHTY MARK | F. Walton | B. Storey | 9/1 | 17 |
| 1989 | ROLL-A-JOINT | C. Popham | B. Powell | 4/1 | 11 |
| 1990 | FOUR TRIX | G. Richards | D. Byrne | 25/1 | 28 |
| 1991 | KILLONE ABBEY | W. A. Stephenson | C. Grant | 40/1 | 18 |

# *Whitbread Gold Cup*

SANDOWN PARK  3 MILES 5 FURLONGS 18 YARDS  FIRST RUN 1957

| Year | Horse | Trainer | Jockey | SP | Ran |
|---|---|---|---|---|---|
| 1957 | MUCH OBLIGED | N. Crump | H. East | 10/1 | 24 |
| 1958 | TAXIDERMIST | F. Walwyn | Mr J. Lawrence | 100/6 | 31 |
| 1959 | DONE UP | H. R. Price | H. Sprague | 100/6 | 23 |
| 1960 | PLUMMERS PLAIN | L. Dale | R. Harrison | 20/1 | 21 |
| 1961 | PAS SEUL | R. Turnell | D. Dick | 8/1 | 23 |
| 1962 | FRENCHMAN'S COVE | H. T. Jones | S. Mellor | 7/2 | 22 |
| 1963 | HOODWINKED | N. Crump | P. Buckley | 100/7 | 32 |
| 1964 | DORMANT | N. Crump | P. Buckley | 11/4 | 11 |
| 1965 | ARKLE | T. Dreaper | P. Taaffe | 4/9 | 7 |
| 1966 | WHAT A MYTH | H. R. Price | P. Kelleway | 5/4 | 8 |
| 1967 | MILL HOUSE | F. Walwyn | D. Nicholson | 9/2 | 13 |
| 1968 | LARBAWN | M. Marsh | J. Gifford | 8/1 | 16 |
| 1969 | LARBAWN | M. Marsh | J. Gifford | 9/2 | 18 |
| 1970 | ROYAL TOSS | H. Handel | R. Pitman | 20/1 | 17 |
| 1971 | TITUS OATES | G. Richards | R. Barry | 11/1 | 18 |
| 1972 | GREY SOMBRERO | D. Gandolfo | W. Shoemark | 16/1 | 28 |
| 1973 | CHARLIE POTHEEN | F. Walwyn | R. Barry | 11/4 | 21 |
| 1974 | THE DIKLER | F. Walwyn | R. Barry | 5/1 | 16 |
| 1975 | APRIL SEVENTH | R. Turnell | S. Knight | 16/1 | 12 |
| 1976 | OTTER WAY | O. Carter | J. King | 15/2 | 14 |
| 1977 | ANDY PANDY | F. Rimell | J. Burke | 4/1 | 15 |
| 1978 | STROMBOLUS | P. Bailey | T. Stack | 7/1 | 15 |
| 1979 | DIAMOND EDGE | F. Walwyn | W. Smith | 7/1 | 14 |
| 1980 | ROYAL MAIL | S. Mellor | P. Blacker | 8/1 | 12 |
| 1981 | DIAMOND EDGE | F. Walwyn | W. Smith | 5/1 | 18 |
| 1982 | SHADY DEAL | J. Gifford | R. Rowe | 4/1 | 9 |
| 1983 | DRUMLARGAN | E. O'Grady | Mr F. Codd | 11/1 | 15 |
| 1984 | SPECIAL CARGO | F. Walwyn | K. Mooney | 8/1 | 13 |
| 1985 | BY THE WAY | Mrs M. Dickinson | R. Earnshaw | 11/2 | 20 |
| 1986 | PLUNDERING | F. Winter | S. Sherwood | 14/1 | 16 |
| 1987 | LEAN AR AGHAIDH | S. Mellor | G. Landau | 6/1 | 9 |
| 1988 | DESERT ORCHID | D. Elsworth | S. Sherwood | 6/1 | 12 |
| 1989 | BROWN WINDSOR | N. Henderson | M. Bowlby | 12/1 | 18 |
| 1990 | MR FRISK | K. Bailey | Mr M. Armytage | 9/2 | 13 |
| 1991 | DOCKLANDS EXPRESS* | K. Bailey | A. Tory | 4/1 | 10 |

* 1991: Cahervillahow finished first but was disqualified

# INTERNATIONAL                              Ireland
## *Irish Grand National*

FAIRYHOUSE                    3 MILES 5 FURLONGS          FIRST RUN 1870

| YEAR | HORSE | TRAINER | JOCKEY | SP | RAN |
|------|-------|---------|--------|-----|-----|
| 1946 | GOLDEN VIEW | R. O'Connell | M. Molony | 7/1 | 11 |
| 1947 | REVELRY | J. Doyle | D. Moore | 6/1 | 17 |
| 1948 | HAMSTAR | W. O'Grady | E. Kennedy | 6/1 | 17 |
| 1949 | SHAGREEN | T. Dreaper | E. Newman | 5/1 | 20 |
| 1950 | DOMINICK'S BAR | T. Hyde | M. Molony | 8/1 | 12 |
| 1951 | ICY CALM | W. O'Grady | P. Doyle | 100/6 | 19 |
| 1952 | ALBERONI | M. V. O'Brien | L. Stephens | 6/1 | 11 |
| 1953 | OVERSHADOW | C. Magnier | A. Power | 20/1 | 15 |
| 1954 | ROYAL APPROACH | T. Dreaper | P. Taaffe | evens | 11 |
| 1955 | UMM | G. Wells | P. Taaffe | 100/7 | 16 |
| 1956 | AIR PRINCE | J. McClintock | T. O'Brien | 20/1 | 19 |
| 1957 | KILBALLYOWN | P. Norris | G. Robinson | 10/1 | 26 |
| 1958 | GOLD LEGEND | J. Brogan | J. Lehane | 100/8 | 21 |
| 1959 | ZONDA | M. Geraghty | P. Taaffe | 5/1 | 15 |
| 1960 | OLYMPIA | T. Dreaper | P. Taaffe | 6/1 | 16 |
| 1961 | FORTRIA | T. Dreaper | P. Taaffe | 17/2 | 14 |
| 1962 | KERFORO | T. Dreaper | L. McLoughlin | 9/1 | 11 |
| 1963 | LAST LINK | T. Dreaper | P. Woods | 7/1 | 10 |
| 1964 | ARKLE | T. Dreaper | P. Taaffe | 1/2 | 7 |
| 1965 | SPLASH | T. Dreaper | P. Woods | 6/4 | 4 |
| 1966 | FLYINGBOLT | T. Dreaper | P. Taaffe | 8/11 | 6 |
| 1967 | VULPINE | P. Mullins | M. Curran | 7/1 | 12 |
| 1968 | HERRING GULL | P. Mullins | J. Crowley | 5/2 | 12 |
| 1969 | SWEET DREAMS | K. Bell | R. Coonan | 10/1 | 18 |
| 1970 | GAROUPE | F. Flood | C. Finnegan | 10/1 | 13 |
| 1971 | KING'S SPRITE | G. Wells | A. Moore | 7/1 | 19 |
| 1972 | DIMWIT | P. Mullins | M. Curran | 15/2 | 14 |
| 1973 | TARTAN ACE | T. Costello | J. Cullen | 10/1 | 14 |
| 1974 | COLEBRIDGE | J. Dreaper | F. Wright | 11/5 | 10 |
| 1975 | BROWN LAD | J. Dreaper | T. Carberry | 6/4 | 8 |
| 1976 | BROWN LAD | J. Dreaper | T. Carberry | 7/2 | 15 |
| 1977 | BILLYCAN | A. Maxwell | M. Morris | 8/1 | 20 |
| 1978 | BROWN LAD | J. Dreaper | G. Dowd | 5/1 | 19 |
| 1979 | TIED COTTAGE | D. Moore | Mr A. Robinson | 13/2 | 20 |
| 1980 | DALETTA | G. St John Williams | J. Harty | 11/1 | 25 |
| 1981 | LUSKA | P. Mullins | T. Finn | 11/1 | 20 |
| 1982 | KING SPRUCE | M. O'Brien | G. Newman | 20/1 | 25 |
| 1983 | BIT OF A SKITE | E. O'Grady | T. Ryan | 7/1 | 27 |
| 1984 | BENTOM BOY | W. Rooney | Mrs A. Ferris | 33/1 | 29 |
| 1985 | RHYME 'N' REASON | D. Murray-Smith | G. Bradley | 6/1 | 23 |
| 1986 | INSURE | P. Hughes | M. Flynn | 16/1 | 15 |
| 1987 | BRITTANY BOY | K. Hitchmough | T. Taaffe | 14/1 | 26 |
| 1988 | PERRIS VALLEY | D. Weld | B. Sheridan | 12/1 | 18 |
| 1989 | MAID OF MONEY | J. Fowler | A. Powell | 10/1 | 22 |
| 1990 | DESERT ORCHID | D. Elsworth | R. Dunwoody | evens | 14 |
| 1991 | OMERTA | M. Pipe | Mr A. Maguire | 6/1 | 22 |

# *Irish Two Thousand Guineas*

THE CURRAGH                     I MILE                FIRST RUN 1921

| YEAR | HORSE | TRAINER | JOCKEY | SP | RAN |
|------|-------|---------|--------|-----|-----|
| 1946 | CLARO | H. Hartigan | J. Canty | 100/8 | 13 |
| 1947 | GRAND WEATHER | E. McGrath | T. Burns | 3/1 | 8 |
| 1948 | BEAU SABREUR | C. Brabazon | T. Burns | 7/1 | 12 |
| 1949 | SOLONAWAY | M. Collins | M. Hartnett | 100/6 | 12 |
| 1950 | MIGHTY OCEAN | D. Rogers | A. Brabazon | 10/1 | 10 |
| 1951 | SIGNAL BOX | D. Rogers | M. Molony | 5/4 | 16 |
| 1952 | D.C.M. | J. Rogers | L. Ward | 7/4 | 11 |
| 1953 | SEA CHARGER | K. Kerr | W. Johnstone | 6/1 | 13 |
| 1954 | ARCTIC WIND | J. Rogers | J. Mullane | 25/1 | 14 |
| 1955 | HUGH LUPUS | J. Lenehan | W. Johnstone | 13/8 | 20 |
| 1956 | LUCERO | H. Wragg | E. Mercer | 5/1 | 13 |
| 1957 | JACK KETCH | E. Quirke | C. Smirke | 7/4 | 13 |
| 1958 | HARD RIDDEN | J. Rogers | C. Smirke | 9/2 | 13 |
| 1959 | EL TORO | M. V. O'Brien | T. Burns | 100/9 | 15 |
| 1960 | KYTHNOS | P. Prendergast | R. Hutchinson | 5/4 | 14 |
| 1961 | LIGHT YEAR | A. O'Brien | G. Bougoure | 6/1 | 21 |
| 1962 | ARCTIC STORM | J. Oxx | W. Williamson | 20/1 | 17 |
| 1963 | LINACRE | P. Prendergast | P. Matthews | 40/1 | 14 |
| 1964 | SANTA CLAUS | J. Rogers | W. Burke | evens | 16 |
| 1965 | GREEN BANNER | K. Kerr | N. Brennan | 100/7 | 21 |
| 1966 | PAVEH | T. Ainsworth | T. Burns | 9/4 | 15 |
| 1967 | ATHERSTONE WOOD* | S. Quirke | R. Parnell | 100/7 | 19 |
| 1968 | MISTIGO | S. Quirke | R. Parnell | 10/1 | 15 |
| 1969 | RIGHT TACK | J. Sutcliffe, jr | G. Lewis | evens | 15 |
| 1970 | DECIES | B. van Cutsem | L. Piggott | 8/13 | 13 |
| 1971 | KINGS COMPANY | G. Robinson | F. Head | 9/2 | 14 |
| 1972 | BALLYMORE | P. Prendergast | C. Roche | 33/1 | 14 |
| 1973 | SHARP EDGE | W. R. Hern | J. Mercer | 5/2 | 16 |
| 1974 | FURRY GLEN | S. McGrath | G. McGrath | 10/1 | 10 |
| 1975 | GRUNDY | P. Walwyn | P. Eddery | 10/11 | 12 |
| 1976 | NORTHERN TREASURE | K. Prendergast | G. Curran | 33/1 | 17 |
| 1977 | PAMPAPAUL | H. Murless | G. Dettori | 16/1 | 21 |
| 1978 | JAAZEIRO | M. V. O'Brien | L. Piggott | 11/4 | 12 |
| 1979 | DICKENS HILL | M. O'Toole | A. Murray | 5/2 | 9 |
| 1980 | NIKOLI | P. Prendergast | C. Roche | 5/1 | 13 |
| 1981 | KINGS LAKE | M. V. O'Brien | P. Eddery | 5/1 | 13 |
| 1982 | DARA MONARCH | L. Browne | M. Kinane | 20/1 | 14 |
| 1983 | WASSL | J. Dunlop | A. Murray | 12/1 | 10 |
| 1984 | SADLER'S WELLS | M. V. O'Brien | G. McGrath | 10/1 | 9 |
| 1985 | TRIPTYCH | D. O'Brien | C. Roche | 7/1 | 16 |
| 1986 | FLASH OF STEEL | D. Weld | M. Kinane | 9/2 | 6 |
| 1987 | DON'T FORGET ME | R. Hannon | W. Carson | 6/4 | 8 |
| 1988 | PRINCE OF BIRDS | M. V. O'Brien | D. Gillespie | 9/1 | 14 |
| 1989 | SHAADI | M. Stoute | W. R. Swinburn | 7/2 | 12 |
| 1990 | TIROL | R. Hannon | P. Eddery | 5/4 | 9 |
| 1991 | FOURSTARS ALLSTAR | L. O'Brien | M. Smith | 9/1 | 12 |

* 1967: Kingfisher finished first but was disqualified

## Irish One Thousand Guineas

THE CURRAGH                    I MILE                    FIRST RUN 1922

| YEAR | HORSE | TRAINER | JOCKEY | SP | RAN |
|------|-------|---------|--------|-----|-----|
| 1946 | ELLA RETFORD | H. Hartigan | J. Canty | 100/8 | 13 |
| 1947 | SEA SYMPHONY | H. Hartigan | M. Wing | 11/2 | 20 |
| 1948 | MORNING WINGS | E. McGrath | J. Canty | 5/1 | 16 |
| 1949 | SUNLIT RIDE | R. Fetherstonhaugh | H. Holmes | 6/1 | 18 |
| 1950 | PRINCESS TRUDY | P. Prendergast | M. Molony | evens | 18 |
| 1951 | QUEEN OF SHEBA | H. Persse | H. Holmes | 3/1 | 16 |
| 1952 | NASHUA | H. Hartigan | C. Smirke | 7/2 | 14 |
| 1953 | NORTHERN GLEAM | D. Rogers | T. Burns | 5/2 | 15 |
| 1954 | PANTOMIME QUEEN | H. Hartigan | W. Nevett | 6/1 | 16 |
| 1955 | DARK ISSUE | D. Rogers | P. Canty | 6/1 | 17 |
| 1956 | PEDEROBA | A. Head | W. Johnstone | 4/1 | 16 |
| 1957 | EVEN STAR | R. Day | F. Durr | 6/1 | 15 |
| 1958 | BUTIABA | A. Head | J. Massard | 2/1 | 15 |
| 1959 | FIORENTINA | A. Head | G. Moore | evens | 19 |
| 1960 | ZENOBIA | T. Shaw | L. Ward | 100/8 | 15 |
| 1961 | LADY SENATOR | P. Ashworth | T. Gosling | 6/4 | 12 |
| 1962 | SHANDON BELLE | R. Fetherstonhaugh | T. Burns | 20/1 | 16 |
| 1963 | GAZPACHO | P. Prendergast | F. Palmer | 9/1 | 18 |
| 1964 | ROYAL DANSEUSE | S. McGrath | J. Roe | 7/4 | 13 |
| 1965 | ARDENT DANCER | T. Gosling | W. Rickaby | 5/1 | 13 |
| 1966 | VALORIS | M. V. O'Brien | J. Power | 9/1 | 15 |
| 1967 | LACQUER | H. Wragg | R. Hutchinson | 4/1 | 15 |
| 1968 | FRONT ROW | R. Jarvis | E. Eldin | 7/1 | 13 |
| 1969 | WENDUYNE | P. Prendergast | N. Williamson | 2/1 | 13 |
| 1970 | BLACK SATIN | J. Dunlop | R. Hutchinson | 3/1 | 13 |
| 1971 | FAVOLETTA | H. Wragg | L. Piggott | 5/2 | 17 |
| 1972 | PIDGET | K. Prendergast | W. Swinburn | 20/1 | 16 |
| 1973 | CLOONAGH | H. Cecil | G. Starkey | 7/1 | 12 |
| 1974 | GAILY | W. R. Hern | R. Hutchinson | 11/5 | 17 |
| 1975 | MIRALLA | Sir H. Nugent | R. Parnell | 14/1 | 11 |
| 1976 | SARAH SIDDONS | P. Prendergast | C. Roche | 9/2 | 14 |
| 1977 | LADY CAPULET | M. V. O'Brien | T. Murphy | 16/1 | 14 |
| 1978 | MORE SO | P. Prendergast | C. Roche | 2/1 | 17 |
| 1979 | GODETIA | M. V. O'Brien | L. Piggott | 4/6 | 12 |
| 1980 | CAIRN ROUGE | M. Cunningham | A. Murray | 5/1 | 18 |
| 1981 | ARCTIQUE ROYALE | K. Prendergast | G. Curran | 7/1 | 15 |
| 1982 | PRINCE'S POLLY | D. Weld | W. Swinburn | 12/1 | 24 |
| 1983 | L'ATTRAYANTE | O. Douieb | A. Badel | 4/1 | 18 |
| 1984 | KATIES | M. Ryan | P. Robinson | 20/1 | 23 |
| 1985 | AL BAHATHRI | H. T. Jones | A. Murray | 7/1 | 15 |
| 1986 | SONIC LADY | M. Stoute | W. R. Swinburn | 4/1 | 19 |
| 1987 | FOREST FLOWER | I. Balding | T. Ives | 4/1 | 11 |
| 1988 | TRUSTED PARTNER | D. Weld | M. Kinane | 10/1 | 16 |
| 1989 | ENSCONSE | L. Cumani | R. Cochrane | 13/8 | 13 |
| 1990 | IN THE GROOVE | D. Elsworth | S. Cauthen | 5/1 | 12 |
| 1991 | KOOYONGA | M. Kauntze | W. O'Connor | 4/1 | 12 |

## *Irish Derby*

THE CURRAGH      I MILE 4 FURLONGS      FIRST RUN 1866

| YEAR | HORSE | TRAINER | JOCKEY | SP | RAN |
|------|-------|---------|--------|-----|-----|
| 1946 | BRIGHT NEWS | Capt. D. Rogers | M. Wing | 100/8 | 14 |
| 1947 | SAYAJIRAO | F. Armstrong | E. Britt | evens | 11 |
| 1948 | NATHOO | F. Butters | W. Johnstone | 7/2 | 12 |
| 1949 | HINDOSTAN | F. Butters | W. Johnstone | 7/1 | 12 |
| 1950 | DARK WARRIOR | P. Prendergast | J. Thompson | 4/1 | 8 |
| 1951 | FRAISE DU BOIS | H. Wragg | C. Smirke | 5/2 | 16 |
| 1952 | THIRTEEN OF DIAMONDS | P. Prendergast | J. Mullane | 10/1 | 10 |
| 1953 | CHAMIER | M. V. O'Brien | W. Rickaby | 5/4 | 13 |
| 1954 | ZARATHUSTRA | M. Hurley | P. Powell, jr | 50/1 | 11 |
| 1955 | PANASLIPPER | S. McGrath | J. Eddery | 4/1 | 13 |
| 1956 | TALGO | H. Wragg | E. Mercer | 9/2 | 10 |
| 1957 | BALLYMOSS | M. V. O'Brien | T. Burns | 4/9 | 8 |
| 1958 | SINDON | M. Dawson | L. Ward | 100/8 | 12 |
| 1959 | FIDALGO | H. Wragg | J. Mercer | 1/2 | 11 |
| 1960 | CHAMOUR | A. O'Brien | G. Bougoure | 3/1 | 7 |
| 1961 | YOUR HIGHNESS | H. Cottrill | H. Holmes | 33/1 | 18 |
| 1962 | TAMBOURINE II | E. Pollet | R. Poincelet | 15/2 | 24 |
| 1963 | RAGUSA | P. Prendergast | G. Bougoure | 100/7 | 16 |
| 1964 | SANTA CLAUS | J. Rogers | W. Burke | 4/7 | 19 |
| 1965 | MEADOW COURT | P. Prendergast | L. Piggott | 11/10 | 21 |
| 1966 | SODIUM | G. Todd | F. Durr | 13/2 | 23 |
| 1967 | RIBOCCO | R. F. J. Houghton | L. Piggott | 5/2 | 23 |
| 1968 | RIBERO | R. F. J. Houghton | L. Piggott | 100/6 | 14 |
| 1969 | PRINCE REGENT | E. Pollet | G. Lewis | 7/2 | 15 |
| 1970 | NIJINSKY | M. V. O'Brien | L. Ward | 4/11 | 13 |
| 1971 | IRISH BALL | P. Lallei | A. Gibert | 7/2 | 15 |
| 1972 | STEEL PULSE | A. Breasley | W. Williamson | 10/1 | 14 |
| 1973 | WEAVERS' HALL | S. McGrath | G. McGrath | 33/1 | 15 |
| 1974 | ENGLISH PRINCE | P. Walwyn | Y. Saint-Martin | 8/1 | 13 |
| 1975 | GRUNDY | P. Walwyn | P. Eddery | 9/10 | 13 |
| 1976 | MALACATE | F. Boutin | P. Paquet | 5/1 | 17 |
| 1977 | THE MINSTREL | M. V. O'Brien | L. Piggott | 11/10 | 15 |
| 1978 | SHIRLEY HEIGHTS | J. Dunlop | G. Starkey | 5/4 | 11 |
| 1979 | TROY | W. R. Hern | W. Carson | 4/9 | 9 |
| 1980 | TYRNAVOS | B. Hobbs | A. Murray | 25/1 | 13 |
| 1981 | SHERGAR | M. Stoute | L. Piggott | 1/3 | 12 |
| 1982 | ASSERT | D. O'Brien | C. Roche | 4/7 | 10 |
| 1983 | SHAREEF DANCER | M. Stoute | W. R. Swinburn | 8/1 | 12 |
| 1984 | EL GRAN SENOR | M. V. O'Brien | P. Eddery | 2/7 | 8 |
| 1985 | LAW SOCIETY | M. V. O'Brien | P. Eddery | 15/8 | 13 |
| 1986 | SHAHRASTANI | M. Stoute | W. R. Swinburn | evens | 11 |
| 1987 | SIR HARRY LEWIS | B. Hills | J. Reid | 6/1 | 8 |
| 1988 | KAHYASI | L. Cumani | R. Cochrane | 4/5 | 11 |
| 1989 | OLD VIC | H. Cecil | S. Cauthen | 4/11 | 8 |
| 1990 | SALSABIL | J. Dunlop | W. Carson | 11/4 | 9 |
| 1991 | GENEROUS | P. Cole | A. Munro | evens | 6 |

# *Irish Oaks*

THE CURRAGH          1 MILE 4 FURLONGS          FIRST RUN 1895

| YEAR | HORSE | TRAINER | JOCKEY | SP | RAN |
|------|-------|---------|--------|-----|-----|
| 1946 | LINARIA | A. McCormick | C. Smirke | 10/11 | 10 |
| 1947 | DESERT DRIVE | D. Rogers | M. Molony | 2/1 | 14 |
| 1948 | MASAKA | H. Hartigan | A. Brabazon | evens | 10 |
| 1949 | CIRCUS LADY | R. Fetherstonhaugh | H. Holmes | 3/1 | 12 |
| 1950 | COREJADA | C. Semblat | W. Johnstone | 4/7 | 16 |
| 1951 | DJEBBELLICA | C. Clout | C. Smirke | 4/1 | 13 |
| 1952 | FIVE SPOTS | P. Prendergast | J. Mullane | 11/2 | 13 |
| 1953 | NOORY | R. Carver | C. Smirke | 2/1 | 11 |
| 1954 | PANTOMIME QUEEN | H. Hartigan | G. Cooney | 100/7 | 15 |
| 1955 | AGAR'S PLOUGH | R. Fetherstonhaugh | H. Holmes | 10/1 | 12 |
| 1956 | GARDEN STATE | H. Wragg | E. Mercer | 13/2 | 8 |
| 1957 | SILKEN GLIDER | S. McGrath | J. Eddery | 11/4 | 15 |
| 1958 | AMANTE | A. Head | L. Ward | 11/4 | 11 |
| 1959 | DISCOREA | H. Wragg | E. Mercer | 100/7 | 9 |
| 1960 | LYNCHRIS | J. Oxx | W. Williamson | 11/4 | 17 |
| 1961 | AMBERGRIS | H. Wragg | J. Lindley | 6/4 | 10 |
| 1962 | FRENCH CREAM | G. Brooke | W. Rickaby | 100/9 | 12 |
| 1963 | HIBERNIA | J. Oxx | W. Williamson | 6/4 | 15 |
| 1964 | ANCASTA | M. V. O'Brien | J. Purtell | 3/1 | 9 |
| 1965 | AURABELLA | M. V. O'Brien | L. Ward | 22/1 | 10 |
| 1966 | MERRY MATE | J. Oxx | W. Williamson | 100/9 | 10 |
| 1967 | PAMPALINA | J. Oxx | J. Roe | 100/8 | 14 |
| 1968 | CELINA | N. Murless | A. Barclay | 4/1 | 12 |
| 1969 | GAIA | M. V. O'Brien | L. Ward | 4/1 | 7 |
| 1970 | SANTA TINA | C. Milbank | L. Piggott | 5/2 | 13 |
| 1971 | ALTESSE ROYALE | N. Murless | G. Lewis | 1/2 | 13 |
| 1972 | REGAL EXCEPTION | J. Fellows | M. Philipperon | 4/1 | 12 |
| 1973 | DAHLIA | M. Zilber | W. Pyers | 8/1 | 12 |
| 1974 | DIBIDALE | B. Hills | W. Carson | 7/4 | 8 |
| 1975 | JULIETTE MARNY | J. Tree | L. Piggott | 5/2 | 14 |
| 1976 | LAGUNETTE | F. Boutin | P. Paquet | 3/1 | 18 |
| 1977 | OLWYN | R. Boss | J. Lynch | 11/1 | 8 |
| 1978 | FAIR SALINIA | M. Stoute | G. Starkey | 3/1 | 12 |
| 1979 | GODETIA | M. V. O'Brien | L. Piggott | 6/4 | 13 |
| 1980 | SHOOT A LINE | W. R. Hern | W. Carson | 6/4 | 8 |
| 1981 | BLUE WIND | D. Weld | W. Swinburn | 4/6 | 10 |
| 1982 | SWIFTFOOT | W. R. Hern | W. Carson | 4/1 | 10 |
| 1983 | GIVE THANKS | J. Bolger | D. Gillespie | 7/4 | 12 |
| 1984 | PRINCESS PATI | C. Collins | P. Shanahan | 9/2 | 11 |
| 1985 | HELEN STREET | W. R. Hern | W. Carson | 3/1 | 9 |
| 1986 | COLORSPIN | M. Stoute | P. Eddery | 6/1 | 8 |
| 1987 | UNITE | M. Stoute | W. R. Swinburn | 8/13 | 8 |
| 1988 | { DIMINUENDO | H. Cecil | S. Cauthen | 2/9 | 9 |
|      | MELODIST | M. Stoute | W. R. Swinburn | 11/1 | |
| 1989 | ALYDARESS | H. Cecil | M. Kinane | 7/4 | 5 |
| 1990 | KNIGHT'S BARONESS | P. Cole | T. Quinn | 13/8 | 10 |
| 1991 | POSSESSIVE DANCER | A. Scott | S. Cauthen | 8/1 | 10 |

The great chaser Mandarin in his retirement role as hack to the
legendary trainer Fulke Walwyn.

Democrat, the top two-year-old of 1899, with Lord Kitchener in India.

The final jumping meeting at Hurst Park in March 1962.

Eph Smith winning on Saphira at Alexandra Park in May 1959. The television mast at Alexandra Palace can be seen beyond the stand.

Course specialist Red Cast in action at Wye.

Remittance Man (Richard Dunwoody), winner of the Channel Four Trophy for the 1990/91 National Hunt season, at the last in the Waterford Castle Arkle Challenge Trophy at Cheltenham.

# *Irish St Leger*

THE CURRAGH      1 MILE 6 FURLONGS      FIRST RUN 1915

| YEAR | HORSE | TRAINER | JOCKEY | SP | RAN |
|------|-------|---------|--------|-----|-----|
| 1946 | CASSOCK | R. Fetherstonhaugh | J. Moylan | 4/1 | 9 |
| 1947 | ESPRIT DE FRANCE | H. Hartigan | M. Wing | 4/9 | 5 |
| 1948 | BEAU SABREUR | C. Brabazon | T. Burns | 9/2 | 8 |
| 1949 | BROWN ROVER | C. Boyd-Rochfort | W. Carr | 3/1 | 13 |
| 1950 | MORNING MADAM | P. Connolly | P. Canty | 20/1 | 12 |
| 1951 | DO WELL | M. Wing | L. Ward | 10/11 | 10 |
| 1952 | JUDICATE | C. Boyd-Rochfort | W. Carr | 6/4 | 7 |
| 1953 | SEA CHARGER | K. Kerr | W. Johnstone | 5/2 | 10 |
| 1954 | ZARATHUSTRA | M. Hurley | P. Powell | 7/4 | 5 |
| 1955 | DIAMOND SLIPPER | H. Nugent | D. Page | 100/8 | 9 |
| 1956 | MAGNETIC NORTH | D. Hastings | W. Elliott | 8/1 | 8 |
| 1957 | OMMEYAD | A. Head | J. Massard | 5/4 | 11 |
| 1958 | ROYAL HIGHWAY | H. Murless | N. Brennan | 7/4 | 6 |
| 1959 | BARCLAY | M. V. O'Brien | G. Bougoure | 1/2 | 7 |
| 1960 | LYNCHRIS | J. Oxx | W. Williamson | 4/6 | 8 |
| 1961 | VIMADEE | T. Burns | T. Burns | 100/9 | 10 |
| 1962 | ARCTIC VALE | P. Prendergast | P. Matthews | 40/1 | 9 |
| 1963 | CHRISTMAS ISLAND | P. Prendergast | G. Bougoure | 6/1 | 10 |
| 1964 | BISCAYNE | J. Oxx | W. Williamson | 4/1 | 8 |
| 1965 | CRAIGHOUSE | W. R. Hern | J. Mercer | 6/1 | 14 |
| 1966 | WHITE GLOVES | M. V. O'Brien | L. Ward | 4/1 | 14 |
| 1967 | DAN KANO | J. Lenehan | L. Piggott | evens | 8 |
| 1968 | GIOLLA MEAR | M. Hurley | F. Berry | 8/1 | 10 |
| 1969 | REINDEER | M. V. O'Brien | L. Ward | 5/2 | 9 |
| 1970 | ALLENGRANGE | S. McGrath | G. McGrath | 9/1 | 8 |
| 1971 | PARNELL | S. Quirke | A. Simpson | 11/5 | 8 |
| 1972 | PIDGET | K. Prendergast | T. Burns | 13/2 | 7 |
| 1973 | CONOR PASS | K. Prendergast | P. Jarman | 5/1 | 7 |
| 1974 | MISTIGRI | P. Prendergast | C. Roche | 9/1 | 7 |
| 1975 | CAUCASUS | M. V. O'Brien | L. Piggott | 3/1 | 13 |
| 1976 | MENEVAL | M. V. O'Brien | L. Piggott | 4/5 | 11 |
| 1977 | TRANSWORLD | M. V. O'Brien | T. Murphy | 13/2 | 9 |
| 1978 | M-LOLSHAN | H. R. Price | B. Taylor | 2/1 | 8 |
| 1979 | NINISKI | W. R. Hern | W. Carson | 11/10 | 10 |
| 1980 | GONZALES | M. V. O'Brien | R. Carroll | 4/7 | 8 |
| 1981 | PROTECTION RACKET | J. Hindley | B. Taylor | 6/4 | 7 |
| 1982 | TOUCHING WOOD | H. T. Jones | P. Cook | 5/4 | 10 |
| 1983 | MOUNTAIN LODGE | J. Dunlop | D. Gillespie | 13/2 | 10 |
| 1984 | OPALE | A. Stewart | D. McHargue | 11/4 | 9 |
| 1985 | LEADING COUNSEL | M. V. O'Brien | P. Eddery | 7/4 | 12 |
| 1986 | AUTHAAL | D. O'Brien | C. Roche | 8/1 | 6 |
| 1987 | EUROBIRD | J. Oxx | C. Asmussen | 9/4 | 8 |
| 1988 | DARK LOMOND | M. V. O'Brien | D. Gillespie | 10/1 | 13 |
| 1989 | PETITE ILE | J. Oxx | R. Quinton | 3/1 | 10 |
| 1990 | IBN BEY | P. Cole | T. Quinn | 5/1 | 12 |
| 1991 | TURGEON | J. Pease | A. Cruz | 3/1 | 10 |

## *Irish Champion Stakes*

LEOPARDSTOWN          1 MILE 2 FURLONGS          FIRST RUN 1984

| YEAR | HORSE | TRAINER | JOCKEY | SP | RAN |
|------|-------|---------|--------|-----|-----|
| 1984 | SADLER'S WELLS | M. V. O'Brien | P. Eddery | 3/1 | 12 |
| 1985 | COMMANCHE RUN | L. Cumani | L. Piggott | 11/10 | 11 |
| 1986 | PARK EXPRESS | J. Bolger | J. Reid | 11/2 | 13 |
| 1987 | TRIPTYCH | P. Biancone | A. Cruz | 5/4 | 12 |
| 1988 | INDIAN SKIMMER | H. Cecil | M. Roberts | 9/4 | 9 |
| 1989 | CARROLL HOUSE | M. Jarvis | M. Kinane | 5/1 | 9 |
| 1990 | ELMAAMUL | W. R. Hern | W. Carson | 2/1 | 8 |
| 1991 | SUAVE DANCER | J. Hammond | C. Asmussen | 4/6 | 7 |

# France
## *Prix du Jockey-Club [French Derby]*

| YEAR | HORSE | TRAINER | JOCKEY | SP | RAN |
|------|-------|---------|--------|-----|-----|
| 1946 | PRINCE CHEVALIER | E. Boullenger | C. Bouillon | 6/10 | 15 |
| 1947 | SANDJAR | C. Semblat | R. Poincelet | 1/2 | 13 |
| 1948 | BEY | R. Carver | W. Johnstone | 39/2 | 22 |
| 1949 | GOOD LUCK | H. Delavaud | P. Blanc | 18/1 | 7 |
| 1950 | SCRATCH | C. Semblat | W. Johnstone | 38/10 | 15 |
| 1951 | SICAMBRE | M. Bonaventure | P. Blanc | 8/10 | 14 |
| 1952 | AURIBAN | C. Semblat | W. Johnstone | 7/10 | 13 |
| 1953 | CHAMANT | C. Bartholomew | M. Garcia | 29/2 | 20 |
| 1954 | LE PETIT PRINCE | C. Semblat | R. Bertiglia | 10/1 | 19 |
| 1955 | RAPACE | R. Wallon | F. Palmer | 6/1 | 15 |
| 1956 | PHILIUS | C. Elliott | S. Boullenger | 13/1 | 16 |
| 1957 | AMBER | R. Carver | M. Garcia | 21/2 | 14 |
| 1958 | TAMANAR | J. Cunnington | J. Deforge | 59/2 | 17 |
| 1959 | HERBAGER | P. Pelat | G. Chancelier | 8/10 | 16 |
| 1960 | CHARLOTTESVILLE | A. Head | G. Moore | 28/10 | 16 |
| 1961 | RIGHT ROYAL | E. Pollet | R. Poincelet | 8/10 | 15 |
| 1962 | VAL DE LOIR | M. Bonaventure | F. Palmer | 28/10 | 18 |
| 1963 | SANCTUS | E. Pollet | M. Larraun | 14/1 | 13 |
| 1964 | LE FABULEUX | W. Head | J. Massard | 28/10 | 14 |
| 1965 | RELIANCE | F. Mathet | Y. Saint-Martin | 5/10 | 9 |
| 1966 | NELCIUS | M. Clément | Y. Saint-Martin | 79/10 | 13 |
| 1967 | ASTEC | A. Lieux | A. Jézébel | 61/10 | 13 |
| 1968 | TAPALQUÉ | F. Mathet | Y. Saint-Martin | 91/10 | 22 |
| 1969 | GOODLY | W. Head | F. Head | 62/10 | 17 |
| 1970 | SASSAFRAS | F. Mathet | Y. Saint-Martin | 22/10 | 15 |
| 1971 | RHEFFIC | F. Mathet | W. Pyers | 21/2 | 14 |
| 1972 | HARD TO BEAT | R. Carver, jr | L. Piggott | 36/10 | 13 |
| 1973 | ROI LEAR | A. Head | F. Head | 11/2 | 16 |
| 1974 | CARACOLERO | F. Boutin | P. Paquet | 414/10 | 15 |
| 1975 | VAL DE L'ORNE | A. Head | F. Head | 4/5 | 11 |
| 1976 | YOUTH | M. Zilber | F. Head | 19/10 | 18 |
| 1977 | CRYSTAL PALACE | F. Mathet | G. Dubroeucq | 6/4 | 14 |
| 1978 | ACAMAS | G. Bonnaventure | Y. Saint-Martin | 6/4 | 20 |
| 1979 | TOP VILLE | F. Mathet | Y. Saint-Martin | 13/10 | 11 |
| 1980 | POLICEMAN | C. Milbank | W. Carson | 538/10 | 14 |
| 1981 | BIKALA | P. Biancone | S. Gorli | 172/10 | 12 |
| 1982 | ASSERT | D. O'Brien | C. Roche | 22/10 | 14 |
| 1983 | CAERLEON | M. V. O'Brien | P. Eddery | 14/10 | 12 |
| 1984 | DARSHAAN | A. de Royer-Dupré | Y. Saint-Martin | 14/10 | 17 |
| 1985 | MOUKTAR | A. de Royer-Dupré | Y. Saint-Martin | 1/5 | 11 |
| 1986 | BERING | Mme C. Head | G. Moore | 1/2 | 13 |
| 1987 | NATROUN | A. de Royer-Dupré | Y. Saint-Martin | 41/10 | 17 |
| 1988 | HOURS AFTER | P. Biancone | P. Eddery | 161/10 | 16 |
| 1989 | OLD VIC | H. Cecil | S. Cauthen | 47/10 | 12 |
| 1990 | SANGLAMORE | R. Charlton | P. Eddery | 95/10 | 12 |
| 1991 | SUAVE DANCER | J. Hammond | C. Asmussen | 3/5 | 7 |

# Prix de l'Arc de Triomphe

LONGCHAMP                    1 MILE 4 FURLONGS                    FIRST RUN 1920

| YEAR | HORSE | TRAINER | JOCKEY | SP | RAN |
|------|-------|---------|--------|-----|-----|
| 1920 | COMRADE | P. Gilpin | F. Bullock | 34/10 | 13 |
| 1921 | KSAR | W. Walton | G. Stern | 115/10 | 12 |
| 1922 | KSAR | W. Walton | F. Bullock | 3/10 | 11 |
| 1923 | PARTH | J. Crawford | F. O'Neill | 17/2 | 13 |
| 1924 | MASSINE | E. Cunnington | A. Sharpe | 23/20 | 9 |
| 1925 | PRIORI | P. Carter | M. Allemand | 40/1 | 15 |
| 1926 | BIRIBI | J. Torterolo | D. Torterolo | 5/2 | 16 |
| 1927 | MON TALISMAN | F. Carter | C. Semblat | 24/10 | 10 |
| 1928 | KANTAR | R. Carver | A. Esling | 32/10 | 11 |
| 1929 | ORTELLO | W. Carter | P. Caprioli | 13/1 | 13 |
| 1930 | MOTRICO | M. d'Okhuysen | M. Fruhinsholtz | 83/10 | 10 |
| 1931 | PEARL CAP | F. Carter | C. Semblat | 32/10 | 10 |
| 1932 | MOTRICO | M. d'Okhuysen | C. Semblat | 38/10 | 15 |
| 1933 | CRAPOM | F. Regoli | P. Caprioli | 22/10 | 15 |
| 1934 | BRANTÔME | L. Robert | C. Bouillon | 11/10 | 13 |
| 1935 | SAMOS | F. Carter | W. Sibbritt | 19/1 | 12 |
| 1936 | CORRIDA | J. Watts | C. Elliott | 4/5 | 10 |
| 1937 | CORRIDA | J. Watts | C. Elliott | evens | 12 |
| 1938 | ECLAIR AU CHOCOLAT | L. Robert | C. Bouillon | 26/10 | 10 |
| 1939–40 | *No race* | | | | |
| 1941 | LE PACHA | J. Cunnington | P. Francolon | 18/10 | 7 |
| 1942 | DJEBEL | C. Semblat | J. Doyasbère | 18/10 | 9 |
| 1943 | VERSO II | C. Clout | G. Duforez | 6/5 | 13 |
| 1944 | ARDAN | C. Semblat | J. Doyasbère | 6/4 | 11 |
| 1945 | NIKELLORA | R. Pelat | W. Johnstone | 10/1 | 11 |
| 1946 | CARACALLA | C. Semblat | C. Elliott | 3/10 | 9 |
| 1947 | LE PAILLON | W. Head | F. Rochetti | 23/2 | 12 |
| 1948 | MIGOLI | F. Butters | C. Smirke | 10/1 | 14 |
| 1949 | CORONATION | C. Semblat | R. Poincelet | 37/10 | 28 |
| 1950 | TANTIÈME | F. Mathet | J. Doyasbère | 5/2 | 12 |
| 1951 | TANTIÈME | F. Mathet | J. Doyasbère | 17/10 | 19 |
| 1952 | NUCCIO | A. Head | R. Poincelet | 74/10 | 18 |
| 1953 | LA SORELLINA | E. Pollet | M. Larraun | 65/4 | 25 |
| 1954 | SICA BOY | P. Pelat | W. Johnstone | 41/10 | 21 |
| 1955 | RIBOT | U. Penco | E. Camici | 88/10 | 23 |
| 1956 | RIBOT | U. Penco | E. Camici | 6/10 | 20 |
| 1957 | OROSO | D. Lescalle | S. Boullenger | 52/1 | 24 |
| 1958 | BALLYMOSS | M. V. O'Brien | A. Breasley | 39/10 | 17 |
| 1959 | SAINT CRESPIN | A. Head | G. Moore | 17/1 | 25 |
| 1960 | PUISSANT CHEF | C. Bartholomew | M. Garcia | 4/1 | 17 |
| 1961 | MOLVEDO | A. Maggi | E. Camici | 18/10 | 19 |
| 1962 | SOLTIKOFF | R. Pelat | M. Depalmas | 40/1 | 24 |
| 1963 | EXBURY | G. Watson | J. Deforge | 36/10 | 15 |
| 1964 | PRINCE ROYAL II | G. Bridgland | R. Poincelet | 16/1 | 22 |
| 1965 | SEA BIRD II | E. Pollet | T. Glennon | 12/10 | 20 |
| 1966 | BON MOT | W. Head | F. Head | 53/10 | 24 |

| YEAR | HORSE | TRAINER | JOCKEY | SP | RAN |
|------|-------|---------|--------|----|----|
| 1967 | TOPYO | C. Bartholomew | W. Pyers | 82/1 | 30 |
| 1968 | VAGUELY NOBLE | E. Pollet | W. Williamson | 5/2 | 17 |
| 1969 | LEVMOSS | S. McGrath | W. Williamson | 52/1 | 24 |
| 1970 | SASSAFRAS | F. Mathet | Y. Saint-Martin | 19/1 | 15 |
| 1971 | MILL REEF | I. Balding | G. Lewis | 7/10 | 18 |
| 1972 | SAN SAN | A. Penna | F. Head | 37/2 | 19 |
| 1973 | RHEINGOLD | B. Hills | L. Piggott | 17/10 | 27 |
| 1974 | ALLEZ FRANCE | A. Penna | Y. Saint-Martin | 1/2 | 20 |
| 1975 | STAR APPEAL | T. Grieper | G. Starkey | 119/1 | 24 |
| 1976 | IVANJICA | A. Head | F. Head | 71/10 | 20 |
| 1977 | ALLEGED | M. V. O'Brien | L. Piggott | 39/10 | 26 |
| 1978 | ALLEGED | M. V. O'Brien | L. Piggott | 14/10 | 18 |
| 1979 | THREE TROIKAS | Mme C. Head | F. Head | 88/10 | 22 |
| 1980 | DETROIT | O. Douieb | P. Eddery | 67/10 | 20 |
| 1981 | GOLD RIVER | A. Head | G. Moore | 53/1 | 24 |
| 1982 | AKIYDA | F. Mathet | Y. Saint-Martin | 11/1 | 17 |
| 1983 | ALL ALONG | P. Biancone | W. R. Swinburn | 17/1 | 26 |
| 1984 | SAGACE | P. Biancone | Y. Saint-Martin | 39/10 | 22 |
| 1985 | RAINBOW QUEST | J. Tree | P. Eddery | 71/10 | 15 |
| 1986 | DANCING BRAVE | G. Harwood | P. Eddery | 11/10 | 15 |
| 1987 | TREMPOLINO | A. Fabre | P. Eddery | 20/1 | 11 |
| 1988 | TONY BIN | L. Camici | J. Reid | 14/1 | 24 |
| 1989 | CARROLL HOUSE | M. Jarvis | M. Kinane | 189/10 | 19 |
| 1990 | SAUMAREZ | N. Clement | G. Mossé | 15/1 | 21 |
| 1991 | SUAVE DANCER | J. Hammond | C. Asmussen | 37/10 | 14 |

# Prix de l'Abbaye de Longchamp

LONGCHAMP                     5 FURLONGS                    FIRST RUN 1958

| YEAR | HORSE | TRAINER | JOCKEY | SP | RAN |
|------|-------|---------|--------|-----|-----|
| 1958 | EDELLIC | F. Mathet | M. Garcia | 41/10 | 4 |
| 1959 | SLY POLA | E. Pollet | J. Massard | 61/10 | 6 |
| 1960 | HIGH BULK | E. Pollet | J. Massard | 21/10 | 6 |
| 1961 | L'EPINAY | E. Pollet | R. Poincelet | 28/10 | 7 |
| 1962 | FORTINO | F. Mathet | Y. Saint-Martin | 28/10 | 7 |
| 1963 | TEXANITA | F. Mathet | Y. Saint-Martin | 13/10 | 10 |
| 1964 | TEXANITA | F. Mathet | T. Glennon | 8/10 | 8 |
| 1965 | SILVER SHARK | F. Mathet | Y. Saint-Martin | 7/10 | 6 |
| 1966 | FARHANA | F. Mathet | Y. Saint-Martin | 1/2 | 5 |
| 1967 | PENTATHLON | H. Danner | F. Head | 21/1 | 8 |
| 1968 | BE FRIENDLY | C. Mitchell | G. Lewis | 33/10 | 11 |
| 1969 | TOWER WALK | G. Barling | L. Piggott | 28/10 | 12 |
| 1970 | BALIDAR | J. Winter | L. Piggott | 16/10 | 9 |
| 1971 | SWEET REVENGE | T. Corbett | G. Lewis | 38/10 | 5 |
| 1972 | DEEP DIVER | P. Davey | W. Williamson | 18/10 | 8 |
| 1973 | SANDFORD LAD | H. R. Price | A. Murray | 6/5 | 12 |
| 1974 | MOUBARIZ | F. Mathet | H. Samani | 91/10 | 9 |
| 1975 | LIANGA | A. Penna | Y. Saint-Martin | 6/5 | 12 |
| 1976 | GENTILHOMBRE | N. Adam | T. McKeown | 179/10 | 10 |
|      | MENDIP MAN | A. Paus | A. Gibert | 46/10 | — |
| 1977 | GENTILHOMBRE | N. Adam | P. Cook | 3/1 | 11 |
| 1978 | SIGY | Mme C. Head | F. Head | 19/10 | 7 |
| 1979 | DOUBLE FORM | R. F. J. Houghton | J. Reid | 39/10 | 13 |
| 1980 | MOORESTYLE | R. Armstrong | L. Piggott | 17/10 | 9 |
| 1981 | MARWELL | M. Stoute | W. R. Swinburn | 42/10 | 10 |
| 1982 | SHARPO | J. Tree | P. Eddery | 4/5 | 13 |
| 1983 | HABIBTI | J. Dunlop | W. Carson | 2/5 | 8 |
| 1984 | COMMITTED | D. Weld | S. Cauthen | 16/10 | 12 |
| 1985 | COMMITTED | D. Weld | M. Kinane | 84/10 | 12 |
| 1986 | DOUBLE SCHWARTZ | C. Nelson | P. Eddery | 6/4 | 13 |
| 1987 | POLONIA | J. Bolger | C. Roche | 63/10 | 9 |
| 1988 | HANDSOME SAILOR* | B. Hills | M. Hills | 19/10 | 10 |
| 1989 | SILVER FLING | I. Balding | J. Matthias | 3/1 | 16 |
| 1990 | DAYJUR | W. R. Hern | W. Carson | 1/10 | 6 |
| 1991 | KEEN HUNTER | J. Gosden | S. Cauthen | 115/10 | 14 |

* 1988: Cadeaux Genereux finished first but was disqualified and placed last

# United States of America
## *Winners of US Triple Crown Races*

| YEAR | KENTUCKY DERBY | PREAKNESS STAKES | BELMONT STAKES |
|------|----------------|------------------|----------------|
|      | 1M2F, CHURCHILL DOWNS | 1M1½F, PIMLICO | 1M4F, BELMONT PARK |
| 1946 | **Assault** | **Assault** | **Assault** |
| 1947 | Jet Pilot | Faultless | Phalanx |
| 1948 | **Citation** | **Citation** | **Citation** |
| 1949 | Ponder | Capot | Capot |
| 1950 | Middleground | Hill Prince | Middleground |
| 1951 | Count Turf | Bold | Counterpoint |
| 1952 | Hill Gail | Blue Man | One Count |
| 1953 | Dark Star | Native Dancer | Native Dancer |
| 1954 | Determine | Hasty Road | High Gun |
| 1955 | Swaps | Nashua | Nashua |
| 1956 | Needles | Fabius | Needles |
| 1957 | Iron Liege | Bold Ruler | Gallant Man |
| 1958 | Tim Tam | Tim Tam | Cavan |
| 1959 | Tomy Lee | Royal Orbit | Sword Dancer |
| 1960 | Venetian Way | Bally Ache | Celtic Dancer |
| 1961 | Carry Back | Carry Back | Sherluck |
| 1962 | Decidedly | Greek Money | Jaipur |
| 1963 | Chateaugay | Candy Spots | Chateaugay |
| 1964 | Northern Dancer | Northern Dancer | Quadrangle |
| 1965 | Lucky Debonair | Tom Rolfe | Hail To All |
| 1966 | Kauai King | Kauai King | Amberoid |
| 1967 | Proud Clarion | Damascus | Damascus |
| 1968 | Forward Pass | Forward Pass | Stage Door Johnny |
| 1969 | Majestic Prince | Majestic Prince | Arts and Letters |
| 1970 | Dust Commander | Personality | High Echelon |
| 1971 | Canonero | Canonero | Pass Catcher |
| 1972 | Riva Ridge | Bee Bee Bee | Riva Ridge |
| 1973 | **Secretariat** | **Secretariat** | **Secretariat** |
| 1974 | Cannonade | Little Current | Little Current |
| 1975 | Foolish Pleasure | Master Derby | Avatar |
| 1976 | Bold Forbes | Elocutionist | Bold Forbes |
| 1977 | **Seattle Slew** | **Seattle Slew** | **Seattle Slew** |
| 1978 | **Affirmed** | **Affirmed** | **Affirmed** |
| 1979 | Spectacular Bid | Spectacular Bid | Coastal |
| 1980 | Genuine Risk | Codex | Temperence Hill |
| 1981 | Pleasant Colony | Pleasant Colony | Summing |
| 1982 | Gato Del Sol | Aloma's Ruler | Conquistador Cielo |
| 1983 | Sunny's Halo | Deputed Testamony | Caveat |
| 1984 | Swale | Gate Dancer | Swale |
| 1985 | Spend A Buck | Tank's Prospect | Creme Fraiche |
| 1986 | Ferdinand | Snow Chief | Danzig Connection |
| 1987 | Alysheba | Alysheba | Bet Twice |
| 1988 | Winning Colours | Risen Star | Risen Star |
| 1989 | Sunday Silence | Sunday Silence | Easy Goer |
| 1990 | Unbridled | Summer Squall | Go And Go |
| 1991 | Strike the Gold | Hansel | Hansel |

Triple Crown winners in bold type.

## *Arlington Million*

ARLINGTON, CHICAGO  1 MILE 2 FURLONGS          FIRST RUN 1981

| YEAR | HORSE | TRAINER | JOCKEY | SP | RAN |
|------|-------|---------|--------|-----|-----|
| 1981 | JOHN HENRY | R. McAnally | W. Shoemaker | 11/10 | 12 |
| 1982 | PERRAULT | C. Whittingham | L. Pincay, jr | 13/10 | 14 |
| 1983 | TOLOMEO | L. Cumani | P. Eddery | 382/10 | 14 |
| 1984 | JOHN HENRY | R. McAnally | C. McCarron | 11/10 | 12 |
| 1985 | TELEPROMPTER | J. Watts | T. Ives | 142/10 | 13 |
| 1986 | ESTRAPADE | C. Whittingham | F. Toro | 21/10 | 14 |
| 1987 | MANILA | L. Jolley | A. Cordero | evens | 8 |
| 1988 | MILL NATIVE | A. Fabre | C. Asmussen | 406/10 | 14 |
| 1989 | STEINLEN | D. W. Lukas | J. Santos | 53/10 | 13 |
| 1990 | GOLDEN PHEASANT | C. Whittingham | G. Stevens | 66/10 | 11 |
| 1991 | TIGHT SPOT | R. McAnally | L. Pincay, jr | 18/10 | 10 |

# THE BREEDERS' CUP

The venue for the Breeders' Cup moves each year. The eight Breeders' Cups run to date (on the Flat) have been held at:

1984  Hollywood Park, California
1985  Aqueduct, New York
1986  Santa Anita, California
1987  Hollywood Park, California
1988  Churchill Downs, Kentucky
1989  Gulfstream Park, Florida
1990  Belmont Park, New York
1991  Churchill Downs, Kentucky

## *Breeders' Cup Sprint*

6 FURLONGS (DIRT)

| YEAR | HORSE | TRAINER | JOCKEY | SP | RAN |
|------|-------|---------|--------|-----|-----|
| 1984 | EILLO | B. Lepman | C. Perret | 13/10 | 11 |
| 1985 | PRECISIONIST | L. Fenstermaker | C. McCarron | 34/10 | 14 |
| 1986 | SMILE | F. Schulhofer | J. Vasquez | 11/1 | 9 |
| 1987 | VERY SUBTLE | M. Stute | P. Valenzuela | 164/10 | 13 |
| 1988 | GULCH | D. W. Lukas | A. Cordero, jr | 58/10 | 13 |
| 1989 | DANCING SPREE | C. McGaughey | A. Cordero, jr | 166/10 | 13 |
| 1990 | SAFELY KEPT | A. Goldberg | C. Perret | 122/10 | 14 |
| 1991 | SHEIKH ALBADOU | A. Scott | P. Eddery | 263/10 | 11 |

# Breeders' Cup Juvenile Fillies

1 MILE 110 YARDS (DIRT)

| Year | Horse | Trainer | Jockey | SP | RAN |
|------|-------|---------|--------|-----|-----|
| 1984 | OUTSTANDINGLY* | F. Martin | W. Guerra | 228/10 | 11 |
| 1985 | TWILIGHT RIDGE | D. W. Lukas | J. Velasquez | 6/10 | 12 |
| 1986 | BRAVE RAJ | M. Stute | P. Valenzuela | 4/1 | 12 |
| 1987 | EPITOME | P. Hauswald | P. Day | 304/10 | 12 |
| 1988 | OPEN MIND | D. W. Lukas | A. Cordero, jr | 7/10 | 12 |
| 1989 | GO FOR WAND | W. Badgett, jr | R. Romero | 5/2 | 12 |
| 1990 | MEADOW STAR | L. Jolley | J. Santos | 1/5 | 13 |
| 1991 | PLEASANT STAGE | C. Speckert | E. Delahoussaye | 58/10 | 14 |

* 1984: Fran's Valentine finished first but was disqualified

# Breeders' Cup Distaff

1 MILE 1 FURLONG (DIRT)

| Year | Horse | Trainer | Jockey | SP | RAN |
|------|-------|---------|--------|-----|-----|
| 1984 | PRINCESS ROONEY | N. Drysdale | E. Delahoussaye | 7/10 | 7 |
| 1985 | LIFE'S MAGIC | D. W. Lukas | A. Cordero, jr | 2/5 | 7 |
| 1986 | LADY'S SECRET | D. W. Lukas | P. Day | 1/2 | 8 |
| 1987 | SACAHUISTA | D. W. Lukas | R. Romero | 29/10 | 6 |
| 1988 | PERSONAL ENSIGN | C. McGaughey | R. Romero | 1/2 | 9 |
| 1989 | BAYAKOA | R. McAnally | L. Pincay, jr | 7/10 | 10 |
| 1990 | BAYAKOA | R. McAnally | L. Pincay, jr | evens | 7 |
| 1991 | DANCE SMARTLY | J. Day | P. Day | 1/2 | 13 |

# Breeders' Cup Mile

1 MILE (TURF)

| Year | Horse | Trainer | Jockey | SP | RAN |
|------|-------|---------|--------|-----|-----|
| 1984 | ROYAL HEROINE | J. Gosden | F. Toro | 17/10 | 10 |
| 1985 | COZZENE | J. Nerud | W. Guerra | 36/10 | 14 |
| 1986 | LAST TYCOON | R. Collet | Y. Saint-Martin | 359/10 | 14 |
| 1987 | MIESQUE | F. Boutin | F. Head | 36/10 | 14 |
| 1988 | MIESQUE | F. Boutin | F. Head | 2/1 | 12 |
| 1989 | STEINLEN | D. W. Lukas | J. Santos | 18/10 | 11 |
| 1990 | ROYAL ACADEMY | M. V. O'Brien | L. Piggott | 5/2 | 13 |
| 1991 | OPENING VERSE | R. Lundy | P. Valenzuela | 267/10 | 14 |

## *Breeders' Cup Juvenile*

1 MILE (TURF)

| YEAR | HORSE | TRAINER | JOCKEY | SP | RAN |
|------|-------|---------|--------|-----|-----|
| 1984 | CHIEF'S CROWN | R. Laurin | D. MacBeth | 7/10 | 10 |
| 1985 | TASSO | N. Drysdale | L. Pincay, jr | 56/10 | 13 |
| 1986 | CAPOTE | D. W. Lukas | L. Pincay, jr | 12/5 | 13 |
| 1987 | SUCCESS EXPRESS | D. W. Lukas | J. Santos | 41/10 | 13 |
| 1988 | IS IT TRUE | D. W. Lukas | L. Pincay, jr | 92/10 | 10 |
| 1989 | RHYTHM | C. McGaughey | C. Perret | 26/10 | 12 |
| 1990 | FLY SO FREE | F. Schulhofer | J. Santos | 7/5 | 11 |
| 1991 | ARAZI | F. Boutin | P. Valenzuela | 21/10 | 14 |

## *Breeders' Cup Turf*

1 MILE 4 FURLONGS (TURF)

| YEAR | HORSE | TRAINER | JOCKEY | SP | RAN |
|------|-------|---------|--------|-----|-----|
| 1984 | LASHKARI | A. de Royer-Dupré | Y. Saint-Martin | 534/10 | 11 |
| 1985 | PEBBLES | C. Brittain | P. Eddery | 22/10 | 14 |
| 1986 | MANILA | L. Jolley | J. Santos | 88/10 | 9 |
| 1987 | THEATRICAL | W. Mott | P. Day | 9/5 | 14 |
| 1988 | GREAT COMMUNICATOR | T. Ackel | R. Sibille | 124/10 | 10 |
| 1989 | PRIZED | N. Drysdale | E. Delahoussaye | 88/10 | 14 |
| 1990 | IN THE WINGS | A. Fabre | G. Stevens | 9/5 | 11 |
| 1991 | MISS ALLEGED | P. Bary | E. Legrix | 421/10 | 13 |

## *Breeders' Cup Classic*

1 MILE 2 FURLONGS (DIRT)

| YEAR | HORSE | TRAINER | JOCKEY | SP | RAN |
|------|-------|---------|--------|-----|-----|
| 1984 | WILD AGAIN | V. Timphony | P. Day | 313/10 | 8 |
| 1985 | PROUD TRUTH | J. Veitch | J. Velasquez | 74/10 | 8 |
| 1986 | SKYWALKER | C. Whittingham | L. Pincay, jr | 101/10 | 11 |
| 1987 | FERDINAND | C. Whittingham | W. Shoemaker | evens | 12 |
| 1988 | ALYSHEBA | J. van Berg | C. McCarron | 6/4 | 9 |
| 1989 | SUNDAY SILENCE | C. Whittingham | C. McCarron | 2/1 | 8 |
| 1990 | UNBRIDLED | C. Nafzger | P. Day | 6/1 | 14 |
| 1991 | BLACK TIE AFFAIR | E. Poulos | J. Bailey | 4/1 | 11 |

# PATTERN RACES

THE FLAT

The Pattern was first implemented in 1971, dividing the top events in the major European racing countries into Group One (Classics and other races of prime international importance), Group Two (races of international importance but just below championship standard) and Group Three (usually preparatory contests for the higher groups). Below Group races are Listed races, for horses just short of Group standard.

The Pattern races in Great Britain in 1992 are listed here, with 1991 winners given in parentheses.

**Group One**
(24 races)

ONE THOUSAND GUINEAS, Newmarket (*Shadayid*)
TWO THOUSAND GUINEAS, Newmarket (*Mystiko*)
DERBY STAKES, Epsom (*Generous*)
CORONATION CUP, Epsom (*In The Groove*)
OAKS STAKES, Epsom (*Jet Ski Lady*)
ST JAMES'S PALACE STAKES, Royal Ascot (*Marju*)
CORONATION STAKES, Royal Ascot (*Kooyonga*)
ASCOT GOLD CUP, Royal Ascot (*Indian Queen*)
ECLIPSE STAKES, Sandown Park (*Environment Friend*)
JULY CUP, Newmarket (*Polish Patriot*)
KING GEORGE VI AND QUEEN ELIZABETH DIAMOND STAKES, Ascot
   (*Generous*)
SUSSEX STAKES, Goodwood (*Second Set*)
INTERNATIONAL STAKES, York (*Terimon*)
YORKSHIRE OAKS, York (*Magnificent Star*)
NUNTHORPE STAKES, York (*Sheikh Albadou*)
SPRINT CUP, Haydock Park (*Polar Falcon*)
ST LEGER, Doncaster (*Toulon*)
QUEEN ELIZABETH II STAKES, Ascot (*Selkirk*)
FILLIES' MILE, Ascot (*Culture Vulture*)

CHEVELEY PARK STAKES, Newmarket (*Marling*)
MIDDLE PARK STAKES, Newmarket (*Rodrigo De Triano*)
DEWHURST STAKES, Newmarket (*Dr Devious*)
CHAMPION STAKES, Newmarket (*Tel Quel*)
RACING POST TROPHY, Doncaster (*Seattle Rhyme*)

## Group Two
(27 races)

FORTE MILE, Sandown Park (*In The Groove*)
JOCKEY CLUB STAKES, Newmarket (*Rock Hopper*)
DANTE STAKES, York (*Environment Friend*)
YORKSHIRE CUP, York (*Arzanni*)
LOCKINGE STAKES, Newbury (*Polar Falcon*)
TEMPLE STAKES, Sandown Park (*Elbio*)
QUEEN ANNE STAKES, Royal Ascot (*Sikeston*)
PRINCE OF WALES'S STAKES, Royal Ascot (*Stagecraft*)
KING EDWARD VII STAKES, Royal Ascot (*Saddlers' Hall*)
RIBBLESDALE STAKES, Royal Ascot (*Third Watch*)
KING'S STAND STAKES, Royal Ascot (*Elbio*)
HARDWICKE STAKES, Royal Ascot (*Rock Hopper*)
PRINCESS OF WALES'S STAKES, Newmarket (*Rock Hopper*)
FALMOUTH STAKES, Newmarket (*Only Yours*)
RICHMOND STAKES, Goodwood (*Dilum*)
NASSAU STAKES, Goodwood (*Ruby Tiger*)
GEOFFREY FREER STAKES, Newbury (*Drum Taps*)
GREAT VOLTIGEUR STAKES, York (*Corrupt*)
GIMCRACK STAKES, York (*River Falls*)
LOWTHER STAKES, York (*Culture Vulture*)
CELEBRATION MILE, Goodwood (*Bold Russian*)
CHAMPAGNE STAKES, Doncaster (*Rodrigo De Triano*)
FLYING CHILDERS STAKES, Doncaster (*Paris House*)
MILL REEF STAKES, Newbury (*Showbrook*)
ROYAL LODGE STAKES, Ascot (*Made Of Gold*)
SUN CHARIOT STAKES, Newmarket (*Ristna*)
CHALLENGE STAKES, Newmarket (*Mystiko*)

## Group Three
(55 races)

NELL GWYN STAKES, Newmarket (*Crystal Gazing*)
EARL OF SEFTON STAKES, Newmarket (*Terimon*)
CRAVEN STAKES, Newmarket (*Marju*)
FRED DARLING STAKES, Newbury (*Shadayid*)
GREENHAM STAKES, Newbury (*Bog Trotter*)
JOHN PORTER STAKES, Newbury (*Rock Hopper*)
GORDON RICHARDS STAKES, Sandown Park (*Noble Patriarch*)
CLASSIC TRIAL, Sandown Park (*Hailsham*)
SAGARO STAKES, Ascot (*Teamster*)
PALACE HOUSE STAKES, Newmarket (*Elbio*)
CHESTER VASE, Chester (*Toulon*)
ORMONDE STAKES, Chester (*Per Quod*)
DERBY TRIAL, Lingfield Park (*Corrupt*)
MUSIDORA STAKES, York (*Gussy Marlowe*)
DUKE OF YORK STAKES, York (*Green Line Express*)
HENRY II STAKES, Sandown Park (*Top Of The World*)
BRIGADIER GERARD STAKES, Sandown Park (*Stagecraft*)
DIOMED STAKES, Epsom (*Sylva Honda*)
COVENTRY STAKES, Royal Ascot (*Dilum*)
JERSEY STAKES, Royal Ascot (*Satin Flower*)
QUEEN MARY STAKES, Royal Ascot (*Marling*)
QUEEN'S VASE, Royal Ascot (*Jendali*)
CORK AND ORRERY STAKES, Royal Ascot (*Polish Patriot*)
NORFOLK STAKES, Royal Ascot (*Magic Ring*)
CRITERION STAKES, Newmarket (*La Grange Music*)
LANCASHIRE OAKS, Haydock Park (*Patricia*)
CHERRY HINTON STAKES, Newmarket (*Musicale*)
JULY STAKES, Newmarket (*Showbrook*)
SCOTTISH CLASSIC, Ayr (*Zoman*)
PRINCESS MARGARET STAKES, Ascot (*Bezelle*)
BEESWING STAKES, Newcastle (*Bold Russian*)
GORDON STAKES, Goodwood (*Stylish Senor*)
GOODWOOD CUP, Goodwood (*Further Flight*)
KING GEORGE STAKES, Goodwood (*Title Roll*)
LANSON CHAMPAGNE STAKES, Goodwood (*Dr Devious*)
MOLECOMB STAKES, Goodwood (*Sahara Star*)
ROSE OF LANCASTER STAKES, Haydock Park (*Lord Of Tusmore*)
HUNGERFORD STAKES, Newbury (*Only Yours*)

PRESTIGE STAKES, Goodwood (*Musicale*)
SOLARIO STAKES, Sandown Park (*Chicmond*)
SEPTEMBER STAKES, Kempton Park (*Young Buster*)
PARK HILL STAKES, Doncaster (*Patricia*)
MAY HILL STAKES, Doncaster (*Midnight Air*)
KIVETON PARK STAKES, Doncaster (*Bog Trotter*)
DONCASTER CUP, Doncaster (*Great Marquess*)
SELECT STAKES, Goodwood (*Filia Ardross*)
CUMBERLAND LODGE STAKES, Ascot (*Drum Taps*)
DIADEM STAKES, Ascot (*Shalford*)
SUPREME STAKES, Goodwood (*Osario*)
JOCKEY CLUB CUP, Newmarket (*Further Flight*)
PRINCESS ROYAL STAKES, Ascot (*Always Friendly*)
CORNWALLIS STAKES, Ascot (*Magic Ring*)
ROCKFEL STAKES, Newmarket (*Musicale*)
HORRIS HILL STAKES, Newbury (*Lion Cavern*)
ST SIMON STAKES, Newbury (*Further Flight*)

## NATIONAL HUNT

The current Pattern for steeplechasing and hurdling was first implemented for the 1990/91 season to give a more balanced structure to the
jumping season by strengthening the mid-term period and thus counter-
acting the overwhelming importance of the late-season meetings at Cheltenham and Liverpool.

The racing programme is divided into twelve sections:

juvenile hurdles
2 mile novice hurdles
2½ mile novice hurdles
2 mile hurdles
2½ mile hurdles
3 mile hurdles

2 mile novice chases
2½ mile novice chases
3 mile novice chases
2 mile chases
2½ mile chases
3 mile chases

In each of these sections there are two Grade One races, spaced in order
to provide realistic targets for the top performers. The Grade Two events
include a few limited handicaps but primarily consist of good-class conditions races, and Grade Three consists of the top fourteen open handicaps. The gradings listed below are as for the 1991/92 season.

## Grade one
(24 races)

LONG WALK HURDLE, Ascot (3¼ mile hurdle)
FINALE JUNIOR HURDLE, Chepstow (2 mile juvenile hurdle)
FELTHAM NOVICES' CHASE, Kempton Park (3 mile novice chase)
KING GEORGE VI CHASE, Kempton Park (3 mile chase)
CHRISTMAS HURDLE, Kempton Park (2 mile hurdle)
CASTLEFORD CHASE, Wetherby (2 mile chase)
NORTHUMBERLAND GOLD CUP, Newcastle (2 mile novice chase)
CHALLOW HURDLE, Newbury (2½ mile novice hurdle)
NEWTON CHASE, Haydock Park (2½ mile chase)
TOLWORTH HURDLE, Sandown Park (2 mile novice hurdle)
BISHOPS CLEEVE HURDLE, Cheltenham (2½ mile hurdle)
SCILLY ISLES NOVICES' CHASE, Sandown Park (2½ mile novice chase)
SUPREME NOVICES' HURDLE, Cheltenham (2 mile novice hurdle)
ARKLE CHASE, Cheltenham (2 mile novice chase)
CHAMPION HURDLE, Cheltenham (2 mile hurdle)
STAYERS HURDLE, Cheltenham (3 mile hurdle)
SUN ALLIANCE NOVICES' HURDLE, Cheltenham (2½ mile novice
   hurdle)
QUEEN MOTHER CHAMPION CHASE, Cheltenham (2 mile chase)
SUN ALLIANCE CHASE, Cheltenham (3 mile novice chase)
TRIUMPH HURDLE, Cheltenham (2 mile juvenile hurdle)
GOLD CUP, Cheltenham (3¼ mile chase)
MELLING CHASE, Liverpool (2½ mile chase)
AINTREE HURDLE, Liverpool (2½ mile hurdle)
FUTURE CHAMPION NOVICES' CHASE, Ayr (2½ mile novice chase)

## Grade Two
(63 races)

DESERT ORCHID CHASE, Wincanton
CHARLIE HALL CHASE, Wetherby
WEST YORKSHIRE HURDLE, Wetherby
WENSLEYDALE JUVENILE HURDLE, Wetherby
HALDON GOLD CUP CHASE, Devon and Exeter
AGA WORCESTER NOVICE CHASE, Worcester
RACECALL ASCOT HURDLE, Ascot
HURST PARK NOVICE CHASE, Ascot
H & T WALKER HANDICAP CHASE, Ascot

KENNEL GATE NOVICE HURDLE, Ascot
NEWBURY LONG DISTANCE HURDLE, Newbury
GERRY FEILDEN HURDLE, Newbury
FIGHTING FIFTH HURDLE, Newcastle
REYNOLDSTOWN NOVICE HURDLE, Wolverhampton
PETERBOROUGH CHASE, Huntingdon
CROWN GAP WINTER NOVICE HURDLE, Sandown Park
TINGLE CREEK HANDICAP CHASE, Sandown Park
HENRY VIII NOVICE CHASE, Sandown Park
REHEARSAL HANDICAP CHASE, Chepstow
BULA HURDLE, Cheltenham
A. F. BUDGE NOVICE HURDLE, Cheltenham
SUMMIT JUVENILE HURDLE, Lingfield Park
DECEMBER NOVICE CHASE, Lingfield Park
WATERLOO HURDLE, Haydock Park
ROVACABIN NOEL NOVICE CHASE, Ascot
PML LIGHTNING NOVICE CHASE, Ascot
VICTOR CHANDLER HANDICAP CHASE, Ascot
DIPPER NOVICE CHASE, Newcastle
PETER MARSH HANDICAP CHASE, Haydock Park
PREMIER LONG DISTANCE HURDLE, Haydock Park
CHAMPION HURDLE TRIAL, Haydock Park
ROSSINGTON MAIN NOVICE HURDLE, Doncaster
RIVER DON NOVICE HURDLE, Doncaster
FINESSE JUVENILE HURDLE, Cheltenham
WEST OF SCOTLAND NOVICE CHASE, Ayr
AGFA DIAMOND HANDICAP CHASE, Sandown Park
MARSTON MOOR HANDICAP CHASE, Wetherby
REYNOLDSTOWN NOVICE CHASE, Ascot
GAME SPIRIT CHASE, Newbury
PERSIAN WAR NOVICE HURDLE, Chepstow
NOTTINGHAMSHIRE NOVICE CHASE, Nottingham
REGENCY HURDLE, Warwick
KINGWELL HURDLE, Wincanton
RENDLESHAM HURDLE, Kempton Park
TOTE PLACEPOT JUVENILE HURDLE, Kempton Park
GALLOWAY BRAES NOVICE CHASE, Kempton Park
DOVECOTE NOVICE HURDLE, Kempton Park
CAVALIER CHASE, Worcester
BERKSHIRE HURDLE, Newbury
OPAL NOVICE CHASE, Lingfield Park

LETHEBY AND CHRISTOPHER LONG DISTANCE HURDLE, Ascot
GLENLIVET ANNIVERSARY JUVENILE HURDLE, Liverpool
MARTELL CUP CHASE, Liverpool
MUMM MILDMAY NOVICE CHASE, Liverpool
HEIDSIECK DRY MONOPOLE NOVICE HURDLE, Liverpool
SEAGRAM 100 PIPERS NOVICE HURDLE, Liverpool
SANDEMAN MAGHULL NOVICE CHASE, Liverpool
CAPTAIN MORGAN HANDICAP CHASE, Liverpool
JANNEAU MERSEY NOVICE HURDLE, Liverpool
SCOTTISH CHAMPION HURDLE, Ayr
SW SHOWERS SILVER TROPHY CHASE, Cheltenham
STAFFORDSHIRE HURDLE, Uttoxeter
PERTEMPS KINGMAKER NOVICE CHASE, Warwick

**Grade Three**
(14 races)

MACKESON GOLD CUP, Cheltenham
HENNESSY GOLD CUP, Newbury
WILLIAM HILL HANDICAP HURDLE, Sandown Park
A. F. BUDGE HANDICAP CHASE, Cheltenham
WELSH NATIONAL, Chepstow
TOTE JACKPOT HANDICAP HURDLE, Sandown Park
TOTE GOLD TROPHY, Newbury
RACING POST CHASE, Kempton Park
COUNTY HURDLE, Cheltenham
GRAND NATIONAL, Liverpool
SCOTTISH NATIONAL, Ayr
EBF NOVICE HURDLE FINAL, Cheltenham
WHITBREAD GOLD CUP, Sandown Park
SWINTON INSURANCE HANDICAP HURDLE, Haydock Park

# BIG RACES IN 1992

## JANUARY

4 Sat **Anthony Mildmay, Peter Cazalet Memorial Chase,** Sandown Park
**Newton Chase,** Haydock Park

11 Sat **Victor Chandler Chase,** Ascot

18 Sat **Bic Razor Lanzarote Handicap Hurdle,** Kempton Park

## FEBRUARY

1 Sat **Agfa Diamond Handicap Chase,** Sandown Park

8 Sat **Tote Gold Trophy,** Newbury

22 Sat **Racing Post Chase,** Kempton Park
**Tote Placepot Hurdle,** Kempton Park

## MARCH

7 Sat **Sunderland Imperial Cup,** Sandown Park

10 Tue **Smurfit Champion Hurdle,** Cheltenham
**Bonusprint Stayers Hurdle,** Cheltenham
**Waterford Castle Arkle Challenge Trophy,** Cheltenham

11 Wed **Queen Mother Champion Chase,** Cheltenham
**Sun Alliance Chase,** Cheltenham

12 Thu **Daily Express Triumph Hurdle,** Cheltenham
**Tote Cheltenham Gold Cup,** Cheltenham

21 Sat **William Hill Lincoln Handicap,** Doncaster

## APRIL

2 Thu **Martell Cup Chase,** Liverpool

3 Fri **Glenlivet Melling Chase,** Liverpool

4 Sat **Martell Grand National,** Liverpool
**Sandeman Aintree Hurdle,** Liverpool

10 Fri **Gainsborough Stud Fred Darling Stakes,** Newbury

11 Sat **William Hill Scottish National,** Ayr
**Singer & Friedlander Greenham Stakes,** Newbury

14 Tue **Shadwell Stud Nell Gwyn Stakes,** Newmarket

15 Wed **Ladbroke European Free Handicap,** Newmarket

16 Thu **Craven Stakes,** Newmarket

24 Fri **Forte Mile,** Sandown Park

25 Sat **Whitbread Gold Cup,** Sandown Park
**Thresher Classic Trial,** Sandown Park

30 Thu **General Accident One Thousand Guineas,** Newmarket

## MAY

1 Fri **General Accident Jockey Club Stakes,** Newmarket

2 Sat **General Accident Two Thousand Guineas,** Newmarket

**Kentucky Derby,** Churchill
Downs, Kentucky
4 Mon **Jubilee Handicap,**
Kempton Park
5 Tue **Dalham Chester Vase,**
Chester
6 Wed **Ladbroke Chester Cup,**
Chester
9 Sat **Derby Trial,** Lingfield Park
12 Tue **Tattersalls Musidora
Stakes,** York
13 Wed **Dante Stakes,** York
14 Thu **Polo Mints Yorkshire Cup,**
York
15 Fri **Juddmonte Lockinge
Stakes,** Newbury
16 Sat **Airlie/Coolmore Irish
Two Thousand Guineas,**
The Curragh
23 Sat **Goffs Irish One Thousand
Guineas,** The Curragh

## JUNE

3 Wed **Ever Ready Derby Stakes,**
Epsom
4 Thu **Hanson Coronation Cup,**
Epsom
6 Sat **Gold Seal Oaks Stakes,**
Epsom
16 Tue **St James's Palace Stakes,**
Royal Ascot
**Prince of Wales's Stakes,**
Royal Ascot
17 Wed **Coronation Stakes,** Royal
Ascot
**Royal Hunt Cup,** Royal
Ascot
18 Thu **Gold Cup,** Royal Ascot
**Ribblesdale Stakes,** Royal
Ascot
19 Fri **King's Stand Stakes,** Royal
Ascot
**Wokingham Stakes,** Royal
Ascot
**Hardwicke Stakes,** Royal
Ascot

27 Sat **Newcastle 'Brown Ale'
Northumberland Plate,**
Newcastle
28 Sun **Budweiser Irish Derby,**
The Curragh

## JULY

4 Sat **Coral-Eclipse Stakes,**
Sandown Park
7 Tue **Princess of Wales's Stakes,**
Newmarket
**Hillsdown Cherry Hinton
Stakes,** Newmarket
8 Wed **Anglia Television July
Stakes,** Newmarket
9 Thu **July Cup,** Newmarket
11 Sat **John Smith's Magnet Cup,**
York
**Kildangan Stud Irish
Oaks,** The Curragh
25 Sat **King George VI and
Queen Elizabeth Diamond
Stakes,** Ascot
28 Tue **William Hill Stewards'
Cup,** Goodwood
29 Wed **Sussex Stakes,** Goodwood
30 Thu **Dickins & Jones
Goodwood Cup,**
Goodwood
**Schweppes Golden Mile,**
Goodwood

## AUGUST

1 Sat **Vodafone Nassau Stakes,**
Goodwood
15 Sat **Ibn Bey Geoffrey Freer
Stakes,** Newbury
18 Tue **Juddmonte International
Stakes,** York
**Great Voltigeur Stakes,**
York
19 Wed **Aston Upthorpe Yorkshire
Oaks,** York
**Tote Ebor Handicap,** York
**Scottish Equitable**

Gimcrack Stakes, York
20 Thu  **Keeneland Nunthorpe
Stakes**, York
**Lowther Stakes**, York
21 Fri  **Solario Stakes**, Sandown
Park
29 Sat  **Beefeater Gin Celebration
Mile**, Goodwood

## SEPTEMBER

5 Sat  **Sprint Cup**, Haydock Park
9 Wed  **A.F. Budge Park Hill
Stakes**, Doncaster
**May Hill Stakes**, Doncaster
10 Thu  **Doncaster Cup**, Doncaster
**Kiveton Park Stakes**,
Doncaster
11 Fri  **Laurent Perrier
Champagne Stakes**,
Doncaster
12 Sat  **Coalite St Leger Stakes**,
Doncaster
**Meadow Meats Irish
Champion Stakes**,
Leopardstown
18 Fri  **Ladbrokes Ayr Gold Cup**,
Ayr
19 Sat  **Jefferson Smurfit Irish
St Leger**, The Curragh
26 Sat  **Queen Elizabeth II Stakes**,
Ascot
**Fillies' Mile**, Ascot
30 Wed  **Tattersalls Cheveley Park
Stakes**, Newmarket

## OCTOBER

1 Thu  **Newgate Stud Middle
Park Stakes**, Newmarket
3 Sat  **William Hill
Cambridgeshire**,
Newmarket
**Cheveley Park Stud Sun
Chariot Stakes**, Newmarket
4 Sun  **Ciga Prix de l'Arc de
Triomphe**, Longchamp

**Ciga Prix de l'Abbaye**,
Longchamp
16 Fri  **Dewhurst Stakes**,
Newmarket
17 Sat  **Dubai Champion Stakes**,
Newmarket
**Tote Cesarewitch**,
Newmarket
24 Sat  **Racing Post Trophy**,
Doncaster
31 Sat  **Breeders' Cup**, Gulfstream
Park, Florida

## NOVEMBER

7 Sat  **William Hill November
Handicap**, Doncaster
14 Sat  **Mackeson Gold Cup**,
Cheltenham
21 Sat  **H. & T. Walker Gold Cup**,
Ascot
28 Sat  **Hennessy Cognac Gold
Cup**, Newbury
**Bellway Homes 'Fighting
Fifth' Hurdle**, Newcastle

## DECEMBER

5 Sat  **William Hill Handicap
Hurdle**, Sandown Park
12 Sat  **A.F. Budge Gold Cup**,
Cheltenham
19 Sat  **SGB Handicap Chase**,
Ascot
**Northumberland Gold
Cup**, Newcastle
26 Sat  **King George VI Chase**,
Kempton Park
**Rowland Meyrick
Handicap Chase**, Wetherby
28 Mon  **Christmas Hurdle**,
Kempton Park
**Coral Welsh National**,
Chepstow
**Castleford Chase**,
Wetherby

# BRITISH AND IRISH FIXTURES, 1992

Fixtures on the Flat are shown in bold type, National Hunt in roman, Irish in italic. An asterisk denotes an evening meeting, and 'AW' indicates racing on all-weather surfaces.

'C4' after a fixture indicates that it is scheduled for coverage by Channel Four Racing.

The dates and Channel Four coverage are subject to alteration.

## JANUARY

1 Wed **Southwell (AW)**, Catterick, Cheltenham, Devon & Exeter, Leicester, Windsor (C4), *Fairyhouse, Tramore*

2 Thu Ayr, Lingfield (AW), Nottingham

3 Fri **Southwell (AW)**, Edinburgh, Newton Abbot

4 Sat **Lingfield (AW)**, Haydock, Market Rasen, Sandown (C4), *Naas*

6 Mon Lingfield, Southwell (AW), Wolverhampton, *Thurles*

7 Tue Chepstow, Leicester, Lingfield (AW), Wolverhampton

8 Wed Kelso, Plumpton, Southwell (AW)

9 Thu Edinburgh, Lingfield (AW), Wincanton, *Punchestown*

10 Fri **Southwell (AW)**, Ascot, Wetherby

11 Sat **Lingfield (AW)**, Ascot, Market Rasen, Newcastle, Warwick, *Leopardstown*

13 Mon Carlisle, Fontwell, Southwell (AW)

14 Tue Folkestone, Lingfield (AW), Sedgefield

15 Wed **Southwell (AW)**, Ludlow, Windsor

16 Thu Lingfield (AW), Taunton, *Gowran Park*

17 Fri **Southwell (AW)**, Catterick, Kempton, Towcester

18 Sat **Lingfield (AW)**, Catterick, Kempton (C4), Haydock, Warwick, *Punchestown*

19 Sun *Navan*

20 Mon Leicester, Lingfield, Southwell (AW)

21 Tue **Lingfield (AW)**, Chepstow, Nottingham

22 Wed Sedgefield, Southwell (AW), Wolverhampton, *Fairyhouse*

23 Thu Huntingdon, Lingfield (AW), Newton Abbot, *Tramore*

24 Fri **Southwell (AW)**, Wincanton, Uttoxeter

25 Sat **Lingfield (AW)**, Ayr, Cheltenham, Doncaster (C4), *Naas*

27 Mon Plumpton, Southwell (AW)

28 Tue Leicester, Lingfield (AW), Sedgefield

29 Wed **Southwell (AW)**, Nottingham, Windsor, *Naas*

30 Thu Edinburgh, Lingfield (AW),

Towcester, *Tramore*

31 Fri    **Southwell (AW)**, Kelso,
Lingfield

## FEBRUARY

1 Sat    **Lingfield (AW)**, Chepstow,
Sandown (C4), Stratford,
Wetherby, *Leopardstown*

3 Mon    Fontwell, Southwell (AW),
Wolverhampton

4 Tue    **Lingfield (AW)**, Carlisle,
Warwick

5 Wed    Ascot, Ludlow, Southwell
(AW), *Down Royal*

6 Thu    Huntingdon, Lingfield
(AW), Wincanton, *Clonmel*

7 Fri    **Southwell (AW)**, Bangor-
on-Dee, Newbury,
Sedgefield

8 Sat    **Lingfield (AW)**, Ayr,
Catterick, Newbury,
Uttoxeter (C4), *Fairyhouse*

10 Mon    Hereford, Plumpton,
Southwell (AW)

11 Tue    Newton Abbot, Lingfield
(AW), Towcester

12 Wed    **Southwell (AW)**,
Folkestone, Worcester

13 Thu    Leicester, Lingfield (AW),
Sandown, *Thurles*

14 Fri    **Southwell (AW)**,
Edinburgh, Fakenham,
Sandown

15 Sat    **Lingfield (AW)**, Chepstow,
Newcastle (C4),
Nottingham, Windsor,
*Navan*

16 Sun    *Leopardstown*

17 Mon    Fontwell, Southwell (AW),
Wolverhampton

18 Tue    **Lingfield (AW)**,
Huntingdon, Sedgefield

19 Wed    Folkestone, Southwell (AW),
Warwick, *Downpatrick*

20 Thu    Catterick, Lingfield (AW),
Wincanton, *Thurles*

21 Fri    **Southwell (AW)**, Kelso,
Kempton

22 Sat    **Lingfield (AW)**, Doncaster,
Edinburgh, Kempton (C4),
Stratford, *Punchestown*

24 Mon    Doncaster, Leicester,
Southwell (AW)

25 Tue    Lingfield (AW), Nottingham

26 Wed    **Southwell (AW)**, Plumpton,
Wetherby, Worcester,
*Gowran Park*

27 Thu    Lingfield (AW), Ludlow,
*Tipperary*

28 Fri    **Southwell (AW)**, Haydock,
Newbury

29 Sat    **Lingfield (AW)**, Haydock,
Hereford, Market Rasen,
Newbury, *Naas*

## MARCH

1 Sun    *Fairyhouse*

2 Mon    Leicester, Southwell (AW),
Windsor

3 Tue    **Lingfield (AW)**, Sedgefield,
Warwick

4 Wed    Bangor-on-Dee, Catterick,
Folkestone, Southwell (AW)

5 Thu    **Lingfield (AW)**, Stratford,
Wincanton, *Clonmel*

6 Fri    **Southwell (AW)**, Carlisle,
Market Rasen, Sandown

7 Sat    **Lingfield (AW)**,  Ayr,
Chepstow, Doncaster,
Sandown (C4), *Navan*

9 Mon    Southwell (AW), Plumpton,
Taunton

10 Tue    **Lingfield (AW)**,
Cheltenham, Sedgefield

11 Wed    Cheltenham, Newton Abbot

12 Thu    Cheltenham, Hexham

13 Fri    Fakenham, Lingfield,
Wolverhampton

14 Sat    **Southwell (AW)**, Chepstow,
Lingfield, Newcastle,
Uttoxeter (C4), *Leopardstown*

16 Mon    Newcastle, Wolverhampton

17 Tue    Fontwell, Nottingham,
*Leopardstown, Limerick, Down
Royal*

18 Wed    **Southwell (AW)**, Kelso,

Worcester

19 Thu **Doncaster (C4)**, Devon &
Exeter, Towcester, *Wexford*

20 Fri **Doncaster (C4)**, Ludlow,
Newbury

21 Sat **Doncaster (C4)**, **Lingfield
(AW)**, Bangor-on-Dee,
Hexham, Newbury, *Naas*

23 Mon **Folkestone**, Hexham

24 Tue **Leicester**, Sandown

25 Wed **Catterick**, Worcester,
*Downpatrick*

26 Thu **Brighton**,
**Wolverhampton**, Taunton,
*Thurles*

27 Fri **Beverley**, Plumpton,
Wincanton

28 Sat **Beverley**, **Warwick**, Ascot,
Southwell, *The Curragh*

30 Mon **Folkestone**, **Newcastle**

31 Tue **Leicester**, Sedgefield

## APRIL

1 Wed **Hamilton**, Worcester,
*Gowran Park*

2 Thu **Brighton**, Liverpool

3 Fri **Kempton**, Liverpool, Devon
& Exeter

4 Sat **Lingfield (AW)**, Hereford,
Liverpool, *Tramore*

5 Sun *Naas*

6 Mon **Wolverhampton**, Kelso,
*Roscommon*

7 Tue **Pontefract**, Southwell

8 Wed **Ripon**, Ascot, Ludlow,
*Navan*

9 Thu **Hamilton**, Taunton,
*Clonmel*

10 Fri **Newbury**, **Thirsk**, Ayr

11 Sat **Newbury**, **Thirsk**, Ayr
**(C4)**, Bangor-on-Dee,
Stratford, *The Curragh*, *Down
Royal*

13 Mon **Brighton**, **Edinburgh**,
**Nottingham**, Huntingdon,
*Limerick*

14 Tue **Newmarket (C4)**, Fontwell,
Sedgefield

15 Wed **Newmarket (C4)**,
**Pontefract**, Cheltenham

16 Thu **Newmarket (C4)**, **Ripon**,
Cheltenham, *Ballinrobe*

18 Sat **Haydock**, **Kempton (C4)**,
**Newcastle**, Carlisle,
Newton Abbot, Plumpton,
Southwell, Towcester,
*Leopardstown*, *Mallow*

20 Mon **Kempton (C4)**, **Newcastle**,
**Nottingham**, **Warwick**,
Carlisle, Chepstow,
Fakenham, Hereford,
Huntingdon, Market Rasen,
Newton Abbot, Plumpton,
Towcester, Uttoxeter,
Wetherby, Wincanton,
*Fairyhouse*, *Mallow*

21 Tue **Warwick**, Chepstow,
Uttoxeter, Wetherby,
*Fairyhouse*

22 Wed **Catterick**, **Folkestone**,
*Ludlow, Perth, *Fairyhouse*

23 Thu **Beverley**, Perth, *Tipperary*

24 Fri **Carlisle**, **Sandown (C4)**,
Perth, *Taunton

25 Sat **Leicester**, **Ripon**,
**Sandown (C4) (mixed)**,
Hexham, Market Rasen,
*Worcester, *The Curragh*

27 Mon **Pontefract**,
**Wolverhampton**,
*Windsor, *Hexham, *Sligo*

28 Tue **Bath**, **Nottingham**, *Ascot,
*Sedgefield, *Punchestown*

29 Wed **Ascot**, *Cheltenham, Kelso,
*Punchestown*

30 Thu **Redcar**, **Newmarket (C4)**,
**Salisbury**, *Punchestown*

## MAY

1 Fri **Hamilton**, **Newmarket
(C4)**, *Bangor-on-Dee,
Newton Abbot

2 Sat **Haydock**, **Newmarket
(C4)**, **Thirsk**, *Hexham,
*Hereford, Uttoxeter, *Naas*

3 Sun *Gowran Park*

4 Mon  **Pontefract, Haydock (mixed), Kempton (C4), Warwick**, Devon & Exeter, Fontwell, Ludlow, Newcastle, Southwell, Towcester, *Down Royal*, *Navan*

5 Tue  **Chester (C4), *Sandown**, Chepstow, *Sedgefield*, *Limerick*

6 Wed  **Chester (C4), Salisbury**, *Wetherby*, *Worcester*, *Navan*

7 Thu  **Brighton, Carlisle, Chester (C4)**, *Uttoxeter*, *Tramore*

8 Fri  **Beverley, Carlisle, Lingfield**, *Stratford*, *Wincanton*

9 Sat  **Beverley, Bath, Lingfield**, Bangor-on-Dee, *Market Rasen*, *Newcastle*, *Warwick*, *Leopardstown*

11 Mon  **Hamilton**, *Windsor*, **Wolverhampton**, *Killarney*

12 Tue  **York (C4)**, *Folkestone*, Newton Abbot, *Towcester*, *Killarney*

13 Wed  *Kempton, **York (C4)**, Hereford, *Newton Abbot*, *Perth*, *Killarney*, *Leopardstown*

14 Thu  **York (C4)**, *Huntingdon*, Perth, *Limerick*

15 Fri  **Newbury, Newmarket, Thirsk**, *Stratford*, *Downpatrick*

16 Sat  *Hamilton, **Newbury, Newmarket (C4), Thirsk**, *Southwell*, *Lingfield*, *Warwick, The Curragh, Downpatrick*

18 Mon  **Bath, Edinburgh** *Roscommon*

19 Tue  **Beverley, Goodwood**, *Mallow*

20 Wed  **Goodwood**, *Perth*, Worcester, *Mallow*, *Leopardstown*

21 Thu  **Goodwood, Catterick**, *Clonmel*

22 Fri  **Haydock, Salisbury**, *Pontefract, Towcester, *Dundalk*

23 Sat  **Doncaster, Haydock, Kempton (C4)**, *Lingfield*, *Southwell*, *Warwick*, Hexham, Cartmel, *The Curragh*

25 Mon  **Chepstow, Doncaster, Leicester, Redcar, Sandown (C4)**, Cartmel, Hereford, *Hexham*, Huntingdon, Fakenham, Fontwell, Uttoxeter, Wetherby, *Down Royal*, *Kilbeggan*

26 Tue  **Leicester, Redcar**, *Sandown*, *Uttoxeter*, *Wexford*

27 Wed  **Brighton**, *Ripon*, Cartmel, *Tipperary*

28 Thu  **Brighton, Carlisle**, *Tipperary*

29 Fri  *Goodwood, **Hamilton, Newcastle, Nottingham**, *Stratford*, *Dundalk*

30 Sat  **Edinburgh, Lingfield**, *Wolverhampton*, *Market Rasen*, Stratford, *Fairyhouse*

## JUNE

1 Mon  **Leicester, Redcar**, *Leopardstown, Tralee*

2 Tue  **Folkestone**, *Newbury*, **Yarmouth**, *Tramore*

3 Wed  *Beverley, **Epsom (C4)**, Yarmouth, *The Curragh*

4 Thu  **Beverley, Epsom (C4)**, *Clonmel*

5 Fri  **Catterick, Epsom (C4), Goodwood**, *Haydock*, Southwell

6 Sat  *Carlisle, **Catterick, Epsom (C4), Haydock**, *Leicester, The Curragh*

7 Sun  *Roscommon*

8 Mon Nottingham, Pontefract,
*Roscommon*
9 Tue Salisbury, Pontefract,
*Mallow*
10 Wed Beverley, *Hamilton,
*Kempton, Southwell,
*Leopardstown*
11 Thu *Chepstow, Hamilton,
Newbury, *Tipperary*
12 Fri *Doncaster, *Goodwood,
Sandown, Southwell, York
(C4), *Dundalk*
13 Sat Bath, *Lingfield,
*Nottingham, Sandown
(C4), York (C4),
*Wolverhampton, *Naas*
15 Mon Brighton, Edinburgh,
*Windsor, *Clonmel*
16 Tue Royal Ascot, Thirsk
17 Wed Royal Ascot, Ripon
18 Thu Royal Ascot, Ripon,
*Ballinrobe, *Naas*
19 Fri Royal Ascot, Ayr, Redcar,
*Newmarket, *Gowran Park*
20 Sat Ascot, Ayr, *Lingfield,
Redcar, *Southwell,
*Warwick, *Gowran Park*
21 Sun *Gowran Park*
22 Mon Edinburgh, Nottingham,
*Windsor,
*Wolverhampton,
*Kilbeggan*
23 Tue Brighton, *Newbury,
Yarmouth, *Sligo*
24 Wed Carlisle, *Chester,
*Kempton, Salisbury,
*Sligo, *Wexford*
25 Thu Carlisle, Salisbury,
*Thurles*
26 Fri *Bath, Doncaster,
*Goodwood, *Newcastle,
Newmarket, Lingfield
27 Sat Chepstow, *Doncaster,
*Lingfield, Newcastle
(C4), Newmarket (C4),
*Warwick, *The Curragh*
28 Sun *The Curragh*
29 Mon Hamilton, Pontefract,
*Windsor,

Wolverhampton, *Limerick*
30 Tue Chepstow, Folkestone,
*Bellewstown*

## JULY

1 Wed *Catterick, *Epsom,
Warwick, Yarmouth,
*Bellewstown*
2 Thu *Brighton, Catterick,
*Haydock, Yarmouth,
*Bellewstown*
3 Fri *Beverley, Haydock,
Southwell, Sandown (C4),
*Wexford*
4 Sat Bath, Beverley, Haydock,
*Nottingham, Sandown
(C4), *Naas*
6 Mon Edinburgh, Leicester,
Ripon, *Windsor,
*Roscommon*
7 Tue Newmarket (C4),
Pontefract
8 Wed Bath, *Kempton,
Newmarket (C4), *Redcar
9 Thu *Chepstow, Newmarket
(C4), Redcar, *Tipperary,
*Dundalk*
10 Fri *Chester, Lingfield,
Warwick, York (C4),
*Tipperary*
11 Sat Chester, Lingfield,
Salisbury, *Southwell,
York (C4), *The Curragh*
12 Sun *Dundalk, The Curragh*
13 Mon *Beverley, Edinburgh,
*Windsor,
Wolverhampton, *Down
Royal, *Killarney*
14 Tue Beverley, Folkestone,
*Leicester, *Down Royal,
*Killarney*
15 Wed Catterick, *Sandown,
Southwell, *Yarmouth,
*Killarney*
16 Thu Catterick, *Chepstow,
*Hamilton, Sandown,
*Killarney*
17 Fri *Hamilton, Newbury,

*Newmarket, Southwell,
Thirsk

18 Sat   Ayr, *Lingfield,
Newmarket (C4),
Newbury, Ripon,
*Wolverhampton,
*Leopardstown*

20 Mon  Bath, Ayr, *Nottingham,
*Windsor, *Ballinrobe,
*Wexford*

21 Tue   Ayr, Folkestone, *Ballinrobe*

22 Wed  Doncaster, *Hamilton,
*Redcar, *Sandown,
Yarmouth, *Naas*

23 Thu   Brighton, *Doncaster,
*Hamilton, Yarmouth,
*Tipperary*

24 Fri    Ascot, *Ayr, Carlisle,
*Pontefract, Yarmouth

25 Sat    Ayr, Ascot, Newcastle,
*Warwick, *Southwell,
*Leopardstown*

27 Mon  Newcastle, Lingfield,
*Windsor,
*Wolverhampton, *Galway*

28 Tue   Beverley, *Leicester,
Goodwood, *Galway*

29 Wed  Catterick, *Epsom,
*Southwell, Goodwood,
*Galway*

30 Thu   Goodwood, *Salisbury,
Yarmouth, *Galway*

31 Fri    *Edinburgh, Thirsk,
*Newmarket, Goodwood,
Bangor-on-Dee, *Galway*

# AUGUST

1 Sat    Thirsk, *Windsor,
Newmarket (C4),
Goodwood, Newton Abbot,
*Market Rasen, *Galway*

3 Mon   Ripon, *Nottingham,
Newton Abbot, *Leopardstown*,
*Tipperary*

4 Tue    Redcar, Brighton,
*Nottingham, *Roscommon*

5 Wed   Pontefract, Brighton,
*Kempton, Devon &

Exeter, *Fairyhouse*

6 Thu    Pontefract, Brighton,
*Mallow*

7 Fri     *Haydock, *Newmarket,
Redcar, Wolverhampton,
Plumpton, *Kilbeggan*

8 Sat     *Lingfield, Newmarket
(C4), Haydock, Redcar,
*Southwell, *Worcester,
*Leopardstown*

9 Sun    *Leopardstown*

10 Mon  *Thirsk, *Leicester,
Windsor, Worcester,
*Laytown*

11 Tue   Bath, Yarmouth,
*Catterick, *Fontwell,
*Gowran Park*

12 Wed  Beverley, Salisbury,
*Leopardstown*, *Tramore*

13 Thu   Beverley, Salisbury,
Newton Abbot, *Tramore*

14 Fri    Folkestone, Southwell,
Newbury, *Haydock,
*Tramore*

15 Sat    Ripon, Newbury,
*Wolverhampton,
*Lingfield, Bangor-on-Dee,
*Market Rasen, *The Curragh*,
*Tramore*

17 Mon  Hamilton, Windsor,
*Roscommon*

18 Tue   Folkestone, York (C4),
*Wexford*

19 Wed  Yarmouth, York (C4),
*Kempton, *Sligo*

20 Thu   *Salisbury, Yarmouth,
York (C4), *Sligo, Tipperary*

21 Fri    Chester, Sandown (C4),
Perth

22 Sat    Chester, Ripon, Sandown
(C4), *Hereford, Perth, *The
Curragh*

23 Sun   *Tralee*

24 Mon  Nottingham, Hexham,
*Tralee*

25 Tue   Brighton, Pontefract,
*Tralee*

26 Wed  Redcar, Brighton, Devon &
Exeter, *Tralee*

27 Thu Lingfield, Worcester, *Tralee*
28 Fri *Edinburgh, Goodwood, Newmarket (C4), Thirsk, *Tralee*
29 Sat Goodwood (C4), Newcastle, Newmarket, *Windsor, Cartmel, *Hereford, *Leopardstown*
30 Sun *The Curragh*
31 Mon Chepstow, Epsom (C4), Newcastle, Ripon, Warwick, Wolverhampton, Cartmel, Huntingdon, Newton Abbot, Plumpton, Southwell, *Galway*, *Downpatrick*

## SEPTEMBER

1 Tue Epsom, Ripon, Newton Abbot, *Galway*
2 Wed York, Fontwell, Newton Abbot, *Galway*
3 Thu York, Salisbury, *Tipperary*
4 Fri Haydock, Kempton (C4), Sedgefield
5 Sat Haydock, Kempton (C4), Thirsk, Stratford, *The Curragh*
7 Mon Hamilton, Wolverhampton, *Roscommon*
8 Tue Carlisle, Leicester, Lingfield, *Limerick*
9 Wed Doncaster (C4), Devon & Exeter, *Fairyhouse*
10 Thu Doncaster (C4), Folkestone, Newton Abbot, *Gowran Park*
11 Fri Doncaster (C4), Goodwood, Worcester
12 Sat Chepstow, Doncaster (C4), Goodwood, Bangor-on-Dee, Worcester, *Leopardstown*
14 Mon Bath, Leicester, Plumpton, *Ballinrobe*
15 Tue Sandown, Yarmouth, Sedgefield

16 Wed Ayr, Beverley, Sandown, Yarmouth, Devon & Exeter, *Dundalk*
17 Thu Ayr, Beverley, Lingfield, Yarmouth, Uttoxeter, *Clonmel*
18 Fri Ayr (C4), Newbury, Southwell, Huntingdon
19 Sat Ayr (C4), Catterick, Newbury, Market Rasen, Worcester, *The Curragh*, *Down Royal*
21 Mon Edinburgh, Folkestone, Nottingham, Pontefract, *Listowel*
22 Tue Kempton, Nottingham, *Listowel*
23 Wed Brighton, Perth, Southwell, *Listowel*
24 Thu Ascot, Perth, Taunton, *Listowel*
25 Fri Ascot, Haydock, Redcar, Hereford, *Listowel*
26 Sat Ascot, Haydock, Redcar, Carlisle, Market Rasen, Stratford, *The Curragh*, *Downpatrick*
28 Mon Bath, Hamilton, Wolverhampton, Carlisle, Fontwell, *Sligo*
29 Tue Brighton, Newcastle, Devon & Exeter
30 Wed Newmarket (C4), Salisbury, Cheltenham, Sedgefield, *Fairyhouse*

## OCTOBER

1 Thu Lingfield, Newmarket (C4), Cheltenham, *Mallow*
2 Fri Goodwood, Newmarket (C4), Hexham
3 Sat Goodwood, Newmarket (C4), Chepstow, Kelso, Uttoxeter, *Fairyhouse*
4 Sun *Tipperary*
5 Mon Pontefract, Warwick, Southwell, *Roscommon*
6 Tue Folkestone, Redcar,

**Warwick,** Newton Abbot, *Roscommon*

7 Wed **Haydock, York,** Towcester, *Gowran Park*

8 Thu **Haydock, York,** Ludlow, Wincanton, *Punchestown*

9 Fri **Ascot,** Carlisle, Market Rasen

10 Sat **Ascot, York (C4),** Ayr, Bangor-on-Dee, Southwell, Worcester, *The Curragh, Down Royal*

11 Sun *The Curragh*

12 Mon **Leicester,** Fontwell, *Dundalk*

13 Tue **Chepstow, Leicester,** Devon & Exeter, Sedgefield

14 Wed **Redcar,** Cheltenham, Wetherby, *Navan*

15 Thu **Newmarket (C4),** Hexham, Taunton, Uttoxeter, *Thurles*

16 Fri **Catterick, Newmarket (C4),** Ludlow

17 Sat **Catterick, Newmarket (C4),** Kelso, Kempton, Southwell, Stratford, *Naas*

18 Sun *Limerick*

19 Mon **Edinburgh, Folkestone, Nottingham,** Fakenham

20 Tue **Chepstow, Chester,** Plumpton, *The Curragh*

21 Wed **Chester,** Ascot, Newcastle, *Navan*

22 Thu **Newbury, Pontefract,** Wincanton, *Tipperary*

23 Fri **Doncaster,** Devon & Exeter, Hereford, Newbury

24 Sat **Doncaster (C4), Newbury,** Catterick, Huntingdon, Worcester, *Leopardstown*

26 Mon **Leicester, Lingfield,** *Leopardstown, Galway*

27 Tue **Leicester, Redcar,** *Punchestown*

28 Wed **Yarmouth,** Fontwell, Sedgefield, *Punchestown*

29 Thu **Nottingham,** Kempton, Stratford, *Wexford*

30 Fri **Newmarket,** Bangor-on-

Dee, Wetherby

31 Sat **Newmarket (C4),** Sandown, Warwick, Wetherby, *Down Royal, Naas*

## NOVEMBER

1 Sun *Clonmel*

2 Mon **Newcastle,** Plumpton, Wolverhampton

3 Tue **Hamilton,** Devon & Exeter, Hereford

4 Wed Newbury, Kelso, *The Curragh*

5 Thu **Edinburgh, Lingfield (AW),** Uttoxeter, Wincanton, *Gowran Park*

6 Fri **Doncaster,** Hexham, Market Rasen

7 Sat **Doncaster (C4),** Chepstow, Newcastle, Windsor, *Navan*

8 Sun *Punchestown*

9 Mon Carlisle, Folkestone, Wolverhampton

10 Tue **Southwell (AW),** Sedgefield

11 Wed Haydock, Worcester, *Downpatrick*

12 Thu Kelso, Taunton, Towcester, *Clonmel*

13 Fri Ayr, Cheltenham, Huntingdon

14 Sat **Lingfield (AW),** Ayr, Cheltenham, Nottingham, *Naas*

15 Sun *Leopardstown*

16 Mon Leicester, Windsor

17 Tue **Southwell (AW),** Newton Abbot, Warwick, Wetherby

18 Wed Haydock, Kempton, *Fairyhouse*

19 Thu Haydock, Ludlow, Wincanton, *Tipperary*

20 Fri Ascot, Leicester, Sedgefield

21 Sat Ascot, Liverpool, Catterick, Market Rasen, Towcester, *Navan*

23 Mon Catterick, Folkestone, Wolverhampton

24 Tue Devon & Exeter,

Huntingdon, Stratford
25 Wed  Hereford, Hexham
Plumpton, *Naas*
26 Thu  Carlisle, Nottingham,
Taunton, *Thurles*
27 Fri  **Southwell (AW)**, Bangor-
on-Dee, Newbury
28 Sat  **Lingfield (AW)**, Newbury,
Newcastle (C4), Warwick,
*Fairyhouse*
29 Sun  *Fairyhouse*
30 Mon  Kelso, Worcester

## DECEMBER

1 Tue  Fontwell, Newcastle
2 Wed  **Southwell (AW)**, Catterick,
Huntingdon, Ludlow
3 Thu  **Lingfield (AW)**, Windsor,
Uttoxeter, *Thurles*
4 Fri  Devon & Exeter, Hereford,
Nottingham, Sandown
5 Sat  Chepstow, Sandown (C4),
Towcester, Wetherby,
*Punchestown*
7 Mon  Edinburgh, Warwick
8 Tue  Plumpton, Sedgefield,
*Clonmel*
9 Wed  Haydock, Worcester
10 Thu  **Southwell (AW)**, Haydock,
Taunton, *Punchestown*
11 Fri  Cheltenham, Doncaster,
Hexham
12 Sat  Cheltenham, Doncaster

(C4), Edinburgh, Lingfield,
*Navan*
14 Mon  Ludlow, Newton Abbot
15 Tue  **Southwell (AW)**,
Folkestone
16 Wed  **Lingfield (AW)**, Bangor-
on-Dee, *Fairyhouse*
17 Thu  Kelso, Towcester, *Clonmel*
18 Fri  Catterick, Fakenham,
Uttoxeter
19 Sat  **Lingfield (AW)**, Ascot,
Newcastle, Nottingham,
Uttoxeter, *Navan*
21 Mon  Edinburgh, Lingfield
22 Tue  **Lingfield (AW)**, Hereford
26 Sat  Huntingdon, Kempton (C4),
Market Rasen, Newton
Abbot, Sedgefield,
Wetherby, Wincanton,
Wolverhampton,
*Leopardstown, Limerick, Down
Royal*
27 Sun  *Leopardstown*
28 Mon  **Southwell (AW)**, Chepstow,
Kempton (C4), Wetherby.
Wolverhampton,
*Leopardstown, Limerick*
29 Tue  Plumpton, Stratford,
*Leopardstown, Limerick*
30 Wed  Carlisle, Fontwell, Taunton,
Warwick
31 Thu  **Lingfield (AW)**, Catterick,
Cheltenham, Folkestone,
Leicester, *Punchestown*

# QUIZ ANSWERS

1   Gary Carter. On 14 June he emulated the feat of Paul Cook in 1981, winning on Luvly Jubly at Southwell (1.30), Romany Rye at York (4.40) and Able Susan at Doncaster (8.15).

2   Remittance Man.

3   Carvill's Hill.

4   Lester Piggott, on Golan Heights.

5   Christy Roche, on Jet Ski Lady.

6   A man and child were sitting on the course about two furlongs from the start, forcing the field to take avoiding action.

7   Newcastle.

8   Fourstars Allstar, in the Irish Two Thousand Guineas.

9   Steinbeck, on Arazi's racecourse debut at Chantilly in May.

10   Sheikh Albadou, in the Breeders' Cup Sprint.

11   Dancing Brave.

12   Leopardstown.

13   Walter Swinburn, in the Budweiser Irish Derby.

14   Kempton Park, where they were transferred from Epsom due to the rebuilding works.

15   Swiss.

16   Ray Cochrane, for 'intentional riding'.

17   Sikeston, the Clive Brittain-trained five-year-old who won Group One races in Italy in May, October and November.

18   Sarcita.

19   Mike Channon with Affair of State.

20   Culture Vulture in the Brent Walker Fillies' Mile at Ascot and the Prix Marcel Boussac at Longchamp.

21   French-based John Hammond, trainer of Suave Dancer.

22   Sweden – on the German-trained Tao.

23   Indian Queen.

24   Corrupt and Toulon, at 4-1.

25   He was the most expensive yearling of all time, sold in 1985 for $13.1 million.

26   Sabin du Loir.

27   Trio – the 1-2-3 in any order on nominated races.

28   Reference Point.

29   Marju.

30   Sanglamore.

31   Alex Greaves, on Amenable.

32   He became only the fifth jockey to have ridden 3000 winners in Britain. The others are Sir Gordon Richards, Lester Piggott, Willie Carson and Doug Smith.

33   Ladbroke Sprint Cup (Polar Falcon), St Leger (Toulon) and Champion Stakes (Tel Quel).

34   Gold Seal Oaks (Jet Ski Lady) and Coronation Stakes (Kooyonga).

35   Jenny Pitman, in the Grunwick Decade Celebration Stakes (a National Hunt Flat Race) at Warwick on 16 November.

36   Folkestone.

37   Bangor-on-Dee.

38   Steve Smith Eccles.

39   Cahervillahow and Docklands Express.

40   Francis Norton, who rode Deposki.

41   None.

42   1989 St Leger – run at Ayr due to subsidence at Doncaster.

43   6-4.

44   33-1.

45   Wolverhampton.

46   West Tip.

47   Troy, in 1979.

48   1984.

49   Morley Street – Breeders' Cup Steeplechase in 1990 and 1991.

50   Miesque (Mile 1987 and 1988) and

Bayakoa (Distaff 1989 and 1990).

51   Colin Brown, Richard Linley, Brian Rouse (in Desert Orchid's one and only race on the Flat in the Sagaro Stakes at Ascot in 1985), Simon Sherwood, Richard Dunwoody and Graham Bradley.

52   1982 (Lester Piggott).

53   Aliysa.

54   The two-year-olds Provideo (16 wins in 1984) and Timeless Times (16 wins in 1990), both trained by Bill O'Gorman.

55   Harrow.

56   Japan Cup, in 1981.

57   Racing Post – current sponsor of the Group One race for two-year-olds over one mile at Doncaster in October, run as the Racing Post Trophy since 1989.

58   A. F. Budge – current sponsor of the 2½-mile handicap chase at Cheltenham in December, run as the A. F. Budge Gold Cup since 1988.

59   1961.

60   Dawn Run.

61   The Whitbread Gold Cup at Sandown Park in 1957.

62   Cheltenham, 1957–59.

63   Kribensis, winner of the Triumph Hurdle in 1988 and the Champion Hurdle in 1990.

64   Golden Miller, Arkle and Dawn Run.

65   Liverpool and Ayr.

66   Kempton Park.

67   Robert Sangster.

68   Khalid Abdullah.

69   Richard Burridge, part owner of Desert Orchid.

70   Newmarket (Rowley Mile course).

71   Sandown Park.

72   Liverpool (Grand National course).

73   Bangor-on-Dee and Chepstow.

74   Sandown Park.

75   York.

76   Kelso.

77   Kelso.

78   Roberto, in the 1972 Benson and Hedges Gold Cup at York.

79   Teleprompter.

80   Stockton, in 1981.

81   Henry Cecil.

82   Jack Berry.

83   David Nicholson.

84   Old Vic, in 1989.

85   Melbourne Cup.

86   Ayr, Edinburgh, Hamilton Park, Kelso and Perth.

87   Twelve.

88   Eighteen.

89   Lettoch.

90   250-1.

91   Sigy, in 1978.

92   Kentucky Derby (Churchill Downs), Preakness Stakes (Pimlico), Belmont Stakes (Belmont Park).

93   Affirmed, in 1978.

94   Happy Valley and Sha Tin.

95   Gay Future.

96   11-2.

97   26.

98   Empery, in 1976.

99   Slip Anchor, who had just one race as a four-year-old in 1986.

100   Tap On Wood, in the 1979 Two Thousand Guineas.

# ADDRESSES
# AND TELEPHONE
# NUMBERS

(For address and telephone numbers of individual racecourses, please consult the entries on pages 75–135.)

**Channel Four Racing:** South Bank Television Centre, London SE1 9LT. Tel 071-261 3434

**Federation of British Racing Clubs:** 4 Bosley Crescent, Wallingford, Oxfordshire. Tel 0491 32399

**Horseracing Advisory Council:** 52 Grosvenor Gardens, London SW1W 0AU. Tel 071-730 4540

**Injured Jockeys Fund:** PO Box 9, Newmarket, Suffolk CB8 8JG. Tel 0638 662246

**Jockey Club:** 42 Portman Square, London W1H 0EN. Tel 071-486 4921

**Jockeys' Association of Great Britain:** 1 Bridge Street, Newbury, Berkshire RG14 5BL. Tel 0635 44102

**Levy Board:** Horserace Betting Levy Board, 52 Grosvenor Gardens, London SW1W 0AU. Tel 071-730 4540

**National Horseracing Museum:** 99 High Street, Newmarket, Suffolk CB8 8JL. Tel 0638 667333

**Press Association:** 85 Fleet Street, London EC4P 4BE. Tel 071-353 7440

**Racecourse Association:** Winkfield Road, Ascot, Berkshire SL5 7HX. Tel 0344 25912

**Racecourse Technical Services:** 88 Bushey Road, London SW20 0JH Tel 081-947 3333

**Raceform:** Compton, Newbury, Berkshire RG16 0NL. Tel 0635 578080

**Racegoers Club:** Flagstaff House, High Street, Twyford, Berkshire RG10 9EA. Tel 0734 341666

**Racehorse Owners Association:** 42 Portman Square, London W1H 9FH. Tel 071-486 6977

**Racing Post:** Cannon House, 112-120 Coombe Lane, Raynes Park, London SW20 0BA. Tel 081-879 3377

**Satellite Information services (SIS):** 17 Corsham Street, London N1 6DR. Tel 071-253 2232

**Sporting Life:** 33 Holborn, London EC1P 1DQ. Tel 071-353 0246

**Tote:** The Horserace Totalisator Board, Tote House, 74 Upper Richmond Road, Putney, London SW15 2SU. Tel 081-874 6411

**Timeform:** Timeform House, Halifax, West Yorkshire HX1 1XE. Tel 0422 330330

**Turf Newspapers:** 19 Clarges Street, London W1Y 7PG. Tel 071-499 4391

**Weatherbys:** Sanders Road, Finedon Road Industrial Estate, Wellingborough, Northants NN8 4BX. Tel 0933 440077